Research Series on the Chinese Dream and China's Development Path

Drawing on a large body of empirical studies done over the last two decades, the *Research Series on the Chinese Dream and China's Development Path* seeks to provide its readers with in-depth analyses of the past and present, and forecasts for the future course of China's development. Thanks to the adoption of Socialism with Chinese characteristics, and the implementation of comprehensive reform and opening, China has made tremendous achievements in areas such as political reform, economic development, and social construction, and is making great strides towards the realization of the Chinese dream of national rejuvenation. In addition to presenting a detailed account of many of these achievements, the authors also discuss what lessons other countries can learn from China's experience. This series will be an invaluable companion to every researcher who is trying to gain a deeper understanding of the development model, path, and experience unique to China.

More information about this series at http://www.springer.com/series/13571

Ya'nan Wang • Puning Hao • Ting Liu •
Juan Zhao • Yu Fang

Annual Evaluation Report of China's Cultural Consumption Demand

SSAP

Springer

Ya'nan Wang
Yunnan Academy of Social Sciences
Kunming, Yunnan
China

Puning Hao
Northwest China's Foreign Opening and Bo
Yunnan Normal University
Kunming, Yunnan
China

Ting Liu
Research Center for Cultural Development
Yunnan Academy of Social Sciences
Kunming, Yunnan
China

Juan Zhao
Yunnan Academy of Social Sciences
Kunming, Yunnan
China

Yu Fang
China Ministry of Civil Affairs Center
China

ISSN 2363-6866 ISSN 2363-6874 (electronic)
Research Series on the Chinese Dream and China's Development Path
ISBN 978-981-10-0729-3 ISBN 978-981-10-0730-9 (eBook)
DOI 10.1007/978-981-10-0730-9

Printed on acid-free paper

This Springer imprint is published by Springer Nature
The registered company is Springer Science+Business Media Singapore Pte Ltd.

Series Preface

Since China's reform and opening began in 1978, the country has come a long way on the path of Socialism with Chinese characteristics, under the leadership of the Communist Party of China. Over 30 years of reform efforts and sustained spectacular economic growth have turned China into the world's second largest economy and wrought many profound changes in the Chinese society. These historically significant developments have been garnering increasing attention from scholars, governments and the general public alike around the world since the 1990s, when the newest wave of China studies began to gather steam. Some of the hottest topics have included the so-called China miracle, Chinese phenomenon, Chinese experience, Chinese path and the Chinese model. Homegrown researchers have soon followed suit. Already hugely productive, this vibrant field is putting out a large number of books each year, with Social Sciences Academic Press alone having published hundreds of titles on a wide range of subjects.

Because most of these books have been written and published in Chinese, readership has been limited outside China – even among many who study China – for whom English is still the lingua franca. This language barrier has been an impediment to efforts by academia, business communities and policy-makers in other countries to form a thorough understanding of contemporary China, of what is distinct about China's past and present may mean not only for her future but also for the future of the world. The need to remove such an impediment is both real and urgent, and the *Research Series on the Chinese Dream and China's Development Path* is my answer to the call.

This series features some of the most notable achievements from the last 20 years by scholars in China in a variety of research topics related to reform and opening. They include both theoretical explorations and empirical studies, and cover economy, society, politics, law, culture and ecology, the six areas in which reform and opening policies have had the deepest impact and farthest-reaching consequences for the country. Authors for the series have also tried to articulate their visions of the "Chinese Dream" and how the country can realize it in these fields and beyond.

All the editors and authors for the *Research Series on the Chinese Dream and China's Development Path* are both long-time students of reform and opening and recognized authorities in their respective academic fields. Their credentials and expertise lend credibility to these books, each of which having been subject to a rigorous peer-review process for inclusion in the series. As part of the Reform and Development Programme under the State Administration of Press, Publication, Radio, Film and Television of the People's Republic of China, the series is published by Springer, a Germany-based academic publisher of international repute, and distributed overseas. I am confident that it will help fill a lacuna in studies of China in the era of reform and opening.

Xie Shouguang

Preface

The year 2000 was a turning point in the development course of modern China. This was not because of its significance in the Western calendar, where it marks the end of the twentieth century and the beginning of a new millennium; rather it was significant because it was, in the course of China's unique history, the year that marked the realization of a "Basically Prosperous Society" and the starting point of the next leg of China's journey towards a "Fully Prosperous Society". According to the traditional concept of "prosperity" that has prevailed in China for thousands of years, its complete achievement involves two steps, the realization of "sufficiency", followed by hints of "affluence". From "Basic Prosperity" to "Full Prosperity", the "two-step" process of China's modernization has captured the spirit of the "Chinese Dream", with all its rich and deep cultural import. It is in this process of moving from "Basic Prosperity" to "Full Prosperity" that China has realized its transformation from a traditional to a modern society.

The modern transformation of Chinese society has had two prominent markers: one is the construction and gradual improvement of the market economy system which has brought continued growth in the Chinese economy for several years, integrating the global market economy system effectively and deeply affecting the Chinese economy, society and lifestyle in every aspect; the second marker is the construction and steady progress of the systems of public finance, public service and social security – the society is public, the government is public, finances are public and so the government's primary responsibility is to provide public services and basic social security for the whole of society. These two aspects are inevitably linked, because a complete market economy system must be accompanied by a sound social security system. In the process of implementing, in the face of the international financial crisis, the national policy of "stimulating domestic demand, broadening consumption and improving the livelihood of its people", Chinese society fully became aware of this point.

In the past, China has had a tradition of formulating an economic plan every 10 years, whereby all production and consumption was carried out in accordance with the plan, and provisions were organized according to the plan. After the transference to a market economy system, Chinese economic development has faced a long-term difficulty of lack of domestic demand, especially in the case of the growth of cultural production being restricted by the insufficiency in cultural consumption demands. The reason for this was the lag in construction of a social security system. If we say that the driving force in the substance of economic development in manufacturing is still reliant on the so-called triumvirate, and that besides investment and domestic demand, there is also foreign demand; then the driving force behind the development of cultural industry, besides investment, basically can only rely on foreign demand.

Due to social traditions, the Chinese public generally maintains the classic characteristic of a traditional agricultural society, which goes along with the notion of "relying on the weather for sustenance", which leads to unpredictability year after year. The idea that "the heavens call the shots" makes future livelihoods difficult to grasp, and Chinese people focus on saving extra money, leading to a high rate of savings in Chinese society. While social safeguards are not sufficient, the public must focus more on saving money, leading to measures of self-protection, such as funds for purchasing a home, funds for children's education, funds for sickness and old age and similar situations. That is to say, that in addition to maintaining a level of essential expenses, Chinese people also prepare for savings for future contingencies. This situation is bound to suppress a broadening step in consumption, as necessary consumption remains fixed, with spiritual and cultural consumption inevitably being the first to be left aside. Therefore, within the scope of the Chinese nation, the public's cultural consumption status grows negatively in relation to the growth in savings.

The valuable lessons China learned from the international financial crisis is that the country should focus on "stimulating domestic demand, expanding consumption and improving livelihoods" within the socialist market economy system. These points should become basic Chinese long-term national policies followed in the construction of the Chinese-style socialist economy and the construction of culture and society. This has become the basic idea behind the national Twelfth Five-Year Plan. Developments in the cultural domain raise the level of scientific development and should adhere more to the concept of "people first" and the basic principles of making quality of life an equal priority; stimulating domestic cultural demand, broadening cultural consumption, improving culture and quality of life and using the promotion of socialist cultural development to satisfy the cultural needs of the urban and rural populations on a broader scale.

Within the socialist market economy system, the so-called demands are mainly shown as consumer demands, including the most basic needs for food, clothing and shelter; it makes a little sense, therefore, to talk about "meeting demands" outside of consumer demands. Cultural development that takes "meeting the spiritual and cultural needs of the public as a starting and ending point" needs to be translated into promoting consumption across urban and rural areas and allowing all to share in the benefits. In order to measure the effects of cultural development and production through the increase in popular consumer demands, is not only necessary – the results of cultural development must be implemented it the cultural consumption demands of residents of rural and urban areas, something which is also feasible – among cultural production and cultural consumption there is an interaction of supply and demand which cannot be avoided. The ultimate power of cultural production can only come from popular cultural consumption needs, and cultural production's actual results can only be verified if they meet cultural consumption demands.

The essence of continuing to deepen cultural reform and mechanisms for innovation lies in bringing the cultural manufacturing industry completely into a unified socialist market economy system; changing from a plan-based orientation to a market-based orientation; from a manufacturing orientation to a consumer orientation; from a goal of supply to a goal of demand. The space for development of China's culture industry must be brought out by the enhancement of "endogenous power", and more so should be implemented from its own "starting and ending point". The development of the culture industry and the enhancement of cultural consumption should form good relations of coordinated growth of supply and demand. In the process of fully constructing a prosperous society, the results of cultural development cannot just be measured by per capita "cultural GDP". Promoting cultural industry as a pillar of the national economy is just a means; enhancing and satisfying the cultural consumption demand of the populace is the ultimate goal; the "GDP culture chase" stemming from "GDP worship" must stop.

Yunnan, China
March 26, 2014

Wang Ya'nan

Acknowledgments

After a relatively short gestation period, the *Research Series on the Chinese Dream and China's Development Path* has started to bear fruits. We have, first and foremost, the books' authors and editors to thank for making this possible. And it was the hard work by many people at Social Sciences Academic Press and Springer, the two collaborating publishers, that made it a reality. We are deeply grateful to all of them.

Mr. Xie Shouguang, president of Social Sciences Academic Press (SSAP), is the mastermind behind the project. In addition to defining the key missions to be accomplished by it and setting down the basic parameters for the project's execution, as the work has unfolded, Mr. Xie has provided critical input pertaining to its every aspect and at every step of the way. Thanks to the deft coordination by Ms. Li Yanling, all the constantly moving parts of the project, especially those on the SSAP side, are securely held together, and as well synchronized as is feasible for a project of this scale. Ms. Gao Jing, unfailingly diligent and meticulous, makes sure every aspect of each Chinese manuscript meets the highest standards for both publishers, something of critical importance to all subsequent steps in the publishing process. That high-quality if also at times stylistically as well as technically challenging scholarly writing in Chinese has turned into decent, readable English that readers see on these pages is largely thanks to Ms. Liang Fan, who oversees translator recruitment and translation quality control.

Ten other members of the SSAP staff have been intimately involved, primarily in the capacity of in-house editor, in the preparation of the Chinese manuscripts. It is time-consuming work that requires attention to details, and each of them has done this and is continuing to do this with superb skills. They are, in alphabetical order: Mr. Cai Jihui, Ms. Liu Xiaojun, Mr. Ren Wenwu, Ms. Shi Xiaolin, Ms. Song Yuehua, Mr. Tong Genxing, Ms. Wu Dan, Ms. Yao Dongmei, Ms. Yun Wei and Ms. Zhou Qiong. In addition, Xie Shouguang and Li Yanling have also taken part in this work.

Mr. RenWenwu is the SSAP in-house editor for the current volume.

Our appreciation is also owed to Ms. Li Yan, Mr. Chai Ning, Ms. Wang Lei and Ms. Xu Yi from Springer's Beijing Representative Office. Their strong support for the SSAP team in various aspects of the project helped to make the latter's work that much easier than it would have otherwise been.

We thank Ms. Ivy Goldstein for translating this book.

Last, but certainly not least, it must be mentioned that funding for this project comes from the Ministry of Finance of the People's Republic of China. Our profound gratitude, if we can be forgiven for a bit of apophasis, goes without saying.

Social Sciences Academic Press
Springer

This research project has received support from the following institutions and projects:

Chinese Academy of Social Sciences Innovation Project
Yunnan Province CCP Committee Propaganda Department
Yunnan Province Innovation Project of Philosophy and Social Sciences
Yunnan Academy of Social Sciences Chinese Cultural Development Research and Key Evaluation Laboratory
Yunnan Normal University Key Research Project in the Humanities and Social Sciences

Publisher: Assessment Center for Chinese Cultural Consumption Demands

Cooperating Institutions:

Yunnan Academy of Social Sciences Cultural Development Research Center
China Academy of Social Sciences Center for Cultural Research
National School of Administration's Social and Cultural Research Department
Yunnan Normal University Public Cultural Services and Cultural Industry Development Research Institute
Social Sciences Academic Press
Guangming Daily Cultural Industry Research Center

Allied Institutions:

National Cultural Industry Innovation and Development Research Center of Shanghai Jiaotong University
Communication University of China Institute for Cultural Industries
National Innovation Center for Cultural Research, Wuhan University

Consultants: Wang Weiguang

Zhou Wenzhang
Zhao Jin

Chief Scientists: Wang Ya'nan

Zhang Xiaoming
Qi Shuyu

Academic Committee

Wang Ya'nan
Deng Yonghong
Yin Hong
Bao Xiaolin
Ren Jia
Xiang Yong
Liu Wei
Liu Yuzhu
Qi Yongfeng
Qi Shuyu
Hua Jian
Li Tao
Li Kanghua
Fan Zhou
Yang Lin
Yang Zhengquan
Yang Fuquan
Song Jianwu
Zhang Xiaoming
Zhang Ruicai
Chen Shaofeng
Jin Yuanpu
Zheng Hai
Zheng Xiaoyun
Hao Puning
Hu Huilin
Gao Shusheng
Yin Guojun
Cui Chengquan
Zhang Jiangang
Fu Caiwu
Tong Huai
Xie Shouguang
Kuai Dashen
Xiong Chengyu

Acknowledgem

Introduction

What standards should be used to measure the construction of a prosperous society? Clearly, we cannot again, as in the year 2000, simply and crudely apply the standard of a per capita GDP of 800 USD equaling "basic prosperity". Rather, "livelihood indicators" will play an undoubtable, irreplaceable role. In the process of building a prosperous society, the targets of cultural development should be implemented within its own "starting and ending points".

In 2012, nationwide consumption demands across urban and rural areas maintained high growth, with a total accumulated growth of 12.64 %, reaching 1.140597 trillion yuan; per capita growth was 12.08 %, reaching 844.45 yuan. Using per capita as a measure, the growth in urban and rural cultural consumption was significantly higher than the output value and significantly lower than the growth in income among urban and rural inhabitants; it was slightly lower than the total growth in consumption and significantly lower than the accumulated growth. The urban–rural gap in cultural consumption decreased 1.97 % from the last year, and the regional gap in cultural consumption between provinces and rural areas decreased by 1.04 %.

Total cultural consumption growth in urban and rural areas of 21 provinces was greater than 10 %; among those, urban and rural areas in 11 provinces experienced a total growth of greater than 15 %, and urban and rural areas in 3 provinces experienced a total growth greater than 20 %. It was just the high growth of consumption demand across urban and rural areas in most provinces that resulted in the high growth of countrywide overall cultural consumption demand in urban and rural areas.

The status ranking for cultural consumption demand among provinces is as follows: Jiangsu, Beijing and Shanghai ranked top three in the "2012 Annual Provincial Leaders"; Jiangsu, Qinghai and Liaoning ranked top three in the "2000–2012 Provincial Runners-Up"; Jiangsu, Tianjin and Qinghai ranked top three in the "2005–2012 Provincial Runners-Up"; Tianjin, Xinjiang and Ningxia ranked top three in the "2010–2012 Provincial Runners-Up"; Tianjin, Jilin and Henan ranked top three in the "2012 Annual Provincial Runners-Up".

The status ranking of cultural and educational consumption demand among key cities is as follows: Guangzhou, Xi'an and Nanjing ranked top three in the "2012 Annual Major City Leaders"; Hefei, Kunming and Fuzhou ranked top three in the "2005–2012 Major City Runners-Up"; Wuhan, Kunming and Nanning ranked top three in the "2010–2012 Major City Runners-Up"; Tianjin, Hefei and Changchun ranked top three in the "2012 Annual Major City Runners-Up".

Abstract

In 2012, the countrywide cultural consumption demand in urban and rural areas maintained high growth: the total cultural consumption went up by 12.64 %, reaching 11405.97 hundred million yuan; the per capita value went up by 12.09 %, reaching 844.45 yuan. As measured by per capita value, the annual growth of the cultural consumption in urban and rural areas was higher than the GDP growth, lower than residents' income growth and slightly lower than the total consumption growth, also significantly lower than savings growth. The disparity of cultural consumption between urban and rural areas shrank by 1.97 %; the regional gap of cultural consumption in urban and rural areas among various provinces shrank by 1.04 % over the previous year.

The total cultural consumption in urban and rural areas increased in 21 provinces by over 10 %, in 11 of which by over 15 % and in 3 of which by over 20 %; the per capita value of cultural consumption in urban and rural areas increased in 19 provinces by over 10 %, in 10 of which by over 15 % and in 3 of which by over 20 %. It was just the high growth of consumption demand across urban and rural areas in most provinces that resulted in the high growth of countrywide overall cultural consumption demand in urban and rural areas.

The status ranking for cultural consumption demand among provinces is as follows: Jiangsu, Beijing and Shanghai ranked top three in the "2012 Annual Provincial Leaders"; Jiangsu, Qinghai and Liaoning ranked top three in the "2000–2012 Provincial Runners-Up"; Jiangsu, Tianjin and Qinghai ranked top three in the "2005–2012 Provincial Runners-Up"; Tianjin, Xinjiang and Ningxia ranked top three in the "2010–2012 Provincial Runners-Up"; Tianjin, Jilin and Henan ranked top three in the "2012 Annual Provincial Runners-Up".

The rankings of the status evaluation of the cultural and educational consumption demand among key cities are as follows: Guangzhou, Xi'an and Nanjing ranked top three in the "2012 annual key cities leaders"; Hefei, Kunming and Fuzhou ranked top three in the "2005–2012 Major City Runners-Up"; Wuhan,

Kunming and Nanning ranked top three in the "2010–2012 Major City Runners-Up"; Tianjin, Hefei and Changchun ranked top three in the "2012 Major City Runners-Up".

Keywords Cultural consumption • Demand and sharing • Status evaluation • Analysis and forecast

Contents

Contributing Authors

Wang Ya'nan completed a Bachelor of Arts Degree and is a researcher at Yunnan Academy of Social Sciences and Director of the Cultural Development Research Center. Wang's academic research is in the areas of cultural theory, cultural strategy and cultural industry. Wang is nationally recognized among academic circles for the following contributions: (1) defining the concept of "Oral Culture" and completing systematic research; (2) analyzing the rite of passage of "Rituals Towards in Taking on the Identity of a Parent"; (3) putting forth the discourse of "High Cultural Content"; of "Human Economics" that is (4) putting forth the argument that "The Modern Chinese Nation Is Comprised of 56 Equal Ethnicities which Have Built a National Community"; (5) research and innovation on an "Evaluation System for Chinese Cultural Consumption Demands".

Hao Puning completed a Bachelor of Arts degree and is a professor at Yunnan Normal University's Northwest China's Foreign Opening and Border Security Research Center and the Deputy Director of the Research Institute for Public Cultural Services and the Development of Cultural Industries, his academic directions being: Film and Television Arts, Cultural Industry and Journalism Studies. He has presided over the National Social Science Fund Project, "Research in the National Culture's Original Media", and presided over the Provincial Academy's Cooperative Project, "Yunnan Ethnic Cultural Relics and Forms of Industrial Society and Cultural and Economic Construction". He has participated in the filming of several television series and was the head writer and planner of the television documentary, *Leaping Across* (Part Six).

Liu Ting is a PhD candidate and a research associate at the Research Center for Cultural Development at the Yunnan Academy of Social Sciences, the Associate Editor of *The Blue Book on Yunnan's Cultural Development* and the Secretary General of the Yunnan Association of Young Social Scientists. Her academic areas are the anthropology of art and leisure culture and leisure industry research, a representative work in which is *Folk Leisure Culture*. She was in charge of the National Social Science Association's Western Project "New Thinking on the

Protection of Folk Customs of Yunnan's Ethnic Minorities". She was a participant in the entire process of research and innovation for the "Evaluation System of the Chinese Cultural Consumption" and participated in authoring *The Report on the Evaluation System of the Boom in Chinese Cultural Consumption*,as well as being responsible for proofreading and editing the entire volume.

Zhao Juan, MA, is an Assistant Researcher at the Research Center for Cultural Development at the Yunnan Academy of Social Sciences and an Associate Editor for *The Blue Book on Yunnan's Cultural Development*, as well as the Chief Officer for the Yunnan Association of Young Social Scientists. Her research interests include ethnic culture and cultural industry. She participated in the entire process for research and innovation in "Evaluation System of the Chinese Cultural Consumption Demands" and was a coauthor of *The Report on the Evaluation System of the Boom in Chinese Cultural Consumption*, as well as being responsible for proofreading and editing the entire volume.

Fang Yu, PhD, is a Research Assistant at the China Ministry of Civil Affairs Center for the Aging and is the Executive Editor of the *Report on Developments in Caring for the Aged in China*, and was the recipient of The Department of Education's Award for Newcomers in PhD Scholarship. Her research areas are oral traditions, culture of the ageing and cultural industry. She participated in research and innovation during the entire process of "Evaluation System on the Chinese Cultural Consumption Demands" and was involved in *The Report on the Evaluation System of the Boom in Chinese Cultural Consumption* in the capacity of translator and document revisor.

Other Contributors

Zhang Yongde, Researcher, Yunnan Academy of Social Sciences Religion Department
Rao Yuan, Professor, Yunnan Normal University Physical Education Department
Song Xihui, Professor, Yunnan Normal University Departments of Philosophy and Political Science
Zou Jianda, Executive Dean and Professor, Yunnan Normal University Media Department
Wei Haiyan, Editor-in-Chief, Yunnan Province Political Consultative Conference Information Center
Li Yufeng, Lecturer, Yunnan Normal University, Media Department
Xiao Qing, Associate Professor, Yunnan Normal University, Media Department
Kong Zhijian, Research Associate, Yunnan Academy of Social Sciences, Southeast Asia Research Institute
Li Miao, Yunnan Normal University, Lecturer, Media Department
Yuan Chunsheng, Research Assistant, Yunnan Academy of Social Sciences,

Chang Fei, Office Director and Director of Research, Yunnan Academy of Social Sciences
Lu Shuang Mei, Associate Professor, Yunnan Academy of Social Sciences, Media Department
Li Wenjuan, Deputy Director of Personnel and Research Associate, Yunnan Academy of Social Sciences
Wang Yang, Assistant Director and Assistant Researcher, Yunnan Academy of Social Sciences
Deng Yunfei, Assistant Researcher, Yunnan Academy of Social Sciences, Southeast Asia Research Institute
Chen Zongtao, Assistant Researcher, Yunnan Academy of Social Sciences Information Center

Chapter 1
The Overall Status Evaluation of China's Cultural Consumption Demand in Urban and Rural Areas: An Analysis for Period Beginning in 1991 and the 2012 Annual Assessment

Abstract In 2012, the countrywide overall cultural consumption demand in urban and rural areas continued to maintain high growth: the total cultural consumption went up by 12.64 %, reaching 11,405.97 hundred million yuan; the per capita value went up by 12.09 %, reaching 844.45 yuan. As measured by per capita value, the annual growth of cultural consumption in urban and rural areas was significantly higher than GDP growth, significantly lower than residents' income growth, slightly lower than total consumption growth, and significantly lower than savings growth. The disparity of cultural consumption between urban and rural areas shrank by 1.97 %; the regional gap of cultural consumption in urban and rural areas among various provinces shrank by 1.04 % from the previous year. The status evaluations of countrywide overall cultural consumption demand in urban and rural areas in 2012 are as follows: the value of the vertical assessment is remarkably higher than the base value since the "Ninth Five-Year Plan" period; it is slightly lower than the base value since the "Tenth Five-Year Plan" period; is significantly lower than the base value since the "Eleventh Five-Year Plan" period and is slightly higher than the base value of the previous year; the annual horizontal assessment without urban and rural and regional gaps is remarkably lower than the ideal value, because of the continuous presence of the urban and rural and the regional gaps.

Keywords National urban and rural areas • Cultural consumption • Status evaluation • Integrative measure

In 2012, nationwide cultural consumption demand across urban and rural areas continued to maintain high growth, with a total accumulated growth of 12.64 %, reaching 1.140597 trillion yuan; per-capita growth was 12.08 %, reaching 844.45 yuan. Using per-capita as a measure, the growth in urban and rural cultural consumption was significantly higher than the output value, and significantly lower than the growth in income among urban and rural inhabitants; it was slightly lower than the total growth in consumption and significantly lower than the accumulated growth. The urban-rural gap in cultural consumption decreased

Y. Wang et al., *Annual Evaluation Report of China's Cultural Consumption Demand*, Research Series on the Chinese Dream and China's Development Path,
DOI 10.1007/978-981-10-0730-9_1

1.97 % from the last year, and the regional gap in cultural consumption between provinces and rural areas decreased by 1.04 %.

What standards should we use to measure the construction of a prosperous society? Clearly, we cannot again, as in the year 2000, simply and crudely apply the standard of a per capita GDP of 800 USD equaling "basic prosperity". Rather, "livelihood indicators" will undoubtedly play an irreplaceable role. In the process of building a prosperous society, the targets of cultural development should be implemented within its own "starting and ending points".

The third plenary session of the 18th CPC Central Committee's decision to "Promote the Innovation of Cultural and Institutional Mechanisms" emphasized that the direction of the work would adhere to being people-centered, would further deepen cultural reform, construct a modern public system of cultural services, promote the standardization and equalization of basic public cultural services, promote beneficial cultural projects and effectively connect the cultural needs of the public. The section about "Promoting Innovative Reform in Social Enterprise" emphasized striving hard to provide diverse services for society, better meeting the needs of the populace, and achieving results in the development of more equitable benefits for all people. This is also applicable to cultural development. Meeting the populace's needs within the socialist market economy system should mainly be expressed through meeting consumption needs, including the most typical need of "basic protection", or minimum livelihood protection, and protection of the consumer needs of food and clothing consumption amongst the impoverished populace, rather than the physical implementation of a rationing system of food and clothing. Therefore, it is the cultural consumption demands of the populace which reflect the basic aspects of a cultural livelihood.

This paper analyzes the overall growth trend of nationwide cultural consumption demands among the urban and rural populace since 1991, and also evaluates the overall situation of nationwide cultural consumption demand across urban and rural areas for the year 2012. This is both an overall evaluation of nationwide cultural consumption demand across urban and rural areas and also a basic calculation for the ranking of each urban and rural area's cultural consumption. Due to space limitations, the first and last year of each 5-year period will be combined in the charts throughout the book, but the annual data growth will still be indexed. When this paper analyzes the growth trend in the calendar year, the evaluation for this calculation filters out the highest and lowest annual values.

1.1 Growth Trends in Nationwide Urban and Rural Cultural Consumption Over the Last 21 Years

Total cultural consumption demand is the concrete manifestation of how much cultural industry and production has actually entered the daily life of citizens, and is also the concrete manifestation of the development of cultural industry and production actually entering into the cultural consumption demands of the masses. The total increase in nationwide urban and rural demand in cultural consumption can offer a wide-ranging perspective which is conducive to understanding the overall urban and rural trend. This paper's analysis and evaluation begins with the overall nationwide growth in cultural consumption in urban and rural areas.

1.1.1 Overall Growth Trends in Urban and Rural Cultural Consumption

The overall nationwide growth trend in urban and rural cultural consumption from 1991 to 2012 is shown in Fig. 1.1. Included are the comprehensive urban and rural cultural consumption demand growth trends as well as single-line cultural consumption demand growth trends of urban and rural (towns and villages) across three levels. The sum for cities/towns and villages is the comprehensive urban and rural total amount, and the two correspond to each other to constitute the overall nationwide pattern, and are necessary to place together for analysis.

Figure 1.1 converts national urban and rural cultural consumption absolute values into direct graphic area proportions, and also shows the relationship of growth between urban and rural areas since 1991; the third curve between the two exponential growth curves is the comprehensive urban and rural growth index.

From 1991 to 2012, total nationwide urban and rural cultural consumption increased from 66.821 billion yuan to 1.140597 trillion yuan, which was a growth over the 21 years of 1.073776 trillion yuan and 1606.94 %, and an average annual increase of 14.47 %. The highest growth occurred during 2002 at a rate of 31.89 %; the smallest growth occurred during 2001, at a rate of 2.60 %. During the years of the "Ninth Five-Year Plan" there was an average annual growth of 14.26 %, and during the years of the "Tenth Five-Year Plan" there was an average annual growth of 11.36 %. The average annual growth rate during the "Eleventh Five-Year Plan" was lower than that during the "Tenth Five-Year Plan" by 2.29 percentage points, and lower than that during the "Ninth Five-Year Plan" by 2.90 percentage points.

Over the same period, total national cultural consumption rose from 25.796 to 851.3 billion yuan, which was a total growth of 3,200.12 % over 21 years, with an average annual growth of 18.12 %. The year of highest growth was 2002, with a growth rate of 62.66 %; the smallest growth occurred during 1992 when there was a growth rate of 2.92 %. During the years of the "Ninth Five-Year Plan" there was an average annual growth rate of 18.36 %, and during the time of the "Tenth Five-Year Plan" there was an average annual growth rate of 19.68 %. During the "Eleventh Five-Year Plan" period, there was an average annual growth rate of 16.51 %. The annual average growth rate during the "Eleventh Five-Year Plan" period was lower than that during the "Tenth Five-Year Plan" by 3.17 percentage points, and lower than that during the "Ninth Five-Year Plan" by 1.85 percentage points.

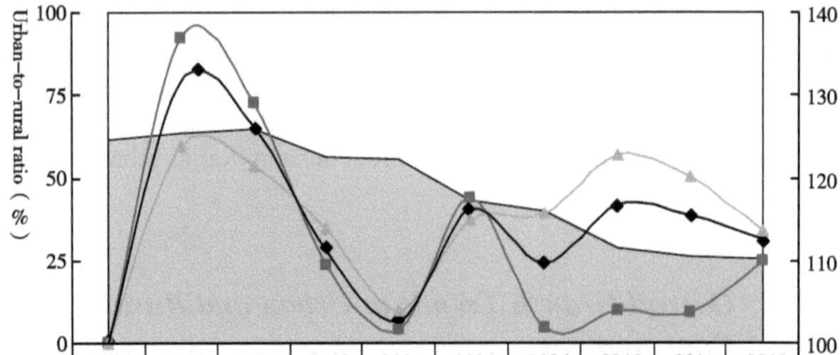

	1991	1995	1996	2000	2001	2005	2006	2010	2011	2012
Urban Total	257.96	509.71	619.51	1183.75	1229.64	2906.79	3366.50	6240.56	7494.97	8513.00
Rural Total	410.25	878.65	1132.74	1520.60	1544.97	2219.78	2262.33	2537.72	2631.22	2892.97
Urban–Rural Total	668.21	1388.36	1752.25	2704.35	2774.61	5126.57	5628.83	8778.28	10126.19	11405.97
Urban–Rural Annual Growth	100.00	131.69	126.21	111.27	102.60	116.09	109.80	116.71	115.36	112.64
Urban Annual Growth	100.00	123.73	121.54	113.81	103.88	115.03	115.82	122.86	120.10	113.58
Rural Annual Growth	100.00	136.80	128.92	109.37	101.60	117.52	101.92	103.91	103.68	109.95

Fig. 1.1 Overall growth trends in nationwide urban and rural cultural consumption demand. *LHS area*: the total amount of cultural consumption in urban and rural areas (each 100 million yuan converted to %), ratio between changes in urban and rural areas, representing urban and rural totals; *RHS curve*: urban and rural annual growth coefficient (previous year = 100). Data is calculated according to related volumes of the National Statistical Bureau's *China Statistical Yearbook*; in this, Chongqing was not counted as a province before 1997, Tibet is missing urban data in 1993, 1995 and from 1997 to 1998, so they are not included in corresponding year totals

Over the same period, total nationwide rural cultural consumption increased from 41.025 to 289.297 billion yuan, an increase of 248.272 billion yuan. This was a total growth rate of 605.17 % over the 21 years, with an average annual growth rate of 9.75 %. The largest growth occurred in 1995, at a rate of 36.80 %; the smallest growth occurred in 2000 with a negative growth of 1.04 %. During the years of the "Ninth Five-Year Plan", there was an average annual growth of 11.59 %; during the "Tenth Five-Year Plan" period there was an average annual growth of 7.86 %; and during the "Eleventh Five-Year Plan" period there was an average annual growth rate of 2.71 %. Average annual growth during the "Eleventh Five-Year Plan" period was lower than that during the "Tenth Five-Year Plan" period by 5.15 percentage points, and lower than that of the "Ninth Five-Year Plan" period by 8.88 percentage points.

Comparing nationwide cultural consumption growth rates between urban and rural areas shows that during the "Ninth Five-Year Plan" period, total urban growth was 1.81 times total rural growth, and average annual urban growth was higher than rural growth by 6.77 percentage points; during the "Tenth Five-Year Plan" period, total urban growth was 3.17 times total rural growth, and average annual urban growth was higher than rural growth by 11.82 percentage points. In the last 21 years, total nationwide urban growth was 5.29 times the total rural growth, and the average annual urban growth was 8.37 percentage points higher than that in rural areas. This is sufficient to show that nationwide rural cultural consumption demand has experienced weak growth. However, in order to obtain the reason why there is an imbalance in nationwide urban and rural growth, we still need to rule out the factor of changes in population distribution brought about my urbanization in order to precisely measure per capita growth trends in urban and rural areas.

Whether looking only at the "Ninth Five-Year Plan", "Tenth Five-Year Plan" and "Eleventh Five-Year Plan" periods, or viewing the last 21 years as a whole, the average annual growth of total nationwide urban cultural consumption is much higher than that of rural growth. It can therefore be inferred that total nationwide urban and rural cultural consumption as well as average annual growth has been influenced by changes in urban and rural population proportions brought about by the process of urbanization. This perhaps can explain why rural growth, across all time periods, is much lower than urban growth, and also lower than urban and rural comprehensive growth. However, there is another fact that cannot be ignored: whether looking solely at urban areas or rural areas, or a mix of both, compared with the "Ninth Five-Year Plan" and "Tenth Five-Year Plan" periods, during the "Eleventh Five-Year Plan" period, there was a significant drop in the average annual growth of nationwide total cultural consumption.

During the first 2 years of the "Twelfth Five-Year Plan", the average annual total nationwide urban and rural cultural consumption demand grew 13.99 %, which was 0.27 percentage points lower than the average annual growth during the "Ninth Five-Year Plan" period, but 0.34 percentage points higher than the average annual growth during the "Tenth Five-Year Plan" period and 2.63 percentage points higher than the average annual growth during the "Eleventh Five-Year Plan" period; total urban growth was 16.80 %, with a total average annual rural growth of 6.77 % . The urban annual total is 2.60 times higher than the rural year total, and the difference in cultural consumption demand in nationwide urban and rural areas continues to expand significantly.

1.1.2 Growth Trends in Urban and Rural Per Capita Cultural Consumption

National per capita values undoubtedly will be influenced by changes in population distribution brought about by urbanization, and are conducive to doing a comparison both of this time period and between urban and rural areas. See Fig. 1.2 for national urban and rural per capita cultural consumption demand trends from 1991 to 2012.

Figure 1.2 shows trends in changes in national urban and rural cultural consumption, and also shows the per capita cultural consumption growth index on three levels for urban and rural areas together, and urban and rural areas separately.

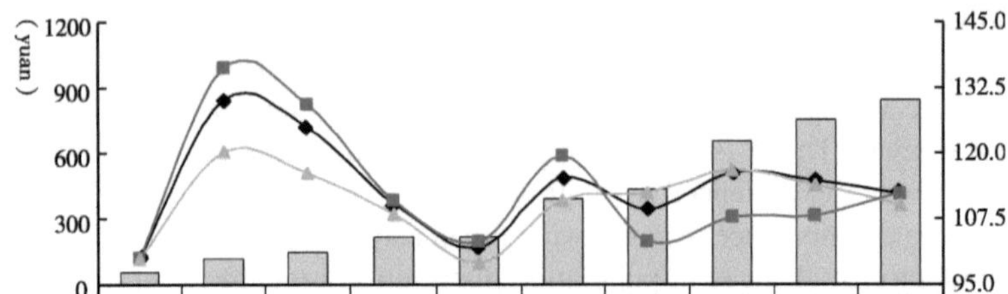

	1991	1995	1996	2000	2001	2005	2006	2010	2011	2012
Urban and Rural Per Capita	58.07	115.23	143.92	214.18	218.16	393.23	429.35	656.16	753.36	844.45
Urban and Rural Annual Growth	100.00	130.27	124.89	110.39	101.86	115.41	109.19	116.15	114.81	112.09
Urban Annual Growth	100.00	120.16	116.28	108.35	99.11	111.04	112.34	116.86	114.02	110.18
Rural Annual Growth	100.00	136.32	129.37	110.92	103.17	119.32	103.27	107.68	108.08	112.40

Fig. 1.2 Growth trends in national urban and rural per capita cultural consumption. *LHS cylindrical*: urban and rural per capita cultural consumption (yuan); *RHS curve*: urban and rural (including city/town, village/rural) annual growth coefficient (previous year = 100, lower than 100 is negative growth)

From 1991 to 2012, nationwide urban and rural per capita consumption rose from 58.07 to 844.45 yuan, growing 1,354 % in 21 years, an average annual growth rate of 13.60 %. The largest annual growth occurred in 2002, at a rate of 31.01 %; the smallest growth occurred in 2001, at a rate of 1.86 %. During the "Ninth Five-Year Plan" period, there was an average annual growth of 13.20 %, during the "Tenth Five-Year Plan" period an average annual growth of 12.92 %, and during the "Eleventh Nine-Year Plan" period there was an average annual growth of 10.78 %. The average annual growth during the "Eleventh Five-Year Plan" period was lower than that during the "Tenth Five-Year Plan" period by 2.14 percentage points, and lower than that during the "Ninth Five-Year Plan" period by 2.42 percentage points.

Nationwide urban per capita cultural consumption (see Fig. 1.6 below for annual absolute values) experienced a growth rate of 1,344.58 % over the same 21 period, with an average annual growth of 13.56 %. The largest annual growth occurred in 2002, with a growth rate of 55.53 %; the smallest annual growth occurred in 2001, with a negative growth of 0.89 %. During the "Ninth Five-Year Plan" period there was an average annual growth of 12.43 %, during the "Tenth Five-Year Plan" period there was an average annual growth of 14.78 %, and during the "Eleventh Five-Year Plan" period there was an average annual growth of 12.93 %. Average annual growth during the "Eleventh Five-Year Plan" period was 1.85 percentage points lower than that during the "Tenth Five-Year Plan" period, and higher than that of "Ninth Five-Year Plan" period by 0.50 percentage points.

During the same period, nationwide rural cultural consumption (annual absolute values can be seen in Fig. 1.6) saw a total increase of 816.27 % over the 21 year period, with an average annual growth rate of 11.12 %. The largest annual growth occurred in 1995, with a growth rate of 36.32 %; the smallest annual growth occurred in 2007, with a growth rate of 0.17 %. During the "Ninth Five-Year Plan" period there was an average annual growth of 12.77 %, during the "Tenth Five-Year Plan" period an average annual growth of 9.61 %, and during the "Eleventh Five-Year Plan" period an average annual growth of 4.41 %. Growth during the "Eleventh Five-Year Plan" period was smaller than that during the "Tenth Five-Year Plan" period by 5.20 percentage points, and lower than that in the "Ninth Five-Year Plan" period by 8.36 percentage points.

In comparing nationwide urban and rural per capita growth in cultural consumption, we see that during the "Ninth Five-Year Plan" period, the total growth of urban per capita values was only 96.69 % of the total growth of rural per capita values, and annual urban per capita growth was lower than that of rural growth by 0.34 percentage points; during the "Tenth Five-Year Plan" period, total growth of urban per capita values was 1.70 times the total growth of rural per capita values, and average annual urban growth was 5.17 percentage points higher than rural growth; during the "Tenth Five-Year Plan" period, total growth of urban per capita values were 3.47 times the total growth of rural per capita values, and average annual urban growth was 8.52 percentage points higher than rural growth. During this 21 year period, total growth of urban per capita values was 1.65 times that of total growth of rural per capita values, and average urban annual growth was higher than average rural annual growth by 2.44 percentage points. The gap in urban and rural national growth in cultural consumption demand is impressive, and shows a serious imbalance in urban and rural growth caused by the sluggish growth of rural areas. However, the gap in urban and rural per capita growth is not as great as the gap in total growth, which signifies that the process of urbanization has had a significant effect on the gap in total urban and rural growth.

In sum, in this 21-year period, growth trends in nationwide per capita cultural consumption demand have exposed two issues to which close attention must be paid: (1) When comparing the "Ninth Five-Year Plan" and the "Tenth Five-Year Plan" periods, the growth rate during the "Eleventh Five-Year Plan" period significantly decreased, both in urban and rural areas; (2) The gap in urban and rural cultural consumption demand has expanded significantly, and expansion has quickened particularly since the "Eleventh Five-Year Plan" period. What leaves one optimistic is that since the "Twelfth Five-Year Period", the above-described problems have been alleviated.

In the first 2 years of the "Twelfth Five-Year Plan" period, nationwide urban and rural average annual growth was 13.44 %, 0.24 percentage points higher than growth during the "Ninth Five-Year Plan" period, and higher than the "Tenth Five-Year Plan" period average annual growth by 0.52 percentage points, and even higher that the "Eleventh Five-Year Plan" growth, by 2.66 percentage points, with an urban per capita growth of 12.08 %; lower than the "Ninth Five-Year Plan" period average annual growth by 0.35 percentage points, and also lower than the "Tenth Five-Year Plan" period average annual growth by 2.70 percentage points; also lower than the "Eleventh Five-Year Plan" period growth by 0.85 percentage points. Rural per capita growth was 10.22 %, lower than the average annual growth during the "Ninth Five-Year Plan" period by 2.55 percentage points, but higher than the average annual growth during the "Tenth Five-Year Plan" period by 0.61 percentage points, and even higher than the average annual growth during the "Eleventh Five-Year Plan" period, by 5.81 percentage points. Urban per capita annual growth was still 1.19 times higher than that of rural growth. The gap between urban and rural areas nationwide in terms of cultural consumption per capita growth has narrowed significantly, but it still exists.

A comparison between urban and rural per capita absolute values and growth is only a kind of preliminary comparison. Nationwide growth in urban and rural per capita cultural consumption demands still needs to be put into the context of economic growth (using per capita GDP), livelihood improvements (shown by per capita income, total consumption, and accumulated savings) in order to make a more convincing comparison. These are facts and mathematics on which this evaluation system and various other assessment indicators are designed and based.

1.2 Background Situation of National Cultural Consumption Over the Last 21 Years

1.2.1 Cultural Consumption and Economic and Social Trends

A nationwide urban and rural overall analysis is the basis of the ranking and evaluation of consumption demand across urban and rural areas, and the treatment of related economic and social factors should begin from a nationwide analysis. See Fig. 1.3 for trends in the relationships between nationwide per capita GDP and urban and rural per capita income, consumption (this study separates non-cultural consumption and cultural consumption into two parts), and accumulated savings.

Figure 1.3 converts the absolute values of nationwide per capita GDP, urban and rural per capita income, consumption and savings since 1991 into a graph, visually showing national urban and rural cultural consumption demand and trends in the relationship between growth and economic and social factors. + Through the various types of numerical calculations in Fig. 1.3, we can see clearly that:

During the "Ninth Five-Year Plan" period, nationwide per capita GDP grew at an average annual rate of 9.26 %, and urban and rural per capita income grew at an average annual rate of 9.34 %; per capita total consumption grew at an average annual rate of 7.88 %, per capita savings grew at an average annual rate of 15.47 %, and per capita cultural consumption grew at an average annual rate of 13.20 %. Average annual growth in urban and rural per capita cultural consumption was higher than average annual growth of per capita GDP over the same period by 3.94 percentage points, higher than average annual growth in urban and rural per capita income by 3.86 percentage points, higher than the average annual growth in total per capita cultural consumption by 5.32 percentage points, and lower than the

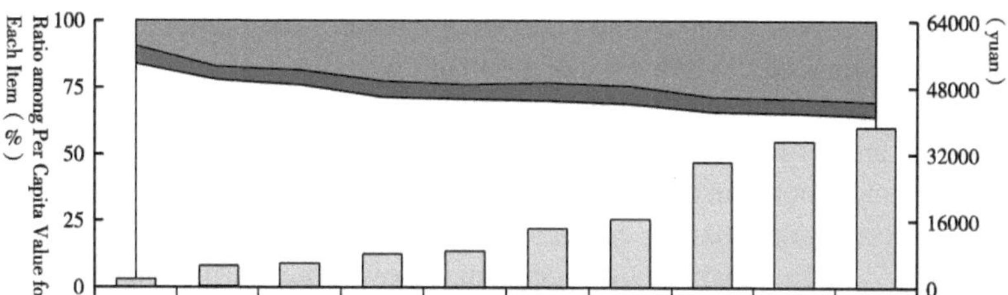

	1991	1995	1996	2000	2001	2005	2006	2010	2011	2012
(1) Per Capita Savings	89.22	404.93	522.29	831.34	967.12	1483.76	1759.43	3516.81	4232.45	5062.52
(2) Cultural Consumption	58.07	115.23	143.92	214.18	218.16	393.23	429.35	656.16	753.36	844.45
(3) Non-Cultural Consumption	784.21	1836.04	2126.84	2637.42	2841.00	4445.22	4948.90	8113.58	9498.43	10653.62
(4) Per Capita GDP	1893.00	5046.00	5846.00	7858.00	8622.00	14185.00	16500.00	30015.00	35198.00	38420.00

Fig. 1.3 Relationship trends between national per capita GDP and urban and rural per capita income, consumption and savings. *LHS area*: urban and rural per capita accumulated savings, per capita cultural consumption, per capita non-cultural consumption (yuan are converted to %), (*1*)+(*2*)+(*3*) = per capita income, (*2*)+(*3*) = total per capita consumption, (*1*)+(*2*) = surplus per capita non-cultural consumption, changes in proportional relationship; *RHS cylinder*: per capita GDP (yuan), according to production data in the calendar year in the 2013 *China Statistical Yearbook*

average annual growth in per capita accumulated savings by 2.27 percentage points. During the "Ninth Five-Year Plan" period, there was a trend of significant growth in nationwide urban and rural cultural consumption demand. This showed the gradual progress that China is making towards the goal of "moderate prosperity" and the social environment through which the spiritual and cultural needs of the people were increasing.

During the "Tenth Five-Year Plan" period, nationwide per capita GDP grew at an average annual rate of 12.54 %, and urban and rural per capita income grew at an average annual rate of 11.41 %; per capita total consumption grew at an average annual rate of 11.15 %, per capita savings grew at an average annual rate of 12.28 %, and per capita cultural consumption grew at an average annual rate of 12.92 %. Average annual growth in urban and rural per capita cultural consumption was higher than average annual growth of per capita GDP over the same period by 0.38 percentage points, higher than average annual growth in urban and rural per capita income by 1.51 percentage points, higher than the average annual growth in total per capita cultural consumption by 1.77 percentage points, and higher than the average annual growth in per capita accumulated savings by 0.64 percentage points. During the "Tenth Five-Year Period", an upsurge in nationwide urban and rural cultural consumption demand was fully apparent. This was in face the period when China's cultural industry was flourishing and the environment and society in which cultural construction reached a climax.

During the "Eleventh Five-Year Plan" period, nationwide per capita GDP grew at an average annual rate of 16.17 %, higher than annual average growth in the

"Tenth Five-Year Plan" by 3.63 percentage points, and higher than average annual growth during the "Ninth Five-Year Plan" by 6.91 percentage points; urban and rural per capita income grew at an average annual rate of 14.21 %, higher than the average annual rate during the "Tenth Five Year Plan" period by 2.80 percentage points and higher than average annual growth during the "Ninth Five-Year Plan" by 4.87 percentage points; per capita total consumption grew at an average annual rate of 12.63 %, higher than the average annual growth rate during the "Tenth Five-Year Plan" period by 1.48 percentage points, and higher than the average annual growth during the "Ninth Five-Year Plan" period by 4.75 percentage points; there was an average annual growth in per capita of accumulated savings of 18.84 %, higher than average annual growth during the "Tenth Five-Year Plan" period by 6.56 percentage points, and higher than average annual growth during the "Ninth Five-Year Plan" period by 3.37 percentage points; the average annual growth of per capita cultural consumption was 10.78 %, lower than average annual growth during the "Tenth Five-Year Plan" period by 2.14 percentage points, and lower than average annual growth during the "Ninth Five-Year Plan" period by 2.42 percentage points. The average annual growth of urban and rural per capita cultural consumption was lower than average annual growth of total per capita GDP over the same period by 5.39 percentage points, lower than average annual growth in urban and rural per capita income by 3.43 percentage points, lower than average annual growth in total per capita consumption by 1.85 percentage points, and in particular, dramatically lower than average annual growth in per capita accumulated savings, by 8.06 percentage points.

At this time, within the environment of increased average annual growth in per capita GDP, income, and total consumption, and the obvious increase in average annual growth of per capita accumulated savings, the average annual growth in per capita cultural consumption has, on the contrary, significantly dropped. The social factors behind this are the influence of the rise in domestic prices in the first 3 years of the "Tenth Five-Year Plan" period, and the international financial crisis which occurred during the last 2 years of the Five-Year plan. Due to the deficits of China's social security system, the general public, for the sake of "Self-Security", had curbed consumption and increased savings; bearing the brunt of decreased spending was "Non-Essential" non-material and cultural consumption.

In the first 2 years of the "Twelfth Five-Year Plan" period, the average annual growth of nationwide per capita GDP was 13.14 %, urban and rural per capita average annual growth was 16.10$, per capita total consumption average annual growth was 14.50 %, per capita accumulated savings average annual growth was 19.98 %, and per capita cultural consumption average annual growth was 13.44 %. Urban and rural per capita cultural consumption average annual growth was higher than per capita GDP average annual growth over the same period by 0.30 percentage points, lower than urban and rural per capita income average annual growth by 2.66 percentage points, lower than per capita total consumption average annual growth by 1.06 percentage points, and lower than per capita accumulated savings average annual growth by 6.54 percentage points.

From 1991 to 2012, nationwide per capita GDP grew at an average annual rate of 15.41 %, urban and rural per capita income grew at an average annual rate of 14.69 %, total per capita consumption grew at an average annual rate of 13.25 %, per capita savings grew at an average annual rate of 21.20 %, and per capita cultural consumption grew at an average annual rate of 13.60 %. Urban and rural per capita cultural consumption average annual growth was significantly lower than per capita GDP growth during the same period, by 1.81 percentage points, moderately lower than urban and rural per capita income average annual growth, by 1.09 percentage points, slightly higher than per capita total consumption average annual growth, by 0.35 percentage points, and very significantly lower than per capita savings average annual growth, by 7.60 percentage points. In the 21 years of study, nationwide urban and rural cultural consumption demand growth lagged behind national economic development, substantially lagging behind livelihood enhancement of the general population, in particular being squeezed by the growth in urban and rural accumulated savings, with a poor coordination of growth. The "Eleventh Five-Year Plan" period's "growth coordination" was significantly less coordinated than that during the "Tenth Five-Year Plan" period, and also significantly less coordinated than that during the "Ninth Five-Year Plan" period; after the "Twelfth Five-Year Plan" period, there was a slight improvement.

In the comprehensive analysis of the growth relationship of the national urban and rural per capita cultural consumption and related background factors, at this point we can only base this on the set indicators of this evaluation system in order to make the next step in expanding the proportion calculation of each related indicator in urban and rural cultural consumption.

1.2.2 Growth Trends in Cultural Consumption and Economic and Social Factors

Here, each absolute value is converted to the annual growth in percent index, where each year has a value of 100, and the starting year of 1991 is the base year. This includes the "Non-Cultural Consumption" and "Savings": values that were carefully set and specially separated out from the base data by this study, revealing trends shown by specific rules. Figure 1.4 shows growth trends in national per capita GDP, urban and rural income, consumption (separated into non-cultural and cultural consumption) and savings.

In the annual growth coefficient chain of data in Fig. 1.4, there are three data items with a specific relationship that are worth noting. Both through the graphics and also the data, the coefficients show strong correlation. The first pair of data items: Reference (1), cylindrical shapes, represent annual growth coefficient, of national per capita GDP; (2), curved lines with diamond shapes, represent annual growth coefficient of urban and rural per capita income. In between the two, from 1992 to 2012, the correlation coefficient was 0.9348, and the growth rate during the

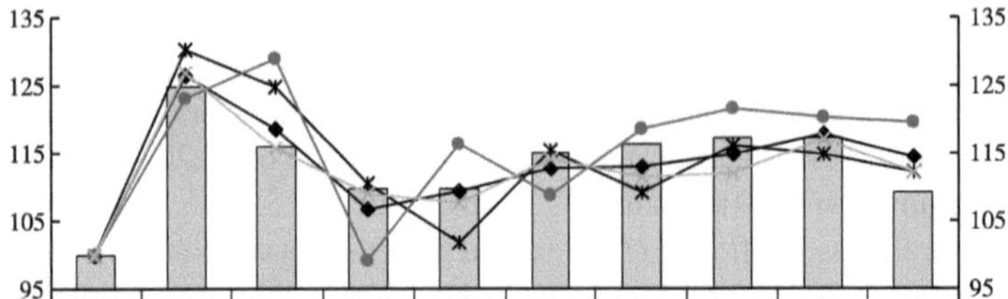

	1991	1995	1996	2000	2001	2005	2006	2010	2011	2012
(1) Per Capita GDP	100	124.78	115.85	109.76	109.72	114.99	116.32	117.21	117.27	109.15
(2) Per Capita Income	100	126.42	118.54	106.70	109.32	112.80	112.90	114.83	117.89	114.34
(3) Non-Cultural Consumption	100	126.92	115.84	109.05	107.72	113.97	111.33	111.99	117.07	112.16
(4) Cultural Consumption	100	130.27	124.89	110.39	101.86	115.41	109.19	116.15	114.81	112.09
(5) Per Capita Savings	100	123.20	128.98	99.08	116.33	108.79	118.58	121.69	120.35	119.61

Fig. 1.4 Growth trends in national per capita GDP, urban and rural income, consumption, and savings. *LHS*: annual growth coefficient (values are in columns, the rest are in the curve), Prior year = 100, lower than 100 represents negative growth. Correlation coefficient for annual growth from 1991 to 2012 (1991, as starting point, is not counted): (*1*) and (2) 0.9348; (2) and (*3*) 0.9483; (*4*) and (*5*) 0.0205. Between 2001 and 2005, 0.9131, between 2001 and 2008, −0.6531, between 2002 and 2008, 0.7123; the "growth of negative savings effect" of cultural consumption was established

calendar year kept pace at a rate of 93.48 %. The correlation coefficient for these data items shows the relationship between "Gross National Income" and the income of urban and rural residents, and the degree of synchronization of their growth.

Second pair of data items: Reference (2) represents the urban and rural per capita income annual growth coefficient, (3), the curved line with squares on it, represents the urban and rural per capita non-cultural consumption annual growth coefficient, and the correlation coefficient between the two from 1992 to 2012 is 0.9483, and the growth rate during the calendar year kept pace at a rate of 93.83 %. The correlation coefficient for these data items shows the relationship between the income of urban and rural residents and essential living expenses (all non-cultural consumption is set as "essential consumption"), as well as the degree of synchronization of their growth.

The third pair of data items: Reference (4), the curved line with circles on it, represents the annual cultural consumption growth index; reference (5), the curved line with triangles on it, represents the annual accumulated savings growth index, and the correlation coefficient between the two from 1992 to 2012 was 0.0205, showing a low degree of correlation. However, studying this time period in depth, there was a negative value from 2001 to 2005 of 0.9131, a negative value from 2001 to 2008 of 0.6531, and a negative value from 2002 to 2008 of 0.7123; here there was a very obvious negative, or inversely proportional, relationship.

The correlation between these two in terms of annual growth may be understood simply as the national urban and rural per capita accumulated savings growing at a rate of 1 %, urban and rural per capita cultural consumption growth decreasing by 0.91 % during the period of 2001–2005, decreasing 0.65 % during the period from 2001 to 2008, decreasing 0.71 % during the period from 2002 to 2008, and vice versa. In a "positive correlation", this degree of correlation does not count as high, but in a "negative correlation", this degree of correlation is quite high. The correlation coefficient for this pair of data shows the degree of growth synchronization between money left over after urban and rural citizens' "essential consumption" and "Non-Essential" non-material and cultural consumption.

The calculations in Fig. 1.4 include the omitted years, and in the list of years on the graph it can be seen that, from 2000 to 2006, on the curved lines of growth in national urban and rural per capita cultural consumption and accumulated savings, there is an almost perfect inverse relationship. Entering the "Twelfth Five-Year Plan", national urban and rural per capita cultural consumption annual growth decreased; corresponding to this was the national urban and rural per capita forming a peak in annual growth in accumulated savings. From the later years of the "Ninth Five-Year Plan" until the beginning of the "Tenth Five-Year Plan", between the cultural consumption annual growth curved line and the accumulated savings annual growth curved line, a corresponding lateral mirror, often called "reflection in the water" shows a negative correlation. This is the "regularity"-an important discovery- that this study revealed many years ago: the trend of China's cultural consumption demand reflect the "effect of the negative growth in accumulated savings". This has been repeatedly confirmed by annual follow-up data and calculations.

The background database for this study was applied fully to each province and region for analysis. If the 20 years since 1992 are analyzed (1991 is not counted, and Tibet and Chongqing, due to lack of corresponding annual data, are not counted), then this "law" is clearly established in 25 of the provinces, and basically established for the remaining provinces of Jilin, Anhui, Hunan, and Guizhou. When looking at the more than 10 years since the "Tenth Five-Year Plan" (corresponding data for Chongqing and Tibet were available and included), there were 23 provinces with a high or very high degree of negative correlation, and this "law" was clearly universally established, and the degree of negative correlation was extremely significant, especially in Beijing, Hebei, Shanghai, Heilongjiang, Hubei, Jiangxi, Ningxia, Gansu, and Sichuan. The degree of negative correlation was relatively high, and the "law" was basically established, in Shandong, Zhejiang, Anhui, Hunan, Chongqing, and Guizhou. Only in Inner Mongolia was the degree of negative correlation relatively low, and in Jilin there was a weak positive correlation. This also revealed a phenomenon: the longer the time of the investigation, the more significant and widespread this "law" seems to be.

At the same time, using the background database to do a complete analysis on each major city from 2006 (the year 2005 is not counted in the annual city data count), there are 27 cities which have a very high degree of negative correlation, universally establishing this "law"; within these, 20 of the cities have an extremely high degree of negative correlation. Dalian and Xi'an have relatively high negative correlations, and this "law" is basically established in those cases; only in Shenyang and Lanzhou were the negative correlations relatively low; in Ningbo, Shenzhen, Haikou, Harbin, and Kunming, there was an extremely low negative correlation or a weak positive correlation. This also reveals a phenomenon: the more the market economy of a region is developed, or the more developed the city, the more universal this "law" is; there are few exceptions among developed provinces, and extremely few exceptions among developed cities.

According to the internal logic of general social and economic development and the current actual situation of China's development, this evaluation study has extracted three pairs of data sets, constituting a complete and concise set of data: national economic growth across all regions → increased income of citizens → increase in essential consumption, but a decrease in terms of proportion of income → an increase in proportion of total income comprised of money left over after necessary living expenditures, but an increase in discretionary spending left over from essential consumption → an increase in "non—essential" spiritual and cultural consumption, but in a ration to output, income, and total consumption, there may be a decrease, and an especially significant decrease compared with accumulated savings. These are original testing methods and ideas for analysis of this evaluation which can show multiple layers of changes in trends.

1.2.3 Changes in the Ratio of Cultural Consumption to Various Factors

Figure 1.5 shows the changing ratio between urban and rural per capita expenditure on cultural consumption.

1.2.3.1 Changes in the Relationship Between Cultural Consumption and GDP

From 1991 to 2012, the proportion of national urban and rural per capita cultural consumption to per capita GDP fell from 3.07 % to 2.20 %, a decrease in 0.87 percentage points. This ratio was highest in 1991 at a rate of 3.0 %, and lowest in 2008 at a rate of 2.13 %; overall there was a downward trend. In the annual items listed in Fig. 1.5, it can be seen that the ratio appeared higher only in 1996, 2000, 2005, and 2012, and was lower during the other years.

In studying national urban and rural ratio dynamics over different time periods, we can see that during the "Ninth Five-Year Plan" period, there was a 0.44 percentage point increase from 1995 to 2000; during the "Tenth Five-Year Plan" period, there was a 0.05 percentage point increase from 2000 to 2005; during the "Eleventh Five-Year Plan" period, there was a decrease of 0.59 percentage points from 2005 to 2010. During each 5-year period there was a shift in national urban and rural ratios; the "Tenth Five-Year Plan" period was significantly worse than the

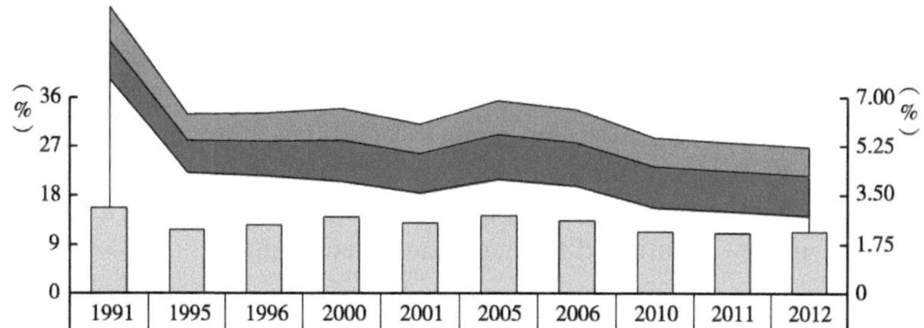

	1991	1995	1996	2000	2001	2005	2006	2010	2011	2012
Proportion of Income	6.2336	4.8905	5.1527	5.8155	5.4183	6.2198	6.0152	5.3405	5.2013	5.0992
Proportion of Total Consumption	6.8939	5.9054	6.3378	7.5109	7.1312	8.1271	7.9830	7.4821	7.3486	7.3443
Ratio to Non-Surplus	39.4237	22.1527	21.6024	20.4855	18.4055	20.9498	19.6159	15.7241	15.1102	14.2959
Ratio to GDP	3.0674	2.2836	2.4618	2.7256	2.5302	2.7721	2.6021	2.1861	2.1404	2.1979

Fig. 1.5 Changes national urban and rural per capita cultural consumption ratios. *LHS area*: ratio (%) of urban and rural per capita cultural comparison and per capita income, per capita total consumption, per capita non-cultural consumption surplus (abbreviated in the chart as "non-surplus"). Annual changes to the various ratios are visually represented; *RHS cylinder*: ratio of urban and rural per capita cultural consumption and per capita GDP (%)

"Ninth Five-Year Plan" period, and the "Eleventh Five-Year Plan" period was again significantly worse than the "Tenth Five-Year Plan" period.

During the first 2 years of the "Eleventh Five-Year Plan" period, the proportional value between national urban and rural per capita cultural consumption and per capita GDP increased by 0.0118 percentage points, and there was a slight increase in the reverse coordination between the growth in urban and rural cultural consumption demand and national economic development.

1.2.3.2 Changes in Cultural Consumption as Proportion of Income

From 1991 to 2012, national urban and rural per capita cultural consumption decreased from 6.23 % of per capita income to 5.10 %, a decrease of 1.13 percentage points. The national urban and rural ratio was at its highest in 2002 at a rate of 6.38 %, and at its lowest in 1994 at a rate of 4.75 %; overall there was a downward trend. Looking at the years shown in Fig. 1.5, this ratio increased only in 1996, 2000, and 2005, and decreased during all of the other years.

When looking at changes in national urban and rural ratios by time period, we can see that in the "Ninth Five-Year Plan" period, there was an increase of 0.93 percentage points from 1995 to 2000; in the "Tenth Five-Year Plan" period, there was an increase of 0.40 percentage points from 2000 to 2005; in the "Eleventh Five-Year Plan" period, there was a decrease of 0.88 percentage points from 2005 to 2010. In each 5-year period there was a change in the national urban and rural ratio, the "Tenth Five-Year Plan" period being significantly worse-off than the "Ninth

Five-Year Plan" period, and the "Eleventh Five-Year Plan" period again being significantly worse-off than the "Tenth Five-Year Plan" period.

During the first 2 years of the "Eleventh Five-Year Plan" period, the proportion of national urban and rural per capita cultural consumption to per capita income decreased by 0.24 percentage points, and the coordination between the growth in urban and rural cultural consumption demand, and the growth in urban and rural citizens' income, continued to significantly decrease.

1.2.3.3 Changes in Cultural Consumption as Proportion of Total Consumption

From 1991 to 2012, proportion of national urban and rural cultural consumption to total consumption went up from 6.89 to 7.34 %, an increase of 0.45 percentage points. The national urban and rural proportion was highest in 2002, at a rate of 8.30 %, and lowest in 1994, at a rate of 5.76 %; there was a general upward trend. When looking at all of the years listed in Fig. 1.5, we can see that there was an increase only in the years 1996, 2000, and 2005, and a decrease during the other years.

When looking at changes in ratio over time period, during the "Ninth Five-Year Plan" period, from 1995 to 2000 there was an increase of 1.61 percentage points; during the "Tenth Five-Year Plan" period from 2000 to 2005, there was an increase of 0.62 percentage points; during the "Eleventh Five-Year Plan" period from 2005 to 2010, there was a decrease of 0.65 percentage points. There were shifts in national urban and rural ratios over every 5-year period, with the "Tenth Five-Year Period" being significantly worse-off than the "Ninth Five-Year Period", and the "Eleventh Five-Year Plan" period being yet again worse-off than the "Tenth Five-Year Plan" period.

During the first 2 years of the "Twelfth Five-Year Plan" period, the ratio of national urban and rural cultural consumption to per capita total consumption decreased by 0.14 percentage points, with a significant decrease in the coordination of urban and rural cultural consumption demand growth and urban and rural total consumption growth.

1.2.3.4 The Changing Relationship Between Cultural Consumption and Non-cultural Consumption Surplus

From 1991 to 2012, the proportionate value between national urban and rural per capita cultural consumption and per capita non-cultural consumption surplus decreased from 39.42 % to 14.30 %, a decrease of 25.12 percentage points. The national urban and rural ratio was at its highest point in 1991 at 39.42 %, and at its lowest in 2012 at 14.30 %, with a general downward trend. Of the years listed in Fig. 1.5, only in 2005 was there a growth in this proportion, while in all other years there was a decrease.

When looking at the national urban and rural changes in ration over time periods, we see that during the "Ninth Five-Year Plan" period, 1995–2000, it was lowered by 1.67 percentage points; during the "Tenth Five-Year Plan" period, it was increased by 0.46 percentage points; During the "Eleventh Five-Year Plan" period from 2005 to 2010, it decreased by 5.23 percentage points. Each 5-year period showed changes in national urban and rural ratio; the "Tenth Five-Year Plan" period was significantly better than the "Ninth Five-Year Plan" period, and the "Eleventh Five-Year Plan period was significantly worse than the "Tenth Five-Year Plan" period.

During the first 2 years of the "Twelfth Five-Year Plan" period, the ratio between national urban and rural per capita cultural consumption and per capita non-cultural consumption surplus decreased by 1.43 percentage points, with a significant decrease in the coordination of growth of urban and rural cultural consumption demand with the increase in urban and rural citizens' money left over after essential expenses.

The analysis of to the relationship between the values of urban and rural cultural consumption demand shows coordinated growth and national economic development and advances in livelihood, an upward trend from 1991 to 2012 in the share of cultural consumption in total consumption and a downward trend in surplus . In the "Ninth Five-Year Plan" period, the ratio of cultural consumption to GDP, to proportion of income, and to total consumption showed an upward trend, while the ratio to non-cultural surplus showed a downward trend; in the "Tenth Five-Year Plan" period, there was a slight upward trend across all proportions of cultural consumption values; in the "Eleventh Five-Year Plan" period, there was a significant downward trend across all proportions of cultural consumption values. In the first 2 years of the "Twelfth Five-Year Plan" period, national urban and rural cultural consumption growth was slightly higher than GDP growth, significantly lower than urban and rural income growth, moderately lower than total consumption growth, and much lower than accumulated savings growth. Cultural consumption and GDP ratio saw an upward trend, whereas proportion of income ratio, proportion of total consumption ratio, and non-cultural consumption surplus ratio saw a downward trend.

1.3 Coordination Between National Urban and Rural and Regional Cultural Consumption Over 21 Years

This study's uniquely designed assessment detects the coordination of growth between urban and rural cultural consumption demand, and also detects the coordination of regional growth in cultural consumption demand. By then placing national urban and rural cultural consumption demand growth in the context of coordination with the growth in urban and rural areas, and across regions, we can also see comparable conditions and warning trends, which are useful for progressing with analysis and assessment. For a comparison between urban and rural areas of national cultural consumption, and for trends of change among urban and rural cultural consumption across regions, from the years 1991 to 2012, see Fig. 1.6.

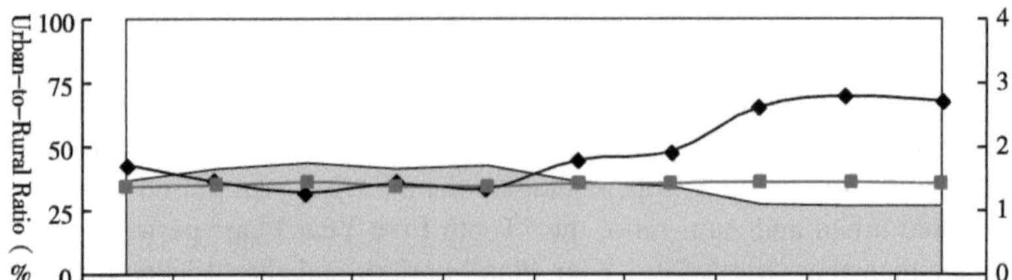

	1991	1995	1996	2000	2001	2005	2006	2010	2011	2012
Urban–to–Rural Ratio	84.03	147.01	170.95	264.07	261.71	526.14	591.04	966.30	1101.74	1213.88
Rural Per Capita	48.62	102.39	132.46	186.72	192.64	295.48	305.13	366.72	396.36	445.49
Urban–to–Rural Ratio	1.7283	1.4358	1.2906	1.4143	1.3585	1.7806	1.9370	2.6350	2.7796	2.7248
Urban–Rural Gap	1.3642	1.3886	1.4342	1.3836	1.3794	1.4140	1.4260	1.4422	1.4445	1.4295

Fig. 1.6 National per capita cultural consumption urban and rural ratios and changing trends across regions. *LHS area*: rural per capita cultural consumption (yuan converted to %), ratio between changes in urban and rural areas; *RHS curve*: per capita urban and rural cultural consumption (rural = 1), Regional discrepancy in urban per capita cultural consumption (no gap = 1)

1.3.1 Cultural Consumption Trends of Expansion in Urban and Rural Areas

From 1991 to 2012 the ratio between urban and rural national cultural consumption broadened from 1.7283 to 2.7248, or 57.66 %. The national per capita cultural consumption ratio in cities and rural areas was at its lowest in 1996 at 1.2906, and at its highest in 2011 at 2.7796; overall there was a continued significant expansion trend. Of all the cities listed in Fig. 1.6, only from 1995 to 1996, and in 2001 and 2012 was there a reduced ratio between urban and rural areas; in the rest of the years there were expansions. In the last 10 years, China has made the resolution of the "Three Rural Issues" a national priority. One cannot help but be shocked at the development and changing situation during these years, as well as its continuity in the areas of the exemption of agricultural taxes that have been in existence for thousands of years and the guarantee of accelerating development across rural regions. Many major cities are committed to the implementation of the "International Catching-Up" policy, constructing and development with greater acceleration, imperceptibly sacrificing the balanced developmental success of national urban and rural areas.

Looking at different times period, during the "Ninth Five-Year Plan" period, the proportion of per capita urban to rural cultural consumption from 1995 to 2000 was reduced by 1.50 %; during the "Tenth Five-Year Plan" period, from 2000 to 2005, was expanded by 25.90 %; during the "Eleventh Five-Year Plan" period, from 2005 to 2010, there was an expansion of 47.98 %. In terms of the changes in ratio between urban and rural areas in national per capita cultural consumption, during the “Tenth Five-Year Plan” period, a significant expansion began; during the “Eleventh Five-Year Plan” period, the degree of expansion was more serious than that during the “Tenth Five-Year Plan” period. The gap in urban and rural per capita cultural consumption is rapidly expanding.

The calculations for the ratio of national cultural consumption between urban and rural areas come from the differing per capita cultural consumption absolute values and growth changes in the two areas. Changes have occurred in the national cultural consumption urban and rural ratio, and the ratio has been affected by the national urban and rural annual cultural consumption demand.

From 1991 to 2012, national urban per capita cultural consumption rose from 84.03 to 1,213.88 yuan, an increase of 1,129.85 yuan and a total percentage increase over 21 years of 1,344.58 %, a annual average growth of 13.56 %; rural per capita cultural consumption rose from 48.62 to 445.49 yuan, an increase of 396.87 yuan, and a total percentage increase over 21 years of 816.27 %, with a annual average growth of 11.12 %. In the 21 years, the average annual growth of total urban per capita cultural consumption demand was higher than that in rural areas by 2.44 percentage points; the average annual growth rate for rural areas was only 82.01 % that of urban areas, leading the continued expansion of the gap between cultural consumption in urban and rural areas.

Looking at this over time periods, during the “Ninth Five-Year Plan” period, national urban and rural per capita consumption increased at a total rate of 79.63 %, with an average annual increase of 12.43 %; rural per capita consumption increased at a total rate of 82.36 %, with an average annual increase of 12.77 %. Average annual rural growth was higher than average annual urban growth by 0.34 percentage points, and the urban and rural ratio of cultural consumption narrowed.

During the “Tenth Five-Year Plan” period, national urban per capita cultural consumption increased at a total rate of 99.24 %, with an average annual growth of 14.78 %; rural per capita cultural consumption increased at a total rate of 58.25 %, with an average annual growth of 9.61 %. The average rural annual growth was lower than urban average annual growth by 5.17 percentage points, and the urban and rural ratio of cultural consumption significantly expanded.

During the “Eleventh Five-Year Plan” period, national urban per capita cultural consumption grew at a total rate of 83.66 %, with a annual average increase of 12.93 %; rural per capita cultural consumption grew at a total rate of 24.11 %, with an average annual increase of 4.41 %. The average annual rural growth was lower than the average annual urban growth by 8.52 percentage points, and the urban and rural ratio of cultural consumption significantly expanded.

During the first 2 years of the “Twelfth Five-Year Plan” period, national urban per capita cultural consumption grew at a rate of 12.08 %, and rural per capita cultural consumption grew at a rate of 10.22 %. Average annual rural growth was lower than average annual urban growth by 1.86 percentage points, and over the 2 year period there was an expansion in the ration of urban to rural cultural consumption of 3.41 %.

1.3.2 Trends in Regional Gaps in Urban and Rural Cultural Consumption

From 1991 to 2012, the gap in per capita cultural consumption between urban and rural areas expanded from 1.3642 to 1.4295, an expansion of 4.79 %. The smallest difference in per capita cultural consumption between urban and rural areas took place in 1992 at a value of 1.3490, and the largest was in 2008 at 1.4593; there was an overall trend of continued gradual expansion. Looking at the years listed in Fig. 1.6, we see that the gap between urban and rural regions was reduced only from 2000 to 2001, and in 2012; during the other years, there was an expansion annual. Over the past decade, China has been undertaking development of the western part of the country, raising the level of central China, implementing several strategic policies for revitalizing the old industrial base in northeast China, promoting development of these areas to keep pace with the rest of this country. This situation, occurring and continuing for many years, cannot help but make one feel surprised. Several provinces in the east have implemented the "Modernization First" strategy, seizing the advantage of this initiative to construct and develop, while sacrificing balanced development in all regions across the nation.

Looking at this across time periods, during the "Ninth Five-Year Plan" period, the nationwide per capita cultural consumption gap between urban and rural regions narrowed by 0.36 % from 1995 to 2000; during the "Tenth Five-Year Plan" period, the gap widened by 2.20 % from 2000 to 2005; during the "Eleventh Five-Year Plan" period, the gap widened by 1.99 % from 2005 to 2010. In terms of the nationwide growth in the per capita cultural consumption gap between urban and rural regions, the "Eleventh Five-Year Period" gap was slightly reduced from that during the "Tenth Five-Year Plan" period, but the per capita cultural consumption demand gap between urban and rural regions has continued the general trend of gradual expansion.

The basis for calculation of nationwide difference between urban and rural consumption is the difference in absolute values of urban and rural per capita cultural consumption across provinces and regions as well as the change in growth. Nationwide differences in regional urban and rural cultural consumption changes are also affected by annual growth in urban and rural cultural consumption demand across China's 31 provinces. The expansion of nationwide urban and rural per capita cultural consumption difference among regions indicates that the urban and rural per capita cultural consumption in a fairly large number of provinces or regions, compared with the national urban and rural average, tended to be polarized, being either higher or lower.

During the first 2 years of the "Twelfth Five-Year Plan" period, the regional gap in urban and rural per capita cultural consumption narrowed by 0.88 %. The trends in expansion and narrowing of the regional gap in cultural consumption in urban and rural areas does not have as many negative effects as the changes in expansion and narrowing of the ratio of cultural consumption in urban areas to that in rural areas, but it is still worth examining.

1.4 Evaluation of Nationwide Urban and Rural Cultural Consumption Demand Over 21 Years

In a comprehensive analysis, over the 21 years, the total average annual growth of nationwide urban and rural cultural consumption demand was 14.47 %, with an average annual growth in per capita demand of 13.60 %; urban and rural cultural consumption growth was significantly lower than GDP growth, fairly significantly lower than urban and rural income growth, slightly higher than total consumption growth, and much lower than growth in savings; the gap between urban and rural areas in per capita cultural consumption expanded by 57.66 %, with a regional gap of 4.78 %. These are shown in the comprehensive evaluation calculation of the national urban and rural cultural consumption demand index.

Trends of change in the nationwide urban and rural cultural consumption demand index from 1991 to 2012 can be seen in Fig. 1.7. The nationwide urban and rural cultural consumption demand index is based on various types of evaluation results from different time periods and references values, implemented in 2012. The index percentile measures the horizontal and vertical percentage levels.

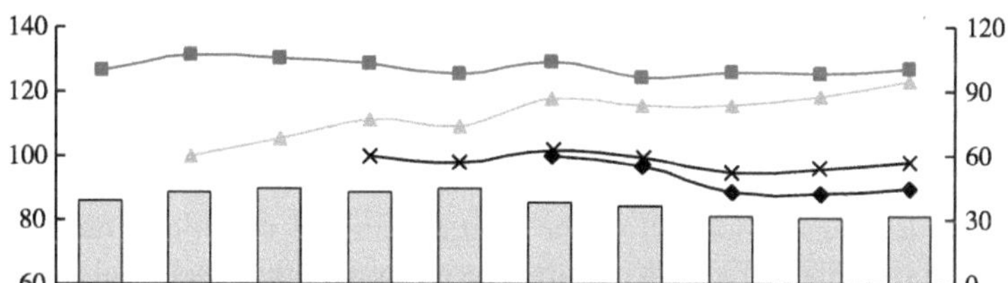

	1991	1995	1996	2000	2001	2005	2006	2010	2011	2012
Horizontal Assessment	86.19	88.59	89.95	88.87	89.55	85.38	84.27	81.10	80.64	80.93
Vertical Assessment (1)	—	100.00	105.35	111.61	109.16	117.77	115.70	115.64	118.57	122.99
Vertical Assessment (2)	—	—	—	100.00	97.82	101.84	99.19	94.76	95.65	98.00
Vertical Assessment (3)	—	—	—	—	—	100.00	96.62	88.61	88.24	89.59
Vertical Assessment (4)	100.00	106.83	105.35	102.81	97.82	103.62	96.62	99.29	98.49	100.77

Fig. 1.7 Index of trends of change in nationwide urban and rural per capita cultural consumption demand. *LHS cylindrical*: horizontal assessment ideal value with no discrepancy = 100); *RHS curve*: vertical assessment (starting annual base value = 100), (*1*) 1995 as starting point; (*2*) 2000 as starting point; (*3*) 2005 as starting point; *Right axis curve*: longitudinal assessment (*4*), starting from previous year

1.4.1 *Annual Horizontal Assessment Index*

In each annual horizontal assessment of ideal values, urban and rural cultural consumption total share values are measured based on nationwide urban and rural total base values (the national share is = 100 % of the base value). Per capita absolute values and each item's proportionate value is measured based on nationwide urban and rural average values. When the share rises or is higher than the national average value, then there are "plus points". When the share lowers or is lower than the average national value, then there are "minus points". The ratio of urban and rural cultural consumption, as well as regional gaps, are measured against an ideal status with no gaps; whether it is the country as a whole or separate regions, as long as there is an urban and rural ration and regional difference, a "deduction" will be implemented.

In the nationwide cultural consumption demand for urban and rural areas, as well as regions, the "ideal value" for be 100, indicating zero difference. In 2012 that value was 80.93, lower than the zero-difference ideal by 19.07, but higher than the previous year, 2011, by 0.29. When comparing this ratio across different years, Fig. 1.7 shows that it falls short of the ideal value in all ten listed years zero-difference. Among these years, the highest value was in 1996 at 89.95, and the lowest value was in 2011 at 80.64. This is because nationwide urban and rural overall per capita cultural consumption absolute values and proportionate values become the overall baseline as well as its own baseline. The urban and rural cultural consumption proportion and regional discrepancy became the main overall national measurement indicator, and the urban and rural ration and regional discrepancy is generally continuously widening.

In this evaluation, all of the overall national urban and rural "loss in points" came from the per capita cultural consumption urban and rural ratio, and the urban and rural per capita cultural consumption regional gap that exists and is widening. Only if the urban and rural ration and the regional gap narrows can the nationwide urban and rural overall prosperity index rise; only if the urban and rural ratio and regional gap is completely eliminated can the national urban and rural index reach the "ideal value" of 100.

1.4.2 *Vertical Assessment Indexes Since the "Ninth Five-Year Plan"*

In a vertical assessment vertical assessment since the "Ninth Five-Year Plan", national urban and rural cultural consumption total shares, per capita absolute values, each item's proportional values, and urban and rural ratio and regional discrepancies begin with the corresponding values from 1995 as a starting point to measure the base value. Whether it is the overall national values, or regional values, the numerical indicators that are higher than those in 1995 will be "plus points", and those lower than in 1995 will be "minus points" with the indicators ultimately being balanced. Each of the following vertical assessment vertical assessments will be evaluated in this way, with the difference being that the starting year will be different.

The last year of the "Eighth Five-Year Plan", 1995, has a base value of 100 as a starting point. In 2012, this national urban and rural index was 122.99, higher than the base starting value in 1995 by 22.99, and also higher than that in 2011 by 4.42. Since the "Ninth Five-Year Plan", in looking at the annual index, Fig. 1.7 shows that in the list of years, all 8 had annual averages higher than the starting base value of 100. Among these, the highest value was in 2012 at 122.99, and the lowest value was in 1996 at 105.35. Entering into the "Eleventh Five-Year Plan", the national urban and rural index decreased slightly, but it came up again in 2011 and in 2012 continued to rise.

1.4.3 Vertical Assessment Vertical Assessment Indexes Since the "Tenth Five-Year Plan"

With the last year of the "Ninth Five-Year Plan", 2000, having a starting base value of 100, the national urban and rural index for 2012 was 98.00, lower than the starting base in 2000 by a value of 2.00, but higher than the previous year 2011 by 2.35. Looking at the indexes of each since the "Tenth Five-Year Plan" period, of the years listed in Fig. 1.7, 2005 was higher than the starting annual base value of 100, while the other 5 years were lower than the base value. Among these, the highest value was in 2005 at 101.84, and the lowest was in 2010 at 94.76. Entering into the "Eleventh Five-Year Plan" period, the national urban and rural index went down, coming back up again in 2011, and continuing to rise in 2012.

1.4.4 Vertical Assessment Since the "Eleventh Five-Year Plan"

Setting the last year, 2005, of the "Tenth Five-Year Plan" as a starting value of 100, the national urban and rural index in 2012 was 89.59, lower than the base value of 2005 by 10.41, but higher than the previous year, 2011, by 1.35. Looking at each year's index since the "Eleventh Five-Year Plan", Fig. 1.7 shows that there were 4 years with a value lower than the base value of 100. Among these, the highest was in 2006 at 96.62, and the lowest was in 2011 at 88.24. As the "Eleventh Five-Year Plan" period began, the national urban and rural index dropped significantly, basically bottoming out in 2011. This shows that China's continued implementation in recent years of the "stimulating domestic demand, expanding consumption, and improving the people's livelihood" strategies has been shown to have an effect on actually accomplishing the increase in national urban and rural cultural consumption demand.

1.4.5 Annual Vertical Index Assessment

Starting from the last year, 2011, with a base value of 100, the national urban and rural index for 2012 was 100.77, higher than the 2011 base value by 0.77. In Fig. 1.7, the years 1995–1996, 2000, 2005, and 2010 were higher than the previous year base value of 100, and the remaining four listed years were lower than the base value. Among these, the highest was in 1995 at 106.83, and the lowest was in 2006 at 96.62.

In each type of vertical assessment vertical assessment, "minus points" came from the decrease of the share value of urban and rural cultural consumption totals (the national base share did not play a role), negative growth of per capita absolute values (total rural growth in 2007 at the national level and previous urban per capita negative value growth in 2001), the decrease in each index's proportionate value, the expansion of urban and rural ratios and regional gaps; on the other hand, "gaining points" came from the increase of the share value of urban and rural cultural consumption totals, positive growth of per capita absolute values, the increase in each index's proportional value, and the narrowing of urban and rural rations and regional gaps.

In Fig. 1.7, the vertical assessment vertical assessment numbers (1)–(3) evaluated the national urban and rural cultural consumption status since the "Ninth Five-Year Plan", Tenth Five-Year Plan", and "Eleventh Five-Year Plan". When comparing these three, a phenomenon can be seen: from 1995 as the starting point, the index improved significantly; from the starting point of 2000, the index has fluctuated; from the starting point of 2005, the index significantly decreased. This may reflect the "diminishing effect of growth", the so-called "low starting point, big progress"; conversely this is a "large base with difficult growth". When the country and all of its regions decide to really put into place and implement as quickly as possible economic development and basic human needs, as well as the coordinated growth of culture and livelihood, and ensure the "Sharing of Development Among the People", curbing urban and rural discrepancies, curbing the expanding trend of the "reverse action" of regional discrepancies over many years, continuing with reducing and eliminating urban-rural discrepancies and regional discrepancies, then the main focal point of "Comprehensive, Coordinated, and Sustainable Development" will be realized.

Chapter 2
Evaluation System and Technical Report on Chinese Cultural Consumption Demand

Abstract This paper, a technical report on the "Evaluation System on the Chinese Cultural Consumption Demand" is based on comprehensively calculated, nationwide urban and rural data. The report discusses the underlying data source, the methods of data deduction, relevant numerical relationships, and specifics indicators, measures, and explanations; the report also analyzes how the various types of data is reflected in the general trends in nationwide urban and rural cultural consumption. This evaluation system comprehensively evaluates provincial, urban and rural areas and provides city, town and village single-line evaluations. Assessments of city centers, towns, villages are done is omorphically with similar calculation methods.

Keywords Cultural consumption • Status evaluation • Integrative measure of urban and rural areas • Index and method

This paper, a technical report on the "Evaluation System on the Chinese Cultural Consumption Demand", elaborates on the index system and calculation method of the evaluation. At the same time, the text is based on the nationwide urban and rural comprehensive calculations and data, and offers explanations of the base data sources, data deduction methods, related numerical relationships, specific indicators calculations and measures, and also analyzes the nationwide urban and rural general cultural consumption trends that are reflected in all types of data. The detailed analysis in this general report on growth in total cultural consumption and per capita growth, the gap in growth in urban and rural areas, as well as the relationships between cultural consumption and output, income, total consumption, and savings, and the growth discrepancy between regions, will be investigated further.

2.1 Sources for Base Data and Calculation Methods

The evaluation system uses provincial information (all provincial administration regions excluding Taiwan, Hong Kong, Macau, and including provinces, autonomous regions, and municipalities) an urban and rural comprehensive evaluation, an

Y. Wang et al., *Annual Evaluation Report of China's Cultural Consumption Demand*,
Research Series on the Chinese Dream and China's Development Path,
DOI 10.1007/978-981-10-0730-9_2

urban and rural single-line evaluation, and an evaluation of key cities (four municipalities, 22 province capitals, five autonomous region capitals, and five non-capital sub-provincial cities). All of the base data used came from the official publication of the National Bureau of Statistics' *China Statistical Yearbook*; the National Bureau of Statistics' urban social and economic survey, *China City Statistical Yearbook*, and *China Urban (Town) Life and Price Yearbook* (which in 2013 was changed to *China Price Statistical Yearbook*; there were major changes brought about here; details to be discussed later). Statistical Yearbooks of varying relevant data can be used as auxiliary reference checks. Data from the same source with the same caliber of identity and standard of identity under the statistical system can ensure that the data and calculations between each city in the evaluation results are comparable. The three above-mentioned kinds of yearbooks are typically published each year at the end of the year (with some being published at the beginning of the next year) with the official announcement being made of the previous year's statistics. The 2012 statistical data is published as the newest information in the 2013 statistical yearbook.

The base data used for this evaluation system includes: GDP of all regions nationwide, income of all regions nationwide, total consumption (with a distinction being made between cultural consumption and non-cultural consumption), savings (consumption surplus; i.e., the difference between income and total consumption).

2.1.1 Calculating Total Cultural Consumption

The data for the total in cultural consumption was obtained through a multi-calculated derivative.

Under the existing statistical system, the statistics for total consumption nationwide and on a regional level (among which cultural consumption is included) were divided into urban and rural aspects; thus, the comprehensive data for urban and rural areas requires the combination of the corresponding range of urban and rural population distribution data, and an extrapolation of the total comprehensive urban and rural data and per capita values. Various types of data from the four main regions of the eastern Midwest and Northeast have been, for many years, lacking in the *China Statistical Yearbook* and therefore recalculations need to be made in accordance with data from these provinces and regions. The relationships between the data and the calculation methods are shown in Table 2.1. It also should be explained that the 2005 *China Statistical Yearbook* first provided data on the eastern Midwest and northeastern region's urban and rural total consumption, as well as comprehensive data on education and culture per capita, etc., but because there was no prospective for previous years, this research paper will use its own calculation methods to obtain relevant data in order to remain consistent through the years.

Table 2.1 Calculation methods for urban and rural comprehensive values and the relationship between urban and rural statistical data

Scope and content	**Base data**	**Population paramenters**	**Aggregate**	**Population parameters**	**Scope and content**
National urban cultural consumption	Urban per capita	Urban total	Aggregate	**Urban and rural per capita**	National urban and rural comprehensive cultural consumption
National rural cultural consumption	Rural per capita	Rural total			
Scope and content	**Calculations of demographic parameters**	**Related provincial sums**	**Sum of towns and villages**	**Calculations of population parameters**	**Scope and content**
Urban cultural consumption of the four major regions	Urban per capita	Total in urban areas	Aggregate	**Per capita across urban and rural areas**	Eastern, Midwestern, and Northeaster urban-rural comprehensive cultural consumption
Rural cultural consumption of the four major regions	Rural per capita	Total in rural areas			
Scope and content	**Basic data**	**Population parameters**	**Aggregate**	**Population parameters**	**Scope and content**
Provincial and urban cultural consumption	Urban per capita	Urban total	Aggregate	**Per capita across urban and rural areas**	Provincial/regional urban and rural cultural consumption
Provincial and rural cultural consumption	Rural per capita	Rural total			
Scope and content	**Basic data**	**Population parameters**			
Spending on culture and education of city centers	Urban per capita	Urban total			

Note: Total calculations only derived from consumption in national and provincial/regional and major cities. Each assessment and ranking is based on per capita values, and total values from each region cannot be compared

Regarding the basic significance of the population data on calculating various types of total values and per capita values, the following explanation is necessary:

1. The National Bureau of Statistics' *National Statistical Database* previously revised the *China Statistical Yearbook* annual volume on nationwide urban and rural population data, including provincial population data, whose calculations and database this evaluation system promptly adopted; at the same time, according to statistical norms, the calculations were done according to average population data; the corresponding calculated value will have a slight discrepancy with the early results of this study (using year-end population data).
2. The *China Statistical Yearbook*'s volume of national urban and rural total populations includes the military and other special groups (included in the urban population), and does not include a distinction among regions (including urban population) ultimate needs of the national population were converted to average annual population. The national annual average population is not strictly equal to the provincial and regional average population, and therefore there will be discrepancies in the calculation of the national total value and provincial and regional totals which were not balanced and were retained as-is.
3. The *China Statistical Yearbook* does not provide urban and rural population data by region. This study carried out annual calculations for the purposes of the evaluation. In accordance with the annual provincial, urban and rural population growth rate from 2000 to 2005, provincial, urban and rural annual population growth values from 2001 to 2004 were projected; also, in accordance with the provincial, urban and rural annual population growth rate from 2005 to 2009, provincial, urban and rural population growth rates for 2010 were projected. Lastly, the process of balancing was conducted according to the total population of provincial, urban and rural areas, obtaining the corresponding annual urban and rural population distribution values, which were then separately converted to urban and rural annual average populations, and according to this relevant calculations were made.
4. In the last couple years, the *China City Statistical Yearbook* changed its statistical calibrations and no longer offers data on the urban population by major city, instead offering data on municipal districts. This evaluation system obtained calibrations according to the changing population (and also converted it to annual average population data), and then projected the total values for municipal districts. It should be sufficient for main cities of municipal districts to represent the whole city, and for residents of the municipal district to represent the city's residents.

In addition, before 1997 Chongqing was treated as a separate province, and there is a lack of data for Tibet for 1995 and 1997–1998, so related national annual total data calculations do not include these two places, and corresponding deductions should be made when calculating the total population base.

2.1.2 Specific Sources for Per-capita Base Data

2.1.2.1 Per-capita GDP

1. National Per-Capita GDP: For national per capita GDP data from 2009 and all previous years, see the *China Statistical Yearbook* from 2010, *1–2 Gross Domestic Product*, which has the following description: "Data from 2009 has been preliminarily verified; data from 2005 to 2008 has been revised after the second economic census." Hereafter each year's national per capita GDP data will be dealt with in the same manner; the current 2012 data will serve as the preliminary data put forth in the 2013 *China Statistical Yearbook*; next year, it will then be necessary to make adjustments again according to the 2014 *China Statistical Yearbook*.
2. Provincial Per Capita GDP: Annual provincial per capita GDP can be seen in the *China Statistical Yearbook*'s annually-published *Gross Regional Product* (figure/table numbers in each year's volume vary and are not standardized). Also, the National Bureau of Statistics' *National Statistics Database* has revised the annual provincial and regional per capita GDP data, and this evaluation system will use these revisions; therefore, the outcomes for related provincial and regional numerical calculations and the earlier research for this project may have slight discrepancies.
3. Per Capita GDP of Major Cities: This evaluation system did not use the per capita GDP data for each key city put forth in the *China City Statistical Yearbook*. The reason for this is that the per capita GDP of a few cities is calculated according to the permanent resident population (but there is no data), and the remaining cities are calculated according to the population of households; therefore, the two different calibrations of data cannot be used simultaneously. This evaluation system used household populations in major cities (converted to an average annual population) and the total value of the data to recalculate the per capita GDP. Wherein, the 2011–2013 versions are based on the data for each city's municipal district population on the "2–1 Population" table in the *China City Statistical Yearbook* (converted to the annual average population); and made calculations according to the data on each city's total GDP by area on table "2–13, Comprehensive Economics (I)". Because the China City Statistical Yearbook's publishing date was delayed, the 2014 volume was changed to be in accordance to the data from *China Statistical Yearbook's* "City Overview".

This method is consistent with this evaluation system's concept for index design, as it can examine from ancient times in China, the gap between urban and rural areas: the regional divide that continues today and is built into society's third social divide – the hundreds of millions of working-class "blue collar" (urban household workers) within the army system, and the (so-called "migrant workers"), and those with an in-between identity of non-uniformity of "National Treatment".

In present-day China, this problem has become more serious in more developed and large cities. On the one hand, the growth in GDP signifies that the wealth in society is growing; this is what the hundreds of millions of "migrant workers" have participated in creating. However, when GDP statistics are calculated by region, the labor output is not connected to those who do the work. Though the wealth created by these laborers was desired, but residence statuses for these "New Industrial Workers" and their families was refused. On the other hand, the "People Sharing in the Fruits of Development" in each city mainly benefits the local residents of the city, and the excluded hundreds of millions of "migrant workers" are forced to return home each year in the hustle and bustle, creating a strange phenomenon during the Chinese New Year; they are not rewarded for their work and their families cannot come live with them; instead they must use the "Return on Chinese New Year" method to share the fruits of urban development with their families.

In this evaluation system, the resulting relatively high per capita GDP of the major cities will serve as the calculation denominator, converted to a relatively low cultural consumption and output ratio, giving a number for the "savings" of this kind of "development defect". In this sense, these evaluation indicators can be counted as this evaluation system's implied third calibration target (details to follow). In reality, in the process of evaluating and analyzing provinces and regions, even though the balanced data on regional per capita GDP from the *China Statistical Yearbook* was used directly, the relatively high per capita of developed provinces served as the calculated denominator, and was converted into a low ratio of cultural consumption and output, and to a certain extent reflects the significance of this layer.

This implied third calibration index touches upon fair employment in the nation and society as a whole. Within the current institutional structure, so-called "employment" only refers to statistics on urban employment and does not include statistics on migrant workers. In 2013, 6.99 million students graduated from college, and this year was referred to as "the most difficult year for employment". In actuality, nowadays every year is "the most difficult year for employment"; the actual "most difficult" thing is for the hundreds of millions of "migrant workers" (which includes workers who have migrated to the cities as well as [those working in] enterprises in rural areas) to get fair employment, to formally receive an identity of "industrial worker", to get an income for supporting the family that is equal to that of an urban local, and to settle his/her family in the city (or town) (and only in this way the equity issue of compulsory education of children could be resolved). To not do this, or to not do this well, causes a natural deduction in the effectiveness of urban development.

2.1.2.2 Per Capita Income

The *China Statistical Yearbook*'s volume, Per Capita Annual Income of Urban Households by Sources and Region has data on the calendar year national and provincial per capita disposable income of urban residents; for data on the per capita net income of rural residents over the calendar year, see Per Capita Annual Net Income of Rural Households by Sources AND Region. Combining the corresponding annual national and provincial urban and rural population distribution data calculations, you can get a comprehensive national and provincial per capita income of urban and rural values. For per capita calendar-year disposable income of residents of key cities, see the *China City (town) Life Price Yearbook*'s calendar year volume, "Basic Situations of Urban Households in the Five Largest Cities".

2.1.2.3 Total Per Capita Consumption

For data on per capita cultural consumption of national and provincial urban residents, see the *China Statistical Yearbook*'s volume, Per Capita Annual Living Expenditure Of Urban Residents By Region; for data on per capita cultural consumption data for rural residents over the calendar year, see Per Capita Living Expenditure Of Rural Households. Combining the corresponding annual national and provincial urban and rural population distribution data calculations, you can get a comprehensive value for national and provincial urban and rural per capita expenditure values. For per capita expenditure for the calendar year of residents of major cities, see the *China City (town) Life Price Yearbook*'s volume "Basic Situations of Urban Households in the Five Largest Cities".

The total value of per capita expenditure can be separated into per capita non-cultural consumption and per capita cultural consumption numerical values.

2.1.2.4 Per Capita Cultural Consumption

Data on per capita cultural consumption for residents in towns, cities, provinces, and nationwide over the calendar year can be seen in the *China Statistical Yearbook*, Annual Per Capital Living Expenditures of Urban Households Per Region and Education, Recreational And Cultural Services' as well as the two sections, "Cultural and Recreational Supplics" and "Cultural and Recreational Services". Data on per capita cultural consumption for rural residents can be seen in the statistical items, "Annual Per Capita Living Expenditures of Rural Households per Region" and "Cultural and Recreational Supplies". The 2012 *China Statistical Yearbook* was the first to unify urban and rural "Cultural and Educational Consumption", of which the statistical item name is collectively referred to as "Culture, Education and Recreation"; other than this, nothing has been changed.

Therefore it can be seen that the "Cultural Consumption" and "Educational Consumption" of urban residents have been separated from one another, yet "Cultural Consumption" and "Educational Consumption" of rural residents have not. This is the reason why the proportion of rural income spent on "Cultural Consumption" seems higher than that of urban income. In the *Statistical Yearbook* of earlier in the year, the section titled "Non-Commodity Expenditures" in the table "Annual Per Capita Living Expenditures of Rural Households per Region" there is a numerical breakdown, and if the "Education Spending" part were excluded, then the rural "cultural consumption" numbers would have nothing left in them. This is perhaps the reason that "Cultural and Educational Consumption" of rural residents is not separated [into two categories].

The annual per capita educational, recreational, and services consumption among residents of major cities can be seen in *China City (town) Life Price Yearbook*'s ""Basic Situations of Urban Households in the Five Largest Cities"". The consumption statistics on "Education, Culture, Recreation and Service" in major cities have not been subdivided into "Cultural Consumption" and "Educational Consumption"; the related data for "Cultural and Educational Consumption" has been combined in the statistics.

What comes by particular surprise is that when the 2013 *China City (town) Life Price Yearbook* changed its name to the *China Price Statistical Yearbook*, the "Life" section was completely dropped, and there was never a volume published called "China City Life Statistical Yearbook". Upon asking, it was discovered that the livelihood statistics in the "Life" section – per capita income of city residents, total consumption (which includes cultural and educational consumption) were controversial, and some cities had objections. Therefore, these statistics were simply not published anymore. This leads to several big problems: (1) The Statistics Bureau is using taxpayer money to conduct a life sample survey of urban residents; if questions come up about the data then the science of the sample survey methods should be researched and resolved. The regulations of the sample selections, the representativeness of the sample population and various issues still must be publicly published, otherwise this would be considered a breach of government information disclosure regulations. (2) The current "Moderately Prosperous Society in all Respects" plan is sprinting through its last years, and livelihood statistics are unmatched in importance in terms of investigating the effectiveness of the this plan. Things cannot again be like the vision of the years during the "Basic Prosperity" plan, when GDP was only used as an afterthought. Put simply, the Statistics Bureau's unauthorized refusal to publicly publish this data is unreasonable and unacceptable!

To ensure the regular undertaking of this evaluation study, we must use previous years' data on per capita income of residents of major cities, total consumption, average annual growth rate of educational and cultural consumption, deduce an estimated per capita value for 2012, and then make subsequent calculations accordingly (including the total amount of cultural and educational consumption). This is unfortunate and upsetting, but it has been forced upon us.

2.1.2.5 Per Capita Accumulations

The difference between income data and total consumption data is the accumulations data. This study used the concept of "accumulations" to distinguish between "savings" which are put into the bank. "Accumulations" includes extra money no matter where it is put, and is usually a much higher amount than "savings"; it also takes the place of the oft-used concept in economics, "surplus". The term "surplus", which came originally from Western economists, emphasizes proactive consumption; "surplus" is the passive result of consumption. A sound market economy system must have a sound social security system, and along with that, only a "welfare state" can produce the low accumulation of "consumerism".

The importance that the Chinese people have always placed on "accumulation" serves as an active way of controlling consumption, and the lags in the social security system have caused the general public to increase their accumulation of savings in order to strive for "self-protection"; accumulating savings has therefore become a "must" in current Chinese society. This means that besides "essential expenses" (those which this study places in the non-cultural consumption category), there is also "essential accumulation", such as: funds for purchasing the family home, funds for the children's education, funds for medical expenses and old age, etc. Therefore, "non-essential" spiritual and cultural spending becomes the "left-over accumulation" from "essential accumulation". The long-term development of the Chinese economy faces the worry of insufficient domestic consumption demand; during the few years before the Eleventh Five-Year Plan period, the urban and rural cultural consumption demand experienced a decline in growth, yet the accumulated savings of urban and rural residents experienced a widespread surge, the root cause of this being the lack of a sound social security system.

2.2 Evaluation Indexes and Their Design Concepts

This evaluation system designed and used assessment indicators split into three categories and eight items. Due to the difficulty in finding references for domestic and foreign existing empirical data and calculation methods, many of the indicators from this study come from real life.

2.2.1 Basic Indicators: The Absolute Value of Cultural Consumption

The absolute value of cultural consumption is separated into two types of values: the total absolute value and the per capita absolute value. Each total value needs to be converted to the national total share value.

2.2.1.1 The Total Cultural Consumption Share Value

The total urban cultural consumption demand is the concrete manifestation of the actual entrance of the total industrial production into daily-life consumption, and is also the concrete manifestation of the conversion of cultural development and production into the cultural consumption demands of the masses. However, whether it is overall total production or total consumption value that is behind this, there is the size of the provinces, difference in population sizes, regional economic scales, and the industrial base, etc., which all contain great differences; the total values are not comparable between places. This study mainly focuses on overall urban and rural cultural consumption growth trends on a national level.

The overall urban and rural cultural consumption total value is not comparable itself, but the urban and rural overall total growth margin and the changes in national share can be compared. In actuality, the overall average annual growth rate and additions and changes in share are related, and the order of total annual average growth and the order of additions and changes in share are also related.

Among the indicators measured in this study, national urban and rural totals will be the base, and the proportion of national totals among national annual changes in share will be used to measure. In the horizontal assessment for the calendar year, the base is the total proportion share nationwide for a year or more; for example, setting the year 2011 as having a national share of 100 (for percentages in this paper, the decimal point usually retains two places for convenient expression), because of the situation of change detected in the last year, the 2012 share will earn "extra points" for increasing, and when the share declines there will be a "loss of points". In the vertical assessment for the calendar year, the total proportion of the country share of all regions in the start of the year serves as the base; as an example, since the evaluation of the "tenth fifth-year plan", if the country share of the year 2000 is 100, according to the changes detected in the last 12 years, the 2012 share will earn "extra points" for increasing, and when the share declines there will be a "loss of points".

2.2.1.2 Per Capita Cultural Consumption Absolute Values

The cultural consumption value index proportion and value index differential, both need to be calculated based on the per capita absolute value of cultural consumption. Therefore, the per capita absolute value of cultural consumption is a base indicator. The *China Statistical Yearbook* presents statistical data on national, provincial, urban and rural per capita cultural consumption, but the national and urban and rural comprehensive per capita values still need to be calculated from the urban and rural comprehensive assessment.

In the annual horizontal assessment of this index, the total per capita national urban and rural values are the basis which is balanced by the discrepancy between the per capita values of each region and the national percapita values. For example, if 2012 is set with a national urban and rural per capita value of 100; if a region has a per capita value higher than the national urban and rural one, this index will be assigned "plus points". If any region has a per capita value lower than the national urban and rural per capita value, than this index will be assigned "minus points".

Generally speaking, there has been sustained growth in total per capita cultural consumption across the nation; this indicator is the most powerful "plus" factor within the vertical assessment. However, once a annual negative growth occurs, or if the entire 5-year period is one of negative growth, or even if there is a cumulative negative growth over two 5-year periods (in a minority of provincial or rural areas that is the case), the this indicator will become a "minus point" factor. In each year of "The Eleventh Five-Year Plan" the negative growth of the absolute value of per capita cultural consumption resulted in the "negative points" situation province-wide rural areas being not uncommon, even being visible province-wide in urban areas.

2.2.2 Balancing Indicators: Proportionate Value of Cultural Consumption

The basic method of this evaluation system for establishing an evaluation index system from reality is to use, as much as possible, various nationally-issued statistical data items under the existing statistical system, and to construct and measure the various resulting ratio relationships. An analysis of the relationships between per capita cultural consumption value and per capita output value, income, total consumption, and data on accumulated savings, especially economic reflections, background factors in. societal development, are the basis on which the standards for the proportionate value of per capita cultural consumption are set in this evaluation system.

2.2.2.1 Ratio of Per Capita Cultural Consumption and Per Capita Output

The ratio between the total consumption of citizens and the GDP (the consumption rate of citizens) can measure the pulling effect that domestic livelihood spending has on the GDP; the ratio between cultural consumption and GDP (the rate of livelihood and cultural consumption) at the same time can measure the pulling effect that cultural consumption has on the GDP. Looked at another way, this is the actual effect of China's economic growth driving the growth in livelihood and cultural livelihood consumption demand. If the livelihood consumption and cultural consumption livelihood demands of urban residents of an area were not effectively enhanced, then production growth and cultural production growth would depart from the basic purpose of their interdependence, and would unfortunately only be able to be seen as the invalid production of "a tool becoming a purpose".

Within the calculation of this indicator, if the per capita production values of an area continue to climb, and the growth in per capita cultural consumption demands of urban and rural residents lowers year after year, then the assessment values will undoubtedly get lower. As for the increase in cultural production values across regions, there is a particular need to make such a measure, and to crack open the intensifying "Cultural Industry Chase" phenomenon occurring across various regions in recent years; the development of cultural production is for satisfying cultural consumption demands; unfortunately, there is no unified standard for the numerical values and statistical data of the annual growth across regions in cultural production.

In the annual horizontal assessment of these indicators, the overall proportion of nationwide urban and rural values will serve as a reference, and the discrepancy between regional ratios will be weighed by nationwide ratios. For example, if the 2012 nationwide urban and rural ratio in this study is 100, if the value in a certain area is higher than the national urban and rural average ratio, this indicator will earn "plus points"; if the value in a certain area is lower than the national urban and rural average ratio, than this detected indicator will get "minus points". Of this study's indicators in the calendar year vertical assessment, the nationwide and regional urban and rural ratios in the beginning of the year will serve as the base measure of this study. For example, the nationwide urban and rural ratios for 1995, 2000, 2005, and 2010 the value in this study is 100; investigating changes throughout and between the past 17, 12, 7, and 2 years, the overall value for nationwide urban and rural households is lower, and the indicator detected multiple "minus points". Each area showed the same pattern.

It is clear that due to the continued fluctuation of the proportional values of nationwide urban and rural per capita cultural consumption and per capita GDP, the indicators in this vertical assessment become a component of the heavier "minus points" factor, and only in a few years was there a weak "plus factor" when compared with the previous year. Investigation of the 2 years since the "Twelfth Five-Year Plan" shows "plus points", embodying the power of the binding targets of the "Twelfth Five-Year Plan's" "Achievement of Income Growth of the People Along With Economic Development". This is indeed gratifying!

2.2.2.2 The Proportion of Per Capita Income That Is Accounted for by Cultural Consumption

Admittedly, behind the absolute value of per capita cultural consumption exist differences in income levels of the population; this is comparable to the proportion of the income of local people that per capita cultural consumption accounts for. The proportion of local people's income that accounts for per capita cultural consumption is analogous to the changes in proportion of per capita food consumption under a certain income level, which is known as "Engel's Law"; this is reflected in the cultural consumption needs under a certain level of income, which might as well become a kind of "Cultural Livelihood Coefficient" calculation base.

If we suppose that the proportion of an area's urban and rural citizens' per capita cultural consumption is a relatively high proportion of the income of the local people, then the idea that local urban and rural cultural consumption demand is relatively strong is brought into heavy doubt. On the contrary, if a region's urban and rural per capita cultural consumption absolute value is perhaps not low, but its proportion of the local per capita income is low, this then does not demonstrate that the local urban and rural cultural consumption demand is strong. This is the reason why proportion is more demonstrative of the issue than absolute value is.

In the horizontal annual assessment of this study's index the total proportional value of nationwide urban and rural areas serves as the baseline, and the difference between each region's proportional values and the proportional values of the entire country are the index measures. For example, if the proportional value for the nation's urban and rural areas in this study is 100, and a certain region is higher than the national urban and rural proportional value then this indicator will be detected as having "plus points"; if a particular region is lower than the national urban and rural proportional value, then this indicator will be detected as having "minus points". In this annual vertical assessment, the original annual national and regional urban and rural proportional value will serve as the base measure. For example, the proportional values for the years 1995, 2000, 2005 and 2010 are set at 100, and the changes in status in the last 17, 12, 7 and 2 years were studied; the overall ratio of national urban and rural areas was mostly lowered, so the index was detected as "minus points"; each area showed the same pattern.

Because the proportion of national urban and rural per capita cultural consumption in the per capita income has been continuously decreasing substantially in the last 21 years, the indicators in the vertical assessment has mainly become a "minus points" factor, and only in a few years did it become a weak "plus point" factor when compared with the previous year.

2.2.2.3 Ratio of Per Capita Cultural Consumption to Total Cultural Consumption

Likewise, at the background of the regional per capita cultural consumption absolute value is the difference in consumption levels among local people. The proportion of per capita cultural consumption to total per capita consumption is more comparable. The proportion of per capita cultural consumption to total per capita cultural consumption among local people can be compared to the "Engel Coefficient"- the proportion of per capita spending on food to total spending, which is reflected in the fixed consumption structure of cultural consumption demands, which might as well be viewed as a kind of "Cultural Livelihood Coefficient". Breaking up total consumption into "Non-Cultural Consumption" and Cultural Consumption, the relationships between non-cultural and cultural consumption is shown in the proportion of cultural consumption to total consumption.

If a certain district's per capita cultural consumption makes up a relatively large proportion of total per capita cultural consumption for the local people, then a relatively strong level of cultural consumption demand among local urban and rural people is undoubtable. On the other hand, if a district's urban and rural cultural consumption absolute value is not low, but comprises a low proportion of total per capita consumption of the local people, then this does not show that the local consumption demand across urban and rural areas are strong. In this area, the proportion is more descriptive of the issue than the absolute value.

In this index's annual horizontal assessment, the total proportional value of nationwide urban and rural areas serves as the base, and the difference between each region's proportional values and the proportional values of the entire country are the index measures. For example, if the average ratio for the nation's urban and rural areas for the year 2012 in this study is 100, and a certain region is higher than the national urban and rural average ration then this indicator will be detected as having "plus points"; if a particular region is lower than the national urban and rural average ratio, then this indicator will be detected as having "minus points". In this annual vertical assessment, the original annual national and regional urban and rural average ration will serve as the base measure. The value for the national urban and rural overall values in 1995, 2000, 2005, and 2010 is 100, and when looking at changes in the situation between the past 17, 12, 7 and 2 years, there was an overall decrease in national urban and rural value, and the indicator detected multiple "minus points". Each area showed the same pattern.

Because the proportion of national urban and rural per capita cultural consumption in the per capita income has been continuously decreasing in a substational way in the last 21 years, the indicators in the vertical assessment have mainly become a "minus points" factor, and only in a few years did it become a weak "plus point" factor when compared with the previous year.

2.2.2.4 Ratio of Per Capita Cultural Consumption to Per Capita Non-cultural Consumption Surplus

Corresponding to "Non-Cultural Consumption", there is "Non-Cultural Surplus Consumption"; cultural consumption and accumulated savings make up "Non-Cultural Surplus Consumption"; that is, the difference between per capita income and non-cultural consumption. This is an original line of thinking and a modified design in this evaluation system, the aim of which is to focus on and assess the specific value relationship between cultural consumption and accumulated savings. If "Non-Cultural Consumption" is posited to be an "essential expense", then cultural consumption, as a "Non-Essential" expense, will naturally be classified along with "accumulated savings" as a "non-cultural consumption surplus". Thus, if the relationship between "Non-Essential" cultural consumption and "Essential" non-cultural consumption is posited as the proportionate value of cultural consumption versus total consumption, and the relationship between cultural consumption and accumulated savings is posited as the proportionate of cultural consumption and non-cultural consumption surplus.

If the per capita accumulated savings of a region's urban and rural citizens grows at a high rate, it is bound to bear the brunt of the direct pressure of the "Non-Essential" cultural consumption from accumulated savings, so then it is obvious that local consumption demand across urban and rural areas would shrink. This is the "negative effect of the growth in accumulated savings" of the cultural consumption demands of the Chinese people.

There is also a technical reason why the relationship between cultural consumption and accumulated savings is processed analytically as the remaining proportionate between cultural consumption and non-cultural consumption: the index design of this evaluation system needs to separately evaluate an integration of urban and rural areas; cities and towns; and rural areas. Rural household consumption expenditure includes goods consumption, and the income is referred to as "net income"; in a minority of places, over a minority of the years, per capita consumption of rural residents was slightly larger than per capita income, and per capita accumulated savings became negative; therefore, an illogical negative index will appear in the evaluation calculations. The flexible design of the proportion of cultural consumption and non-cultural consumption surplus has avoided this difficult technical problem.

In this index's annual horizontal assessment, the total proportionate value of nationwide urban and rural areas serves as the base, and the difference between each region's proportionate values and the proportionate values of the entire country are the index measures. For example, if the average ratio for the nation's urban and rural areas for the year 2012 in this study is 100, and a certain region is higher than the national urban and rural average ratio then this indicator will be detected as having "plus points"; if a particular region is lower than the national urban and rural average ratio, then this indicator will be detected as having "minus points". In this annual vertical assessment, the original annual national and regional urban and rural average ratio will serve as the base measure. The value for the national urban and rural overall values in 1995, 2000, 2005, and 2010 is 100, and when looking at changes in the situation between the past 17, 12, 7 and 2 years, there was an overall decrease in national urban and rural value, and the indicator detected multiple "minus points". Each area showed the same pattern.

Because of the marked continuous decrease in proportional value of national urban and rural per capita cultural consumption and per capita non-cultural consumption surplus over the last 21 years, this index has become a heavy "minus points" factor within this vertical assessment, and only in a small number of years was it a weak "plus points" factor compared to the previous year.

Looking at the changes in proportional values among national urban and rural cultural consumption, a consistent trend was shown, which can become a mutually authenticated intrinsic link. This is sufficient to show the targets chosen and what this evaluation system has been.

2.2.3 *Correction Indicators: The Ratio Difference of Cultural Consumption*

Eliminating as soon as possible gaps and regional discrepancies in urban and rural livelihood development across all areas and realizing "Urban-Rural Integration" and "Balanced Regional Development", as well as ensuring equal "Treatment of

National Citizens" nationwide across all urban and rural regions, should become national and local achievements as well as the main targets of performance evaluations of all levels of government. This is also the largest priority of "maintaining stability" in the current construction of the nation and social governance. The essence of livelihood depends first of all on a just society; this is especially true in the case of human development; livelihood-oriented, balanced priorities must form the basic principles of cultural construction and development.

This evaluation system created an "urban-to-rural ratio" reciprocal statistical index in order to calculate and make the "urban-to-rural ratio" become the evaluation index; and also has created a "regional gap" evaluation index to measure regional discrepancies, as well as completed calculations for nationwide, cross-major regions, provinces and major cities. With the background of "Integrated and Coordinated Scientific Development", these two indexes can serve as two important standards for examining cultural consumption demand equity. The urban-rural and regional gaps in cultural consumption reflect the serious defect of uneven growth in cultural consumption demand across urban and rural areas and across regions; this "Growth Defect" is essentially a natural detractor of increasing effectiveness. These two indicators are similar to the "energy-saving" converted deduction of a "Green GDP", which is intended to promote cultural development that is shared equally in urban and rural areas and regions, contributing to needed institutions and feasible mechanisms for social equality.

2.2.3.1 Ratio of Per Capita Urban-to-Rural Cultural Consumption Ratio

In today's China, there is a stark contrast between cities that are "like Europe" and rural areas that are "like Africa", in fact strengthening the deep-rooted and ancient "Wild Country Divided" traditional pattern of social stratification. In recent years, the nation has vigorously promoted solutions to the "top-priority" "Three Rural Issues" problem, promoting "Urban Areas Nurturing Rural Areas", with which significant progress has been made. However, overall urban development has increased at a greater speed, and the urban-rural gap has not changed, but has in fact widened rapidly.

The urban-to-rural ratio of cultural consumption is expressed in the rural per capita value of 1 measuring multiple urban per capita values. The ideal value for the urban-to-rural ratio is set at 1; with no gap between urban and rural areas, the urban-rural per capita value ratio would be rendered as 1:1. With the reciprocal value of the urban-to-rural ratio as a weighted index, in the ideal situation the reciprocal of 1 would still be 1, and using 1 as weight, any value will still be its original value. As long as the urban-to-rural ratio is greater than 1, and the index value of the reciprocal number is less than 1, then the weighted reduction will play a role. To the contrary, if the urban-to-rural ratio is less than 1, and an "inversion" takes place, with rural per capita cultural consumption being higher than urban, the weighted method will promote the principle of "Being too Positive in Righting a Wrong", and "plus points" will naturally be given.

In the annual horizontal assessment of this indicator, when measuring with the ideal of zero for urban-ruralgap, whether nationwide or regional, as long as the urban-to-rural ratio is bigger than 1 there will be "minus points", but when the urban-to-rural ratio is "reversed" (less than 1) then "plus points" will be obtained. For example, if the 1995, 2000, 2005 and 2010 national overall urban-to-rural ratios are set at 100, when examining the changes within the previous 17, 12, 7, and 2-year periods, the overall national urban-to-rural l ratios have all significantly expanded, and these indexes are detected as being significant "minus points". This holds across all regions.

Due to the continuous widening of the urban-rural gap in terms of per capita cultural consumption across the country over the 21 years, these indicators became heavily weighted "minus points" factors in horizontal and vertical evaluations. However, when the "urban-rural reversal" in local areas becomes a "plus points" factor in the horizontal assessment, some years also become national "plus points" factors in the vertical evaluation when compared to the previous year.

It is necessary to clarify that rural per capita "cultural consumption" and "educational consumption" are not differentiated from one another, as the National Bureau of Statistics views these related statistics as "cultural consumption"; actually, "educational consumption", might be a more suitable label some of the time. If urban areas also measured "cultural and educational consumption" together, then the urban-rural gap would be even larger—the urban-to-rural ratio for cultural and educational consumption for 2012 was higher than 4.5646 nationwide (the urban-to-rural ratio and regional differences were slight, so four decimal points were used in expressing it). Even with rural "cultural and educational consumption" generalized together as "cultural consumption", the urban-to-rural ratio of cultural consumption has already broadened to the degree that it demands high priority.

2.2.3.2 Differences in Regional Per Capita Cultural Consumption

In today's China, the "pioneering" development of the East and the lagging development of the West are in sharp contrast. The national development in economy, society, and people's livelihoods suggest an extremely unfavorable "quasi-federalist" aspect of unitary republican national governance. In the last more than 10 years, China has implemented the policies of "Western Development", "The Rise of Central China", and "Revitalization of the Old Industrial Base of the Northeast" but the eastern region has already declared itself "Taking the Lead in Realizing Modernization", and the developmental discrepancies among regions continues to widen.

A reference value needs to be determined to measure regional differences; this is the national average per capita cultural consumption. This is needed to make a comparison between national regions. When setting the average national per capita cultural consumption at 1 to measure each region's per capita cultural consumption value, and obtaining each values's distance from the national average values as the discrete absolute value, the average value can be obtained from the discrete absolute values of the 31 provinces. Adding the discrete absolute values or average values to the base index of 1, there will be no gap between those regions, then the average value of the regions would be rendered as 1:1:1. At the same time, the reciprocal values of the regional differences become a weighted index, the difference from an urban-rural reversed ratio calculation being that here there is no "inversion": any place that is higher than the national average deviation will be deducted as a "failure to drive balanced growth; those that are lower than the national average deviation will be deducted as "dragging behind balanced growth". That is to say, that "leading" growth and "lagging" growth are the same, as they both deviate from "balanced growth, and both will "lose points".

In the annual horizontal assessment of these indicators, with no difference in regional disparities as measured by the ideal value, whether national or regional, as long as there exists a regional differences there will be a "loss of points", with no "upside-down" exceptions. For example, if the no-gap ideal value is set at 100, then the total estimated value for 2012 ($1/N \times 100$, $N =$ regional difference) would be 69.95, and this indicator would detect a "loss of points" reaching 30.05 %. In the annual vertical evaluation of these indicators, the national and regional averages themselves will be the starting annual regional difference base measures. For example, if the overall urban and rural regional discrepancy values for the years 1995, 2000, 2005 and 2010 are set at 100, then studying the change in status between the last 17, 12, 7, and 2 years, then we see that the overall national urban and rural regional differences are gradually expanding, and the indicator is detected as having mostly "minus points". This was the case across all regions.

Due to the overall gradual expansion of national urban and rural discrepancy over the 21 years, the indicators in the vertical and horizontal assessments have mainly become heavily weighted "minus point" factors. However, in the annual vertical assessment, there were several years where there was a "plus points" factor when compared with the previous year. In the 2 years since the "Twelfth Five-Year Plan" period, a slight "plus points" aspect has been shown, reflecting the "Twelfth Five-Year Plan" mandate of "strengthening coordinated regional development", bringing about the first step to narrowing the regional gap.

The urban-rural gap in cultural consumption demand and the regional gap has been brought about by the imbalance in urban and rural, and regional development of livelihood and cultural livelihood. All provinces and regions should be held accountable for this and receive appropriate deductions. This applies to all four major regions of the East, Middle, West, and Northeast, with provinces sharing responsibility. The national urban-to-rural ratio and regional discrepancy leading to a "loss of points" is of course something the entire country bears responsibility for, and is deducted at the national level. The essence of human development and livelihood comes first from the coordination of justice and equality; this is the proper meaning of a "scientific concept of development".

2.3 Index Weight Distribution and Evaluation Calculation Methods

The evaluation method must fully consider the current situation of unbalanced regional development to ensure that results are reasonable and comparable.

China's economic and social development across regions is extremely unbalanced, with an extreme difference in economic growth, income levels, consumption structures, and savings habits among regions. At the same time, using various measures to produce a comprehensive evaluation, a level of balance between regions may be reached. Each region may have its strong points in different indicators; no matter what aspect, there are always advantageous indicators that manifest, and in the end different indicators are integrated to form the same evaluation result, forming a simple and direct comprehensive comparison among regions.

In the process of these various kinds of quantifications of cultural consumption demand, per capita absolute values, the proportions of all four values are all quantitative reactions to reality; there is no theoretical or ideal value to follow and the national averages should be used to measure each region; the ideal for urban-to-rural ratio and regional discrepancies is zero-difference. Therefore, the evaluation method obviously should be designed around national averages and no-gap ideal values. However, this is still not enough; in order to realize a fair evaluation with the same starting point between regions which have an extreme imbalance in development, this evaluation system specially designed a kind of diachronic base value vertical assessment based on the statuses of previous years.

2.3.1 Weight Distribution of Each Evaluation Index

When several indexes are used to expand a comprehensive evaluation, the weight distribution between each index is of pivotal significance.

Weighted values usually do not follow theoretical or ideal values, but are mainly empirical values. The comparability of regional per capita cultural consumption absolute values is not very high, though the relative proportions of cultural consumption are more comparable and can measure differences in regional economic situations surrounding cultural consumption demand: income levels, consumption structures, and saving habits. Therefore, the proportional value index weight is higher than the absolute value index. The continued expansion of the urban-rural gap and regional discrepancies is the most significant developmental defect of today's China. The index weight of urban-to-rural ratios and regional discrepancies are based on the inverted comprehensive calculation results of the ideal, no-gap urban and rural and regional values: because other indicators of some regions may have relatively high scores, making the integrated score higher, and urban-to-rural ratio and regional discrepancies are still a reality, the weights of these corrected indexes should be heavier in order to regulate the comprehensive scores so that there won't be too many regions reaching the "ideal value of 100", and "super ideal" scores that go over the "ideal value of 100" won't be too high. At the same time, during a relatively long period of vertical assessment for example, during the entire "Tenth Five-Year Plan" period vertical evaluation, it can be ensured that most regions in the nation will have rising indexes in the end. After repeated tests, relative balance is looked for between the "leniency" of the vertical evaluation and the "strictness" of the horizontal assessment, and after attempting to use to the evaluation for 4 years between 2008 and 2010, from the start of the evaluation in 2011, this evaluation system has arranged the distributed weight of the eight indexes of cultural consumption total values: per capita absolute values, four scale values, urban-to-rural ratio and regional discrepancies, as 2:1:2:2:2:2:4:3.

Indeed, the evaluation indexes can continue to grow, and the weights among the indexes might as well be adjusted (adding evaluation indexes itself indicates that the original weight distribution proportion has changed), so the evaluation result percentiles will not have the significance of absolute values. However, as long as the same index is used, and the calculations are made according to the same weight, and the same evaluation method is used to obtain the result, a vertical comparison of the annual increase and a horizontal comparison of the level of proportional values among regions are comparable.

This kind of weight distribution of indexes also takes into account the calculation model compatibility of this multi-level, multi-perspective analytical evaluation. Actually, strictly speaking of the base data in the *China Statistical Yearbook*, because the cultural consumption and educational consumption values of cross-region rural citizens are not separated, the actual urban-to-rural ratio of cultural consumption should be much larger, so therefore presumably doing an analytical evaluation of cultural and educational consumption would be more reasonable and comparable. In light of this, this evaluation system must also use the three aspects (comprehensive urban and rural, and urban and rural numbers separately) and the three types of analytical evaluation (cultural consumption, educational consumption and cultural/educational consumption) to make the evaluation index system and model as one.

See Table 2.2 for this evaluation system's indexes and weighted calculations, as well as the evaluation methods. All of the index calculation evaluations use the overall national, 4 main areas, and 31 provinces and 36 major cities. Three levels of cultural consumption evaluation ranking from the 31 provinces are: urban and rural integrated evaluation; a separate urban evaluation, and a separate rural evaluation. Also, there is a cultural and educational consumption evaluation ranking from the 36 major cities.

Table 2.2 National cultural consumption demand evaluation index and weighted calculations and evaluation methods

	Evaluation index			Synchronic ideal value	Diachronic base value
No.	Classification	(Integrated urban/rural or single-line)	Weighted calculation	Horizontal assessment	Vertical evaluation
1	Absolute value	Change in cultural (cultural/educational or educational) consumption proportion of national total	2	Weighted with previous year's base value	Measuring using its own starting annual base value
2		Per capita cultural (cultural/educational or educational) consumption	1		
3	Proportional value	And per capita GDP ratio	2	Using national average value as benchmark measure	
4		Per capita income ratio	2		
5		Per capita total Consumption ratio	2		
6		And per capita non-cultural consumption surplus ratio	2		
7	Correction value	Urban-to-rural ratio	4	Using no-gap ideal value as weight	
8		Regional discrepancy	3		

Using its own starting annual value of itself as benchmark measure

2.3.2 *Special Clarifications Regarding the Urban and Rural Single-Line Evaluations*

It is necessary to specifically clarify that in the process of separating the cultural consumption of urban versus rural citizens to create single-line evaluations, the two indicators of per capita cultural consumption and per capita GDP proportional values, and the urban-to-rural ratio of per capita cultural consumption, both have some particularities.

1. The national per capita GDP data by province published by the *China Statistical Yearbook* does not differentiate between urban and rural areas. In calculating and evaluating urban and rural data, per capita cultural consumption is calculated as an integrated urban and rural value, and the per capita GDP value forms the urban and rural composite proportional value; also, in the single-line urban and rural calculation and evaluation, the separate urban or rural per capita cultural consumption values form the proportional value along with the urban and rural integrated per capita GDP value. This can reveal the enhanced gap between consumption demands in urban and in rural areas within the background of the same economic growth. There are obviously differences between them, which are reflected in the relationship between the composited and different sides.

2. This evaluation system uses statistical data to show the urban and rural discrepancy and set the "urban-to-rural ratio" as a corrective index. In the calculation and evaluation of the composite urban and rural values, the urban-to-rural ratio of per capita cultural consumption reveals the urban-rural gap that actually exists with the urban and rural composite values; also, in the urban and rural single-line calculations and evaluations, the per capita cultural consumption urban-to-rural ratio reveals another corresponding formation of a discrepancy. There are obvious differences between them, reflected in the relationship between the whole and different parts.

In the process of doing the actual calculations in this evaluation system, the three types of eight indicators all used the urban-rural composite evaluation, urban and rural single-line evaluation, and the major cities evaluation. These mathematical ideas come from the fact that, in the final measures and calculations of this evaluation—the cultural consumption demand index – are not looking for an absolute significance, the focus rather being on generalizing and getting a comparable result; its technical feasibility comes from the fact that per capita cultural consumption and per capita GDP proportion, and per capita cultural consumption urban – rural ratio are all proportional values, and therefore, when deducting the isomorphic value relationship, the calculation can be generalized and the results will have comparability. Whether it is the urban-rural composite calculation, urban and rural single-line calculations, or major city calculations, as long as the evaluation indexes are the same and the same calculation methods between all regions and years, the calculations process can be generalized, and the calculation results can be compared.

2.3.3 *Evaluation Methods and Result Rankings*

2.3.3.1 Horizontal Assessment of Synchronic Ideal Value

The ideal value evaluation of the horizontal synchronic comparison between each region is used to compare cultural consumption demand value levels nationally across regions and in the same years. In this evaluation method, the total cultural consumption surplus value is measured from the previous year's base value, and if the share increases, there are "plus points", and if it decreases, "minus points". Per capita cultural consumption absolute value, proportion with per capita GDP, the proportionate value of per capita income, the proportionate value of total per capita consumption, and the proportionate value of per capita non-cultural consumption surplus, together are the five indicators. Using the national average value for the year as the reference value for measurement, the values of each region corresponding to the reference value's weighted index to do the weighted calculations, those higher than the national average benchmark will receive "plus points", while those lower than the national average benchmark will receive "minus points".

The two discrepancy indexes of urban-to-rural ratio and regional discrepancy are measured according to the no-gap ideal value. Whether towards national, the four big regions (east, middle, west, and northeast), or towards each province and major city (the urban-to-rural ratio evaluation is based on the location of the provinces), as long as there is an urban-rural gap and a regional discrepancy, then "minus points" will be implemented (except for the special situation of an urban-to-rural "upside-down" ratio). Thus, each region will correspond to its base value (the national total can also be understood as making up a "share" of 100 % or 1:1). This point is also equal, and the proportional value of each region, province, and major city in the corresponding national average benchmark is also equal, and the regional ratio and regional discrepancy in the corresponding no-gap ideal value is also equal. A uniformly equal evaluation ensures that the evaluation results will be reasonable and comparable and the levels can be seen at a glance.

In the ideal value horizontal assessment, due to the cultural consumption absolute value (including the total share value and the per capita absolute value), related proportional values based on national average benchmarks (relative to the regional proportion of the national share, the national as a "share" of 100 % can also be understood as the national average value; the calculation methods are interlinked) to measure. The urban-to-rural ratio and regional discrepancies are measured according to the no-gap ideal value; if the national total is realized among urban and rural areas and there are no gaps between regions, then the "ideal value of 100" will be reached, and the "loss of points" will certainly come from the urban-rural gap and regional discrepancies which cannot be avoided. Therefore, in the current situation of a significant urban-rural ration and regional discrepancy that even may continue to widen, the country overall will have a difficult time reaching the "ideal value of 100"; only when the urban-rural ratio and regional discrepancies actually become smaller can the national overall evaluation score rise.

2.3.3.2 Vertical Evaluation of Diachronic Base Values

The base value evaluation of each region's diachronic vertical parallel uses the annual regional cultural consumption demand index fluctuations. With this evaluation method, the eight indicators: total cultural consumption share values, per capita cultural consumption absolute values, proportional values with per capita GDP, the proportionate value of per capita income, the proportionate value of total per capita consumption, the proportional value of per capita non-cultural consumption surplus, urban-to-rural ratio and regional discrepancies, all use the national regional starting related annual values as a base index for measuring (The national total 100 % "share" standard can also be understood as the base value), the final annual corresponding values corresponding to the weighted number's base value to get a weighted calculation; the base numbers that have increased received "plus points" and the ones that are lower than the base value receive "minus points". In this way, all regions will be equal in their annual starting points, and when evaluating the changes within the final year, the same standards will be used for each, and the gains and losses will be easy to see.

In the base value vertical evaluation, since all of the indicators are measured by the annual base value, the national total will not simply wait for a "loss of points" from the urban-to-rural ratio and regional disparity to deduct, rather will possibly, in the case of an increase in absolute values or proportional values, or in the case of the urban-rural ratio or regional disparity becoming narrower, and the base figure will have an upward trend surpassing that of previous years, thus obtaining "plus points".

This evaluation system contains the national evaluations from 1991 to 2012, an evaluation and ranking from the four big districts of the east, middle, west, and northeast, a comprehensive evaluation of urban and rural citizens from 31 provinces, single-line evaluations of cultural consumption from urban and rural citizens, and educational consumption and educational/cultural consumption demand. There is also an evaluation and ranking of cultural/educational consumption from 2005 to 2012 of citizens from major cities and municipalities. According to need, calculations and values can be obtained from any year range, regional distribution, population distribution, and evaluation content areas, in order to construct the necessary figure to analyze changing trends. The (Comprehensive Urban-Rural Assessment) provincial and regional paper from this book can viewed, as well as the articles on major cities.

Lastly, there are two points which should be given extra explanation:

1. This evaluation is oriented towards the humanities research community and the academic community, and it is necessary for it to maintain a natural language style, avoiding any kind of calculation formulas or complicated calculation symbols, with an effort to use elementary mathematical methods to solve problems. In this way natural language can be used to express it. Of course, in a society of compulsory education, Arabic numerals and simple arithmetic numerals are public common knowledge, and are deemed to already be a part of natural language.
2. All of the calculations of this evaluations system were made one time in the evaluation database, the decimals were not limited; the figures in this book only keep two or four decimal places in the values listed. By relying on the values listed in the figures for checking, there may be subtle differences after the decimal points, but these are no calculation errors. In particular, the figures described in the text (the evaluation database synchronization algorithms generated automatic calibration), because of the practice of only taking two decimal places, after each is rounded multiple times, so cannot be checked according to this.

Technical Report on the Status Evaluation System of the China's Cultural Consumption Demand —*Analysis of the Basic Situation from 1991 to 2012*

Abstract: This paper is a technical report on "The Status Evaluation System of China's Cultural Consumption Demand". Based on the comprehensive data calculation of the overall urban and rural areas, it illustrates the basic data source, the data inference method, the related numerical relationship and the specific index calculation. Thus, it analyses the basic situation of the countrywide cultural consumption demand in urban and rural areas revealed by these types of data. This evaluation system is in common use of the integrative measure of the urban and rural areas across the provinces, the single measure of the city-towns, and the rural areas, also the key cities. The index and the calculation methods are the same in the above measure.

Chapter 3
Urban and Rural Cross Province Cultural Consumption Demand Evaluation and Ranking: 2000–2012 Evaluation and Predictions for Subsequent Years

Abstract In 2012, the total cultural consumption in urban and rural areas increased by over 10 % in 21 provinces, in 11 of which it increased by over 15 % and in 3 of which it increased by over 20 %; the per capita value of cultural consumption in urban and rural areas increased by over 10 % in 19 provinces, in 10 of which it increased by over 15 % and in 3 of which it increased by over 20 %. The evaluation rankings of the cultural consumption demand in urban and rural areas across the provinces are as follows: in the horizontal assessment of ideal value without urban and rural and regional gaps, Jiangsu, Beijing, and Shanghai ranked top three in "2012 Annual Urban and Rural Leaders"; in the vertical assessment of their own base values throughout the past years, Jiangsu, Qinghai, and Liaoning ranked top three as the "2000–2012 Urban and Rural Runners-Up"; Jiangsu, Tianjin, and Qinghai ranked top three in the "2005–2012 Urban and Rural Runners-Up"; Tianjin, Xinjiang, and Ningxia ranked top three as the "2010–2012 Urban and Rural Runners-Up"; Tianjin, Jilin, and Henan ranked top three as the "2012 Annual Urban and Rural Runners-Up".

Keywords Cross-province urban and rural areas • Cultural consumption • Integrative evaluation • Status ranking

This evaluation system applied the national cross-province urban and rural integrated cultural consumption demand status evaluation and, after having been undertaken for several years, has many years' worth of actual evaluation results. The annual evaluation ranking only goes to 2011, but has continuous applications and can be used as a reference.

This paper has expanded the 2012 integrated cultural consumption status evaluation analysis, calculation, evaluation and ranking of nationwide 31 provinces and four major regions (east, middle, west, and northeast). Given the detailed investigation within the province-wide urban and rural sub-report, this paper focuses on the analysis on a comparison of the four major regions (east, middle, west, and northeast), and focuses on a ranking and evaluation of the provinces.

Y. Wang et al., *Annual Evaluation Report of China's Cultural Consumption Demand*, Research Series on the Chinese Dream and China's Development Path,
DOI 10.1007/978-981-10-0730-9_3

3.1 Basic Status of Cultural Consumption Demand Growth in Urban and Rural Areas Across Provinces

The total growth trends in province-wide urban and rural cultural consumption demand can provide a macro perspective, so this paper analyzes and estimates according each provinces' proportion of urban and rural total cultural consumption, beginning with the changes in increasing and decreasing of the national share.

3.1.1 Increases and Decreases of the Total Share of Each Province Across Urban and Rural Areas

Table 3.1 shows the total growth in cultural consumption for each provinces' urban and rural areas, from 2000 to 2012, as well as other changes in the national share. The national urban and rural overall data makes up the base numbers listed in the first row of the calculation and evaluation. In this figure, the provinces are mainly ranked in order of 1,2,3. . ...., with the four major regions added to the ranking as [1], [2], [3], [4] (etc.).

From 2000 to 2012, the national urban and rural cultural consumption total grew from 270.435 billion yuan to 1.140597 trillion yuan, a total growth in absolute value of 870.162 billion yuan and a total growth percentage of 321.76 %, with an average annual growth of 12.74 %. Over the same period, the overall annual average growth of the eastern region was 14.16 %, higher than the national urban and rural annual average growth, growing from 47.05 to 54.67 % in percentage of the national urban and rural share accounted for, an increase of 16.19 %; the overall average annual growth of the northeast region was 13.20 %, higher than the national urban and rural average annual growth, growing from 6.53 to 6.85 % in percentage of the national urban and rural share, an increase of 5.02 %; the overall average annual growth of the middle region was 11.33 %, lower than the national urban and rural average annual growth, decreasing from 23.40 % to 20.12 % in percentage of the national urban and rural share, a decrease of 14.00 %; the overall average annual growth of the western region was 10.79 %, lower than the national urban and rural average annual growth, decreasing from 23.68 % to 19.20 %, a decrease of 18.92 %.

When comparing across time periods, during the "Tenth Five-Year Plan" period, the average annual growth of national urban and rural total cultural consumption was 13.65 %. Average annual growth in the Eastern region was 15.43 %, higher than the national annual average; average annual growth in the Northeastern region was 13.77 %, higher than the national average annual growth; average annual growth in the Middle region was 11.82 %, lower than the national average annual growth; average annual growth in the Western region was 11.24 %, lower than the national average annual growth. During the "Eleventh Five-Year Plan" period, the average annual growth of national urban and rural total cultural consumption was 11.36 %. Average annual growth in the Eastern region was 12.49 %, higher than the

Table 3.1 Each province and urban and rural region's total cultural consumption growth and amount it accounts for in changes in status of China's total share

Region	Total growth in cultural consumption				Changes accounting for national urban and rural share			
			Average annual growth over 12 Years				Changes in share over 12 years	
	Totals in the year 2000 (hundred million yuan)	Totals in the year 2012 (hundred million yuan)	Growth index (previous year = 100)	Index ranking	Share in the year 2000 (5)	Share in the year 2012 (%)	Percentage change	Rank of change
National	**2,704.35**	**11,405.97**	**112.74**	–	**100**	**100**	–	–
Jiangsu	202.36	1322.84	116.94	1	7.4828	11.5978	54.99	**1**
Beijing	81.78	469.77	115.68	2	3.0240	4.1186	36.20	**2**
Shanghai	98.46	548.12	115.38	3	3.6408	4.8056	31.99	**3**
Guangdong	267.89	1437.53	115.36	4	9.9059	13.0417	31.66	**4**
Tianjin	34.17	169.16	114.26	6	1.2635	1.4831	17.38	**6**
Fujian	86.32	383.33	113.23	9	3.1919	3.3608	5.29	**9**
Zhejiang	170.15	712.28	112.67	13	6.2917	6.2448	−0.75	**13**
Hebei	100.30	382.55	111.80	19	3.7088	3.3539	−9.57	**19**
Hainan	12.64	44.61	111.08	21	0.4674	0.3911	−16.32	**21**
Shandong	218.34	715.17	110.39	25	8.0737	6.2701	−22.34	**25**
East	1272.42	6235.34	114.16	[1]	47.0509	54.6673	16.19	**[1]**
Liaoning	75.83	378.00	114.32	5	2.8040	3.3141	18.19	**5**
Jilin	44.79	189.29	112.76	12	1.6562	1.6596	0.21	**12**
Heilongjiang	55.79	214.10	111.86	17	2.0630	1.8771	−9.01	**17**
Northeast	176.41	781.40	113.20	[2]	6.5232	6.8508	5.02	**[2]**
Shanxi	49.95	231.82	113.65	7	1.8470	2.0324	10.04	**7**
Henan	134.13	569.43	112.80	11	4.9598	4.9924	0.66	**11**
Anhui	98.99	394.09	112.20	16	3.6604	3.4551	−5.61	**16**
Jiangxi	72.90	278.97	111.83	18	2.6957	2.4458	−9.27	**18**
Hubei	120.16	389.08	110.29	26	4.4432	3.4112	−23.23	**26**

(continued)

Table 3.1 (continued)

Region	Total growth in cultural consumption				Changes accounting for national urban and rural share			
			Average annual growth over 12 Years				Changes in share over 12 years	
	Totals in the year 2000 (hundred million yuan)	Totals in the year 2012 (hundred million yuan)	Growth index (previous year = 100)	Index ranking	Share in the year 2000 (5)	Share in the year 2012 (%)	Percentage change	Rank of change
Hunan	156.66	431.87	108.82	30	5.7929	3.7864	−34.64	**30**
Middle	632.79	2295.25	111.33	[3]	23.3990	20.1232	−14.00	**[3]**
Qinghai	5.87	26.65	113.44	8	0.2171	0.2336	7.60	**8**
Inner Mongolia	50.45	223.18	113.19	10	1.8655	1.9567	4.89	**10**
Ningxia	10.32	42.16	112.44	14	0.3816	0.3696	−3.14	**14**
Shanxi	71.69	290.52	112.37	15	2.6509	2.5471	−3.92	**15**
Yunnan	65.05	247.86	111.79	20	2.4054	2.1731	−9.66	**20**
Guizhou	45.94	161.80	111.06	22	1.6987	1.4186	−16.49	**22**
Chongqing	61.05	213.43	110.99	23	2.2575	1.8712	−17.11	**23**
Xinjiang	29.04	98.85	110.75	24	1.0738	0.8667	−19.29	**24**
Tibet	1.0083	3.2214	110.14	27	0.0373	0.0282	−24.40	**27**
Sichuan	159.10	484.38	109.72	28	5.8831	4.2467	−27.82	**28**
Gansu	46.00	137.19	109.53	29	1.7010	1.2028	−29.29	**29**
Guangxi	94.84	260.53	108.79	31	3.5069	2.2842	−34.87	**31**
West	640.36	2189.75	110.79	[4]	23.6789	19.1983	−18.92	**[4]**

Note: (1) Calculations in tables were derived from data; (2) National urban and rural total population statistics include the military, etc. (included in the urban population), regional urban and rural population statistics are not related; therefore, the total amount from each region does not equal the national total amount; (3) Negative changes in growth of the percentage of the total share of cultural consumption across regions become a decreased percentage; (4) The total for Tibet was too small, so four decimal points were taken (The data calculation was done in accordance with related volumes of the *China Statistical Yearbook*)

national annual average; average annual growth in the Northeastern region was 13.23 %, higher than the national annual average; average annual growth in the Middle region was 9.51 %, lower than the national annual average; average annual growth in the Western region was 8.76 %, lower than the national annual average.

Comparing the urban and rural total cultural consumption growth changes between the two 5-year periods, national average annual growth during the "Eleventh Five-Year Plan" period was lower than that during the "Tenth Five-Year Plan" period by 2.29 percentage points. Each of the four major regions is different, with the annual average growth of the Eastern region over the "Eleventh Five-Year Plan" period being lower than growth during the "Tenth Five-Year Plan" period by 2.94 percentage points; average annual growth in the Northeastern region during the "Eleventh Five-Year Plan" period was lower than that during the "Tenth Five-Year Plan" period by 0.54 percentage points; average annual growth in the Middle region during the "Eleventh Five-Year Plan" period was lower than that during the "Tenth Five-Year Plan" period by 2.31 percentage points; average annual growth in the Western region during the "Eleventh Five-Year Plan" period was lower than that during the "Tenth Five-Year Plan" period by 2.48 percentage points.

Comparing the average annual growth in province-wide and regional urban and rural total cultural consumption demand from the year 2000 to 2012, the 12 provinces of Jiangsu, Beijing, Shanghai, Guangdong, Liaoning, Tianjin, Shanxi, Qinghai, Fujian, Inner Mongolia, Henan, and Jilin are in descending order of average annual growth, and were all had higher average annual growth than the national urban and rural average; the 19 provinces of Zhejiang, Ningxia, Shaanxi, Anhui, Heilongjiang, Jiangxi, Hebei, Yunnan, Hainan, Guizhou, Chongqing, Xinjiang, Shandong, Hubei, Tibet, Sichuan, Gansu, Hunan, and Guangxi, are in descending order of average annual growth, and were all had average annual growth lower than the national urban and rural average. . Among these, Jiangsu Province, in first place for average annual growth, was higher than the national urban and rural average annual growth by 4.20 percentage points; the province in last place for average annual growth, Guangxi, was lower than the national urban and rural annual growth by 3.95 percentage points.

During this 12-year period, in comparing the changes in growth of the share that each province, region, and urban and rural total cultural consumption accounted for of national urban and rural totals, the 12 provinces or regions of Jiangsu, Beijing, Shanghai, Guangdong, Liaoning, Tianjin, Shanxi, Qinghai, Fujian, Inner Mongolia, Henan, and Jilin each increased in share, and are listed in descending order of degree of growth; the 19 provinces or regions of Zhejiang, Ningxia, Shaanxi, Anhui, Heilongjiang, Jiangxi, Hebei, Yunnan, Hainan, Guizhou, Chongqing, Xinjiang, Shandong, Hubei, Tibet, Sichuan, Gansu, Hunan, and Guangxi each decreased in share, and are listed in descending order of degree of decrease. Among these, the province of Jiangsu, which takes first place in national urban and rural share growth, increased by 54.99 %; the province of Guangxi, which takes last place in national urban and rural share growth, decreased by 34.87 %.

In 2012, the national urban and rural cultural consumption total grew by 12.64 %, lower than the average annual growth of the "Tenth Five-Year Plan" period by 1.01 percentage points, and higher than the average annual growth during the "Eleventh Five-Year Plan" period by 1.28 percentage points. In that year, the total growth in cultural consumption of the 16 provinces or regions of Hainan, Gansu, Henan, Beijing, Hubei, Sichuan, Jiangsu, Guizhou, Liaoning, Xinjiang, Shaanxi, Jilin, Jianxi, Shanxi, Yunnan, and Fujian, listed in descending order of growth, were all higher than the national urban and rural annual average growth; the total growth in cultural consumption of the 15 provinces or regions of Guangdong, Anhui, Ningxia, Hebei, Hunan, Tibet, Qinghai, Shandong, Guangxi, Tianjin, Inner Mongolia, Zhejiang, Chongqing, Heilongjiang, and Shanghai, listed in listed in descending order of growth, were all lower than the national urban and rural annual average growth.

The urban and rural cultural consumption total values of each province or region are not in themselves comparable, but the degrees of growth and share changes can be compared. Here we offer an ordered list of the total growth degree and change in share of each region. Because there are large population differences between each region, there are large differences in how much total cultural consumption makes up of the national share, so percent of the shares has significance; therefore, it is easier to rank them when using percent changes in shares. In actuality, total growth and changes in share are connected, and the ranking of total average annual growth and percentage change in shares are consistent.

3.1.2 Provincial, Regional, Urban and Rural Cultural Per Capita Absolute Value Growth Changes

For a provincial and regional, urban and rural per capita cultural consumption absolute value growth situation analysis from 2000 to 2012 see Table 3.2, which contains a ranking in descending order of provincial and regional per capita cultural consumption absolute value annual growth values over those 12 years.

From 2000 to 2012, national urban and rural per capita cultural consumption demand grew from 214.18 to 844.45 yuan, with a per capita absolute value growth of 630.27 yuan and a total growth of 294.27 %, an average annual growth of 12.11 %. During the same period, total per capita absolute value of the Eastern region increased from the national urban and rural per capita value of 138.61–144.04 %, an average annual growth of 12.47 %, higher than the national urban and rural average growth by 0.36 percentage points, a growth of the absolute value that was 145.89 % of the national average; the total per capita absolute value of the Northeastern region increased from the national urban and rural per capita value of 77.36–84.35 %, a annual average of 12.92 %, and higher than the national urban and rural average growth by 0.81 percentage points, the absolute value growth 86.73 % of the national urban and rural average value, with an average annual growth of 86.73 %; the total per capita absolute value of the Middle region decreased from the national urban and rural per capita value of 82.96 % to 75.80 %,

Table 3.2 Provincial/regional, urban and rural per capita cultural consumption absolute value growth situation

Region	Per capita cultural consumption absolute values				Growth change in per capita cultural consumption				
	2000		2012		Total growth and total growth ratios over 12 years			Average annual growth over 12 years	
	Per capita value (yuan)	Rank	Per capita value (yuan)	Rank	Total growth value (yuan)	Total growth ratio (national = 1_	Total growth ratio rank	Growth index (previous year = 100)	Growth index rank
National	**214.18**	–	**844.45**	–	**630.27**	**1**	–	**112.1114**	**–**
Liaoning	181.51	17	861.84	9	680.33	1.0794	9	113.86	**2**
Jilin	167.77	20	683.37	13	520.60	0.8260	12	112.48	**7**
Heilongjiang	146.84	27	558.43	23	411.59	0.6530	22	111.77	**12**
Northeast	165.69	[4]	712.31	[2]	546.62	0.8673	[2]	112.92	**[1]**
Jiangsu	278.35	6	1,672.49	3	1,394.14	2.2120	3	116.12	**1**
Fujian	256.69	7	1,026.59	7	769.90	1.2215	7	112.24	**9**
Guangdong	357.74	4	1,410.06	4	1,052.32	1.6696	4	112.1087	**10**
Beijing	625.71	2	2,298.33	2	1,672.62	2.6538	2	111.45	**15**
Shanghai	632.15	1	2,318.65	1	1,686.50	2.6758	1	111.44	**16**
Tianjin	348.67	5	1,222.22	6	873.55	1.3860	6	111.02	**18**
Hebei	150.96	26	526.63	26	375.67	0.5960	24	110.97	**19**
Zhejiang	375.16	3	1,302.15	5	926.99	1.4708	5	110.93	**21**
Hainan	162.96	21	505.80	27	342.84	0.5440	28	109.90	**25**
Shandong	244.22	8	740.26	11	496.04	0.7870	14	109.68	**26**
East	296.87	[1]	1216.37	[1]	919.50	1.4589	[1]	112.47	**[2]**
Henan	142.12	28	605.97	20	463.85	0.7360	18	112.85	**3**
Anhui	158.10	23	659.23	15	501.13	0.7951	13	112.64	**5**
Shanxi	154.84	24	643.59	18	488.75	0.7755	15	112.61	**6**
Jiangxi	173.98	19	620.45	19	446.47	0.7084	19	111.18	**17**

(continued)

Table 3.2 (continued)

Region	Per capita cultural consumption absolute values				Growth change in per capita cultural consumption				
	2000		2012		Total growth and total growth ratios over 12 years			Average annual growth over 12 years	
	Per capita value (yuan)	Rank	Per capita value (yuan)	Rank	Total growth value (yuan)	Total growth ratio (national = 1_	Total growth ratio rank	Growth index (previous year = 100)	Growth index rank
Hubei	201.98	11	674.51	14	472.53	0.7497	16	110.57	**23**
Hunan	239.28	9	652.65	17	413.37	0.6559	21	108.72	**30**
Middle	177.69	[3]	640.08	[3]	462.39	0.7336	[3]	111.27	**[3]**
Inner Mongolia	213.16	10	897.82	8	684.66	1.0863	8	112.73	**4**
Qinghai	114.34	30	466.91	28	352.57	0.5594	27	112.44	**8**
Sha'anxi	197.43	14	775.16	10	577.73	0.9166	10	112.07	**11**
Guizhou	123.08	29	465.43	29	342.35	0.5432	29	111.72	**13**
Chongqing	198.00	13	727.92	12	529.92	0.8408	11	111.46	**14**
Ningxia	188.11	15	655.32	16	467.21	0.7413	17	110.96	**20**
Yunnan	154.27	25	533.61	25	379.34	0.6019	23	110.89	**22**
Sichuan	185.52	16	600.74	21	415.22	0.6588	20	110.29	**24**
Gansu	180.38	18	533.63	24	353.25	0.5605	26	109.46	**27**
Guangxi	200.44	12	558.65	22	358.21	0.5683	25	108.92	**28**
Xinjiang	160.28	22	445.12	30	284.84	0.4519	30	108.88	**29**
Tibet	39.23	31	105.46	31	66.23	0.1051	31	108.59	**31**
West	177.78	[2]	602.83	[4]	425.05	0.6744	[4]	110.71	**[4]**

Note: Table (1) calculations are derived from comprehensive urban and rural values; (2) The "Growth Ratio" of regional per capita cultural consumption absolute values that are less than 1 are less than the national urban and rural per capita growth; (3) Values for average annual growth over 12 years for the nation as a whole and for Guangdong province used 4 decimals points for comparison and average annual growth of 11.27 %, lower than the national urban and rural average growth by 1.40 percentage points, the absolute value growth 67.44 % of the national urban and rural average absolute value.

Looking at this over time periods, during the "Tenth Five-Year Plan" period, there was a national urban and rural per capita cultural consumption average annual growth of 12.92 %. The average annual growth for the Eastern region was 13.95 %, higher than the national average annual growth; the average annual growth for the Northeastern region was 13.55 %, higher than the national average annual growth; the average annual growth for the Middle region was 11.67 %, lower than the national average annual growth; average annual growth in the Western region was 10.91 %, lower than the national average annual growth. During the "Eleventh Five-Year Plan" period, there was a national urban and rural per capita cultural consumption average annual growth of 10.78 %. The average annual growth for the Eastern region was 10.69 %, lower than the national average annual growth; the average annual growth for the Northeastern region was 12.88 %, higher than the national average annual growth; the average annual growth for the Middle region was 9.64 %, lower than the national annual average growth; the average annual growth for the Western region was 8.85 %, lower than the national average annual growth.

In comparing the urban and rural per capita cultural consumption demand growth changes between these two 5-year periods, we see that the national annual average growth during the "Eleventh Five-Year Plan" period was lower than that during the "Tenth Five-Year Plan" period by 2.14 percentage points. Each of the four major regions had differences, with average annual growth in the Eastern region during the "Eleventh Five-Year Plan" period lower than that during the "Tenth Five-Year Plan" period by 3.26 percentage points; average annual growth in the Northeastern region during the "Eleventh Five-Year Plan" period was lower than that during the "Tenth Five-Year Plan" period by 0.67 percentage points; average annual growth in the Middle region during the "Eleventh Five-Year Plan" period was lower than that during the "Tenth Five-Year Plan" period by 2.03 percentage points; average annual growth in the Western region during the "Eleventh Five-Year Plan" period was lower than that during the "Tenth Five-Year Plan" period by 2.06 percentage points.

In doing a comparison of cross-province and region urban and rural per capita cultural consumption demand average annual growths, we see that the 9 provinces or regions of Jiangsu, Liaoning, Henan, Inner Mongolia, Anhui, Shanxi, Jilin, Qinghai, and Fujian, in descending order of average annual growth, all had annual average growths higher than the national urban and rural average growth; the 22 provinces or regions of Guangdong, Shaanxi, Heilongjiang, Guizhou, Chongqing, Beijing, Shanghai, Jiangxi, Tianjin, Hebei, Ningxia, Zhejiang, Yunnan, Hubei, Sichuan, Hainan, Shandong, Gansu, Guangxi, Xinjiang, Hunan, and Tibet, in descending order of average annual growth, all had annual average growths lower than the national urban and rural average growth. Among these, Jiangsu Province, in first place for average annual growth, was higher than the national urban and rural average growth by 4.01 percentage points; Tibet, in last place for average annual growth, was lower than the national urban and rural average growth by 3.52 percentage points.

When comparing the cross-province and region urban and rural cultural consumption absolute values, in the year 2000, the provinces or regions of Shanghai, Beijing, Zhejiang, Guangdong, Tianjin, Jiangsu, Fujian, Shandong, and Hunan, in descending order of per capita absolute values, were all higher than the national urban and rural average value; the 22 provinces or regions of Inner Mongolia, Hubei, Guangxi, Chongqing, Shaanxi, Ningxia, Sichuan, Liaoning, Gansu, Jiangxi, Jilin, Hainan, Xinjiang, Anhui, Shanxi, Yunnan, Hebei, Heilongjiang, Henan, Guizhou, Qinghai, and Tibet, in descending order of per capita absolute values, were all lower average values than the national urban and rural average value. Among these, Shanghai, in first place, had a per capita value higher than the national urban and rural average value by 298.15 %; Tibet, in last place, had a per capita absolute value only 18.32 % of the national urban and rural average value.

In 2012, the nine provinces or regions of Shanghai, Beijing, Jiangsu, Guangdong, Zhejiang, Tianjin, Fujian, and Inner Mongolia, in descending order of per capita absolute value, were all higher than the national urban and rural average value; the 22 provinces or regions or Shaanxi, Shandong, Chongqing, Jilin, Hubei, Anhui, Ningxia, Hunan, Shanxi, Jiangxi, Henan, Sichuan, Guangxi, Heilongjiang, Gansu, Yunnan, Hebei, Hainan, Qinghai, Guizhou, Xinjiang, and Tibet, in descending order of per capita absolute value, all were higher than the national urban and rural average value. Among these, Shanghai, first place in per capita value, was higher than the national urban and rural average value by 274.57 %; Tibet, last place in per capita value, was only 12.49 % of the national urban and rural average value.

In 2012, the national urban and rural per capita cultural consumption average annual growth was 12.09 %, lower than the average annual growth of the "Tenth Five-Year Plan" period by 0.83 percentage points, and higher than the average annual growth of the "Eleventh Five-Year Plan" period by 1.31 percentage points. In the same year, the 16 provinces or regions of Hainan, Henan, Gansu, Hubei, Sichuan, Jiangsu, Beijing, Guizhou, Liaoning, Shaanxi, Xinjiang, Jilin, Jiangxi, Shanxi, Yunnan, and Anhui, in descending order of average annual growth in cultural consumption, all had growth higher than the national urban and rural average growth; the 15 provinces or regions of Fujian, Guangdong, Ningxia, Hebei, Hunan, Tibet, Shandong, Qinghai, Guangxi, Inner Mongolia, Zhejiang, Tianjin, Heilongjiang, Chongqing, and Shanghai, in descending order of per capita cultural consumption average annual growth, all had lower growth than the national urban and rural annual average.

The basic indicators of per capita cultural consumption absolute values calculated and assessed by this evaluation system, although the final comprehensive evaluation calculations were not calculated at a heavy weight, they are the basis for the following index calculations, and thus actually have a decisive significance. Of course, analysis of national per-province or region urban and rural cultural consumption demand status cannot be done independently, but must be placed with related background factors like national cross-region economic growth, and livelihood enhancement, and also placed with coordination of growth between urban and rural and regional areas, in order to take the next step in analysis.

3.2 Comparison of Provinces and Regions in Context of Related Background Growth

When conducting this evaluation, the national and provincial urban and rural cultural consumption demand and growth needs to be put into context of related economic and livelihood factors in order to investigate the "coordinated growth" status, thereby obtaining extremely important proportional values of basic indicators for numerical calculations.

3.2.1 Changes in Share of GDP

For an analysis of changing trends in proportion of regional urban and rural per capita cultural consumption to per capita GDP see Table 3.3, which is a list in descending order of proportions of urban and rural per capita cultural consumption and per capita GDP in 2012. The table also provides GDP data for the years 2000 and 2012, and when comparing it with the per capita cultural consumption data in Table 3.2, the figures can be rechecked.

From 2000 to 2012, national per capita GDP increased from 7,858 to 38,420 yuan, with an average annual growth of 14.14 %, higher than the national urban and rural per capita cultural consumption average annual growth over the same period by 2.03 percentage points. Within 12 years, the proportion between the national urban and rural per capita cultural consumption and per capita GDP decreased from 2.73 % to 2.20 %, a decrease of 0.53 percentage points and a decline of 19.36 %. Over the same period, the proportion in the Eastern region decreased from 2.41 % to 2.11 %, a decrease of 0.30 percentage points; the proportion in the Northeastern region decreased from 1.81 % to 1.55 %, a decrease of 0.26 percentage points; the proportion in the Middle region decreased from 3.35 % to 1.97 % a decrease of 1.38 percentage points; the proportion in the Western region decreased from 3.75 % to 1.92 %, a decrease of 1.83 percentage points.

When comparing the proportional values of provincial and regional urban and rural per capita cultural consumption to per capita GDP, in the year 2000, the 15 provinces or regions of Guizhou, Hunan, Gansu, Guangxi, Shaanxi, Sichuan, Jiangxi, Chongqing, Ningxia, Anhui, Inner Mongolia, Yunnan, Hubei, Guangdong, and Zhejiang, in descending order of this proportions, all were higher than the national urban and rural total proportional value; the 16 provinces or regions of Shanxi, Shandong, Henan, Beijing, Hainan, Jiangsu, Fujian, Jilin, Qinghai, Xinjiang, Shanghai, Tianjin, Hebei, Heilongjiang, Liaoning, and Tibet, in

Table 3.3 Changes in proportions of provincial and regional per capita cultural consumption and per capita GDP

	2000			2012			Changes in proportional values from 2000 to 2010		
Region	Per capita GDP (yuan)	Ratio of cultural consumption and GDP (%)	Rank of proportional values	Per capita GDP (yuan)	(%) Ratio of cultural consumption and GDP (%)	Rank of proportion	Percentage point increase	Percent increase	Rank
National	**7,858**	**2.73**	–	**38,420**	**2.20**	–	**−0.5277**	**−19.36**	–
Shanghai	29,671	2.13	26	85,373	2.72	1	0.5854	27.48	**1**
Jiangsu	11,765	2.37	21	68,347	2.45	4	0.0812	3.43	**2**
Beijing	24,122	2.59	19	87,475	2.63	2	0.0335	1.29	**3**
Guangdong	12,736	2.81	14	54,095	2.61	3	−0.2023	−7.20	**5**
Fujian	11,194	2.29	22	52,763	1.95	15	−0.3474	−15.15	**7**
Zhejiang	13,416	2.80	15	63,374	2.05	10	−0.7416	−26.52	**10**
Hebei	7,592	1.99	28	36,584	1.44	25	−0.5489	−27.61	**11**
Tianjin	17,353	2.01	27	93,173	1.31	30	−0.6975	−34.71	**15**
Hainan	6,798	2.40	20	32,377	1.56	23	−0.8350	−34.83	**16**
Shandong	9,326	2.62	17	51,768	1.43	26	−1.1887	−45.39	**21**
East	12,305	2.41	[3]	57,722	2.11	[1]	−0.3052	−12.65	**[1]**
Liaoning	11,177	1.62	30	56,649	1.52	24	−0.1026	−6.32	**4**
Heilongjiang	8,294	1.77	29	35,711	1.56	22	−0.2067	−11.68	**6**
Jilin	7,351	2.28	23	43,415	1.59	21	−0.6966	−30.52	**13**
Northeast	9,178	1.81	[4]	46,014	1.55	[4]	−0.2573	−14.25	**[2]**
Henan	5,450	2.61	18	31,499	1.92	16	−0.6840	−26.23	**9**
Shanxi	5,722	2.71	16	33,628	1.91	17	−0.7921	−29.27	**12**
Anhui	4,779	3.31	10	28,792	2.29	8	−1.0186	−30.79	**14**
Jiangxi	4,851	3.59	7	28,800	2.15	9	−1.4321	−39.93	**19**
Hubei	6,293	3.21	13	38,572	1.75	20	−1.4610	−45.52	**22**
Hunan	5,425	4.41	2	33,480	1.95	14	−2.4614	−55.80	**30**

Middle	5,308	3.35	[2]	32,427	1.97	[2]	−1.3741	−41.04	**[3]**
Yunnan	4,769	3.23	12	22,195	2.40	6	−0.8306	−25.68	**8**
Qinghai	5,138	2.23	24	33,181	1.41	27	−0.8183	−36.77	**17**
Xinjiang	7,372	2.17	25	33,796	1.32	29	−0.8571	−39.42	**18**
Gansu	4,129	4.37	3	21,978	2.43	5	−1.9406	−44.42	**20**
Sichuan	4,956	3.74	6	29,608	2.03	11	−1.7144	−45.80	**23**
Tibet	4,572	0.86	31	22,936	0.46	31	−0.3983	−46.42	**24**
Chongqing	5,616	3.53	8	38,914	1.87	18	−1.6550	−46.94	**25**
Guizhou	2,759	4.46	1	19,710	2.36	7	−2.0995	−47.06	**26**
Ningxia	5,376	3.50	9	36,394	1.80	19	−1.6985	−48.54	**27**
Sha'an Xi	4,968	3.97	5	38,564	2.01	12	−1.9640	−49.42	**28**
Guangxi	4,652	4.31	4	27,952	2.00	13	−2.3102	−53.62	**29**
Inner Mongolia	6,502	3.28	11	63,886	1.41	28	−1.8730	−57.13	**31**
West	4,744	3.75	[1]	31,357	1.92	[3]	−1.8249	−48.70	**[4]**

Note: (1) Per capita GDP data comes relevant years of the *China Statistical Yearbook*, and the rest is derived from numerical calculations; (2) a negative increase in ratio percentage points will show a decrease in percentage points. Ranking by an increase in percentage points is more accurate (The following Tables 3.4, 3.5, and 3.6 are the same)

descending order of this ratio, all were lower than the national urban and rural total proportional value. Among these, Guizhou, in first place, had a value higher than the national urban and rural total proportional value by 1.74 percentage points; Tibet, in last place, had a value 1.87 percentage points lower than the national urban and rural total proportional value.

In 2012, only the eight provinces or regions of Shanghai, Beijing, Guangdong, Jiangsu, Gansu, Yunnan, Guizhou, and Anhui, in descending order of this ratio, were higher than the national urban and rural total proportional value; the 23 provinces or regions of Jiangxi, Zhejiang, Sichuan, Shaanxi, Guangxi, Hunan, Fujian, Henan, Shanxi, Chongqing, Ningxia, Hubei, Jilin, Heilongjiang, Hainan, Liaoning, Hebei, Shandong, Qinghai, Inner Mongolia, Xinjiang, Tianjin, and Tibet, in descending order of this ratio, all were lower than the national urban and rural total proportional value. Among these, Shanghai, in first place for this ration, was higher than the national urban and rural total proportional value by 0.52 percentage points; Tibet, in last place, was lower than the national urban and rural total proportional value by 1.74 percentage points.

In comparing the drops and rises in the proportion of provincial and regional urban and rural per capita cultural consumption and per capita GDP from the year 2000 to 2012, only in the three provinces or regions of Shanghai, Jiangsu, and Beijing, in descending order of ratio, did the ratio rise; the 28 provinces of Liaoning, Guangdong, Heilongjiang, Fujian, Yunnan, Henan, Zhejiang, Hebei, Shanxi, Jilin, Anhui, Tianjin, Hainan, Qinghai, Xinjiang, Jiangxi, Gansu, Shandong, Hubei, Sichuan, Tibet, Chongqing, Guizhou, Ningxia, Shaanxi, Guangxi, Hunan, and Inner Mongolia, in descending order of ratio, each decreased. Among these, Shanghai, in first place, had a proportion that increased by 27.48 %; Inner Mongolia, in last place, had a proportion that decreased 57.13 %.

Comparing 2012 to the previous year, the national urban and rural ratio for this indicator increased by 2.69 %. At the same time, the 16 provinces or regions of Hainan, Henan, Beijing, Gansu, Jiangsu, Shanxi, Hubei, Guangdong, Sichuan, Liaoning, Jiangxi, Xinjiang, Hebei, Jilin, Ningxia, and Fujian, in descending order of increase degree for this ratio, all experienced increases; the 15 provinces or regions of Shaanxi, Anhui, Shandong, Zhejiang, Inner Mongolia, Guangxi, Shanghai, Hunan, Yunnan, Guizhou, Qinghai, Heilongjiang, Tianjin, Tibet, and Chongqing, in descending order of increase degree for this ratio, all experienced decreases.

The analysis of this ratio relationship shows that, from 2000 to 2012, in a comparison of the national provincial/regional urban and rural cultural consumption demand growth and GDP growth "growth coordination" was poor. Nationally, and throughout most provinces and regions, the urban and rural cultural consumption demand growth has not kept up with the GDP growth. Economic growth accomplishments did not come with the increase of cultural consumption demand of citizens. In 2012, the situation improved, and this indicator's ratio has increased across most of the nation's provinces and regions.

3.2.2 Changes in Relationship of Proportional Income

For an analysis of the changing status of the proportion that provincial urban and rural per capita cultural consumption makes up of per capita income from the year 2000 to 2012, see Table 3.4, where the proportion that per capita cultural consumption of each province and region makes up of per capita income is ranked in descending order. The table also provides data for per capita income of each province or region, and the comparison Table 3.2 shows regional cultural consumption data; calculations for this can be used to check the data again.

From 2000 to 2012, the national urban and rural per capita income increased from 3,682.95 to 16,569.59 yuan, an average annual increase of 13.35 %, higher than the average annual growth in national urban and rural per capita cultural consumption over the same period by 1.24 percentage points. Over the 12 years, the proportion that national urban and rural per capita cultural consumption makes up of per capita income decreased from 5.82 % to 5.10 %, a decrease of 0.72 percentage points, and 12.37 %. Over the same period, total proportion the Eastern region decreased from 5.52 % to 5.47 %, a decrease of 0.05 percentage points; the total proportion of the Northeastern region decreased from 4.51 % to 4.49 %, a decrease of 0.02 percentage points; the total proportion of the Middle region decreased from 5.90 % to 4.72 %, a decrease of 1.18 percentage points; the total proportion of the Western region decreased from 6.36 % to 4.86 %, a decrease of 1.50 percentage points.

In comparing the proportion of per capita income taken up by urban and rural cultural consumption across provinces, in the year 2000, the 12 provinces or regions of Gansu, Shaanxi, Hunan, Beijing, Ningxia, Guangxi, Inner Mongolia, Sichuan, Shandong, Chongqing, Yunnan, and Jiangxi, in descending order of ratios for this indicator, all had ratios higher than the total national urban and rural ratio; the 19 provinces or regions of Shanghai, Hubei, Jiangsu, Zhejiang, Anhui, Guizhou, Henan, Xinjiang, Shanxi, Fujian, Guangdong, Tianjin, Jilin, Hainan, Hebei, Liaoning, Qinghai, Heilongjiang, and Tibet, in descending order of ratios for this indicator, all had ratios lower than the total national urban and rural ratio. Among these, Gansu Province, in first place of this indicator ratio, had a ratio higher than the national urban and rural total by 2.20 percentage points; Tibet, in last place of this indicator ratio, had a ratio lower than the national urban and rural total by 4.22 percentage points.

In 2012, the seven provinces or regions of Jiangsu, Beijing, Shanghai, Guangdong, Shaanxi, Gansu, and Inner Mongolia, in descending order of this indicator's ratio, all had ratios higher than the national urban and rural total ratio; the 24 provinces or regions of Ningxia, Fujian, Anhui, Zhejiang, Shanxi, Guizhou, Sichuan, Hunan, Henan, Liaoning, Yunnan, Jilin, Jiangxi, Hubei, Tianjin, Chongqing, Guangxi, Qinghai, Shandong, Heilongjiang, Xinjiang, Hebei, Hainan, and Tibet, in descending order of this indicator's ratio, all had ratios lower than the national urban and rural total ratio. Among these, Jiangsu Province, in first place for this indicator's ratio, had a ratio 2.14 percentage points higher than the national urban

Table 3.4 Changes in urban and rural per capita cultural consumption as proportion of per capita total income for each province or region

Region	2000			2012			Changes in proportional values from 2000 to 2010		
	Per capita income (yuan)	Cultural consumption as proportion of income (%)	Rank of proportional value	Per capita income (yuan)	Cultural consumption as proportion of income (%)	Rank of proportional value	Percentage point change	Percentage change	Rank
National	**3,682.95**	**5.8155**	–	**16,560.59**	**5.0992**	–	**−0.7163**	**−12.32**	**–**
Liaoning	3,967.28	4.5753	28	18,358.35	4.6946	17	0.1193	2.61	**4**
Heilongjiang	3,558.14	4.1269	30	13,795.25	4.0480	27	−0.0789	−1.91	**7**
Jilin	3,391.78	4.9463	25	14,815.24	4.6464	19	−0.2999	−6.06	**9**
Northeast	3,676.95	4.5062	[4]	15,875.36	4.4869	[4]	−0.0193	−0.43	**[1]**
Jiangsu	4,892.22	5.6897	15	23,114.85	7.2356	1	1.5459	27.17	**1**
Guangdong	6,930.86	5.1616	23	23,721.57	5.9442	4	0.7826	15.16	**2**
Shanghai	1,0974.50	5.7602	13	37,793.15	6.1351	3	0.3749	6.51	**3**
Beijing	9,033.10	6.9268	4	33,709.72	6.8180	2	−0.1088	−1.57	**6**
Fujian	4,934.26	5.2022	22	20,612.51	4.9804	9	−0.2218	−4.26	**8**
Tianjin	6,854.16	5.0870	24	26,667.83	4.5831	22	−0.5039	−9.91	**10**
Zhejiang	6,633.38	5.6556	16	27,101.01	4.8048	11	−0.8508	−15.04	**16**
Hebei	3,289.30	4.5893	27	13,839.25	3.8054	29	−0.7839	−17.08	**17**
Hainan	3,414.71	4.7724	26	14,305.12	3.5358	30	−1.2366	−25.91	**25**
Shandong	4,068.62	6.0025	9	17,876.78	4.1409	26	−1.8616	−31.01	**29**
East	5,381.09	5.5169	[3]	22,224.91	5.4730	[1]	−0.0439	−0.80	**[2]**
Shanxi	2,869.66	5.3957	21	13,450.50	4.7849	12	−0.6108	−11.32	**11**
Anhui	2,846.20	5.5547	17	13,489.45	4.8870	10	−0.6677	−12.02	**12**
Henan	2,614.77	5.4354	19	12,885.89	4.7026	16	−0.7328	−13.48	**14**
Hubei	3,548.07	5.6928	14	14,691.62	4.5911	21	−1.1017	−19.35	**18**
Jiangxi	2,940.88	5.9158	12	13,436.64	4.6176	20	−1.2982	−21.94	**21**

Hunan	3,363.80	7.1135	3	13,807.33	4.7268	15	−2.3867	−33.55	**30**
Middle	3,010.54	5.9024	[2]	13,572.79	4.7159	[3]	−1.1865	−20.10	**[3]**
Qinghai	2,748.81	4.1598	29	11,081.63	4.2134	25	0.0536	1.29	**5**
Guizhou	2,248.49	5.4737	18	9,730.38	4.7833	13	−0.6904	−12.61	**13**
Inner Mongolia	3,339.74	6.3824	7	16,496.61	5.4424	7	−0.9400	−14.73	**15**
Yunnan	2,583.63	5.9710	11	11,375.76	4.6908	18	−1.2802	−21.44	**19**
Sha'anxi	2,606.24	7.5754	2	13,047.30	5.9412	5	−1.6342	−21.57	**20**
Tibet	2,462.74	1.5931	31	8,517.16	1.2382	31	−0.3549	−22.28	**22**
Chongqing	3,311.66	5.9738	10	16,111.46	4.5180	23	−1.4608	−24.43	**23**
Sichuan	2,943.06	6.3037	8	12,680.43	4.7375	14	−1.5662	−24.85	**24**
Ningxia	2,740.36	6.8644	5	13,036.57	5.0268	8	−1.8376	−26.77	**26**
Xinjiang	2,966.75	5.4027	20	11,438.04	3.8916	28	−1.5111	−27.97	**27**
Gansu	2,251.29	8.0123	1	93,08.23	5.7329	6	−2.2794	−28.45	**28**
Guangxi	2,951.44	6.7914	6	12,508.18	4.4663	24	−2.3251	−34.24	**31**
West	2,796.70	6.3569	[1]	12,416.66	4.8550	[2]	−1.5019	−23.63	**[4]**

Note: The table contains comprehensive urban and rural calculations derived from numerical data; (2) Decreases in ratios are expressed by negative percentage points, and decreases in percentage are expressed by negative percentages

and rural total; Tibet, in last place for this indicator's ratio, had a ratio 3.86 percentage points lower than the national urban and rural total.

In a comparison of changes in provincial/regional urban and rural per capita cultural consumption as proportion of per capita income from 2000 to 2012, only the 5 provinces or regions of Jiangsu, Guangdong, Shanghai, Liaoning, and Qinghai, in descending order of degree of increase, experienced increases in this ratio; the 26 provinces or regions of Beijing, Heilongjiang, Fujian, Jilin, Tianjin, Shanxi, Anhui, Guizhou, Henan, Inner Mongolia, Zhejiang, Hebei, Hubei, Yunnan, Shaanxi, Jiangxi, Tibet, Chongqing, Sichuan, Hainan, Ningxia, Xinjiang, Gansu, Shandong, Hunan, and Guangxi, in descending order of degree of increase, all experienced decreases of this ratio. Among these, Jiangsu Province, in first place, had a ratio of this indicator that increased 27.17 %; Guangxi, in last place, had a ratio that decreased 34.24 %.

When comparing 2012 with the previous year, the national urban and rural ratio decreased 1.96 %. At the same time, only the nine provinces or regions of Hainan, Henan, Beijing, Sichuan, Gansu, Hubei, Jiangsu, Liaoning, and Jilin, in descending order of degree of increase, all experienced increases; the 22 provinces or regions of Jiangxi, Shaanxi, Shanxi, Guizhou, Guangdong, Anhui, Xinjiang, Hebei, Ningxia, Fujian, Yunnan, Hunan, Tibet, Shandong, Inner Mongolia, Guangxi, Tianjian, Zhejiang, Qinghai, Heilongjiang, Shanghai, and Chongqing, in descending order of decline, all experienced decreases.

The analysis of this ratio relationship shows that from 2000 to 2012, in comparing the national urban and rural cultural consumption demand and income growth, the "coordination of growth" was poor. In most of the nation's provinces or regions, the urban and rural cultural consumption demand growth did not keep up with the growth in income of the citizens, and the enhancement of the livelihood of the people did not come about at the same time as the increase in urban and rural cultural consumption demand of citizens.

3.2.3 Changes in the Share of Total Consumption

From 2000 to 2012, the changing trends in provincial/regional urban and rural per capita cultural consumption as proportion of total per capita consumption are analyzed in Table 3.5, where each province or region is ranked in descending order according to the 2012 urban and rural per capita cultural consumption as proportion of total per capita consumption. The table also presents provincial and regional urban and rural per capita total consumption data from 2000 to 2012, which can be compared to the per capita cultural consumption data in Table 3.2 in order to check calculations again.

From 2000 to 2012, national urban and rural per capita total consumption increased from 2,851.61 to 11,498.08 yuan, a 12.32 % increase, higher than the national urban and rural per capita cultural consumption average annual growth over the same period by 0.21 percentage points. Within the 12 years, national urban

Table 3.5 Changes in urban and rural per capita cultural consumption as proportion of per capita total consumption for each province or region

	2000			2012			Change in proportion from 2000 to 2012		
Region	Total per capita consumption	Cultural consumption as proportion of total consumption (%)	Rank of proportion	Total per capita consumption (yuan)	Cultural consumption as proportion of total consumption (%)	Rank of proportion	Percentage point change	Percentage change	Rank
National	**2,851.61**	**7.5109**	–	**11,498.08**	**7.3443**	–	**−0.1666**	**−2.22**	–
Jiangsu	3,545.79	7.8502	11	15,187.64	11.0122	1	3.1620	40.28	**1**
Guangdong	5,527.43	6.4721	26	17,459.70	8.0761	4	1.6040	24.78	**2**
Shanghai	8,293.64	7.6222	12	24,725.28	9.3776	3	1.7554	23.03	**3**
Beijing	7,332.13	8.5338	3	22,366.82	10.2756	2	1.7418	20.41	**4**
Fujian	3,719.03	6.9020	23	13,988.31	7.3389	7	0.4369	6.33	**7**
Zhejiang	5,025.23	7.4655	15	17,487.80	7.4461	6	−0.0194	−0.26	**11**
Tianjin	4,946.50	7.0489	21	17,807.76	6.8634	13	−0.1855	−2.63	**14**
Hebei	2,124.97	7.1039	20	8,675.51	6.0703	26	−1.0336	−14.55	**22**
Hainan	2,492.30	6.5386	25	9,718.36	5.2046	29	−1.3340	−20.40	**27**
Shandong	2,966.95	8.2312	7	11,429.40	6.4768	21	−1.7544	−21.31	**28**
East	4,022.12	7.3808	[3]	14,884.94	8.1718	[1]	0.7910	10.72	**[1]**
Liaoning	3,150.68	5.7611	28	12,869.44	6.6968	15	0.9357	16.24	**5**
Jilin	2,765.45	6.0665	27	10,699.01	6.4339	22	0.3674	6.06	**8**
Heilongjiang	2,705.19	5.4281	29	9,837.59	5.6765	27	0.2484	4.58	**10**
Northeast	2,895.09	5.7232	[4]	11,265.73	6.3228	[4]	0.5996	10.48	**[2]**
Shanxi	2,104.29	7.3582	16	8,920.22	7.2150	8	−0.1432	−1.95	**13**
Henan	1,884.71	7.5409	13	8,643.06	7.0111	11	−0.5298	−7.03	**15**
Jiangxi	2,180.27	7.9796	9	8,693.10	7.1373	10	−0.8423	−10.56	**17**
Hubei	2,769.44	7.2933	17	10,344.94	6.5202	20	−0.7731	−10.60	**18**
Anhui	2111.68	7.4869	14	9,872.63	6.6774	16	−0.8095	−10.81	**19**

(continued)

Table 3.5 (continued)

Region	2000			2012			Change in proportion from 2000 to 2012		
	Total per capita consumption	Cultural consumption as proportion of total consumption (%)	Rank of proportion	Total per capita consumption (yuan)	Cultural consumption as proportion of total consumption (%)	Rank of proportion	Percentage point change	Percentage change	Rank
Hunan	2,893.25	8.2704	5	9,879.28	6.6062	18	−1.6642	−20.12	**26**
Middle	2,312.50	7.6841	[2]	9,384.05	6.8210	[2]	−0.8631	−11.23	**[3]**
Tibet	1,940.69	2.0217	31	4,835.20	2.1811	31	0.1594	7.88	**6**
Qinghai	2,233.07	5.1205	30	8,622.24	5.4152	28	0.2947	5.76	**9**
Guizhou	1,838.84	6.6932	24	7,000.73	6.6483	17	−0.0449	−0.67	**12**
Yunnan	2,163.44	7.1307	19	8,109.39	6.5802	19	−0.5505	−7.72	**16**
Chongqing	2,747.01	7.2078	18	1,1489.65	6.3354	23	−0.8724	−12.10	**20**
Shaanxi	2,206.74	8.9469	2	1,0086.65	7.6850	5	−1.2619	−14.10	**21**
Inner Mongolia	2,588.83	8.2337	6	1,2863.49	6.9796	12	−1.2541	−15.23	**23**
Ningxia	2,304.20	8.1638	8	9,728.86	6.7359	14	−1.4279	−17.49	**24**
Sichuan	2,362.70	7.8521	10	9,499.48	6.3239	24	−1.5282	−19.46	**25**
Guangxi	2,409.09	8.3203	4	8,906.18	6.2726	25	−2.0477	−24.61	**29**
Gansu	1,801.62	10.0121	1	7,448.75	7.1640	9	−2.8481	−28.45	**30**
Xinjiang	2,303.68	6.9578	22	9,060.54	4.9127	30	−2.0451	−29.39	**31**
West	2,274.77	7.8155	[1]	9,236.93	6.5263	[3]	−1.2892	−16.50	**[4]**

and rural per capita cultural consumption has proportion of per capita total consumption decreased from 7.51 % to 7.34 %, a decrease of 0.17 percentage points and a 2.26 % decrease. Over the same period, the proportion of the Eastern region increased from 7.68 % to 8.17 %, an increase of 0.79 percentage points; the proportion from the Northeastern region increased from 5.72 % to 6.32 %, an increase of 0.60 percentage points; the proportion from the Middle region decreased from 7.68 % to 6.82 %, a decrease of 0.86 percentage points; and the proportion from the Western region decreased from 7.82 % to 6.53 %, a decrease of 1.29 percentage points.

In comparing the urban and rural per capita cultural consumption as proportion of per capita total consumption across provinces and regions, in the year 2000, the 13 provinces or regions of Gansu, Shaanxi, Beijing, Guangxi, Hunan, Inner Mongolia, Shandong, Ningxia, Jiangxi, Sichuan, Jiangsu, Shanghai, and Henan, in descending order of this indicator ratio, were all had ratios higher than the national urban and rural total ratio; the 18 provinces or regions of Anhui, Zhejiang, Shanxi, Hubei, Chongqing, Yunnan, Hebei, Tianjian, Xinjiang, Fujian, Guizhou, Hainan, Guangdong, Jilin, Liaoning, Heilongjiang, Qinghai, and Tibet, in descending order of this indicator ratio, all had ratios lower than the national urban and rural total ratio. Among these, Gansu Province, in first place, had a ratio 2.50 percentage points higher than the national urban and rural total ratio; Tibet, in last place, had a ratio 5.49 percentage points lower than the national urban and rural total ratio.

In 2012, the six provinces or regions of Jiangsu, Beijing, Shanghai, Guangdong, Shaanxi, and Zhejiang, in descending order of this indicator's ratio, all had higher ratios than the total urban and rural total ratio; the 25 provinces or regions of Fujian, Shanxi, Gansu, Jiangxi, Henan, Inner Mongolia, Tianjin, Ningxia, Liaoning, Anhui, Guizhou, Hunan, Yunnan, Hubei, Shandong, Jilin, Chongqing, Sichuan, Guangxi, Hebei, Heilongjiang, Qinghai, Hainan, Xinjiang, and Tibet, in descending order of this indicator ratio, all had lower ratios than the national urban and rural total ratio. Among these, Jiangsu Province, in first place, had a ratio higher than the national urban and rural total ratio by 3.67 percentage points; Tibet, in last place, had a ratio lower than the national urban and rural ratio by 5.16 percentage points.

Doing a comparison of each province or region's change in per capita cultural consumption as proportion of per capita total consumption from 2000 to 2012, the 10 provinces or regions of Jiangsu, Guangdong, Shanghai, Beijing, Liaoning, Tibet, Fujian, Jilin, Qinghai, and Heilongjiang, in descending order of increase of this ratio, all experienced increases in ratio; the 21 regions or provinces of Zhejiang, Guizhou, Shanxi, Tianjin, Henan, Yunnan, Jiangxi, Hubei, Anhui, Chongqing, Shaanxi, Hebei, Inner Mongolia, Ningxia, Sichuan, Hunan, Hainan, Shandong, Guangxi, Gansu, and Xinjiang, in ascending order of decrease of this ratio, all experienced decreases n ratio. Among these, Jiangsu Province, in first place, experienced an increase in this ratio of 40.28 %; Xinjiang Province, in last place, experienced a decrease in this ratio of 29.39 %.

When comparing 2012 with the previous year, the national urban and rural ratio for this indicator decreased by 0.06 %. At the same time, the 13 provinces or regions of Hainan, Beijing, Henan, Sichuan, Hubei, Jiangxi, Gansu, Jiangsu, Liaoning,

Tibet, Jilin, Guizhou, and Shaanxi, in descending order of increase of this indicator ratio, all experienced increases in ratio; the 18 provinces or regions of Shanxi, Guangdong, Ningxia, Hebei, Hunan, Zhejiang, Anhui, Shandong, Fujian, Yunnan, Heilongjiang, Shanghai, Xinjiang, Inner Mongolia, Guangxi, Tianjin, Qinghai, and Chongqing, in ascending order of degree of decrease, all experienced decreases in ratio.

An analysis of these ratios shows that, from 2000 to 2012, when comparing the national province/region-wide urban and rural cultural consumption demand growth and total consumption growth, the "Coordination of Growth" between them was poor. In most of the provinces and regions in the nation, the urban and rural cultural consumption demand growth did not keep up with total consumption growth. Stimulating domestic demand and expanding consumption could not come about at the same time as the increase of cultural consumption demand of urban and rural citizens.

3.2.4 Changes in Ratio to Non-cultural Consumption Surplus

For an analysis of changing trends in the proportion between urban and rural per capita cultural consumption and per capita non-cultural consumption surplus in all provinces and regions from 2000 to 2012, see Table 3.6. Each province or region is ranked in descending order of proportion of 2012 per capita cultural consumption and per capita non-cultural consumption surplus. The table also provides data for each province or region's urban and rural per capita cultural consumption surplus for 2000 and 2012, after which, checking with regional per capita cultural consumption data in Table 3.2, recalculations can be made.

From 2000 to 2012, the national urban and rural per capita cultural consumption surplus increased from 1,045.52 to 5,906.97 yuan, an average annual increase of 15.53 %, higher than the national urban and rural per capita cultural consumption average annual growth over the same period by 3.41 percentage points. In 12 years, the national urban and rural per capita cultural consumption and per capita non-cultural consumption surplus proportion decreased from 20.49 % to 14.30 %, a decrease of 6.19 percentage points and 30.21 %. In the same period, the Eastern region proportion decreased from 17.93 % to 14.22 %, a decrease of 3.71 percentage points; the Northeastern region proportion decreased from 17.49 % to 13.38 %, a decrease of 4.11 percentage points; the Middle region proportion decreased from 20.29 % to 13.26 %, a decrease of 7.03 percentage points; the Western region proportion decreased from 25.41 % to 15.94 %, a decrease of 9.47 percentage points.

In comparing the provincial/regional urban and rural per capita cultural consumption and the per capita non-cultural consumption surplus proportions, in the year 2000, the 13 provinces or regions of Hunan, Shaanxi, Ningxia, Gansu,

Table 3.6 Changes in proportions between urban and rural per capita cultural consumption and per capita non-cultural consumption surplus of each province or region

Region	2000			2012			Changes in proportion from 2000 to 2012		
	Per capita non-cultural consumption surplus (yuan) (元)	Ratio of cultural consumption and non-cultural consumption surplus	Proportion rank	Per capita non-cultural consumption surplus	(%) Ratio of cultural consumption and non-cultural consumption surplus	Proportion rank	Change in percentage points	Change in percentage	Rank
National	**1,045.52**	**20.4855**	–	**5,906.97**	**14.2959**	–	**−6.1896**	**−30.21**	**–**
Jiangsu	1,624.78	17.1316	24	9,599.71	17.4223	5	0.2907	1.70	**1**
Guangdong	1,761.16	20.3128	14	7,671.93	18.3794	4	−1.9334	−9.52	**2**
Hebei	1,315.28	11.4771	30	5,690.37	9.2548	30	−2.2223	−19.36	**8**
Shanghai	3313.02	19.0809	16	15386.52	15.0693	12	−4.0116	−21.02	**9**
Tianjin	2,256.33	15.4531	27	10,082.29	12.1225	25	−3.3306	−21.55	**10**
Fujian	1,471.91	17.4391	23	7,650.80	13.4181	21	−4.0210	−23.06	**12**
Hainan	1,085.38	15.0143	28	5,092.56	9.9322	29	−5.0821	−33.85	**17**
Zhejiang	1,983.30	18.9159	17	10915.36	11.9295	26	−6.9864	−36.93	**20**
Beijing	2,326.68	26.8927	6	13641.22	16.8484	6	−10.0443	−37.35	**23**
Shandong	1,345.88	18.1455	21	7,187.64	10.2991	28	−7.8464	−43.24	**25**
East	1,655.83	17.9286	[3]	8,556.34	14.2160	[2]	−3.7126	−20.71	**[1]**
Heilongjiang	999.79	14.6871	29	4,516.09	12.3653	24	−2.3218	−15.81	**6**
Liaoning	998.12	18.1855	19	6,350.76	13.5707	18	−4.6148	−25.38	**14**
Jilin	794.10	21.1267	12	4,804.60	14.3273	14	−6.7994	−32.18	**16**
Northeast	947.55	17.4863	[4]	5,321.95	13.3844	[3]	−4.1019	−23.46	**[2]**
Anhui	892.62	17.7118	22	4,276.05	15.4169	11	−2.2949	−12.96	**5**
Henan	872.18	16.2951	26	4,848.81	12.4973	22	−3.7978	−23.31	**13**

(continued)

Table 3.6 (continued)

Region	2000			2012			Changes in proportion from 2000 to 2012		
	Per capita non-cultural consumption surplus (yuan) (元)	Ratio of cultural consumption and non-cultural consumption surplus	Proportion rank	Per capita non-cultural consumption surplus	(%) Ratio of cultural consumption and non-cultural consumption surplus	Proportion rank	Change in percentage points	Change in percentage	Rank
Shanxi	920.21	16.8265	25	5,173.87	12.4393	23	−4.3872	−26.07	**15**
Hubei	980.61	20.5977	13	5,021.19	13.4333	19	−7.1644	−34.78	**19**
Jiangxi	934.59	18.6153	18	5,364.00	11.5670	27	−7.0483	−37.86	**24**
Hunan	709.84	33.7099	1	4,580.69	14.2478	15	−19.4621	−57.73	**30**
Middle	875.74	20.2909	[4]	4,828.82	13.2555	[4]	−7.0354	−34.67	**[3]**
Inner Mongolia	964.06	22.1101	11	4,530.94	19.8153	3	−2.2948	−10.38	**3**
Qinghai	630.09	18.1474	20	2,926.29	15.9557	8	−2.1917	−12.08	**4**
Xinjiang	823.35	19.4673	15	2,822.61	15.7698	10	−3.6975	−18.99	**7**
Gansu	630.05	28.6297	4	2,393.10	22.2985	1	−6.3312	−22.11	**11**
Sichuan	765.89	24.2230	9	3,781.69	15.8854	9	−8.3376	−34.42	**18**
Guizhou	532.73	23.1032	10	3,195.09	14.5670	13	−8.5362	−36.95	**21**
Shaanxi	596.93	33.0750	2	3,735.82	20.7495	2	−12.3255	−37.27	**22**
Ningxia	624.27	30.1329	3	3,963.03	16.5359	7	−13.5970	−45.12	**26**
Chongqing	762.65	25.9619	8	5,349.73	13.6067	17	−12.3552	−47.59	**27**
Yunnan	574.46	26.8544	7	3,799.98	14.0425	16	−12.8119	−47.71	**28**
Guangxi	742.79	26.9852	5	4,160.66	13.4270	20	−13.5582	−50.24	**29**
Tibet	561.28	6.9901	31	3,787.42	2.7845	31	−4.2056	−60.17	**31**
West	699.71	25.4081	[1]	3,782.56	15.9371	[1]	−9.4710	−37.28	**[4]**

Guangxi, Beijing, Yunnan, Chongqing, Sichuan, Guizhou, Inner Mongolia, Jilin, and Hubei, in descending order of this indicator ration, all had ratios higher than the national urban and rural total ratio; the 18 provinces or regions of Guangdong, Xinjiang, Shanghai, Zhejiang, Jiangxi, Liaoning, Qinghai, Shandong, Anhui, Fujian, Jiangsu, Shanxi, Henan, Tianjin, Hainan, Heilongjiang, Hebei, and Tibet, in descending order of this indicator ratio, all had ratios lower than the national urban and rural total ratio. Among these, Hunan Province, in first place of this indicator ratio, was higher than the national urban and rural total ratio by 13.22 percentage points; Tibet, in last place of this indicator ratio, was lower than the national urban and rural total ratio by 13.50 percentage points.

In 2012, the 14 provinces or regions of Gansu, Shaanxi, Inner Mongolia, Guangdong, Jiangsu, Beijing, Ningxia, Qinghai, Sichuan, Xinjiang, Anhui, Shanghai, Guizhou, and Jilin, in descending order of this ratio indicator, were all had ratios higher than the national urban and rural total ratio; the 17 provinces or regions of Hunan, Yunnan, Chongqing, Liaoning, Hubei, Guangxi, Fujian, Henan, Shanxi, Heilongjiang, Tianjin, Zhejiang, Jiangxi, Shandong, Hainan, Hebei, and Tibet, in descending order of this ratio indicator, all had ratios lower than the national urban and rural total ratio. Among these, Gansu Province, in first place, had a ratio higher than the national urban and rural total ratio by 8.00 percentage points; Tibet, in last place, had a ratio lower than the national urban and rural total ratio by 11.51 percentage points.

In comparing the changes in the provincial/regional urban and rural per capita cultural consumption and per capita non-cultural consumption surplus ratio from 2000 to 2012, only in Jiangsu Province did the ratio of this indicator rise; in the 30 provinces or regions of Guangdong, Inner Mongolia, Qinghai, Anhui, Heilongjiang, Xinjiang, Hebei, Shanghai, Tianjin, Gansu, Fujian, Henan, Liaoning, Shanxi, Jilin, Hainan, Sichuan, Hubei, Zhejiang, Guizhou, Shaanxi, Beijing, Jiangxi, Shandong, Ningxia, Chongqing, Yunnan, Guangxi, Hunan, and Tibet, in ascending order of decline of the ratio, each had a decline. Among these, Jiangsu Province, in first place, had a ratio that increased 1.70 %; Tibet, in last placed, had a ratio that decreased 60.17 %.

In comparing 2012 with the previous year, the national urban and rural indictor for this ratio decreased by 5.39 %. At the same time, only the 5 provinces or regions of Hainan, Henan, Xinjiang, Beijing, and Jiangsu, in descending order of growth of this ratio, experienced an increase; in the 26 provinces or regions of Jilin, Liaoning, Gansu, Anhui, Sichuan, Hubei, Shanxi, Yunnan, Guangdong, Fujian, Tianjin, Qinghai, Guangxi, Shaanxi, Guizhou, Hebei, Jiangxi, Inner Mongolia, Hunan, Shandong, Ningxia, Tibet, Chongqing, Zhejiang, Shanghai, and Heilongjiang, in ascending order of decline of this ratio, experienced decreases.

An analysis of this ratio relationship shows that, from 2000 to 2012, in a comparison of national provincial/regional urban and rural cultural consumption demand growth and non-cultural consumption surplus growth, the "Coordination of Growth" is obviously poor. In most provinces or regions throughout the nation, urban and rural cultural consumption demand growth has not kept up with the growth in surplus money after essential spending that individuals have (this evaluation system puts all non-cultural consumption in the category of non-essential consumption), so that the achievement of building a moderately prosperous society cannot occur along with of the increase in cultural consumption demand.

3.3 Balanced Growth of Each Province and Region, in Urban and Rural Areas

In this evaluation system, cultural consumption demand and its growth need to be placed within the context of urban/rural and regional relationships to investigate the "Balanced Growth" situation, so as to arrive at the indispensable numerical calculations after the corrected index for each item.

3.3.1 Changes in the Urban-Rural Discrepancy in Cultural Consumption Demand

For an analysis of trends of provincial/regional urban-rural ratios of per capita cultural consumption from 2000 to 2012 see Table 3.7, which is a list of per capita cultural consumption urban and rural ratios in ascending order of provinces and regions, from the year 2012. The table also provides base data for provincial/regional urban and rural per capita cultural consumption for the years 2000 and 2012, which can be recalculated.

From 2000 to 2012, national urban per capita cultural consumption grew from 264.07 yuan to 1,213.88 yuan, a total growth of 359.68 %, and an average annual growth of 13.55 %; national rural per capita cultural consumption grew from 186.72 to 445.49 yuan, a total growth of 138.59 %, and an average annual growth of 7.52 %. Over the 12 years, the national urban per capita cultural consumption average annual growth was higher than the rural growth by 6.03 percentage points. The urban-rural ratio for national per capita cultural consumption expanded from 1.4143 to 2.7248, and the urban-rural gap of cultural consumption demand expanded at a rate of 92.66 %.

Over the same period, urban per capita cultural consumption in the Eastern region grew at an average annual rate of 12.91 %, the rural average annual growth was 8.36 %, and the urban average annual growth was higher than the rural average annual growth by 4.55 percentage points; the urban-rural cultural consumption ratio expanded from 1.5405 to 2.5253, an expansion of 63.93 %. In the Northeastern region, urban per capita cultural consumption grew at an average annual rate of 14.66 %, the rural average annual growth rate was 10.22 %, and the average urban annual growth was higher than rural growth by 4.44 percentage points; the urban-rural cultural consumption ratio expanded from 0.9180 to 1.4734, an expansion of

Table 3.7 Changes in the per capita cultural consumption urban-rural gap for each province and region

Region	Cultural consumption urban-rural gap in 2000			Cultural consumption urban-rural gap in 2012			Changes in urban-rural ratio from 2000 to 2012	
	Urban per capita value (yuan)	Rural per capita value (yuan)	Urban-rural ratio (rural = 1)	Urban per capita value (yuan)	Rural per capita value (yuan)	Urban-rural ratio (rural = 1)	Expansion/ reduction percentage	Rank
National	**264.07**	**186.72**	**1.4143**	**1,213.88**	**445.49**	**2.7248**	**92.66**	–
Heilongjiang	143.16	150.67	0.9502	589.27	518.04	1.1375	19.71	**7**
Jilin	163.62	171.77	0.9526	759.59	606.26	1.2529	31.52	**13**
Liaoning	169.55	195.38	0.8678	1,027.31	556.56	1.8458	112.70	**22**
Northeast	158.82	173.01	0.9180	819.87	556.46	1.4734	60.50	**[1]**
Tianjin	393.83	235.22	1.6743	1,328.97	766.08	1.7348	3.61	**3**
Hebei	210.21	130.71	1.6082	722.41	358.49	2.0151	25.30	**8**
Shandong	306.66	207.87	1.4752	963.88	500.98	1.9240	30.42	**11**
Zhejiang	427.60	327.99	1.3037	1,539.55	902.23	1.7064	30.89	**12**
Jiangsu	292.12	268.99	1.0860	1,966.12	1,184.18	1.6603	52.88	**15**
Beijing	667.58	484.86	1.3769	2,481.74	1,152.67	2.1530	56.37	**16**
Shanghai	642.25	559.12	1.1487	2,482.39	952.10	2.6073	126.98	**24**
Fujian	260.19	254.30	1.0232	1,348.74	565.83	2.3836	132.96	**25**
Guangdong	396.00	313.46	1.2633	1,875.74	466.63	4.0198	218.20	**29**
Hainan	144.94	174.39	0.8311	747.25	253.97	2.9423	254.02	**31**
East	369.57	239.90	1.5405	1,587.35	628.57	2.5253	63.93	**[2]**
Tibet	162.56	11.11	14.6319	325.07	40.86	7.9557	−45.63	**1**
Xinjiang	268.12	105.98	2.5299	680.79	261.74	2.6010	2.81	**2**
Qinghai	181.62	79.38	2.2880	675.19	283.28	2.3835	4.17	**4**
Yunnan	317.20	106.14	2.9885	931.36	289.22	3.2202	7.75	**5**
Gansu	298.66	143.87	2.0759	870.89	327.30	2.6608	28.18	**9**
Ningxia	280.31	144.98	1.9334	934.76	373.36	2.5036	29.49	**10**

(continued)

Table 3.7 (continued)

Region	Cultural consumption urban-rural gap in 2000			Cultural consumption urban-rural gap in 2012			Changes in urban-rural ratio from 2000 to 2012	
	Urban per capita value (yuan)	Rural per capita value (yuan)	Urban-rural ratio (rural = 1)	Urban per capita value (yuan)	Rural per capita value (yuan)	Urban-rural ratio (rural = 1)	Expansion/reduction percentage	Rank
Chongqing	288.81	154.52	1.8691	990.06	394.23	2.5114	34.36	**14**
Sichuan	259.26	159.55	1.6249	965.27	329.29	2.9314	80.40	**17**
Guizhou	207.93	97.26	2.1379	896.13	226.44	3.9575	85.11	**18**
Shaanxi	231.28	181.81	1.2721	1,123.04	445.47	2.5210	98.18	**21**
Guangxi	236.74	186.76	1.2676	946.18	270.24	3.5013	176.21	**27**
Inner Mongolia	186.45	232.58	0.8017	1,185.26	513.97	2.3061	187.65	**28**
West	251.46	149.03	1.6873	962.57	321.70	2.9921	77.33	**[3]**
Shanxi	192.25	135.39	1.4200	786.44	498.02	1.5791	11.20	**6**
Hunan	280.36	222.50	1.2600	950.44	400.22	2.3748	88.48	**19**
Anhui	192.03	145.46	1.3202	984.62	385.92	2.5514	93.26	**20**
Henan	173.06	133.08	1.3004	975.48	343.83	2.8371	118.17	**23**
Hubei	189.77	209.89	0.9041	926.08	394.63	2.3467	159.56	**26**
Jiangxi	146.42	184.24	0.7947	938.65	342.70	2.7390	244.66	**30**
Middle	198.85	169.07	1.1762	938.05	382.79	2.4505	108.34	**[4]**

Note: (1) Data for each province or region for urban and rural per capita cultural consumption comes from the related editions of the *China Statistical Yearbook*, and all other calculations are derived from the numbers; (2) Urban-rural ratios under 1 are considered a "reversal", when urban per capita numbers are lower than rural numbers; (3) Negative percentages of urban-rural ratios represent shrinking of urban-rural ratios

60.50 %. In the Middle region, urban per capita cultural consumption grew at an average annual rate of 13.80 %, rural average annual growth was 7.05 %, and the urban average annual growth was higher than the rural average annual growth by 6.75 percentage points; the urban-rural cultural consumption ratio expanded from 1.1762 to 2.4505, an expansion of 108.34 %. In the Western region, urban per capita cultural consumption grew at an average annual rate of 11.84 %, the rural average annual growth was 6.62 %, and the urban average annual growth was higher than rural average annual growth by 5.22 percentage points; the urban-rural cultural consumption ratio expanded from 1.6873 to 2.9921, an expansion rate of 77.33 %.

When doing a comparison among time periods, during the "Tenth Five-Year Plan" period, the urban-rural ratio for national per capita cultural consumption expanded by 25.91 %. During this time, in the Eastern region it expanded 18.13 %, in the Northeastern region, 11.33 %, in the Middle region, 36.85 %, and in the Western region, 20.85 %. During the "Eleventh Five-Year Plan" period, the urban-rural ratio for national per capita cultural consumption expanded by 47.98 %. During this time, in the Eastern region it expanded 34.11 %, in the Northeastern region, 19.24 %, in the Middle region, 47.65 %, and in the Western region, 67.19 %.

When comparing the changes in the urban-rural ratios of per capita cultural consumption between the two 5-year periods, the national urban-rural ratio during the "Eleventh Five-Year Plan" period was 22.07 % larger than that during the "Tenth Five-Year Plan" period. Each of the four major regions was different; in the Eastern region, the urban-rural ratio during the "Eleventh Five-Year Plan" period was 15.98 % larger than that during the "Tenth Five-Year Plan" period; the Northeastern urban-rural ratio during the "Eleventh Five-Year Plan" period was 7.91 % larger than that during the "Tenth Five-Year Plan" period; the urban-rural ratio of the Middle region during the "Eleventh Five-Year Plan" period was 10.80 % larger than that during the "Tenth Five-Year Plan" period; in the Western region, the urban-to-rural ratio during the "Eleventh Five-Year Plan" period was 46.34 % larger than that during the "Tenth Five-Year Plan" period.

When looking at a before and after comparison, in the year 2000, the Northeast and Middle regions had an urban-to-rural ratio that was smaller than the national total urban-to-rural ratio, while the Eastern and Western regions had an urban-to-rural ratio that was larger than the national total urban-to-rural ratio. In 2012, the Eastern, Northeastern, and Middle regions all had urban-to-rural ratios that were smaller than the national total urban-to-rural ratio, while the Western region still had an urban-to-rural ratio larger than the national total urban-to-rural ratio.

In comparing provincial/regional urban and rural per capita cultural consumption, in the year 2000, the 18 provinces or regions of Jiangxi, Inner Mongolia, Hainan, Liaoning, Hubei, Heilongjiang, Jilin, Fujian, Jiangsu, Shanghai, Hunan, Guangdong, Jiangxi, Shaanxi, Henan, Zhejiang, Anhui, and Beijing, in ascending order of urban-to-rural cultural consumption ratios, all had ratios lower than the national total urban-to-rural ratio; the first seven provinces or regions had an "urban-rural reversal", with urban per capita values lower than the rural ones. The 13 provinces or regions of Shanxi, Shandong, Hebei, Sichuan, Tianjin, Chongqing, Ningxia, Gansu, Guizhou, Qinghai, Xinjiang, Yunnan, and Tibet, in ascending order of urban-to-rural cultural consumption ratios, all had larger ratios than the national urban-to-rural ratio. Among these, the urban-to-rural ratio of Jiangxi Province, in first place, was only 56.19 % of the national level; Tibet, in last place, had an urban-to-rural ratio 1,034.60 % higher than the national level.

In 2012, the 22 provinces or regions of Heilongjiang, Jilin, Shanxi, Jiangsu, Zhejiang, Tianjin, Liaoning, Shandong, Hebei, Beijing, Inner Mongolia, Hubei, Qinghai, Fujian, Ningxia, Chongqing, Shaanxi, Anhui, Xinjiang, Shanghai, and Gansu, in ascending order of urban-to-rural cultural consumption ratio, all had smaller ratios than the national total urban-to-rural ratio; the nine provinces or regions of Jiangxi, Henan, Sichuan, Hainan, Yunnan, Guangxi, Guizhou, Guangdong, and Tibet, in ascending order of urban-to-rural cultural consumption ratio, all had ratios larger than the national level. Among these, Heilongjiang Province, in first place, has a ratio that is 41.75 % of the national total urban-to-rural ratio; Tibet, in last place, has a ratio that is 291.97 % higher than the national total urban-to-rural ratio.

From 2000 to 2012, Tibet was the only province or region where the urban-to-rural cultural consumption ratio became smaller; the 30 provinces or regions of Xinjiang, Tianjin, Qinghai, Yunnan, Shanxi, Heilongjiang, Hebei, Gansu, Ningxia, Shandong, Zhejiang, Jilin, Chongqing, Jiangsu, Beijing, Sichuan, Guizhou, Hunan, Anhui, Shaanxi, Liaoning, Henan, Shanghai, Fujian, Hubei, Guangxi, Inner Mongolia, Guangdong, Jiangxi, and Hainan, in ascending order of growth degree of urban-to-rural ratio of cultural consumption, all grew in ratio. Among these, Tibet, in first place, had a ratio that shrunk by 45.63 %; Hainan, in last place, had a ratio that expanded by 254.02 %.

When comparing 2012 with the previous year, the national urban-to-rural ratio of cultural consumption shrunk by 2.01 %. At the same time, the 18 provinces or regions of Tianjin, Jilin, Guangxi, Chongqing, Guizhou, Yunnan, Heilongjiang, Hunan, Ningxia, Hebei, Guangdong, Henan, Fujian, Shanghai, Sichuan, Zhejiang, Xinjiang, and Qinghai, in descending order of degree of decrease of urban-to-rural ratio of cultural consumption, each had a decrease in ratio; the 13 provinces or regions of Hubei, Beijing, Shanxi, Jiangsu, Shaanxi, Shandong, Jiangxi, Gansu, Anhui, Inner Mongolia, Tibet, Hainan, and Liaoning, in ascending order of growth in urban-to-rural ratio of cultural consumption, each experienced a growth in ratio.

This means that, from the year 2000 to 2012, in comparing urban and rural areas nationally across provinces and regions, the "Growth Coordination" in cultural consumption demand among them was significantly poor. In most of the provinces and regions throughout the country, the urban-to-rural ratio of cultural consumption is generally expanding, and the urban-to-rural ratio of many provinces and regions is expanding to an extreme and serious degree. In 2012, the situation became more favorable, with the urban-to-rural cultural consumption ratio of most provinces and regions becoming smaller.

3.3.2 Changes in Regional Discrepancy of Urban and Rural Cultural Consumption Demand

For an analysis of changing trends in regional discrepancies in provincial/regional urban and rural per capita cultural consumption demand in 2000 and 2012, see Table 3.8. The regional discrepancy in urban and rural per capita cultural consumption demand of each province or region or 2012 is ranked in ascending order. Using the calculation method for regional discrepancies in cultural consumption, calculations can be checked again with the corresponding regional per capita cultural consumption data in Table 3.2.

From 2000 to 2012, the regional discrepancy in national urban and rural per capita cultural consumption expanded from 1.3836 to 1.4295, with an increase in regional discrepancy in cultural consumption demand of 3.32 %. During the same period, the regional discrepancy of cultural consumption in the Eastern region expanded by 0.75 %, the regional discrepancy of cultural consumption in the Northeastern region shrunk by 3.79 %, the regional discrepancy of cultural consumption in the Middle region expanded by 2.71 %, and the regional discrepancy of cultural consumption in the Western region expanded by 8.33 %.

Looking at it by time period, during the "Tenth Five-Year Plan" period, national urban and rural per capita regional discrepancy in cultural consumption expanded by 2.20 %. During this period, the Eastern region expanded by 1.01 %, the Northeastern region shrunk by 1.02 %, the Middle region expanded by 0.46 %, and the Western region expanded by 5.21 %. During the "Eleventh Five-Year Plan" period, the national urban and rural per capita regional discrepancy in cultural consumption expanded by 1.99 %. During this time period, the Eastern region expanded 1.46 %, the Northeastern region shrunk by 5.91 %, the Middle region expanded by 2.98 %, and the Western region expanded by 3.97 %.

When comparing the changes in regional discrepancies of per capita cultural consumption during the two 5-year periods, we see that the expansion in national urban and rural regional discrepancy during the "Eleventh Five-Year Plan" period was smaller than that during the "Tenth Five-Year Plan" period by 0.20 %. Each of the four major regions was different, with degree of expansion in urban and rural regional discrepancy during the "Eleventh Five-Year Plan" period in the Eastern region being larger than that during the "Tenth Five-Year Plan" period by 0.45 %; degree of expansion in urban and rural regional discrepancy during the "Eleventh Five-Year Plan" period in the Northeastern region being lower than that during the "Tenth Five-Year Plan" period by 4.89 %; degree of expansion in urban and rural regional discrepancy in the Middle region during the "Eleventh Five-Year Plan" period being larger than that during the "Tenth Five-Year Plan" period by 2.54 %; and degree of expansion in urban and rural regional discrepancy in the Western region during the "Eleventh Five-Year Plan" period being smaller than that during the "Tenth Five-Year Plan" period by 1.24 %.

When comparing the situation before and after, in 2000, the urban and rural regional discrepancies in the Northeastern, Middle, and Western regions were

Table 3.8 Changing trends in regional discrepancies in urban and rural per capita cultural consumption in each province and region

Region	Regional discrepancies in cultural consumption in 2000		Regional discrepancies in cultural consumption in 2012		Changes in regional discrepancies from 2000 to 2012		Annex: rank of urban-to-rural ratios (in accordance with Table 3.7)	
	Regional discrepancy (no discrepancy = 1)	Rank	Regional discrepancy (no discrepancy = 1)	Rank	Percentage change	Rank	2000	2012
National	**1.3836**	–	**1.4295**	–	**3.32**	–	–	–
Liaoning	1.1525	10	1.0206	1	−11.44	**2**	4	7
Jilin	1.2167	14	1.1848	6	−2.62	**9**	7	2
Heilongjiang	1.3144	22	1.3387	17	1.85	**16**	6	1
Northeast	1.2279	[2]	1.1814	[1]	−3.79	**[1]**	[1]	[1]
Zhejiang	1.7516	28	1.5420	26	−11.97	**1**	16	5
Tianjin	1.6279	26	1.4474	23	−11.09	**3**	23	6
Shanghai	2.9515	31	2.7457	31	−6.97	**4**	10	21
Beijing	2.9214	30	2.7217	30	−6.84	**5**	18	10
Shandong	1.1402	9	1.1234	4	−1.47	**10**	20	8
Guangdong	1.6703	27	1.6698	27	−0.03	**12**	12	30
Fujian	1.1985	13	1.2157	8	1.44	**14**	8	15
Hebei	1.2952	20	1.3764	20	6.27	**20**	21	9
Hainan	1.2391	15	1.4010	21	13.07	**25**	3	26
Jiangsu	1.2996	21	1.9806	29	52.40	**31**	9	4
East	1.7095	[4]	1.7224	[4]	0.75	**[2]**	[3]	[3]
Henan	1.3364	23	1.2824	14	−4.04	**6**	15	24
Anhui	1.2618	17	1.2193	9	−3.37	**7**	17	19
Shanxi	1.2771	18	1.2379	12	−3.07	**8**	19	3
Jiangxi	1.1877	12	1.2653	13	6.53	**21**	1	23

Hunan	1.1172	6	1.2271	11	9.84	**24**	11	13
Hubei	1.0570	2	1.2012	7	13.64	**26**	5	12
Middle	1.2062	[1]	1.2389	[2]	2.71	**[3]**	[2]	[2]
Qinghai	1.4661	25	1.4471	22	−1.30	**11**	28	14
Shaanxi	1.0782	5	1.0821	3	0.36	**13**	14	18
Guizhou	1.4254	24	1.4488	24	1.64	**15**	27	29
Tibet	1.8168	29	1.8751	28	3.21	**17**	31	31
Chongqing	1.0756	4	1.1380	5	5.80	**18**	24	17
Inner Mongolia	1.0048	1	1.0632	2	5.81	**19**	2	11
Yunnan	1.2797	19	1.3681	19	6.91	**22**	30	27
Ningxia	1.1217	7	1.2240	10	9.12	**23**	25	16
Sichuan	1.1338	8	1.2886	15	13.65	**27**	22	25
Xinjiang	1.2516	16	1.4729	25	17.68	**28**	29	20
Gansu	1.1578	11	1.3681	18	18.16	**29**	26	22
Guangxi	1.0641	3	1.3384	16	25.78	**30**	13	28
West	1.2396	[3]	1.3429	[3]	8.33	**[4]**	[4]	[4]

Note: (1) Calculations in the table are derived from data; (2) Negative percentages of regional discrepancies represent decreases in regional discrepancies. All ranked urban-to-rural ratios are in accordance with the previous Table 3.7

smaller than the national urban and rural total regional discrepancy, and the urban and rural regional discrepancy of the Eastern region was higher than the national urban and rural total regional discrepancy. In 2012, the urban and rural regional discrepancies in the Northeastern, Middle, and Western regions were still smaller than the national urban and rural total regional discrepancy, and the urban and rural regional discrepancy of the Eastern region was still larger than the national urban and rural total regional discrepancy.

When comparing the regional differences in per capita cultural consumption in each region or province, we see that in the year 2000, the 23 regions and provinces of Inner Mongolia, Hubei, Guangxi, Chongqing, Shaanxi, Hunan, Ningxia, Sichuan, Shandong, Liaoning, Gansu, Jiangxi, Fujian, Jilin, Hainan, Xinjiang, Anhui, Shanxi, Yunnan, Hebei, Jiangsu, Heilongjiang, and Henan, in ascending order of urban and rural cultural consumption regional discrepancy, all had smaller discrepancies than the national urban and rural total regional discrepancy; the eight provinces or regions of Guizhou, Qinghai, Tianjin, Guangdong, Zhejiang, Tibet, Beijing, and Shanghai, in ascending order of urban and rural cultural consumption regional differences, all had larger discrepancies than the national urban and rural total regional discrepancy. Among these, Inner Mongolia, in first place, had a regional discrepancy that was 72.62 % of the national urban and rural total regional discrepancy; Shanghai, in last place, had a regional discrepancy that was 213.32 % larger than the national urban and rural total regional discrepancy.

In 2012, the 21 provinces or regions of Liaoning, Inner Mongolia, Shaanxi, Shandong, Chongqing, Jilin, Hubei, Fujian, Anhui, Ningxia, Hunan, Shanxi, Jiangxi, Henan, Sichuan, Guangxi, Heilongjiang, Gansu, Yunnan, Hebei, and Hainan, in ascending order of urban and rural cultural consumption regional discrepancies, all had lower discrepancies than the national urban and rural total regional discrepancy; the ten provinces or regions of Qinghai, Tianjin, Guizhou, Xinjiang, Zhejiang, Guangdong, Tibet, Jiangsu, Beijing, and Shanghai, in ascending order of urban and rural cultural consumption regional discrepancies, all had higher discrepancies than the national urban and rural total regional discrepancy. Among these, Liaoning Province, in first place, had a regional discrepancy that was 71.39 % of the national urban and rural total regional discrepancy; Shanghai, in last place, had a regional discrepancy that was higher than the national urban and rural total regional discrepancy by 192.07 %.

From 2000 to 2012, the 12 provinces or regions of Zhejiang, Liaoning, Tianjin, Shanghai, Beijing, Henan, Anhui, Shanxi, Jilin, Shandong, Qinghai, and Guangdong, in descending order of degree of decrease in urban and rural cultural consumption regional discrepancy, all decreased in this discrepancy; the 19 provinces or regions of Shaanxi, Fujian, Guizhou, Heilongjiang, Tibet, Chongqing, Inner Mongolia, Hebei, Jiangxi, Yunnan, Ningxia, Hunan, Hainan, Hubei, Sichuan, Xinjiang, Gansu, Guangxi, and Jiangsu, in ascending order of degree of increase in urban and rural cultural consumption regional discrepancy, all increased in this discrepancy. Among these, Zhejiang, in first place, had a regional discrepancy that decreased by 11.97 %; Jiangsu, in last place, had a regional discrepancy that increased 52.40 %.

When comparing 2012 with the previous year, the national urban and rural cultural consumption regional discrepancy decreased by 1.04 %. At the same time, the 19 provinces or regions of Shanghai, Tianjin, Zhejiang, Hainan, Henan, Hubei, Inner Mongolia, Gansu, Sichuan, Shaanxi, Guizhou, Jilin, Jiangxi, Xinjiang, Shanxi, Guangdong, Yunnan, Fujian, and Anhui, in descending order of degree of decrease in regional discrepancy in urban and rural cultural consumption, all had decreases in the discrepancy; the 12 provinces or regions of Tibet, Liaoning, Ningxia, Hebei, Qinghai, Hunan, Guangxi, Shandong, Beijing, Heilongjiang, and Jiangsu, in ascending order of degree of increase in regional discrepancy in urban and rural cultural consumption, all had increases in the discrepancy.

This means that, from 2000 to 2012, when comparing growth in urban and rural per capita cultural consumption demand throughout the nation in different regions, the "Growth Coordination" is relatively poor. In most regions and provinces throughout the nation, regional discrepancies in urban and rural cultural consumption generally increased. The differences lie in the fact that regional discrepancies in urban and rural cultural consumption in developed areas come from the growth in deviation "taking the lead", because the urban and rural regional discrepancies in cultural consumption in developed areas is due to the "lagging" growth deviation. In 2012, the situation improved, and the urban and rural cultural consumption regional discrepancy of most provinces and regions in the country saw a decrease.

3.4 Rankings and Predictions for Urban and Rural Cultural Consumption Demand in Each Province or Region

Based on numerical analysis of the above indicators, according to this evaluation system's assessment methods and weighted calculations, the final estimates for provincial and regional urban and rural comprehensive evaluation and ranking of cultural consumption demand for 2012 were made. Based on different time periods, different reference values of various types of evaluation results were implemented in 2012. The indexes were taken in percentile, using a horizontal measure for percentage points, and a vertical measure for percentage.

3.4.1 2012 Evaluation of Cultural Consumption Demand

For an analysis of a comprehensive calculation of changes in numerical trends of provincial/regional urban and rural cultural consumption demand since the year 2000, see Table 3.9, where, in 2012, each region or province's urban-to-rural and regional gap was ranked against a zero-difference ideal status of a cultural consumption demand index's horizontal assessment.

Table 3.9 Changes in urban and rural cultural consumption demand indexes in each province and region

Region	Starting year base value vertical assessment (starting year base value =100)								Regional horizontal assessment of 2012 urban and rural regional zero-difference ideal value (ideal value = 100)	
	12 years following the "Tenth Five-Year Plan" (2000–2012)		7 years following the "Eleventh Five-Year Plan" (2005–2012)		2 years following the "Twelfth Five-Year Plan" (2010–2012)		(2011–2012) Recent year (2011–2012)			
	Status index	Rank	Status index	Rank	Prosperity index	Rank	Prosperity index	Rank	Prosperity index	Rank
National	**98.00**	–	**89.59**	–	**99.35**	–	**100.77**	–	**80.93**	–
Jiangsu	128.58	1	111.71	1	103.49	14	101.32	13	102.73	**1**
Beijing	110.17	6	99.74	7	103.75	13	103.03	8	100.14	**2**
Shanghai	111.19	5	98.27	8	95.10	26	98.16	25	93.00	**3**
Guangdong	107.21	10	95.16	9	105.29	12	101.69	12	88.52	**6**
Zhejiang	101.91	12	87.18	19	95.42	25	98.63	22	84.26	**9**
Fujian	100.32	13	93.17	12	98.76	18	100.17	19	83.13	**12**
Tianjin	109.51	7	108.62	2	110.78	1	107.80	1	79.50	**16**
Shandong	88.21	24	79.74	26	96.31	22	96.53	29	76.07	**24**
Hebei	98.56	16	87.28	18	98.41	19	100.64	15	69.45	**28**
Hainan	79.23	29	83.31	22	84.83	29	105.26	4	66.52	**30**
East	107.61	[2]	95.10	[1]	100.41	[2]	100.26	[3]	83.50	**[1]**
Jilin	105.41	11	105.70	4	101.82	15	107.47	2	86.62	**8**
Liaoning	111.80	3	94.46	11	95.70	24	98.27	24	84.13	**10**
Heilongjiang	107.85	9	92.09	13	83.50	30	97.67	26	80.85	**15**
East	108.09	[1]	94.90	[2]	92.91	[4]	99.99	[4]	82.53	**[2]**
Shanxi	109.32	8	91.85	14	96.61	21	100.48	17	83.68	**11**
Anhui	99.45	14	87.86	17	90.94	28	97.32	28	82.11	**13**
Hunan	75.25	30	72.58	31	98.25	20	100.30	18	79.33	**17**
Hubei	82.50	28	84.56	21	107.38	4	103.15	7	78.72	**18**
Jiangxi	84.18	26	78.84	27	99.07	17	99.42	21	77.39	**21**

Henan	99.09	15	101.87	6	105.61	9	107.00	3	77.09	**22**
Middle	89.01	[3]	85.54	[3]	99.78	[3]	101.63	[1]	79.02	**[3]**
Shaanxi	91.16	23	86.63	20	94.48	27	99.76	20	91.57	**4**
Gansu	86.46	25	76.40	29	105.90	8	101.92	11	88.98	**5**
Inner Mongolia	92.14	19	90.92	15	101.76	16	95.74	30	86.85	**7**
Ningxia	91.67	22	102.24	5	107.45	3	100.58	16	80.97	**14**
Sichuan	83.60	27	82.37	24	106.36	6	103.87	6	78.70	**19**
Chongqing	91.81	20	82.80	23	106.02	7	98.47	23	78.07	**20**
Yunnan	98.52	17	88.02	16	105.48	11	102.40	10	77.01	**23**
Guizhou	92.32	18	81.08	25	96.28	23	103.90	5	75.41	**25**
Guangxi	70.38	31	75.79	30	106.93	5	102.61	9	72.99	**26**
Qinghai	112.66	2	107.13	3	105.49	10	97.39	27	71.57	**27**
Xinjiang	91.75	21	94.57	10	109.39	2	101.31	14	69.04	**29**
Tibet	111.37	4	78.01	28	80.71	31	95.28	31	33.69	**31**
West	86.20	[4]	83.24	[4]	102.93	[1]	101.06	[2]	77.57	**[4]**

3.4.1.1 Annual Horizontal Assessment Index

With 100 as the "Ideal Value" of a zero-difference status between urban and rural cultural consumption demand and regions, in the annual horizontal assessment, the 2012 national urban and rural cultural consumption demand index was 80.93, lower than the ideal value by 19.07. In this evaluation, because of the national urban and rural cultural consumption total share value (the national share is based on 100 %), per capita absolute value, and each indicator proportion calculated as the base, the national urban and rural total index level, are all due to the urban-to-rural ratio of cultural consumption, and whether the urban-to-rural ratio in cultural consumption and regional discrepancy is increasing or decreasing (p. 57 in Chinese original).

The Eastern urban and rural total index was 83.50, lower than the ideal value by 16.50, and also higher than the national urban and rural total index by 2.56; the Northeastern urban and rural total index was 82.53, lower than the ideal value by 17.47, and also higher than the national urban and rural total index by 1.60; the Middle region urban and rural total index was 79.02, lower than the ideal by 20.98, and also lower than the national urban and rural total index by 1.91; the Western urban and rural total index was 77.57, lower than the ideal by 22.43, and also lower than the national urban and rural total index by 3.36. In this assessment, the urban and rural index level of the four major regions as well as each province and region, besides being due to their own urban-to-rural ratio of cultural consumption, as well as the national regional discrepancy increase and decrease, is mainly based on per capita cultural consumption absolute values and related index proportions being higher or lower than the national overall average value.

When comparing the urban and rural comprehensive = index, the urban and rural prosperity indexes of Jiangsu, Beijing, and Shanghai, in descending order, were in the first three places of the "Leading Economies in Provincial and Regional Cultural Consumption for 2012". Other than these, the 11 provinces or regions of Shaanxi, Gansu, Guangdong, Inner Mongolia, Jilin, Zhejiang, Liaoning, Shanxi, Fujian, Anhui, and Ningxia, in descending order of urban and rural prosperity index, were all higher than the national urban and rural overall prosperity index; the 17 provinces or regions of Heilongjiang, Tianjin, Hunan, Hubei, Sichuan, Chongqing, Jiangxi, Henan, Yunnan, Shandong, Guizhou, Guangxi, Qinghai, Hebei, Xinjiang, Hainan, and Tibet, in descending order of urban and rural prosperity index, were all lower than the national urban and rural overall prosperity index.

3.4.1.2 Vertical Assessment of Prosperity Index Since the "Tenth Five-Year Plan" Period

With the last year of the "Ninth Five-Year Plan" period, the year 2000, having a starting base value of 100, in the vertical assessment in the 12 years since the "Tenth Five-Year Plan" period, the national urban and rural cultural consumption demand prosperity index for 2012 was 98.00, lower than the base value of the year 2000 by 2.00. In this evaluation, the national urban and rural overall prosperity index increased, and compared with the year 2000, the numerical value of the indicators in 2012 increased. This was true across all provinces and regions and across each of the four major regional areas.

The overall urban and rural prosperity index for the Eastern region was 107.61, higher than its 2000 base value by 7.61, and also higher than the national urban and rural overall prosperity index by 9.61; the overall urban and rural prosperity index for the Northeastern region was 108.09, higher than its 2000 base value by 8.09, and also higher than the national urban and rural overall prosperity index by 10.09; the overall urban and rural prosperity index for the Middle region was 89.01, lower than the its base value for the year 2000 by 10.99, and also lower than the national urban and rural overall prosperity index by 8.99; the overall urban and rural prosperity index for the Western region was 86.20, lower than its 2000 base value by 13.80, and also lower than the national urban and rural overall prosperity index by 11.80.

When comparing the urban and rural comprehensive prosperity indexes for each province or region, we see that Jiangsu, Qinghai, and Liaoning, in descending order of urban and rural prosperity index, made up the first three places national of the "Cultural Consumption Demand Prosperity Increase in Provinces and Regions from 2000 to 2012". Besides these, the 14 provinces or regions of Tibet, Shanghai, Beijing, Tianjin, Shanxi, Heilongjiang, Guangdong, Jilin, Zhejiang, Fujian, Anhui, Henan, Hebei, and Yunnan, in descending order of urban and rural prosperity index, were all higher than the national urban and rural overall prosperity index; the 14 provinces or regions of Guizhou, Inner Mongolia, Chongqing, Xinjiang, Ningxia, Shaanxi, Shandong, Gansu, Jiangxi, Sichuan, Hubei, Hainan, Hunan, and Guangxi, in descending order of prosperity index, all had indexes lower than the national urban and rural overall prosperity index.

3.4.1.3 Vertical Assessment of Prosperity Index Since the "Eleventh Five-Year Plan"

When setting the starting base value of 2005, the last year of the "Tenth Five-Year Plan", as 100, in a vertical assessment of the 7 years since the "Eleventh Five-Year Plan", in 2012 the national urban and rural cultural consumption demand prosperity index was 89.59, lower than the 2005 base value by 10.41. In this assessment, the national urban and rural prosperity index increased, and compared with its prosperity index of 2005, the 2012 index value increased. This was true across all four major regions and all the provinces.

The total urban and rural prosperity index for the Eastern region was 95.10, lower than its 2005 base value by 4.90, and also higher than the national urban and rural overall prosperity index by 5.51; the total prosperity index for the Northeastern region was 94.90, lower than its base value in 2005 by 5.10, and also higher than the national urban and rural overall prosperity index by 5.31; the total prosperity index for the Middle region was 85.54, lower than its base value in 2005 by 14.46, and also lower than the national urban and rural overall prosperity index by 4.05; the total prosperity index for the Western region was 83.24, lower than its base value for 2005 by 16.76, and also lower than the national urban and rural total prosperity index by 6.35.

In doing a comparison of the comprehensive urban and rural and provincial/regional prosperity indexes, the provinces or regions of Jiangsu, Tianjin, and Qinghai, in descending order of urban and rural prosperity index, comprised the national top three in "Provincial/Regional Cultural Consumption Demand Prosperity Increase from 2005–2012". Other than these, the 12 provinces of Jilin, Ningxia, Henan, Beijing, Shanghai, Guangdong, Xinjiang, Liaoning, Fujian, Heilongjiang, Shanxi, and Inner Mongolia, in descending order of urban and rural prosperity index, were all higher than the national urban and rural overall prosperity index; the 16 provinces or regions of Yunnan, Anhui, Hebei, Zhejiang Shaanxi, Hubei, Hainan, Chongqing, Sichuan, Guizhou, Shandong, Jiangxi, Tibet, Gansu, Guangxi, and Hunan, in descending order of urban and rural prosperity index, were all lower than the national urban and rural overall prosperity index.

3.4.1.4 Vertical Assessment of Prosperity Index Since the "Eleventh Five-Year Plan"

With the last year of the "Eleventh Five-Year Plan", 2010, having a starting base value of 100, in the vertical assessment of 2 years of the "Twelfth Five-Year Plan", the national urban and rural cultural consumption prosperity index for 2012 was 99.35, lower than the base value of 2010 by 0.65. In this assessment, when it is compared with its own value in 2010, the 2012 national urban and rural total increased across all indexes.. This was the same across all of the four major regions.

The total prosperity index for the Eastern region was 100.41, higher than its base value in 2010 by 0.41, and also higher than the national urban and rural overall prosperity index by 1.06; the total prosperity index for the Northeastern region was 92.91, lower than its base value in 2010 by 7.09, and also lower than the national urban and rural prosperity index by 6.44; the total prosperity index for the Middle region was 99.78, lower than its base value in 2010 by 0.22, and also higher than the national urban and rural overall prosperity index by 0.43; the total prosperity index for the Western region was 102.93, higher than its 2010 base value by 2.93, and also higher than the national urban and rural overall prosperity index by 3.58.

In comparing the comprehensive urban and rural prosperity indexes across provinces and regions, the provinces or regions of Tianjin, Xinjiang, and Ningxia, in descending order of urban and rural prosperity index, comprised the national top three in "Provincial/Regional Cultural Consumption Demand ProsperityIncrease from 2010–2012". Besides these, the 13 provinces or regions of Hubei, Guangxi, Sichuan, Chongqing, Gansu, Henan, Qinghai, Yunnan, Guangdong, Beijing, Jiangsu, Jilin, and Inner Mongolia, in descending order of urban and rural prosperity indexes, all had higher indexes than the national urban and rural overall prosperity index; the 15 provinces and regions of Jiangxi, Xinjiang, Hebei,

Hunan, Shanxi, Shandong, Guizhou, Liaoning, Zhejiang, Shanghai, Shaanxi, Anhui, Hainan, Heilongjiang, and Tibet, in descending order of urban and rural prosperity indexes, all had lower indexes than the national urban and rural total prosperity index.

3.4.1.5 Annual Vertical Assessment of Prosperity Index

Each year started from a base value of 100 based on the previous year, and in the annual vertical assessment, the national urban and rural cultural consumption demand prosperity index for 2012 was 100.77, higher than the last year's base value by 0.77. In this assessment, in terms of increases in the national urban and rural prosperity index, when compared to the previous year, this index saw an increase. This held true for the four major regions and all of the provinces.

The urban and rural prosperity index for the Eastern region was 100.26, higher than the previous year base value by 0.26, and also lower than the national urban and rural prosperity index by 0.51; the urban and rural prosperity index for the Northeastern region was 99.99, lower than the previous year base value by 0.01, and also lower than the national urban and rural prosperity index by 0.78; the urban and rural prosperity index for the Middle region was 101.63, higher than the previous year base value by 1.63, and also higher than the national urban and rural prosperity index by 0.86; the urban and rural prosperity index or the Western region was 101.06, higher than the previous year base value by 1.06, and also higher than the national urban and rural prosperity index by 0.29.

When comparing the overall prosperity indexes for both urban and rural areas of each province or region, the overall prosperity indexes for Tianjin, Jilin, and Henan, in descending order of prosperity index, took up the first three places nationally in the "2012 Cultural Consumption Demand Prosperity Index Increase". Other than these, the 11 provinces or regions of Hainan, Guizhou, Sichuan, Hubei, Beijing, Guangxi, Yunnan, Gansu, Guangdong, Jiangsu, and Xinjiang, in descending order of urban and rural prosperity index, were all had indexes higher than the national urban and rural overall prosperity index; the 17 provinces or regions of Hebei, Ninxia, Shanxi, Hunan, Fujian, Shaanxi, Jiangxi, Zhejiang, Chongqing, Liaoning, Shanghai, Heilongjiang, Qinghai, Anhui, Shandong, Inner Mongolia, and Tibet, in descending order of urban and rural prosperity index, were all had indexes lower than the national urban and rural overall prosperity index.

3.4.2 *Prosperity Forecasts for 2013 and Annual Growth Estimates for 2014*

Given that the statistical data for 2013 has yet to be released, and we have actually already entered into the 2014 year, based on the annual growth rates for per capita

GDP and urban and rural per capita income, total consumption, savings, and cultural consumption for the period from 2000 to 2012, we therefore forecast the 2013 cultural consumption demand prosperity index, and estimate the 2014 provincial/regional urban/rural cultural consumption demand growth. The urban and rural index values are based on calculations (projections) of average annual growth rates for different years of urban and rural per capita values. That is to say, fully implementing the potential of the calculated data from this research evaluation is based on deducting the "maximum" probability of existing data, and, according to the calculated average of changing trends in relevant aspects across provinces and urban and rural areas over the 12 years since the year 2000, forecasting prosperity for 2013, and estimating prosperity growth for 2014.

For the 2012 growth trend forecast in urban and rural comprehensive calculations in cultural consumption demand for each province, and for 2014 growth estimates, see Table 3.10, where the provinces are separated into the four major regions- Northeast, east, Middle, and West, and a geographical distribution arrangement from the north to the south and east to west. Rechecking can be done in accordance with base data from Tables 3.1, 3.2, 3.3, 3.4, 3.5, 3.6, 3.7, and 3.8 in this paper. Given that the numbers in the table are predictions only, they are not to be analyzed or ranked, and are for reference purposes only.

Two points of clarification regarding the report on provinces/regions and urban/rural areas:

1. In Table 3.9 of this paper, provincial/regional urban and rural areas were chosen for the top five categories and the annual horizontal assessment, annual vertical assessment, and vertical assessment for every 5 year period from made up the in-depth provincial and regional analysis report. If a particular region comes in first in several categories, then second place will be used in those categories; if a particular region comes in first and second in several categories, then third place will be used instead of second place. Specifically: Jiangsu took first place in the 2012 urban and rural horizontal assessment, and Tianjin took first place in the 2012 urban and rural vertical assessment; second-place Xinjiang was used in the post-"Twelfth Five-Year Plan" urban and rural vertical assessment (first place was Tianjin), third-place Qinghai was used in the post- "Eleventh Five-Year Plan" urban and rural vertical assessment (first place was Jiangsu, and second place was Tianjin); third-place Liaoning was used in the post-"Tenth Five-Year Plan" urban and rural vertical assessment (first place was Jiangsu and second place was Qinghai). However, in the provincial and regional report for the vertical assessment of the 2 years following the "Twelfth Five-Year Plan", the dynamic curve was too short and the mapping effect was poor, so it was omitted and a special explanation was added.
2. In the provincial and regional report, there was limited space for mapping; the first and last years of the "Tenth Five-Year Plan" period and the last year of are directly compared in the diagram, but the growth of data within is still in an annual growth coefficient. When the annual growth trend is analyzed in this paper, an evaluation database will be used for a background calculation function,

Table 3.10 2013 forecast of cultural consumption demand per province and region and 2014 growth estimates

Region	2013 prosperity forecasts		2014 growth estimates					
			Urban and rural comprehensive forecast		Urban-to-rural ratio and regional discrepancies			
	2012 vertical assessment Base = 100	Ideal zero-difference value for regional horizontal assessment = 100	Total cultural consumption (hundred million yuan)	Cultural consumption per capita values (yuan)	Urban per capita cultural consumption (yuan)	Rural per capita cultural consumption (yuan)	Urban-to-rural ratio (rural = 1)	Regional discrepancy (no discrepancy = 1)
National	**98.79**	**80.44**	**14,498.08**	**1,061.39**	**1,565.26**	**514.97**	**3.0395**	**1.4412**
Heilongjiang	99.98	81.61	267.89	697.68	745.98	636.43	1.1721	1.3427
Jilin	99.60	86.13	240.69	870.98	981.08	748.07	1.3115	1.1794
Liaoning	99.21	83.47	494.06	1,117.33	1,387.08	662.65	2.0932	1.0527
Northeast	99.58	82.33	1,001.38	908.31	1,077.82	676.07	1.5943	1.1916
Beijing	100.08	99.97	628.67	2,854.87	3,088.86	1,331.64	2.3196	2.6897
Tianjin	100.14	80.03	220.84	1,506.40	1,627.61	932.70	1.7451	1.4193
Hebei	99.22	69.13	478.17	648.56	887.44	424.14	2.0923	1.3890
Shandong	97.95	74.86	871.53	890.54	1,166.59	580.09	2.0111	1.1610
Jiangsu	100.58	103.99	1,808.85	2,255.06	2701.58	1,516.00	1.7821	2.1246
Shanghai	99.85	94.77	729.70	2879.41	3,109.79	1,040.43	2.9890	2.7129
Zhejiang	99.49	84.49	904.24	1,602.27	1,905.99	1067.97	1.7847	1.5096
Fujian	98.85	82.81	491.45	1,293.40	1,774.33	646.51	2.7445	1.2186
Guangdong	99.10	89.29	1,979.47	1,772.21	2,430.82	498.62	4.8751	1.6697
Hainan	96.78	63.56	55.04	610.89	982.15	270.39	3.6323	1.4244
East	99.67	83.81	8,126.41	1,538.69	2,023.81	738.03	2.7422	1.7319
Shanxi	99.94	83.53	299.39	816.08	994.56	618.76	1.6073	1.2311
Henan	98.67	75.73	724.59	771.64	1,301.33	402.76	3.2310	1.2730
Anhui	98.82	81.64	496.13	836.36	1,292.96	454.07	2.8475	1.2120

(continued)

Table 3.10 (continued)

	2013 prosperity forecasts		2014 growth estimates					
			Urban and rural comprehensive forecast		Urban-to-rural ratio and regional discrepancies			
Region	2012 vertical assessment Base = 100	Ideal zero-difference value for regional horizontal assessment = 100	Total cultural consumption (hundred million yuan)	Cultural consumption per capita values (yuan)	Urban per capita cultural consumption (yuan)	Rural per capita cultural consumption (yuan)	Urban-to-rural ratio (rural = 1)	Regional discrepancy (no discrepancy = 1)
Hubei	97.29	76.40	473.24	824.65	1,206.11	438.42	2.7510	1.2230
Jiangxi	97.08	75.71	348.89	766.91	1,279.34	380.05	3.3663	1.2774
Hunan	96.67	77.05	511.40	771.45	1,164.91	441.36	2.6394	1.2732
Middle	97.95	77.48	2845.07	792.50	1,214.81	438.65	2.7694	1.2483
Inner Mongolia	97.63	86.19	285.94	1,140.96	1,613.20	586.59	2.7502	1.0750
Shaanxi	98.02	89.97	366.83	973.62	1,461.41	517.23	2.8254	1.0827
Ningxia	98.44	79.78	53.30	806.86	1,142.55	437.12	2.6138	1.2398
Gansu	98.19	86.62	164.59	639.36	1,040.94	375.35	2.7732	1.3976
Qinghai	100.24	72.21	34.28	590.30	8,40.37	350.19	2.3998	1.4438
Xinjiang	98.81	67.93	121.24	527.73	7,95.17	304.31	2.6131	1.5028
Chongqing	98.40	77.64	262.93	904.32	1,215.73	460.83	2.6381	1.1480
Sichuan	97.67	76.52	583.14	730.69	1,201.71	371.56	3.2343	1.3116
Guizhou	98.29	74.09	199.58	580.94	1,143.18	260.69	4.3852	1.4527
Guangxi	96.15	70.99	308.32	662.72	1,191.95	287.40	4.1473	1.3756
Yunnan	99.23	76.29	309.76	656.22	1,114.50	341.81	3.2606	1.3817
Tibet	100.04	33.69	3.91	124.35	364.87	50.76	7.1875	1.8828
West	97.86	76.08	2,687.76	738.89	1,203.90	365.72	3.2919	1.3578

Note: Total estimated population growth is not covered, and there has been no balancing. The sum of each region is not equal to the national sum total

and the estimates will filter out the highest and lowest annual values, including the years omitted in the graph. This is the explanation why each document, in being explained several times, seems to be repeated.

Chapter 4
Evaluation and Ranking of Cultural and Educational Consumption Demand in Major Cities: Annual Assessment of 2005–2012 and Forecast for Latter Years

Abstract In 2012, total cultural and educational consumption increased by over 10 % in 20 major cities, in 8 of which it increased by over 15 % and in one of which in increased by over 20 %; the per capita value of cultural and educational consumption increased by over 10 % in 12 major cities, in 3 of which it increased by over 15 % and in one of which it increased by over 20 %. The rankings of cultural and educational consumption demand in major cities are as follows: in the horizontal assessment of the provincial, urban and rural ideal value without discrepancies in major cities, Guangzhou, Xi'an, and Nanjing were ranked top three in the "2012 Annual Major City Leaders"; in the vertical assessment of their own base values in previous years, Hefei, Kunming, and Fuzhou ranked top three in the "2005–2012 Runner-Up Major Cities"; Wuhan, Kunming, and Nanning ranked top three in the "2010–2012 Runner-Up Major Cities"; Tianjin, Hefei, and Changchun ranked top three in the "2012 Runner-Up Major Cities".

Keywords Major cities • Cultural and educational consumption • Integrative evaluation • Status rankings

This evaluation system uses the assessment of cultural and educational consumption demand for national major cities, and over the years the actual results of several years have been launched, and the annual evaluation ranking previous statistical year of 2011 are ongoing and can be compared to check.

This paper presents an analysis, estimate, evaluation and ranking of national cultural and educational consumption demand of 26 major cities in 2012. As a detailed investigation of other reports on major cities, this paper focuses on an analysis of four municipalities as an example for comparison, and for the rest of the cities, focus is placed on the ranking of indicators.

Y. Wang et al., *Annual Evaluation Report of China's Cultural Consumption Demand*, Research Series on the Chinese Dream and China's Development Path, DOI 10.1007/978-981-10-0730-9_4

4.1 Cultural and Educational Consumption Growth in Each Major City

The cultural and educational consumption demand growth trends of major cities can offer a macro perspective, so this paper uses of the cultural and educational consumption of major cities as proportion of the national share's changes in increase or decrease to begin to do analyses and estimates.

4.1.1 Increase and Decreases of the Total Share of Major Cities

For changes in the total growth in cultural and educational consumption in major cities and proportion of national urban share from 2005 to 2012, see Table 4.1, in which the national total urban data serves as the assessment base calculation and is arranged on the first line. Each city is arranged in numbered order (1,2,3. . ..) of degree of change in cultural and educational consumption as proportion of the national urban share within the 7-year period.

From 2005 to 2012, the national urban cultural and educational consumption total grew from 606.319 billion yuan to 1.426104 trillion yuan, an absolute value growth of 819.785 billion yuan, a total growth of 135.21 %, and an average annual growth of 13.00 %. During the same period, the average annual growth of Beijing was 10.67 %, lower than the national urban average growth, and dropping from 3.97 % of the national urban share to 3.43 % of it, a decrease of 13.55 %; the average annual growth in Tianjin was 9.72 %, lower than the national urban average growth, and dropping from 1.62 % of the national urban share to 1.32 % of it, a decrease of 18.63 %; the average annual growth in Shanghai was 9.48 %, lower than the national urban average growth, and dropping from 4.83 % of the national urban share to 3.87 % of it, a decrease of 19.86 %; the average annual growth of Chongqing was 12.00 %, lower than the national urban average growth, and dropping from 2.35 % of the national urban share to 2.21 % of it, a decrease of 6.00 %.

In comparing the average annual growth of the total cultural and educational consumption demand of each major city from 2005 to 2012, the average annual growth of the 10 cities of Hefei, Kunming, Zhengzhou, Fuzhou, Hohhot, Yinchuan, Guangzhou, Nanjing, Nanning, and Shenyang, in descending order, was higher than the national urban average growth; the average annual growth of the 25 cities of Xi'an, Chongqing, Chengdu, Dalian, Nanchang, Jinan, Beijing, Changchun, Changsha, Harbin, Tianjin, Guiyang, Shanghai, Urumqi, Ningbo, Xiamen, Shijiazhuang, Haikou, Hangzhou, Qingdao, Shenzhen, Taiyuan, Lanzhou, Wuhan, and Xining, in descending order, was lower than the national urban average annual growth. Among these, Hefei, in first place of average annual growth, was had a growth higher than the national urban average growth by 16.76 percentage points; Xining, in last place of average annual growth, had a growth lower than the national urban average growth by 9.73 percentage points.

Table 4.1 Total growth in cultural and educational consumption of each major city and changes in National Urban Share

Region	Growth in total consumption of education and culture				Change in national urban share			
	Total in 2005 (hundred million yuan)	Total for 2012 (hundred million yuan)	Average annual growth over 7 years		(%) 2005 share (%)	(%) 012 share (%)	Share fluctuation over 7 years	
			Growth index (previous year = 100)	Index rank			Percentage fluctuation	Rank fluctuation
National cities	**6,063.19**	**14,261.04**	**113.00**	–	**100**	**100**	–	–
Hefei	9.65	59.76	129.76	1	0.1592	0.4190	163.19	**1**
Kunming	17.23	59.57	119.39	2	0.2842	0.4177	46.97	**2**
Zhengzhou	26.99	90.99	118.96	3	0.4451	0.6380	43.34	**3**
Fuzhou	15.43	46.10	116.92	4	0.2545	0.3233	27.03	**4**
Hohhot	12.36	33.73	115.42	5	0.2039	0.2365	15.99	**5**
Yinchuan	7.41	20.17	115.38	6	0.1222	0.1414	15.71	**6**
Guangzhou	141.74	384.36	115.32	7	2.3377	2.6952	15.29	**7**
Nanjing	88.53	236.14	115.05	8	1.4601	1.6558	13.40	**8**
Nanning	23.19	60.57	114.70	9	0.3825	0.4247	11.03	**9**
Shenyang	51.07	128.36	114.07	10	0.8423	0.9001	6.86	**10**
Xi'an	71.24	157.63	112.01	11	1.1750	1.1053	−5.93	**11**
Chongqing	142.40	314.36	112.00	12	2.3486	2.2078	−6.00	**12**
Chengdu	58.12	124.55	111.50	13	0.9586	0.8734	−8.89	**13**
Dalian	33.25	70.18	111.26	14	0.5484	0.4921	−10.27	**14**
Nanchang	18.45	37.78	110.78	15	0.3043	0.2649	−12.95	**15**
Jinan	40.73	82.84	110.67	16	0.6718	0.5809	−13.53	**16**
Beijing	240.90	489.84	110.67	17	3.9732	3.4348	−13.55	**17**
Changchun	38.40	77.93	110.64	18	0.6333	0.5465	−13.71	**18**
Changsha	34.65	69.44	110.44	19	0.5715	0.4869	−14.80	**19**
Harbin	47.42	93.74	110.23	20	0.7821	0.6573	−15.96	**20**

(continued)

Table 4.1 (continued)

Region	Growth in total consumption of education and culture				Change in national urban share			
	Total in 2005 (hundred million yuan)	Total for 2012 (hundred million yuan)	Average annual growth over 7 years		(%) 2005 share (%)	(%) 012 share (%)	Share fluctuation over 7 years	
			Growth index (previous year = 100)	Index rank			Percentage fluctuation	Rank fluctuation
Tianjin	98.46	188.44	109.72	21	1.6239	1.3214	−18.63	**21**
Guiyang	22.79	43.06	109.52	22	0.3759	0.3019	−19.69	**22**
Shanghai	293.10	552.46	109.48	23	4.8341	3.8739	−19.86	**23**
Urumqi	18.07	33.99	109.45	24	0.2980	0.2383	−20.03	**24**
Ningbo	39.82	74.14	109.29	25	0.6567	0.5199	−20.83	**25**
Xiamen	24.34	43.69	108.72	26	0.4014	0.3064	−23.67	**26**
Shijiazhuang	20.32	36.10	108.56	27	0.3351	0.2531	−24.47	**27**
Haikou	13.03	22.00	107.77	28	0.2149	0.1543	−28.20	**28**
Hangzhou	79.91	121.41	106.16	29	1.3180	0.8513	−35.41	**29**
Qingdao	37.59	56.53	106.00	30	0.6200	0.3964	−36.06	**30**
Shenzhen	54.11	80.76	105.89	31	0.8924	0.5663	−36.54	**31**
Taiyuan	36.88	53.48	105.45	32	0.6083	0.3750	−38.35	**32**
Lanzhou	20.10	28.72	105.23	33	0.3315	0.2014	−39.25	**33**
Wuhan	81.05	114.15	105.01	34	1.3368	0.8004	−40.13	**34**
Xining	7.97	9.98	103.27	35	0.1314	0.0700	−46.73	**35**
Lhasa	–	1.5932	–	–	–	0.0112	–	**–**

Note: (1) Calculations in tables were derived from data; (2) A negative percentage value in each cultural and educational total represents a decrease. The national urban data calculations are based on the *China Statistical Yearbook*; the data calculation for major cities is based on: *China City Statistical Yearbook*, and the *China Urban (Town) Life and Price Yearbook*. The data for major cities has not been differentiated between cultural consumption and educational consumption, and therefore the national urban background statistics are based on “Cultural/Educational Consumption”. Because the total for Lhasa was so small, four decimals points were taken, and where population data is lacking, there is no way to calculate related totals

When comparing the total cultural and educational consumption's fluctuation as part of the national urban share within these 7 years, we see that the 10 cities of Hefei, Kunming, Zhengzhou, Fuzhou, Hohhot, Yinchuan, Guangzhou, Nanjing, Nanning, and Shenzhen, in descending order of degree, each increased in share; the 25 cities of Xi'an, Chongqing, Chengdu, Dalian, Nanchang, Jinan, Beijing, Changchun, Changsha, Harbin, Tianjin, Guiyang, Shanghai, Urumqi, Ningbo, Xiamen, Shijiazhuang, Haikou, Hangzhou, Qingdao, Shenzhen, Taiyuan, Lanzhou, Wuhan, and Xining, in ascending order of degree, each decreased in share. Among these, Hefei, in first place, increased in national urban share by 163.19 %; Xining, in last place, decreased in national urban share by 46.73 %.

In 2012, there was a total growth of 13.21 % in national urban cultural and educational consumption, higher than the average annual growth during the "Eleventh Five-Year Plan" period by 1.58 percentage points. In the same year, the total cultural and educational consumption growth in the 10 cities of Hefei, Kunming, Zhengzhou, Fuzhou, Hohhot, Yinchuan, Guangzhou, Nanjing, Nanning, and Shenyang, in descending order of degree, was higher than the national urban average annual growth; the total cultural and educational consumption growth in the 25 cities of Xi'an, Chongqing, Chengdu, Dalian, Nanchang, Jinan, Beijing, Changchun, Changsha, Harbin, Tianjin, Guiyang, Shanghai, Urumqi, Ningbo, Xiamen, Shijiazhuang, Haikou, Zhengzhou, Qingdao, Shenzhen, Taiyuan, Lanzhou, Wuhan, and Xining, in descending order of degree, was lower than the national urban average annual growth.

The total educational and cultural consumption of all the major cities, in and of itself, is not sufficient for comparison, but the growth degree and change in share can be compared, so we provide ranks of regional growth degree and fluctuation in share. Because the population discrepancies of each city are extremely large, the proportions that each cultural and educational consumption demand makes up of the national share also have great differences, and the fluctuation with shares of percentages points cannot be meaningfully compared. For that reason, when comparing the share fluctuations in percentage points, it is easier to rank them. In actuality, the total growth and the share fluctuations are connected, and the rankings of average annual total growth and share fluctuations percentage are consistent.

4.1.2 Growth Changes in Per Capita Absolute Value of Each Major City

From 2005 to 2012, the per capita cultural and educational consumption absolute value growth trends of each major city are analyzed in Table 4.2. Each city is ranked in descending order by per capita cultural and educational consumption absolute value average annual growth within the 7 year period.

From 2005 to 2012, the national urban per capita cultural and educational consumption demand grew from 1,097.46 to 2,033.50 yuan, a per capita absolute value total growth of 936.05 yuan, and a total growth of 85.29 %, with an average

Table 4.2 Absolute values of growth in per capita cultural and educational consumption of major cities

Region	Per capita cultural and educational consumption absolute values				Growth changes in per capita cultural and educational consumption				
	2005		2012		Increments and increment ratios over 7 years			Average annual per capita growth over 7 years	
	Per capita value (yuan)	Rank	Per capita value (yuan)	Rank	Growth amount (yuan)	Increment ratio (national = 1)	Ranking of growth rate	Growth index (previous year = 100)	Index ranking
National urban areas	**1,097.46**	–	**2,033.50**	–	**936.04**	**1**	–	**109.21**	–
Hefei	569.32	36	2,643.34	10	2,074.02	2.2157	3	124.53	**1**
Kunming	755.08	34	2,174.68	20	1,419.60	1.5166	9	116.31	**2**
Fuzhou	889.69	31	2,400.32	13	1,510.63	1.6139	7	115.23	**3**
Guangzhou	2,328.97	2	5,667.29	1	3,338.32	3.5664	1	113.55	**4**
Nanjing	1,745.15	7	4,236.08	2	2,490.93	2.6611	2	113.51	**5**
Hohhot	1,126.20	21	2,728.41	9	1,602.21	1.7117	6	113.47	**6**
Shenyang	1,033.59	24	2,462.71	12	1,429.12	1.5268	8	113.21	**7**
Wuhan	1,021.21	25	2,366.57	15	1,345.36	1.4373	12	112.76	**8**
Yinchuan	957.20	28	2,026.07	24	1,068.87	1.1419	15	111.31	**9**
Xi'an	1,357.50	13	2,751.66	7	1,394.16	1.4894	11	110.62	**10**
Jinan	1,181.16	18	2,371.29	14	1,190.13	1.2715	13	110.47	**11**
Nanchang	880.31	32	1,736.99	29	856.68	0.9152	20	110.20	**12**
Dalian	1,189.16	17	2,305.98	17	1,116.82	1.1931	14	109.92	**13**
Beijng	2,186.55	4	4,035.67	4	1,849.12	1.9755	4	109.15	**14**
Chengdu	1,228.04	15	2,256.47	19	1,028.43	1.0987	16	109.08	**15**
Nanning	1,160.45	20	2,117.41	21	956.96	1.0223	18	108.97	**16**
Shanghai	2,272.76	3	4,071.82	3	1,799.06	1.9220	5	108.69	**17**
Tianjin	1,283.70	14	2,299.82	18	1,016.12	1.0856	17	108.69	**18**

Changchun	1,177.93	19	2,103.45	22	925.52	0.9888	19	108.64	**19**
Ningbo	1,878.87	6	3,278.93	5	1,400.06	1.4957	10	108.28	**20**
Guiyang	1,112.61	22	1,905.33	26	792.72	0.8469	21	107.99	**21**
Harbin	1,195.16	16	1,931.00	25	735.84	0.7861	24	107.09	**22**
Shijiazhuang	920.75	29	1,446.20	31	525.45	0.5614	27	106.66	**23**
Haikou	897.27	30	1,339.08	34	441.81	0.4720	29	105.89	**24**
Changsha	1,685.70	8	2,465.43	11	779.73	0.8330	22	105.58	**25**
Zhengzhou	1,064.32	23	1,552.79	30	488.47	0.5218	28	105.54	**26**
Xiamen	1,622.58	9	2,313.06	16	690.48	0.7377	25	105.20	**27**
Qingdao	1,435.28	10	2,027.68	23	592.40	0.6329	26	105.06	**28**
Zhengzhou	1,970.32	5	2,739.75	8	769.43	0.8220	23	104.82	**29**
Urumqi	994.94	27	1,361.07	32	366.13	0.3911	31	104.58	**30**
Lanzhou	1,001.01	26	1,359.50	33	358.49	0.3830	33	104.47	**31**
Taiyuan	1,424.62	11	1,851.70	27	427.08	0.4563	30	103.82	**32**
Chongqing	1,391.11	12	1,754.02	28	362.91	0.3877	32	103.37	**33**
Xining	780.98	33	884.14	35	103.16	0.1102	34	101.79	**34**
Lhasa	678.26	35	755.73	36	77.47	0.0828	35	101.56	**35**
Shenzhen	3,118.03	1	2,853.95	6	−264.08	−0.2821	36	98.74	**36**

Note: (1) The national urban per capita cultural and educational consumption data comes from the *China Statistical Yearbook*, and the per capita cultural and educational consumption data for major cities comes from relevant volumes of the *China City (Town) Life and Price Yearbook*, the remaining was derived from numerical calculations; (2) When the "Growth Ratio" of regional cultural and educational consumption absolute values is lower than 1, it is lower than the national urban per capita total growth annual growth of 9.21 %. During the same period, Beijing's per capita absolute value dropped from being 199.24 % of the national urban per capita value to 198.46 %, with an average annual growth of 9.15 %, lower than the national urban average growth by 0.06 percentage points, its absolute value total making up 197.55 % of the national urban average absolute value. Tianjin's per capita absolute value dropped from being 116.97 % of the national urban per capita value to 113.10 %, with an average annual growth of 8.69 %, lower than the national urban average growth by 0.52 percentage points, its absolute value total making up 192.20 % of the national urban absolute value. Shanghai's per capita absolute value dropped from being 207.09 % of the national urban per capita value to 200.24 %, with an average annual growth 8.69 %, lower than the national urban average growth by 0.52 percentage points, its absolute value total making up 192.20 % of the national urban absolute value. Chongqing's per capita absolute value dropped from being 126.76 % of the national urban per capita value to 86.26 %, with an average annual growth of 3.37 %, lower than the national urban average growth by 5.84 percentage points, its absolute value total making up 38.77 % of the national urban absolute value.

In comparing the per capita cultural and educational consumption demand average annual degree of growth among the major cities from 2005 to 2012, we see that the 13 cities of Hefei, Kunming, Fuzhou, Guangzhou, Nanjing, Hohhot, Shenyang, Wuhan, Yinchuan, Xi'an, Jinan, Nanchang, and Dalian, in descending order of average annual growth degree, all experienced higher growth than the national urban average annual growth; the 23 cities of Beijing, Chengdu, Nanning, Shanghai, Tianjin, Changchun, Ningbo, Guiyang, Harbin, Shijiazhuang, Haikou, Changsha, Zhengzhou, Xiamen, Qingdao, Hangzhou, Urumqi, Lanzhou, Taiyuan, Chongqing, Xining, Lhasa, and Shenzhen, in descending order of average annual growth degree, all experienced growth lower than the national urban average annual growth. Among these, Hefei, in first place, had an average annual growth higher than the national urban average annual growth by 15.32 percentage points; Shenzhen, in last place, had a negative average annual growth of 1.26 %.

When comparing the per capita cultural and educational consumption absolute values for each major city in 2005, we see than the 22 cities of Shenzhen, Guangzhou, Shanghai, Beijing, Hangzhou, Ningbo, Nanjing, Changsha, Xiamen, Qingdao, Taiyuan, Chongqing, Xi'an, Tianjin, Chengdu, Harbin, Dalian, Jinan, Changchun, Nanning, Hohhot, and Guiyang, in descending order of per capita absolute values, all had higher values than the national urban average value; the 14 cities of Zhengzhou, Shenyang, Wuhan, Lanzhou, Urumqi, Yinchuan, Shijiazhuang, Haikou, Fuzhou, Nanchang, Xining, Kunming, Lhasa, and Hefei, in descending order of per capita absolute values, all had lower vales than the national urban average value. Among these, Shenzhen, in first place, had a per capita value higher than the national urban average value by 284.11 %; Hefei, in last place, had a per capita value that was only 51.88 % of the national urban average value.

In 2012, the 22 cities of Guangzhou, Nanjing, Shanghai, Beijing, Ningbo, Shenzhen, Xi'an, Hangzhou, Hohhot, Hefei, Changsha, Shenyang, Fuzhou, Jinan, Wuhan, Xiamen, Dalian, Tianjin, Chengdu, Kunming, Nanning, and Changchun, in descending order of per capita absolute values, all had higher values than the national urban average value; the 14 cities of Qingdao, Yinchuan, Harbin, Guiyang, Taiyuan, Chongqing, Nanchang, Zhengzhou, Shijiazhuang, Urumqi, Lanzhou, Haikou, Xining, and Lhasa, in descending order of per capita absolute values, all had lower values than the national urban average value. Among these, Guangzhou, in first place, had a per capita absolute value higher than the national urban average value by 278.70 %; Lhasa, in last place, had a per capita absolute value that was only 37.16 % of the national urban average value.

In 2012, the national urban per capita cultural and educational consumption average annual growth was 9.82 %, higher than the "Eleventh Five-Year Plan" period by 1.62 percentage points. In the same year, the 13 cities of Hefei, Kunming, Fuzhou, Guangzhou, Hohhot, Shenyang, Wuhan, Yinchuan, Xi'an, Jinan, Nanchang, and Dalian, in descending order of per capita cultural and educational consumption average annual growth, all experienced growth higher than the national urban average annual growth; the 23 cities of Beijing, Chengdu, Nanning, Shanghai, Tianjin, Changchun, Ningbo, Guiyang, Harbin,, Shijiazhuang, Haikou, Changsha, Zhengzhou, Xiamen, Qingdao, Hangzhou, Urumqi, Lanzhou, Taiyuan, Chongqing, Lhasa, Xining, and Shenzhen, in descending order of per capita cultural and educational consumption average annual growth, all experienced growth lower than the national urban average annual growth.

Absolute values for per capita cultural and educational consumption as the basic indicator for calculation and assessment in this evaluation, though not being heavily weighted in the final comprehensive evaluation calculation, were the indicators for the base calculation because they had a decisive significance. Of course, the analysis of the cultural and educational consumption situation of the nation and of each major city cannot be undertaken by itself; it needs to be put into context of economic growth of each region in the nation, enhancement of livelihood and other related factors. It also needs to be put into context of coordinated growth of urban and rural areas and across regions, and then can be analyzed further.

4.2 Comparison of Economic and Social Factors with the Coordinated Growth Situation

In this assessment, the national cultural and educational consumption and growth of major cities needs to be placed within a context of economic and livelihood to study the "Coordinated Growth" situation, so as to arrive at extremely important proportional values for the numerical calculations of each indicator.

4.2.1 Changes in Share of GDP

Table 4.3 shows an analysis of each major city's per capita cultural and educational consumption and per capita GDP proportional change trends from 2005 to 2012. Each city is ranked in descending order according to the 2012 per capita cultural

Table 4.3 Per capita cultural and educational consumption in each major city and changes in GDP proportion

Regions	2005			2012			Changes in proportional value from 2005 to 2012		
	Per capita GDP (yuan)	Educational and cultural consumption and ratio to GDP (%)	Proportion rank	Per capita GDP (yuan)	Educational and cultural consumption and ratio to GDP	Proportion Rank	Percentage point change	Percentage change	Rank
National urban areas	**14,185**	**7.7368**	–	**38,420**	**5.2928**	–	**−2.4440**	**−31.59**	–
Hefei	18,960	3.0027	33	58,790	4.4962	4	1.4935	49.74	**1**
Kunming	20,992	3.5970	25	55,376	3.9272	7	0.3302	9.18	**2**
Guangzhou	69,268	3.3623	28	165,574	3.4228	11	0.0605	1.80	**3**
Fuzhou	24,118	3.6888	23	64,664	3.7120	9	0.0232	0.63	**4**
Nanjing	40,887	4.2682	17	112,980	3.7494	8	−0.5188	−12.16	**5**
Shanghai	67,493	3.3674	27	141,811	2.8713	21	−0.4961	−14.73	**6**
Jinan	31,605	3.7372	21	79,018	3.0009	14	−0.7363	−19.70	**7**
Hohhot	34,735	3.2423	31	107,034	2.5491	25	−0.6932	−21.38	**8**
Shenyang	29,935	3.4528	26	91,229	2.6995	23	−0.7533	−21.82	**9**
Beijing	58,767	3.7207	22	138,849	2.9065	18	−0.8142	−21.88	**10**
Nanchang	21,533	4.0882	19	59,250	2.9316	15	−1.1566	−28.29	**11**
Changchun	23,064	5.1073	11	58,691	3.5840	10	−1.5233	−29.83	**12**
Shijiazhuang	19,370	4.7534	12	44,943	3.2178	13	−1.5356	−32.31	**13**
Ningbo	44,156	4.2551	18	114,065	2.8746	20	−1.3805	−32.44	**14**
Wuhan	28,200	3.6214	24	97,078	2.4378	28	−1.1836	−32.68	**15**
Zhengzhou	24,586	4.3290	15	53,297	2.9135	17	−1.4155	−32.70	**16**
Harbin	18,821	6.3500	7	45,804	4.2158	5	−2.1342	−33.61	**17**
Xiamen	67,108	2.4179	34	149,774	1.5444	35	−0.8735	−36.13	**18**
Xi’an	17,319	7.8381	3	54,995	5.0034	3	−2.8347	−36.17	**19**
Yinchuan	20,727	4.6182	13	69,868	2.8999	19	−1.7183	−37.21	**20**
Dalian	38,200	3.1130	32	118,807	1.9409	31	−1.1721	−37.65	**21**

Haikou	20,756	4.3229	16	50,546	2.6492	24	−1.6737	−38.72	**22**
Chengdu	22,139	5.5470	8	69,665	3.2390	12	−2.3080	−41.61	**23**
Nanning	11,057	10.4950	2	35,133	6.0268	1	−4.4682	−42.57	**24**
Guiyang	15,050	7.3925	4	45,302	4.2058	6	−3.1867	−43.11	**25**
Shenzhen	285,306	1.0929	35	466,233	0.6121	36	−0.4808	−43.99	**26**
Hangzhou	44,853	4.3928	14	111,758	2.4515	27	−1.9413	−44.19	**27**
Tianjin	39,507	3.2493	30	129,610	1.7744	32	−1.4749	−45.39	**28**
Taiyuan	26,569	5.3619	10	63,252	2.9275	16	−2.4344	−45.40	**29**
Qingdao	36,627	3.9186	20	95,084	2.1325	30	−1.7861	−45.58	**30**
Lanzhou	18,296	5.4711	9	48,504	2.8028	22	−2.6683	−48.77	**31**
Urumqi	29,597	3.3617	29	79,034	1.7221	33	−1.6396	−48.77	**32**
Changsha	24,688	6.8281	6	97,171	2.5372	26	−4.2909	−62.84	**33**
Chongqing	9,727	14.3017	1	34,195	5.1295	2	−9.1722	−64.13	**34**
Xining	11,398	6.8520	5	40,407	2.1881	29	−4.6639	−68.07	**35**
Lhasa	–	–	–	48,341	1.5633	34	1.5633	–	**–**

Note: (1) National per capita GDP data (national per capita GDP data does not distinguish between urban and rural areas) comes from related volumes of the *China Statistical Yearbook*, and per capita GDP data from major cities is calculated from related volumes of the *China Statistical Yearbook*, and the rest is derived from numerical calculations; (2) Negative percentage point proportions represent a decrease in percentage points, and negative percentages represent decreases in percentages. This makes the ranking of percentage changes more accurate (The following Tables 4.4, 4.5, and 4.6 are the same). GDP data from Lhasa is lacking some years, so there was no way to do related calculations

and educational consumption and per capita GDP proportional values. The table also provides per capita GDP data from 2005 to 2012, and can be compared with regional per capita cultural and educational consumption data from Table 4.2 in order to check computations.

From 2005 to 2012, the national per capita GDP grew from 14,185 to 38,420 yuan, an average annual growth of 15.30 %, higher than the national urban per capita cultural and educational consumption over the same period average annual growth by 6.09 percentage points. In 7 years, the national urban per capita cultural and educational consumption and per capita GDP proportion decreased from 7.74 % to 5.29 %, a decrease of 2.45 percentage points and a 31.59 % decrease. During the same period, Beijing's ratio decreased from 3.72 % to 2.91 %, a decrease of 0.81 percentage points; Tianjin's ratio decreased from 3.25 % to 1.77 %, a decrease of 1.48 percentage points; Shanghai's ratio decreased from 3.37 % to 2.87 %, a decrease of 0.50 percentage points; and Chongqing's ratio decreased from 14.30 % to 5.13 %, a decrease of 9.17 percentage points.

In comparing per capita cultural and educational consumption and per capita GDP of major cities, in 2005, only the three cities of Chongqing, Nanning, and Xi'an, in descending order of this index ratio, were higher than the national urban overall ratio; the 32 cities of Guiyang, Xining, Changsha, Harbin, Chengdu, Lanzhou, Taiyuan, Changchun, Shijiazhuang, Yinchuan, Hangzhou, Zhengzhou, Haikou, Nanjing, Ningbo, Nanchang, Qingdao, Jinan, Beijing, Fuzhou, Wuhan, Kunming, Shenyang, Shanghai, Guangzhou, Urumqi, Tianjin, Hohhot, Dalian, Hefei, Xiamen, and Shenzhen, in descending order of this index ratio, all had lower ratios than the national urban overall ratio. Among these, Chongqing, in first place, had a ratio that was higher than the national urban overall ration by 6.56 percentage points; Shenzhen, in last place, had a ratio that was lower than the national urban overall ratio by 6.64 percentage points.

In 2012, only the city of Nanning had a ratio higher than the national urban overall ratio; the 35 cities of Chongqing, Xi'an, Hefei, Harbin, Guiyang, Kunming, Nanjing, Fuzhou, Changchun, Guangzhou, Chengdu, Shijiazhuang, Jinan, Nanchang, Taiyuan, Zhengzhou, Beijing, Yinchuan, Ningbo, Shanghai, Lanzhou, Shenyang, Haikou, Hohhot, Changsha, Hangzhou, Wuhan, Xining, Qingdao, Dalian, Tianjin, Urumqi, Lhasa, Xiamen, and Shenzhen, in descending order of this ration, all had higher ratios than the national urban overall ratio. Among these, Nanning, in first place, had a ration that was 0.73 percentage points higher than the national urban overall ratio; Shenzhen, in last place, had a ratio that was 4.68 percentage points lower than the national urban overall ratio.

In comparing the fluctuations in the ratio of cultural and educational consumption to per capita GDP for each major city from 2005 to 2012, only the four cities of Hefei, Kunming, Guangzhou, and Fuzhou, in descending order of ratio growth degree, experienced an increase in ratio; the 31 cities of Nanjing, Shanghai, Jinan, Hohhot, Shenyang, Beijing, Nanchang, Changchun, Shijiazhuang, Ningbo, Wuhan, Zhengzhou, Harbin, Xiamen, Xi'an, Yinchuan, Dalian, Haikou, Chengdu, Nanning, Guiyang, Shenzhen, Hangzhou, Tianjin, Taiyuan, Qingdao, Lanzhou, Urumqi, Changsha, Chongqing, and Xi'an, in ascending order of ratio growth degree, all experienced a decrease in ratio. Among these, Hefei, in first place, had a ratio that increased 49.74 %; Xining, in last place, had a ratio that decreased by 68.07 %.

When compared with the previous year, the national urban ratio of this indicator increased by 0.61 % in 2012. At the same time, only the seven cities of Hefei, Guangzhou, Shanghai, Fuzhou, Shenyang, Jinan, and Beijing, in descending order of degree of increase in ratio, experienced increases; the 28 cities of Ningbo, Hohhot, Zhengzhou, Harbin, Nanchang, Xi'an, Yinchuan, Xiamen, Shijiazhuang, Changchun, Nanjing, Dalian, Nanning, Tianjin, Qingdao, Hangzhou, Wuhan, Taiyuan, Kunming, Changsha, Chengdu, Haikou, Guiyang, Shenzhen, Chongqing, Urumqi, Lanzhou, and Xining, in descending order of decrease of this ratio, all experienced decreases.

The analysis of these ratio relationships shows that, from 2005 to 2012, when comparing the cultural and educational consumption in national major cities with GDP growth, the "Coordinated Growth" is poor. In the vast majority of major cities in the nation, cultural and educational consumption demand growth could not keep up with production growth, and economic development could not come about at the same time as the increase in cultural and educational consumption demand of urban citizens. In 2012, the urban ratios experienced a rebound, and there were also more cities where the ratio increased.

4.2.2 Changes in Proportion of Income

For an analysis of the changing trends of per capita cultural and educational consumption of major cities as proportion of per capita income from 2005 to 2012, see Table 4.4, where each city is ranked in descending order of per capita cultural and educational consumption as proportion of per capita income. The table also provides per capita income data for each major city in 2005 and 2012, which can be recalculated after checking with regional per capita cultural and educational consumption data from Table 4.2.

From 2005 to 2012, national urban per capita income grew from 10,493.03 yuan to 24,564.7 yuan, an average annual increase of 12.92 %, and higher than the national urban per capita cultural and educational consumption average annual growth over the same period by 3.71 percentage points. Within the 7 years, the proportion of per capita income made up of national urban per capita cultural and educational consumption fell from 10.46 % to 8.28 %, a decrease of 2.18 percentage points, and a 20.85 % decrease. Over the same period, Beijing's ratio decreased from 12.39 % to 10.40 %, a decrease of 1.99 percentage points; Tianjin's ratio decreased from 10.16 % to 7.53 %, a decrease of 2.63 percentage points; Shanghai's ratio decreased from 12.19 % to 10.06 %, a decrease of 2.13 percentage points; and Chongqing's ratio decreased from 13.58 % to 7.04 %, a decrease of 6.54 percentage points.

In comparing the proportion that per capita cultural and educational consumption makes up of each major city's per capita income, in 2005, the 19 cities of Xi'an,

Table 4.4 Changes in per capita cultural and educational consumption as proportion of income in major cities

Region	2005			2012			Changes in proportion from 2005 to 2012		
	Per capita income (yuan)	Cultural and educational consumption as proportion of income (%)	Proportion rank	Per capita income	Proportion of income made up of cultural consumption (%)	Proportion rank	Fluctuations in percentage points	Fluctuations in percentage	Rank
Nationwide cities	**10,493.03**	**10.4589**	–	**24,564.72**	**8.2781**	–	**−2.1808**	**−20.85**	–
Hefei	9,683.67	5.8792	36	25,839.26	10.2299	5	4.3507	74.00	**1**
Guangzhou	18,287.24	12.7355	5	38,269.61	14.8089	1	2.0734	16.28	**2**
Fuzhou	12,756.78	6.9743	35	30,109.12	7.9721	21	0.9978	14.31	**3**
Kunming	9,515.70	7.9351	33	25,277.04	8.6034	14	0.6683	8.42	**4**
Nanjing	14,997.47	11.6363	12	36,573.17	11.5825	2	−0.0538	−0.46	**5**
Hohhot	12,538.58	8.9819	30	32,158.05	8.4844	17	−0.4975	−5.54	**6**
Wuhan	10,850.10	9.412	26	27,046.71	8.7499	12	−0.6621	−7.03	**7**
Shenyang	10,098.08	10.2355	21	26,819.14	9.1827	8	−1.0528	−10.29	**8**
Nanchang	10,301.28	8.5456	32	23,307.26	7.4526	26	−1.0930	−12.79	**9**
Dalian	11,994.38	9.9143	23	27,303.21	8.4458	18	−1.4685	−14.81	**10**
Yinchuan	8,858.72	10.8052	18	22,215.05	9.1203	9	−1.6849	−15.59	**11**
Beijing	17,652.95	12.3863	6	38,797.74	10.4018	4	−1.9845	−16.02	**12**
Jinan	13,578.46	8.6988	31	32,766.62	7.2369	27	−1.4619	−16.81	**13**
Shanghai	18,645.03	12.1896	7	40,472.43	10.0607	6	−2.1289	−17.46	**14**
Nanning	10,078.20	11.5145	13	22,383.42	9.4597	7	−2.0548	−17.85	**15**
Xi'an	9,627.89	14.0997	1	24,232.12	11.3554	3	−2.7443	−19.46	**16**
Ningbo	17,409.99	10.7919	19	38,088.54	8.6087	13	−2.1832	−20.23	**17**
Guiyang	9,927.97	11.2068	14	21,717.89	8.7731	11	−2.4337	−21.72	**18**

Changchun	10,063.53	11.7049	11	23,064.31	9.1199	10	−2.5850	−22.08	**19**
Chengdu	11,358.81	10.8113	17	27,097.03	8.3274	19	−2.4839	−22.98	**20**
Urumqi	9,604.93	10.3586	20	17,600.10	7.7333	22	−2.6253	−25.34	**21**
Tianjin	12,638.55	10.157	22	30,536.61	7.5313	24	−2.6257	−25.85	**22**
Harbin	10,064.76	11.8747	8	22,465.12	8.5956	15	−3.2791	−27.61	**23**
Shenzhen	28,665.25	10.8774	16	38,006.02	7.5092	25	−3.3682	−30.97	**24**
Shijiazhuang	10,039.83	9.171	29	23,134.69	6.2512	30	−2.9198	−31.84	**25**
Lanzhou	8,529.05	11.7365	10	17,707.30	7.6776	23	−4.0589	−34.58	**26**
Haikou	9,739.50	9.2127	28	22,685.11	5.9029	34	−3.3098	−35.93	**27**
Changsha	12,433.88	13.5573	4	28,718.21	8.5849	16	−4.9724	−36.68	**28**
Zhengzhou	10,977.28	9.6957	25	25,328.12	6.1307	32	−3.5650	−36.77	**29**
Xiamen	16,403.79	9.8915	24	37,819.44	6.1161	33	−3.7754	−38.17	**30**
Taiyuan	10,475.97	13.5989	2	22,469.24	8.2410	20	−5.3579	−39.40	**31**
Hangzhou	16,602.26	11.8678	9	38,400.18	7.1347	28	−4.7331	−39.88	**32**
Qingdao	12,919.84	11.1091	15	32,606.78	6.2186	31	−4.8905	−44.02	**33**
Lhasa	9,431.18	7.1917	34	19,293.68	3.9170	36	−3.2747	−45.53	**34**
Xining	8,397.36	9.3003	27	17,609.34	5.0209	35	−4.2794	−46.01	**35**
Chongqing	10,243.46	13.5805	3	24,929.52	7.0359	29	−6.5446	−48.19	**36**

Note: Data for national urban per capita income comes from the *China Statistical Yearbook*, and data for per capita income of major cities comes from relevant volumes of the *China City (Town) Life Price Yearbook*; the rest is derived from numerical calculations

Taiyuan, Chongqing, Changsha, Guangzhou, Beijing, Shanghai, Harbin, Hangzhou, Lanzhou, Changchun, Nanjing, Nanning, Guiyang, Qingdao, Shenzhen, Chengdu, Yinchuan, and Ningbo, in descending order of ratio, all had higher ratios than the national urban overall ratio; the 17 cities of Urumqi, Shenyang, Tianjin, Xiamen, Zhengzhou, Wuhan, Xining, Haikou, Shijiazhuang, Hohhot, Jinan, Nanchang, Kunming, Lhasa, Fuzhou, and Hefei, in descending order of this ratio, all had lower ratios than the national urban overall ratio. Among these, Xi'an, in first place, had a ratio higher than the national urban overall ratio by 3.64 percentage points; Hefei, in last place, had a ratio lower than the national urban overall ratio by 4.58 percentage points.

In 2012, the 19 cities of Guangzhou, Nanjing, Xi'an, Beijing, Hefei, Shanghai, Nanning, Shenyang, Yinchuan, Changchun, Guiyang, Wuhan, Ningbo, Kunming, Harbin, Changsha, Hohhot, Dalian, and Chengdu, in descending order of this ratio, all had ratios higher than the national urban overall ratio; the 17 cities of Taiyuan, Fuzhou, Urumqi, Lanzhou, Tianjin, Shenzhen, Nanchang, Jinan, Hangzhou, Chongqing, Shijiazhuang, Qingdao, Zhengzhou, Xiamen, Haikou, Xining, and Lhasa, in descending order of ratio, all had ratios lower than the national urban overall ratio. Among these, Guangzhou, in first place, had a ratio that was higher than the national urban overall ratio by 6.53 percentage points; Lhasa, in last place, had a ratio that was lower than the national urban overall ratio by 4.36 percentage points.

In comparing the changes in the proportion that per capita cultural and educational consumption of each major city made up of per capita income from 2005 to 2012, only the four cities of Hefei, Guangzhou, Fuzhou, and Kunming, in descending order of increasing ratio, experienced increases; the 32 cities of Nanjing, Hohhot, Wuhan, Shenyang, Changchun, Chengdu, Urumqi, Tianjin, Harbin, Shenzhen, Shijiazhuang, Lanzhou, Haikou, Changsha, Zhengzhou, Xiamen, Taiyuan, Hangzhou, Qingdao, Lhasa, Xining, and Chongqing, in ascending order of decreasing ratio, all experienced decreases. Among these, Hefei, in first place, had an increase of this ratio by 74.00 %; Chongqing, in last place, had a decrease of this ratio by 48.19 %.

When comparing 2012 with the previous year, the national urban ratio for this indicator decreased by 2.50 %. At the same time, only the four cities of Hefei, Guangzhou, Fuzhou, and Kunming, in descending order of increases in this indicator ratio, experienced increases; the 32 cities of Nanjing, Hohhot, Wuhan, Shenyang, Nanchang, Dalian, Yinchuan, Beijing, Jinan, Nanning, Xian, Ningbo, Guiyang, Changchun, Chengdu, Urumqi, Tianjin, Harbin, Shenzhen, Shijiazhuang, Lanzhou, Haikou, Changsha, Zhengzhou, Lhasa, Xiamen, Taiyuan, Hangzhou, Qingdao, Xining, and Chongqing, in ascending order of decrease in this indicator ratio, all experienced decreases.

The analysis of this ratio shows that, from 2005 to 2012, there was poor "Coordination of Growth" between the growths in cultural and educational consumption demand and income in major cities nationwide. In the vast majority of the major cities throughout the nation, growth in cultural and educational consumption demand could not keep up with the growth in income among citizens, and the enhancement of the people's livelihood has not come about along with the increase in cultural and educational consumption demand of urban citizens.

4.2.3 Changes in the Ratio to Total Consumption

For an analysis of the changing trends in proportion of total per capita consumption made up of per capita cultural and educational consumption in each major city from 2005 to 2012, see Table 4.5, where the proportion of per capita cultural and educational consumption of total per capita consumption for each major city in 2012 is ranked in descending order. The table also provides total per capita consumption data for each major city in 2005 and 2012, and can be compared with per capita cultural and educational consumption data in Table 4.2 for rechecking.

From 2005 to 2012, national urban per capita total consumption increased from 7,942.88 to 16,674.32 yuan, an average annual increase of 11.18 %, and higher than the national urban per capita cultural and educational consumption average annual growth over the same period by 1.97 percentage points. Within 7 years, the proportion of per capita cultural and educational consumption per total per capita consumption decreased from 13.82 % to 12.20 %, a decrease of 1.62 percentage points, and a 11.74 % degree of decrease. Over the same period, the Beijing ratio decreased from 16.51 % to 15.54 %, a decrease of 0.97 percentage points; the Tianjin ration decreased from 13.30 % to 11.21 %, a decrease of 2.09 percentage points; the Shanghai ratio decreased from 16.50 % to 14.68 %, a decrease of 1.82 percentage points; the Chongqing ratio decreased from 16.13 % to 9.37 %, a decrease of 6.76 percentage points.

In comparing the proportion of per capita total consumption made up of by per capita cultural and educational consumption for each major city, in 2005, the 19 cities of Taiyuan, Changsha, Xi'an, Beijing, Shanghai, Nanjing, Chongqing, Guangzhou, Ningbo, Harbin, Nanning, Shenzhen, Hangzhou, Qingdao, Guiyang, Zhengzhou, Changchun, Urumqi, and Lanzhou, in descending order of this indicator ratio, all had higher ratios than the national urban total ratio; the 17 cities of Xiamen, Tianjin, Shenyang, Yinchuan, Jinan, Chengdu, Shijiazhuang, Hohhot, Nanchang, Wuhan, Xining, Haikou, Dalian, Fuzhou, Kunming, Lhasa, and Hefei, in descending order of this indicator ratio, all had lower ratios than the national urban total ratio. Among these, Taiyuan, in first place, had a ratio that was higher than the national urban total ratio by 4.43 percentage points; Hefei, in last place, had a ratio that was lower than the national urban total ratio by 6.12 percentage points.

In 2012, the 13 cities of Nanjing, Guangzhou, Beijing, Hefei, Xi'an, Shanghai, Ningbo, Kunming, Taiyuan, Nanning, Changsha, Hohhot, and Wuhan, in descending order of this indicator ratio, had ratios in this indicator that were higher than the national urban total ratio; the 23 cities of Yinchuan, Guiyang, Shenyang, Jinan, Shenzhen, Changchun, Fuzhou, Chengdu, Tianjin, Hangzhou, Dalian, Urumqi, Harbin, Shijiazhuang, Lanzhou, Nanchang, Zhengzhou, Qingdao,

Table 4.5 Changing trends in proportion of total consumption made up of cultural and educational consumption of each major city

Region	2005			2012			Fluctuations in proportions from 2005 to 2012		
	Total per capita consumption (yuan)	Ratio of cultural and educational consumption to total consumption	Proportion rank	Total per capita consumption (yuan)	Ratio of cultural and educational consumption to total consumption	Proportion rank	Changes in percentage points	Changes in percentage	Rank
National cities	**7,942.88**	**13.8169**	–	**16,674.32**	**12.1954**	–	**−1.6215**	**−11.74**	–
Hefei	7,397.74	7.6959	36	17,793.96	14.8553	4	7.1594	93.03	**1**
Kunming	7,278.48	10.3741	34	16,196.04	13.4273	8	3.0532	29.43	**2**
Nanjing	10,704.34	16.3032	6	23,187.46	18.2688	1	1.9656	12.06	**3**
Guangzhou	14,468.24	16.0971	8	31,530.41	17.9740	2	1.8769	11.66	**4**
Fuzhou	8,427.77	10.5566	33	20,907.82	11.4805	20	0.9239	8.75	**5**
Wuhan	8,234.75	12.4012	29	19,368.65	12.2185	13	−0.1827	−1.47	**6**
Hohhot	8,938.43	12.5995	27	22,127.14	12.3306	12	−0.2689	−2.13	**7**
Beijing	13,244.20	16.5095	4	25,962.07	15.5445	3	−0.9650	−5.85	**8**
Dalian	9,996.41	11.8959	32	20,947.19	11.0086	24	−0.8873	−7.46	**9**
Yinchuan	7,313.67	13.0878	23	16,817.29	12.0476	14	−1.0402	−7.95	**10**
Jinan	9,226.61	12.8017	24	20,179.75	11.7508	17	−1.0509	−8.21	**11**
Chengdu	9,642.45	12.7358	25	19,708.33	11.4493	21	−1.2865	−10.10	**12**
Shenyang	7,862.83	13.1453	22	20,861.25	11.8052	16	−1.3401	−10.19	**13**
Shanghai	13,773.41	16.5011	5	27,743.14	14.6768	6	−1.8243	−11.06	**14**
Nanning	7,881.79	14.7232	11	16,482.79	12.8462	10	−1.8770	−12.75	**15**
Xi'an	7,899.81	17.1840	3	18,599.33	14.7944	5	−2.3896	−13.91	**16**
Ningbo	11,761.59	15.9746	9	24,134.30	13.5862	7	−2.3884	−14.95	**17**
Tianjin	9,653.26	13.2981	21	20,519.72	11.2078	22	−2.0903	−15.72	**18**
Shijiazhuang	7,261.02	12.6807	26	13,708.67	10.5495	27	−2.1312	−16.81	**19**

Guiyang	7,692.62	14.4633	15	15,856.85	12.0158	15	−2.4475	−16.92	**20**
Changchun	8,321.17	14.1558	17	18,269.99	11.5131	19	−2.6427	−18.67	**21**
Nanchang	7,064.14	12.4617	28	17,315.99	10.0311	29	−2.4306	−19.50	**22**
Shenzhen	21,188.84	14.7154	12	24,598.88	11.6020	18	−3.1134	−21.16	**23**
Hangzhou	13,438.99	14.6612	13	24,698.75	11.0927	23	−3.5685	−24.34	**24**
Urumqi	7,051.97	14.1087	18	12,801.53	10.6321	25	−3.4766	−24.64	**25**
Changsha	9,659.86	17.4506	2	19,444.74	12.6792	11	−4.7714	−27.34	**26**
Haikou	7,367.82	12.1782	31	15,134.79	8.8477	34	−3.3305	−27.35	**27**
Lanzhou	7,179.84	13.9420	19	13,521.08	10.0547	28	−3.8873	−27.88	**28**
Taiyuan	7,805.53	18.2514	1	14,294.73	12.9537	9	−5.2977	−29.03	**29**
Lhasa	8,617.11	7.8711	35	13,686.11	5.5219	36	−2.3492	−29.85	**30**
Harbin	7,897.17	15.1340	10	18,303.89	10.5497	26	−4.5843	−30.29	**31**
Xiamen	11,848.83	13.6940	20	24,797.13	9.3279	33	−4.3661	−31.88	**32**
Zhengzhou	7,397.74	14.3871	16	16,358.82	9.4920	30	−4.8951	−34.02	**33**
Qingdao	9,883.45	14.5221	14	21,572.90	9.3992	31	−5.1229	−35.28	**34**
Xining	6,407.86	12.1878	30	11,465.74	7.7112	35	−4.4766	−36.73	**35**
Chongqing	8,623.29	16.1320	7	18,718.78	9.3704	32	−6.7616	−41.91	**36**

Note: Data for national urban per capita total consumption comes from the *China Statistical Yearbook*, and data for urban per capita total consumption comes from related volumes of the *China City (Town) Life Price Yearbook*. All others are derived from calculations

Chongqing, Xiamen, Haikou, Xining, and Lhasa, in descending order of this indicator ratio, all had ratios that were lower than the national urban total ratio. Among these, Nanjing, in first place, had a ratio higher than the national urban total ratio by 6.07 percentage points; Lhasa, in last place, had a ratio lower than the national urban total ratio by 6.67 percentage points.

In comparing changes in per capita cultural and educational consumption of major cities as proportion of per capita total consumption from 2005 to 2012, we see that only the five cities of Hefei, Kunming, Nanjing, Guangzhou, and Fuzhou, in descending order of ratio increase, all experienced increases; the 31 cities of Wuhan, Hohhot, Beijing, Dalian, Yinchuan, Jinan, Chengdu, Shenyang, Shanghai, Nanning, Xi'an, Ningbo, Tianjin, Shijiazhuang, Guiyang, Changchun, Nanchang, Shenzhen, Hangzhou, Urumqi, Changsha, Haikou, Lanzhou, Taiyuan, Lhasa, Harbin, Xiamen, Zhengzhou, Qingdao, Xining, and Chongqing, in ascending order of decrease in growth of this ratio, all experienced decreases. Among these, Hefei, in first place, had a ratio that increased 93.03 %; Chongqing, in last place, had a ratio that decreased 41.91 %.

When comparing 2012 with the previous year, the national urban ratio for this indicator decreased by 0.15 %. At the same time, the five cities of Hefei, Kunming, Nanjing, Guangzhou, and Fuzhou, in descending order of ratio increase, all experienced increases; the 31 cities of Wuhan, Hohhot, Beijing, Dalian, Yinchuan, Jinan, Chengdu, Shenyang, Shanghai, Nanning, Xi'an, Ningbo, Tianjin, Shijiazhuang, Guiyang, Changchun, Nanchang, Shenzhen, Hangzhou, Urumqi, Changsha, Haikou, Lhasa, Lanzhou, Taiyuan, Harbin, Xiamen, Zhengzhou, Qingdao, Xining, and Chongqing, in ascending order of ratio decrease all experienced decreases.

An analysis of these ratio relationships shows that, from 2005 to 2012, when comparing the growth in cultural and educational consumption demand of national major cities and total consumption demand, the "Coordinated Growth" between them is poor. In the vast majority of major cities in the nation, cultural and educational consumption demand growth has not kept up with total consumption growth of citizens. The results of stimulating domestic demand and expanding consumption have not been reflected in an increase of the cultural and educational consumption demands of urban citizens.

4.2.4 Changes in the Ratio to Non-cultural Consumption Surplus

For an analysis of changing trends the proportional relationship between the per capita cultural and educational consumption of each major city and the per capita non-cultural consumption surplus from 2005 to 2012, see Table 4.6, where the ratios of per capita cultural and educational consumption and per capita non-cultural consumption surplus are ranked in descending order. The table also

Table 4.6 Changes in proportion/ratio of per capita cultural and educational consumption and non-cultural surplus of each major city

Region	2005			2012			Changes in proportion from 2005 to 2012		
	Per capita non-cultural consumption surplus (yuan)	Proportion of cultural/ educational consumption to non-cultural consumption Surplus (%)	Proportion rank	Per capita non-cultural consumption surplus (yuan)	Proportion of cultural/ educational consumption to non-cultural consumption surplus o (%)	Proportion rank	Percentage point change	Percentage change	Rank
National cities	**3,647.61**	**30.0871**	–	**9,923.90**	**20.4909**	–	**–9.5962**	**–31.89**	–
Hefei	2,855.25	19.9394	35	10,688.65	24.7304	9	4.7910	24.03	**1**
Fuzhou	5,218.70	17.0481	36	11,601.61	20.6895	22	3.6414	21.36	**2**
Guangzhou	6,147.97	37.8819	9	12,406.49	45.6800	1	7.7981	20.59	**3**
Nanchang	4,117.45	21.3800	33	7,728.26	22.4758	17	1.0958	5.13	**4**
Shenyang	3,268.84	31.6195	19	8,420.61	29.2463	5	–2.3732	–7.51	**5**
Hohhot	4,726.35	23.8281	31	12,759.32	21.3836	20	–2.4445	–10.26	**6**
Harbin	3,362.75	35.5411	12	6,092.24	31.6961	3	–3.8450	–10.82	**7**
Wuhan	3,636.56	28.0818	24	10,044.63	23.5605	15	–4.5213	–16.10	**8**
Nanjing	6,038.28	28.9014	22	17,621.79	24.0389	13	–4.8625	–16.82	**9**
Urumqi	3,547.90	28.0431	25	6,159.64	22.0966	18	–5.9465	–21.20	**10**
Kunming	2,992.30	25.2341	28	11,255.68	19.3208	23	–5.9133	–23.43	**11**
Nanning	3,356.86	34.5695	14	8,018.03	26.4080	8	–8.1615	–23.61	**12**
Ningbo	7,527.27	24.9608	29	17,233.17	19.0269	24	–5.9339	–23.77	**13**
Shanghai	7,144.38	31.8119	18	16,801.10	24.2354	12	–7.5765	–23.82	**14**
Changchun	2,920.29	40.3361	6	6,897.77	30.4947	4	–9.8414	–24.40	**15**
Xi'an	3,085.58	43.9950	3	8,384.45	32.8186	2	–11.1764	–25.40	**16**
Jinan	5,533.01	21.3475	34	14,958.15	15.8528	29	–5.4947	–25.74	**17**

(continued)

Table 4.6 (continued)

Region	2005			2012			Changes in proportion from 2005 to 2012		
	Per capita non-cultural consumption surplus (yuan)	Proportion of cultural/ educational consumption to non-cultural consumption Surplus (%)	Proportion rank	Per capita non-cultural consumption surplus (yuan)	Proportion of cultural/ educational consumption to non-cultural consumption surplus o (%)	Proportion rank	Percentage point change	Percentage change	Rank
Guiyang	3,347.96	33.2325	15	7,766.37	24.5331	10	−8.6994	−26.18	**18**
Beijing	6,595.30	33.1532	16	16,871.33	23.9203	14	−9.2329	−27.85	**19**
Dalian	3,187.13	37.3113	11	8,662.00	26.6218	7	−10.6895	−28.65	**20**
Yinchuan	2,502.25	38.2536	8	7,423.84	27.2914	6	−10.9622	−28.66	**21**
Zhengzhou	4,643.86	22.9189	32	10,522.09	14.7574	33	−8.1615	−35.61	**22**
Tianjin	4,268.99	30.0703	20	12,316.71	18.6723	25	−11.3980	−37.90	**23**
Shenzhen	10,594.44	29.4308	21	16,261.09	17.5508	27	−11.8800	−40.37	**24**
Lanzhou	2,350.22	42.5922	4	5,545.72	24.5144	11	−18.0778	−42.44	**25**
Xiamen	6,177.54	26.2658	27	15,335.37	15.0832	31	−11.1826	−42.57	**26**
Chengdu	2,944.40	41.7076	5	9,645.18	23.3948	16	−18.3128	−43.91	**27**
Changsha	4,459.72	37.7983	10	11,738.90	21.0022	21	−16.7961	−44.44	**28**
Haikou	3,268.95	27.4483	26	8,889.40	15.0638	32	−12.3845	−45.12	**29**
Shijiazhuang	3,699.56	24.8881	30	10,872.22	13.3018	34	−11.5863	−46.55	**30**
Taiyuan	4,095.06	34.7887	13	10,026.21	18.4685	26	−16.3202	−46.91	**31**
Qingdao	4,471.67	32.0972	17	13,061.56	15.5240	30	−16.5732	−51.63	**32**
Chongqing	3,011.28	46.1966	1	7,964.77	22.0223	19	−24.1743	−52.33	**33**
Xining	2,770.48	28.1893	23	7,027.75	12.5807	35	−15.6086	−55.37	**34**
Hangzhou	5,133.59	38.3809	7	16,441.18	16.6640	28	−21.7169	−56.58	**35**
Lhasa	1,492.33	45.4497	2	6,363.30	11.8764	36	−33.5733	−73.87	**36**

Note: Numbers in the table are derived from calculations

provides data for per capita non-cultural consumption surplus for major cities in 2005 and 2012, and can be compare to regional per capita cultural and educational consumption data from Table 4.2 in order to re-calculate.

From 2005 to 2012, the national urban and rural per capita non-cultural consumption surplus increased from 3,647.61 to 9,923.90 yuan, an average annual increase of 15.37 %, higher than the national urban per capita cultural and educational consumption average annual growth over the same period by 6.16 percentage points. In these 7 years, the proportion of national urban per capita cultural and educational consumption within per capita non-cultural consumption surplus decreased from 30.09 % to 20.49 %, a decrease of 9.60 percentage points, and a degree of decrease of 31.89 %. Over the same period, the Beijing proportion decreased from 22.15 % to 23.92 %, a decrease of 9.23 percentage points; the Tianjin proportion decreased from 30.07 % to 18.67 %, a decrease of 11.40 percentage points; the Shanghai proprotion decreased from 31.81 % to 24.24 %, a decrease of 7.57 percentage points; the Chongqing proportion decreased from 46.20 % to 22.02 %, a decrease of 24.18 percentage points.

In comparing the proportion of per capita cultural/educational consumption to per capita non-cultural surplus consumption in major cities, in 2005, the 19 cities of Chongqing, Lhasa, Xi'an, Lanzhou, Chengdu, Changchun, Hangzhou, Yinchuan, Changzhou, Changsha, Dalian, Harbin, Taiyuan, Nanning, Guiyang, Beijing, Qingdao, Shanghai, and Shenyang in descending order of this ratio, all had higher proportions than the national urban overall ratio; the 17 cities of Tianjin, Shenzhen, Nanjing, Xining, Wuhan, Urumqi, Haikou, Xiamen, Kunming, Ningbo, Shijiazhuang, Hohhot, Zhengzhou, Nanchang, Jinan, Hefei, and Fuzhou, in descending order of this proportion, all had proportions lower than the national urban total ratio. Among these, Chongqing, in first place, had a proportion that was higher than the national urban overall proportion by 16.11 percentage points; Fuzhou, in last place, had a proportion that was lower than the national urban overall proportion by 13.04 percentage points.

In 2012, the 22 cities of Guangzhou, Xi'an, Harbin, Changchun, Shenyang, Yinchuan, Dalian, Nanning, Hefei, Guiyang, Lanzhou, Shanghai, Nanjing, Beijing, Wuhan, Chengdu, Nanchang, Urumqi, Chongqing, Hohhot, Changsha, and Fuzhou, in descending order of this proportion, all had proportions higher than the national urban overall proportion; the 14 cities of Kunming, Ningbo, Tianjin, Taiyuan, Shenzhen, Hangzhou, Jinan, Qingdao, Xiamen, Haikou, Zhengzhou, Shijiazhuang, Xining, and Lhasa, in descending order of this proportion, all had proportions lower than the national urban overall proportion. Among these, Guangzhou, in first place, had a proportion higher than the national urban overall proportion by 25.19 percentage points; Lhasa, in last place, had a proportion lower than the national urban overall proportion by 8.61 percentage points.

In comparing the changes in ratio of per capita cultural/educational consumption and per capita non-cultural consumption surplus of major cities from 2005 to 2012, only the four cities of Hefei, Fuzhou, Guangzhou, and Nanchang, in descending order of proportion increase, all experienced increases; the 32 cities of Shenyang, Hohhot, Harbin, Wuhan, Nanjing, Urumqi, Kunming, Nanning, Ningbo, Shanghai,

Changchun, Xi'an, Jinan, Guiyang, Beijing, Dalian, Yinchuan, Zhengzhou, Tianjin, Shenzhen, Lanzhou, Xiamen, Chengdu, Changsha, Haikou, Shijiazhuang, Taiyuan, Qingdao, Chongqing, Xining, Hangzhou, and Lhasa, in ascending order of proportion decrease, all experienced decreases. Among these, Hefei, in first place, had a proportion increase of 24.03 %; Lhasa, in last place, had a proportion decrease of 73.87 %.

When comparing 2012 with the previous year, the national urban ratio decreased by 5.93 %. At the same time, only the four cities of Hefei, Fuzhou, Guangzhou, and Nanchang, in descending order of increase in proportion, all experienced increases; the 32 cities of Shenyang, Hohhot, Harbin, Nanjing, Wuhan, Kunming, Urumqi, Nanning, Shanghai, Ningbo, Changchun, Jinan, Xi'an, Guiyang, Beijing, Dalian, Yinchuan, Zhengzhou, Tianjin, Shenzhen, Chengdu, Lanzhou, Xiamen, Shijiazhuang, Changsha, Haikou, Taiyuan, Qingdao, Lhasa, Hangzhou, Chongqing, and Xining, in ascending order of decrease in proportion, all experienced decreases.

An analysis of this ratio relationship shows that, between 2005 and 2012, when comparing national cultural/educational consumption growth and non-cultural consumption surplus growth in major cities, the "Growth Coordination" between them was poor. In the vast majority of national major cities, the cultural/educational consumption growth did not keep up with the growth in surplus money outside of the necessary consumption of urban citizens (this evaluation system sets total non-cultural consumption as essential consumption). The development of a moderately prosperous society has not been realized in step with the increase in cultural/educational consumption demand of urban citizens.

4.3 Balance of Growth Among Provinces, Cities and Rural Areas

In this evaluation system, cultural/educational consumption demand and growth still needs to be put into the context of the "Coordinated Growth" relationship between urban and rural areas and regional areas, in order to obtain essential ratio differences to correct numerical calculations.

4.3.1 Changes in Difference Between Urban and Rural Cultural/Educational Demand Growth in the Provinces

This evaluation has been specially designed so that the assessment of major cities leads to an urban index ratio. The role that major cities play within the provinces is not only one of stimulating growth in local cities and towns, but also one of driving the growth in local rural areas. As for the analysis and assessment of major cities, there is still a coordinated growth that has been detected between the cultural/educational consumption demand of provinces, regions and urban and rural areas. For ideas about and techniques used for the design, see the B2 technical report.

A province needs the major cities, not for the purpose of "Pioneering Development", but for how they cause the economy, culture, and social construction to radiate and spur on. Any lack of coordination, imbalance, or lack in the development of provinces or regions will inevitably have a negative affect on the development of major cities. Also, it is logical for municipalities and provinces/regions themselves to use the targeted urban/rural ratio. In this analysis, municipalities take all of the data from urban and rural areas, and the remaining cities take related data from provinces/regions to do calculations.

For an analysis of per capita cultural/educational consumption and changing trends of the provinces and regions where each major city is located, see Table 4.7, where a rank of per capita cultural/educational consumption from each province and region from 2012 is provided in ascending order. The table also provides urban and rural per capita cultural/educational consumption base data from 2005 to 2012 for each province and region, which can used for checking calculations.

From 2005 to 2012, the national urban per capita cultural/educational consumption grew from 1,097.46 to 2,033.50 yuan, a total growth of 85.29 %, and an average annual growth of 9.21 %; the national rural per capita cultural/educational consumption grew from 295.48 to 445.49 yuan, a total growth of 50.77 %, and an average annual growth of 6.04 %. In the 7 years, the national urban per capita cultural/educational consumption annual average growth degree was higher than that of rural areas by 3.17 percentage points. The urban-to-rural ratio of national per capita cultural/educational consumption expanded from 3.7142 to 4.5646, and the urban-rural gap of cultural/educational consumption demand expanded by 22.90 %.

Over the same period, Beijing's urban per capita cultural/educational consumption had an average annual growth of 7.79 %, and its rural average annual growth was 5.41 %. The urban average annual growth degree was higher than the rural average annual growth degree by 2.38 percentage points, and the urban-to-rural ratio of cultural/educational consumption expanded from 2.7435 to 3.2085, an expansion of 16.88 %. Tianjin's urban per capita cultural/educational consumption had an average annual growth of 8.38 %, and its rural average annual growth was 12.84 %. The urban average annual growth was lower than that of the rural areas by 4.46 percentage points, and the urban-to-rural ratio of cultural/educational consumption narrowed from 3.9035 to 2.9425, a decrease of 24.62 %. Shanghai's urban per capita cultural consumption had an average urban annual growth of 7.31 %, and an average rural annual growth of 0.24 %, with the urban average annual degree of growth being larger than rural average annual degree of growth by 7.07 percentage points. The urban-to-rural ratio of cultural/educational consumption widened from 2.4268 to 3.9111, an expansion of 61.16. Chongqing's urban per capita cultural/educational consumption had an average annual urban growth of 0.80 %, and an average annual rural growth of 6.74 %. The average annual urban growth degree was lower than the average annual rural growth degree by 5.95 percentage points, and the urban-to-rural ratio of cultural/educational consumption narrowed from 5.5709 to 3.7304, a decrease of 33.04 %.

Table 4.7 Changes in discrepancies of urban-to-rural ratio of per capita cultural/educational consumption in provinces or regions of major cities

Province or region where municipality is located	Urban-rural gap of cultural/educational consumption in 2005			Urban-rural gap of cultural/educational consumption in 2012			Fluctuations in urban-to-rural ratio from 2005 to 2012	
	Urban per capita values (yuan)	Rural per capita value (yuan)	Urban-to-rural ratio (rural = 1)	Urban per capita values (yuan)	Rural Per capita value (yuan)	Urban-to-rural ratio (rural- 1)	Percentage expansion/ decrease	Rank
National	**1,097.46**	**295.48**	**3.7142**	**2,033.50**	**445.49**	**4.5646**	**22.90**	–
Qinghai	803.08	109.53	7.3321	1,097.21	283.28	3.8732	−47.17	**1**
Tibet	678.26	28.20	24.0518	550.48	40.86	13.4723	−43.99	**2**
Chongqing	1,391.11	249.71	5.5709	1,470.64	394.23	3.7304	−33.04	**3**
Tianjin	1,283.70	328.86	3.9035	2,254.22	766.08	2.9425	−24.62	**4**
Heilongjiang	802.49	277.00	2.8971	1,216.56	518.04	2.3484	−18.94	**5**
Jilin	800.22	261.09	3.0649	1,642.70	606.26	2.7096	−11.59	**6**
Shanxi	932.53	279.54	3.3359	1,506.20	498.02	3.0244	−9.34	**7**
Ningxia	769.97	177.90	4.3281	1,515.91	373.36	4.0602	−6.19	**8**
Hebei	795.43	225.79	3.5229	1,203.80	358.49	3.3580	−4.68	**9**
Jiangsu	1,287.90	478.94	2.6891	3,077.76	1,184.18	2.5991	−3.35	**10**
Henan	805.08	177.66	4.5316	1,525.33	343.83	4.4363	−2.10	**11**
Xinjiang	741.35	159.32	4.6532	1,280.81	261.74	4.8934	5.16	**12**
Gansu	942.75	257.88	3.6558	1,388.21	327.30	4.2414	16.02	**13**
Yunnan	775.61	182.62	4.2471	1,434.30	289.22	4.9592	16.77	**14**
Beijing	2,186.55	796.99	2.7435	3,695.98	1,152.67	3.2065	16.88	**15**
Sichuan	909.03	225.16	4.0373	1,587.43	329.29	4.8208	19.41	**16**
Fujian	1,106.95	356.54	3.1047	2,104.83	565.83	3.7199	19.82	**17**
Shandong	1,039.99	377.16	2.7574	1,655.91	500.98	3.3053	19.87	**18**
Guizhou	811.73	160.91	5.0446	1,396.00	226.44	6.1650	22.21	**19**
Inner Mongolia	968.81	309.40	3.1313	1,971.78	513.97	3.8364	22.52	**20**

Hunan	1,138.67	329.28	3.4581	1,737.64	400.22	4.3417	25.55	**21**
Hubei	904.76	271.86	3.3280	1,651.92	394.63	4.1860	25.78	**22**
Shaanxi	1,081.92	297.33	3.6388	2,078.52	445.47	4.6659	28.23	**23**
Zhejiang	1,849.73	722.95	2.5586	2,996.59	902.23	3.3213	29.81	**24**
Guangxi	998.87	226.38	4.4124	1,626.05	270.24	6.0171	36.37	**25**
Guangdong	1,669.09	360.73	4.6270	2,954.13	466.63	6.3308	36.82	**26**
Liaoning	849.53	376.93	2.2538	1,843.89	556.56	3.3130	47.00	**27**
Jiangxi	805.41	276.26	2.9154	1,487.30	342.70	4.3399	48.86	**28**
Hainan	652.03	198.70	3.2815	1,319.54	253.97	5.1957	58.33	**29**
Shanghai	2,272.76	935.51	2.4268	3,723.74	952.10	3.9111	61.16	**30**
Anhui	666.42	256.80	2.5951	1,932.74	385.92	5.0081	92.98	**31**

Note: (1) Data for urban and rural per capita cultural/education for each province and region comes from related volumes of the "*China Statistical Yearbook*", and the rest are derived from numerical calculations; (2) Negative percentages of urban-to-rural ratios represent a decrease in the urban-to-rural ratio

In doing a before and after comparison, in 2005, the urban-to-rural ratios of Beijing and Shanghai were smaller than the national overall urban-to-rural ratio, and the urban-to-rural ratios of Tianjin and Chongqing were larger than the national overall urban-to-rural ratio; in 2012, the urban-to-rural ratios of Beijing, Tianjin, Shanghai and Tianjin were all smaller than the national overall urban-to-rural ratio.

In comparing the urban-to-rural ratio for per capita cultural/educational consumption for each province or region, in 2005, the 23 cities of Shenyang, Dalian, Shanghai, Hangzhou, Ningbo, Hefei, Nanjing, Beijing, Jinan, Qingdao, Harbin, Nanchang, Changchun, Fuzhou, Xiamen, Hohhot, Haikou, Wuhan, Taiyuan, Changsha, Shijiazhuang, Xi'an, and Lanzhou, in ascending order of urban-to-rural ratio of cultural/educational consumption within each province or region, all had smaller ratios than the national overall urban-to-rural ratio; the 13 cities of Tianjin, Chengdu, Kunming, Yinchuan, Nanning, Zhengzhou, Guangzhou, Shenzhen, Urumqi, Guiyang, Chongqing, Xining, and Lhasa, in ascending order of urban-to-rural ratio of cultural/educational consumption within each province or region, all had larger ratios than the national overall urban-to-rural ratio. Among these, Shenyang, in first place of urban-to-rural ratio within the province or region, made up 60.68 % of the national overall urban-to-rural ratio; Lhasa, in last place of urban-to-rural ratio within the province or region, was higher than the national overall urban-to-rural ratio by 647.57 %.

In 2012, the 25 cities of Harbin, Nanjing, Changchun, Tianjin, Taiyuan, Beijing, Jinan, Qingdao, Shenyang, Dalian, Hangzhou, Ningbo, Shijiazhuang, Fuzhou, Xiamen, Chongqing, Hohhot, Xining, Shanghai, Yinchuan, Wuhan, Lanzhou, Nanchang, Changsha, and Zhengzhou, in ascending order of the urban-to-rural ratio within the province or region of cultural/educational consumption, all had smaller ratios than the national overall urban-to-rural ratio; the 11 cities of Xi'an, Chengdu, Urumqi, Kunming, Hefei, Haikou, Nanning, Guiyang, Guangzhou, Shenzhen, and Lhasa, in ascending order of the urban-to-rural ratio within the province or region of cultural/educational consumption, all had larger ratios than the national overall urban-to-rural ratio. Among these, Harbin, in first place of urban-to-rural ratio within the province, was 51.45 % of the national overall urban-to-rural ratio; Lhasa, in last place in urban-to-rural ratio within the province, had a ration that was higher than the national overall urban-to-rural ratio by 25.15 %.

From 2005 to 2012, the provinces or regions in which the 11 cities of Xining, Lhasa, Chongqing, Tianjin, Harbin, Changchun, Taiyuan, Yinchuan, Shijiazhuang, Nanjing, and Zhengzhou are located, in descending order of urban-to-rural ratio of cultural/educational consumption, all experienced decreases; the provinces or regions in which the 25 cities of Urumqi, Lanzhou, Kunming, Beijing, Chengdu, Fuzhou, Xiamen, Jinan, Qingdao, Guiyang, Hohhot, Changsha, Wuhan, Xi'an, Hangzhou, Ningbo, Nanning, Guangzhou, Shenzhen, Shenyang, Dalian, Nanchang, Haikou, Shanghai, and Hefei are located, in ascending order of urban-to-rural ratio of cultural/educational consumption, all experienced increases. In their respective provinces. Among these, Xining, in first place of decrease in urban-to-rural ratio of the province within which it is located, had an urban-to-rural ratio decrease of 47.16 %; Hefei, in last place, had a provincial increase of 92.98 %.

When comparing 2012 with the previous year, the urban-to-rural ratio of national cultural/educational consumption shrunk by 2.35 %. At the same time, the provinces where the 21 cities of Tianjin, Changchun, Chongqing, Guiyang, Nanning, Shijiazhuang, Kunming, Zhengzhou, Yinchuan, Harbin, Taiyuan, Shanghai, Wuhan, Guangzhou, Shenzhen, Nanchang, Beijing, Chengdu, Changsha, Hangzhou, and Ningbo are located, in descending order of urban-rural ratio of cultural/educational consumption, all had ratios that shrunk. The provinces where the 15 cities of Urumqi, Fuzhou, Xiamen, Nanjing, Xi'an, Haikou, Jinan, Qingdao, Xining, Lhasa, Lanzhou, Hohhot, Shenyang, Dalian, and Hefei are located, in ascending order of expansion of urban-to-rural ratio of cultural/educational consumption of the province they are in, all had expanded ratios.

This means that, from 2005 to 2012, when comparing urban and rural areas both national and provincially/regionally, the "Coordinated Growth" of cultural/educational consumption demand is significantly poor. In the vast majority of provinces and regions across the country, there has been a general expansion of the urban-to-rural ratio of cultural/educational consumption, with many provinces and regions experiencing a serious degree of urban-to-rural ratio expansion. In 2012, the urban-to-rural ratio of educational/cultural consumption again being to shrink in most provinces and regions of the country, which was good news.

4.3.2 Changes in Regional Discrepancies in Urban Cultural/ Educational Consumption Demand

The evaluation of major cities show indications of regional discrepancy, and this evaluation system was purposefully designed for this. The reason that national development needs the "Pioneering Trend" of the major cities is not because of their "pioneering development", but because of the role they play in the radiation and stimulation of economy, culture, and society. Any discord, imbalance or lack in national development will inevitably negatively affect the development of major cities.

For an analysis of regional discrepancies and changing trends in per capita cultural/educational consumption in major cities for 2005 and 2012, see Table 4.8, where the regional discrepancies of per capita cultural/educational consumption of each major city in 2012 are ranked in ascending order. In accordance with the calculation method for regional discrepancies in cultural/educational consumption, a re-comparison can be made when looking at per capita cultural/educational consumption data for each region in Table 4.2. Also, using the column spaces in Table 4.8, the ranking results for urban-to-rural ratios of per capita cultural/educational consumption of the provinces where the cities are located, for 2005 and 2012, are attached.

Table 4.8 Changes in regional discrepancies in per capita cultural/educational consumption of major cities

Region	Regional discrepancies in cultural/educational consumption in 2005		Regional discrepancies in cultural/educational consumption in 2005		Fluctuations in regional discrepancy from 2005 to 2012		Attachment: provincial/regional urban-to-rural ratio rank (with Table 4.7)	
	Regional discrepancy (no discrepancy = 1)	Rank (no discrepancy = 1)	Regional discrepancy	Rank	Percentage changes	Rank	2005	2012
= **Nationwide cities**	**1.2915**	–	**1.3069**	–	**1.19**	–	–	–
Shenzhen	2.8411	36	1.4035	29	−50.60	**1**	30	34
Hangzhou	1.7953	32	1.3473	27	−24.95	**2**	4	11
Qingdao	1.3078	24	1.0029	1	−23.31	**3**	9	7
Xiamen	1.4785	27	1.1375	13	−23.06	**4**	14	14
Changsha	1.5360	29	1.2124	19	−21.07	**5**	20	24
Kunming	1.3120	25	1.0694	7	−18.49	**6**	26	29
Taiyuan	1.2981	23	1.0894	8	−16.08	**7**	19	5
Hefei	1.4812	28	1.2999	22	−12.24	**8**	6	30
Yinchuan	1.1278	14	1.0037	2	−11.00	**9**	27	20
Chongqing	1.2676	21	1.1374	12	−10.27	**10**	34	16
Ningbo	1.7120	31	1.6125	31	−5.81	**11**	4	11
Nanchang	1.1979	19	1.1458	14	−4.35	**12**	12	23
Changchun	1.0733	7	1.0344	3	−3.62	**13**	13	3
Harbin	1.0890	11	1.0504	5	−3.54	**14**	11	1
Tianjin	1.1697	16	1.1310	10	−3.31	**15**	24	4
Shanghai	2.0709	34	2.0024	34	−3.31	**16**	3	19
Nanning	1.0574	4	1.0413	4	−1.52	**17**	28	32

Chengdu	1.1190	13	1.1097	9	−0.83	**18**	25	27
Fuzhou	1.1893	18	1.1804	17	−0.75	**19**	14	14
Beijing	1.9924	33	1.9846	33	−0.39	**20**	8	6
Dalian	1.0836	9	1.1340	11	4.65	**21**	1	9
Guiyang	1.0138	1	1.0630	6	4.85	**22**	33	33
Jinan	1.0763	8	1.1661	16	8.34	**23**	9	7
Wuhan	1.0695	6	1.1638	15	8.82	**24**	18	21
Xi'an	1.2369	20	1.3532	28	9.40	**25**	22	26
Shijiazhuang	1.1610	15	1.2888	21	11.01	**26**	21	13
Haikou	1.1824	17	1.3415	25	13.46	**27**	17	31
Shenyang	1.0582	5	1.2111	18	14.45	**28**	1	9
Lhasa	1.3820	26	1.6284	32	17.83	**29**	36	36
Zhengzhou	1.0302	3	1.2364	20	20.02	**30**	29	25
Xining	1.2884	22	1.5652	30	21.48	**31**	35	18
Urumqi	1.0934	12	1.3307	23	21.70	**32**	32	28
Lanzhou	1.0879	10	1.3314	24	22.38	**33**	23	22
Hohhot	1.0262	2	1.3417	26	30.74	**34**	16	17
Nanjing	1.5902	30	2.0831	35	31.00	**35**	7	2
Guangzhou	2.1221	35	2.7870	36	31.33	**36**	30	34

Note: (1) Data in the table is derived from numerical calculations; (2) A negative percentage in regional discrepancy change indicates a shrinkage in regional discrepancy. The urban-to-rural ratio ranking for provinces/regions where the major cities are located are in Table 4.7. Of the corresponding provinces/regions where each city is located, 10 of the cities correspond to 5 provinces, so there are 5 pairs of cities with the same ranking

From 2005 to 2012, regional discrepancy in the national urban per capita cultural/educational consumption expanded from 1.2915 to 1.3069, and the regional gap in cultural/educational consumption expanded by 1.19 %. Over the same period, the cultural/educational consumption regional gap in Beijing shrank by 0.39 %, the cultural/educational consumption regional gap in Tianjin shrunk by 3.31 %, the cultural/educational consumption regional gap in Shanghai shrunk by 3.31 %, and the cultural/educational consumption regional gap in Chongqing shrunk by 10.27 %.

In looking at the before and after, in 2005, the cities of Tianjin and Chongqing had regional gaps that were smaller than the national urban overall regional gap, while Beijing and Shanghai had regional gaps that were larger than the national urban overall regional gap; in 2012, Tianjin and Chongqing still had regional gaps that were smaller than the national urban overall regional gap, while Beijing and Shanghai still had regional gaps that were larger than the national urban overall regional gap.

In comparing the regional discrepancy in per capita cultural/educational consumption of each major city, in 2005, the regional discrepancies in educational/cultural consumption of the 22 major cities of Guiyang, Hohhot, Zhengzhou, Nanning, Shenyang, Wuhan, Changchun, Jinan, Dalian, Harbin, Urumqi, Chengdu, Yinchuan, Shijiazhuang, Tianjin, Haikou, Fuzhou, Nanchang, Xi'an, Chongqing, and Xining, in ascending order of regional discrepancies, all had lower regional discrepancies than the national urban overall regional discrepancy; the 14 major cities of Taiyuan, Qingdao, Kunming, Lhasa, Xiamen, Hefei, Changsha, Nanjing, Ningbo, Hangzhou, Beijing, Shanghai, Guangzhou, and Shenzhen, in ascending order of regional discrepancy in cultural/educational consumption, all had higher discrepancies than the national urban overall regional discrepancy. Among these, Guiyang, in first place, had a regional discrepancy than was only 78.50 % of the national urban overall regional discrepancy; Shenzhen, in last place, had a regional discrepancy that was larger than the national urban overall regional discrepancy by 219.98 %.

In 2012, the regional discrepancies in educational/cultural consumption of the 22 major cities of Qingdao, Yinchuan, Changchun, Nanning, Harbin, Guiyang, Kunming, Taiyuan, Chengdu, Tianjin, Dalian, Chongqing, Xiamen, Nanchang, Wuhan, Jinan, Fuzhou, Shenyang, Changsha, Zhengzhou, Shijiazhuang, and Hefei, in ascending order of regional discrepancies, all were lower than the national urban overall regional discrepancy; the 14 major cities of Urumqi, Lanzhou, Haikou, Hohhot, Hangzhou, Xi'an, Shenzhen, Xining, Ningbo, Lhasa, Beijing, Shanghai, Nanjing, and Guangzhou, in ascending order of regional discrepancies, all had higher regional discrepancies than the national urban overall regional discrepancy. Among these, Qingdao, in first place, had a regional discrepancy that was only 76.74 % of the national urban overall regional discrepancy; Guangzhou, in last place, had a regional discrepancy that was 213.25 % higher than the national urban overall regional discrepancy.

From 2005 to 2012, the regional discrepancies of cultural/educational consumption of the 20 major cities of Shenzhen, Hangzhou, Qingdao, Xiamen, Changsha, Kunming, Taiyuan, Hefei, Yinchuan, Chongqing, Ningbo, Nanchang, Changchun, Harbin, Tianjin, Shanghai, Nanning, Chengdu, Fuzhou, and Beijing, in descending order of reduction degree, all were reduced; the regional discrepancies of cultural/educational consumption of the 16 major cities of Dalian, Guiyang, Jinan, Wuhan, Xi'an, Shijiazhuang, Haikou, Shenyang, Lhasa, Zhengzhou, Xining, Urumqi, Lanzhou, Hohhot, Nanjing, and Guangzhou, in ascending order of degree of expansion, all were expanded. Among these, Shenzhen, in first place, had a reduction in regional discrepancy of 50.60 %; Guangzhou, in last place, had an expansion in regional discrepancy of 31.33 %.

When comparing 2012 with the previous year, we see that the regional discrepancy in national urban cultural/educational consumption shrunk by 0.20 %. Over the same time, the regional discrepancies in cultural/educational consumption of the 14 major cities of Shenzhen, Hangzhou, Xiamen, Changsha, Qingdao, Ningbo, Yinchuan, Changchun, Tianjin, Shanghai, Nanning, Chengdu, Beijing, and Nanchang, in descending order of reduction, all had reduced discrepancies; the regional discrepancies in cultural/educational consumption of the 22 major cities of Dalian, Jinan, Xi'an, Guiyang, Shijiazhuang, Lhasa, Haikou, Xining, Harbin, Zhengzhou, Urumqi, Lanzhou, Wuhan, Shenyang, Hohhot, Nanjing, Guangzhou, Fuzhou, Chongqing, Taiyuan, Kunming, and Hefei, in ascending order of expansion degree, all had expanding regional discrepancies.

This means that, in comparing urban per capita cultural/educational consumption demand growth in nationwide regions from 2005 to 2012, the "Coordinated Growth" was significantly improved. In the majority of major cities, regional discrepancies in cultural/educational consumption were reduced. Compared with regional or provincial discrepancies, between each region of major cities, the growth discrepancy between the "leading" developed areas and the "lagging" underdeveloped areas was not very significant.

4.4 Forecasts and Rankings of Major Cities' Cultural/ Educational Consumption Demand

Based on the numerical analysis for the above indicators, and in accordance with this evaluation system's assessment methods and weighted calculations, the final estimates were made for cultural/educational consumption demand rankings of major cities for 2012. Based on different time periods and different kinds of reference values, survey results for 2012 were obtained. An index percentile was taken, so that the horizontal percentage was measure of high and low, and the vertical percentage was a measure of increase and decrease.

4.4.1 Evaluation of 2012 Cultural/Educational Consumption Demand

For an analysis of changing trends in cultural/educational consumption demand since 2005 as calculated separately per major city, see Table 4.9, where the each city's horizontal assessment of a zero-difference ideal status between regions and urban and rural areas' cultural/educational consumption demand is ranked in descending order.

4.4.1.1 Annual Horizontal Assessment Index

Setting the "ideal value" of cultural/educational consumption demand as 100, which reflects a zero-difference status between urban and rural areas and between regions, in the annual horizontal assessment for national urban cultural/educational consumption demand for 2012, the index number was 78.73, lower than the ideal value by 21.27. In this assessment, due to the national urban cultural/educational consumption total share number (with the national share as 100 % of the base), per capita absolute values and proportions for each indicator being the calculation base, the national urban overall prosperity index level is completely due to the urban-to-rural ratio of cultural/educational consumption and the expansion or narrowing of regional discrepancies in urban cultural/educational consumption.

Beijing's index was 84.41, lower than the ideal value by 15.59, and also higher than the national urban overall index by 5.68; Tianjin's index was 73.51, lower than the ideal value by 26.49, and lower than the national urban overall index by 5.22; Shanghai's index was 81.92, lower than the ideal value by 18.08, and higher than the national urban overall index by 3.19; Chongqing's index was 77.09, lower than the ideal value by 22.91, and lower than the national urban overall index by 1.64. In this evaluation, the prosperity index level of each major city, besides being based on each city's own urban-to-rural ratio of cultural/educational consumption, as well as the changes in expansion/narrowing of the national regional gaps, is probably mostly based on per capita cultural/educational consumption absolute values and their relation in amount (whether higher or lower) to the national overall average value.

In comparing the prosperity indexes for all major cities, the cities of Guangzhou, Xi'an, and Nanjing, in descending order of prosperity index, make up the first three cities nationally among "2012 Leading Cities in Cultural/Educational Consumption Demand". The 10 major cities of Harbin, Nanning, Changchun, Hefei, Beijing, Yinchuan, Shenyang, Shanghai, Kunming, and Guiyang, in descending order of prosperity index, were all higher than the national urban overall prosperity index; the 22 major cities of Dalian, Fuzhou, Chengdu, Wuhan, Chongqing, Taiyuan, Ningbo, Hohhot, Changsha, Jinan, Tianjin, Nanchang, Hangzhou, Lanzhou, Qingdao, Urumqi, Shijiazhuang, Xiamen, Zhengzhou, Shenzhen, Haikou, and Xining, in descending order of prosperity index, all were lower than the national urban overall prosperity index.

Table 4.9 Changes in cultural/educational consumption demand indexes of major cities

Region	Starting year base value vertical assessment (starting year base value = 100)						Horizontal assessment for each region's urban-to-rural ratio and regional no-gap ideal value (ideal value = 100)	
	7 years after the "Eleventh Five-Year Plan" (2005–2012)		2 years after the "Twelfth Five-Year Plan" (2010–2012)		Recent 1 year (2011–2012)			
	Prosperity index	Rank	Prosperity index	Rank	Prosperity index	Rank	Prosperity index	Rank
National cities	**89.73**	–	**99.40**	–	**100.21**	–	**78.73**	–
Guangzhou	105.30	4	103.80	9	102.48	6	104.50	**1**
Xi'an	88.18	21	96.73	24	98.77	22	92.61	**2**
Nanjing	104.31	5	97.97	19	99.85	16	92.51	**3**
Harbin	96.08	9	97.33	22	100.51	14	88.61	**4**
Nanning	89.39	20	110.89	3	102.62	5	88.11	**5**
Changchun	95.83	10	96.77	23	103.11	3	87.71	**6**
Hefei	156.77	1	97.45	20	103.58	2	87.33	**7**
Beijing	92.09	12	99.31	15	100.21	15	84.41	**8**
Yinchuan	101.54	6	105.68	8	102.03	7	83.04	**9**
Shenyang	93.70	11	89.85	34	97.52	27	83.00	**10**
Shanghai	86.88	24	96.16	25	100.83	11	81.92	**11**
Kunming	118.88	2	112.28	2	102.97	4	80.23	**12**
Guiyang	84.97	28	92.50	32	101.84	8	80.09	**13**
Dalian	86.39	25	99.00	17	96.59	31	78.50	**14**
Fuzhou	113.89	3	94.97	27	101.33	9	78.30	**15**
Chengdu	87.02	23	97.44	21	98.88	21	77.83	**16**
Wuhan	90.59	17	112.86	1	99.35	17	77.17	**17**
Chongqing	90.70	16	101.67	10	99.33	18	77.09	**18**
Taiyuan	85.03	27	93.13	29	96.69	30	77.08	**19**
Ningbo	87.59	22	92.59	31	99.33	19	77.00	**20**
Hohhot	97.32	7	107.30	5	97.87	26	76.57	**21**

(continued)

Table 4.9 (continued)

Region	Starting year base value vertical assessment (starting year base value = 100)						Horizontal assessment for each region's urban-to-rural ratio and regional no-gap ideal value (ideal value = 100)	
	7 years after the "Eleventh Five-Year Plan" (2005–2012)		2 years after the "Twelfth Five-Year Plan" (2010–2012)		Recent 1 year (2011–2012)			
	Prosperity index	Rank	Prosperity index	Rank	Prosperity index	Rank	Prosperity index	Rank
Changsha	81.82	31	99.78	13	98.18	24	76.23	**22**
Jinan	91.30	14	99.75	14	98.76	23	73.67	**23**
Tianjin	96.28	8	106.88	6	105.65	1	73.51	**24**
Nanchang	91.27	15	99.14	16	100.54	13	72.77	**25**
Hangzhou	80.34	32	99.99	12	97.49	28	70.83	**26**
Lanzhou	74.44	34	93.12	30	94.49	34	70.44	**27**
Qingdao	80.06	33	95.75	26	96.29	32	69.09	**28**
Urumqi	82.43	30	98.87	18	97.14	29	67.19	**29**
Shijiazhuang	85.72	26	108.58	4	100.63	12	66.12	**30**
Xiamen	84.53	29	91.67	33	98.05	25	65.74	**31**
Zhengzhou	89.60	18	105.70	7	100.92	10	65.40	**32**
Shenzhen	91.40	13	100.69	11	99.28	20	65.03	**33**
Haikou	73.09	35	84.30	35	96.07	33	60.65	**34**
Xining	89.52	19	93.61	28	93.23	35	54.11	**35**
Lhasa	–	–	–	–	–	–	–	**–**

Note: Some of the data is missing for Lhasa, so there was no way to integrate it as an indicator into this assessment

4.4.1.2 Vertical Assessment Index Since the "Eleventh Five-Year Plan"

Setting 2005, the last year of the "Tenth Five-Year Plan", with a starting base value of 100, in vertical assessment of the 7 years since the "Eleventh Five-Year Plan", the national urban cultural/educational consumption demand prosperity index of 2012 was 89.73, lower than the 2005 base value by 10.27. In this evaluation, the increase of the national urban overall prosperity index is due to the fact that when compared to its own index in 2005, every indicator in 2012 increased. This held true for every major city.

Beijing's prosperity index was 92.09, lower than its 2005 index base value by 7.91, and also higher than the national urban overall prosperity index by 2.36; Tianjin's prosperity index was 96.28, lower than its 2005 base index by 3.72, and also higher than the national urban overall prosperity index by 6.55; Shanghai's prosperity index was 86.88, lower than its 2005 base index by 13.12, and also lower than the national urban overall prosperity index by 2.85; Chongqing's prosperity index was 90.70, lower than its 2005 base index by 9.30, and higher than the national urban overall prosperity index by 0.97.

In comparing the prosperity index of each major city, Hefei, Kunming, and Fuzhou, in descending order of prosperity index, comprise the first three places in the "Rise in Urban Cultural/Educational Consumption Demand from 2005–2012". The 14 major cities of Guangzhou, Nanjing, Yinchuan, Hohhot, Tianjin, Harbin, Changchun, Shenyang, Beijing, Shenzhen, Jinan, Nanchang, Chongqing, and Wuhan, in descending order of prosperity index, were all higher than the national urban overall prosperity index; the 18 major cities of Zhengzhou, Xining, Nanning, Xi'an, Ningbo, Chengdu, Shanghai, Dalian, Shijiazhuang, Taiyuan, Guiyang, Xiamen, Urumqi, Changsha, Hangzhou, Qingdao, Lanzhou, and Haikou, in descending order of prosperity index, were all lower than the national urban overall prosperity index.

4.4.1.3 Vertical Assessment Index Since the "Twelfth Five-Year Plan"

Setting 2010, the last year of the "Eleventh Five-Year Plan", with a starting base value of 100, in a vertical assessment of the 7 years since the "Twelfth Five-Year Plan", the national urban cultural/educational consumption demand prosperity index of 2012 was 99.40, lower than the 2010 base value by 0.60. In this evaluation, the increase of the national urban overall prosperity index is due to the fact that when compared to its own index in 2010, every indicator in 2012 increased. This was the case for each major city.

Beijing's prosperity index was 99.31, lower than the 2010 base prosperity index of 0.69, and also lower than the national urban overall index by 0.09; Tianjin's prosperity index was 106.88, higher than the 2010 base index of 6.88, and also higher than the national urban overall prosperity index by 7.48; Shanghai's prosperity index was 96.16, lower than the 2010 base index by 3.84, and also lower than the national urban overall prosperity index by 3.24; Chongqing's prosperity index was 101.67, higher than the base prosperity index of 2010 by 1.67, and also higher than the national urban total prosperity index by 2.27.

In comparing the prosperity indexes of major cities, Wuhan, Kunming, and Nanning, in descending order of prosperity indexes, have the top three highest indexes of the cities ranked in the first three spots of the "2010–2012 Urban Cultural/Educational Consumption Demand Status Increase". The 11 major cities of Shijiazhuang, Hohhot, Tianjin, Zhengzhou, Yinchuan, Guangzhou, Chongqing, Shenzhen, Hangzhou, Changsha, and Jinan, in descending order of prosperity indexes, all had indexes higher than the national urban overall prosperity index; the 20 major cities of Beijing, Nanchang, Dalian, Urumqi, Nanjing, Hefei, Chengdu, Harbin, Changsha, Xi'an, Shanghai, Qingdao, Fuzhou, Xining, Taiyuan, Lanzhou, Ningbo, Guiyang, Xiamen, Shenyang, and Haikou, in descending order of prosperity indexes, all had indexes lower than the national urban overall prosperity index.

4.4.1.4 Vertical Assessment of Annual Prosperity Index

Each year begins with a starting base value which is based on the previous year. In the annual vertical assessment, the 2012 national urban cultural/educational consumption demand index was 100.21, higher than the previous year by 0.21. In this assessment, the national urban overall index rise or fall is due to its comparison with its values in the previous year, and in this year the indicator values increased. This was true across all major cities.

Beijing's prosperity index was 100.21, higher than its previous year base value by 0.21, and unchanged from the national urban overall prosperity index; Tianjin's prosperity index was 105.65, higher than its previous year base value by 5.65, and higher than the national urban overall prosperity index by 5.44; Shanghai's prosperity index was 100.83, higher than its previous year base value by 0.83, and higher than the national urban overall prosperity index by 0.62; Chongqing's prosperity index was 99.33, lower than its previous year base value by 0.67, and also lower than the national urban overall prosperity index by 0.88.

In comparing each major city, Tianjin, Hefei, and Changchun comprised the top three cities, in descending order of prosperity index, in the "2012 Annual Urban Cultural/Educational Consumption Demand Index Increase". The 11 major cities of Kunming, Nanning, Guangzhou, Yinchuan, Guiyang, Fuzhou, Zhengzhou, Shanghai, Shijiazhuang, Nanchang, and Harbin, in descending order of prosperity index, all had higher values than the national urban overall prosperity index; the 21 major cities of Beijing, Nanjing, Wuhan, Chongqing, Ningbo, Shenzhen, Chengdu, Xi'an, Jinan, Changsha, Xiamen, Hohhot, Shenyang, Hangzhou, Urumqi, Taiyuan, Dalian, Qingdao, Haikou, Lanzhou, and Xining, in descending order of prosperity index value, all had lower values than the national urban overall prosperity index.

4.4.2 Status Forecast for 2013 and Growth Estimates for 2014

In view of the fact that statistical data for 2013 is yet to be released, and that we have already entered the 2014 year, the forecast for 2013 cultural/educational consumption prosperity index will be based on per capita GDP and urban per capita income, total consumption, savings, and cultural/educational consumption average annual growth rate in major cities from 2005 to 2012. Growth estimates for cultural/educational consumption demand of major cities in 2014 and the urban-to-rural Ratio ratio forecast numbers will be calculated based on the average annual growth rates in urban and rural per capita data of different years within the provinces and regions. This is to say, fully putting into play the potential of calculated data of this research evaluation will be based on the "largest" probabilities of the calculated base data according to relevant calculations average direction trends from major cities, forecasting the 2013 situation, and estimating 2014 growth trends.

For a forecast of cultural/educational consumption demand for each major city for 2013 and estimates of 2014 growth trends, see Table 4.10, where each city is listed according to province/region of their location, and separated into the four major regions of Northeast, East, Middle, and West, arranged in approximate geographical order from North to South and East to West. In accordance with the base data in Tables 4.1, 4.2, 4.3, 4.4, 4.5, 4.6, 4.7, and 4.8 in this report, computational checks can be made. Given that the figures in the table are forecasts with no analysis or ranking, they are for reference only.

Regarding the sub-reports on major cities, there are two points of clarification to make:

1. The report on major cities chose the top four categories in Table 4.9 from which to draw the annual horizontal assessment, annual vertical assessment, 5-year vertical assessments from near and far, to form the in-depth analysis in the city report. Specifically: the 2012 city horizontal assessment used Guangzhou, in first place, and the 2012 city vertical assessment used Tianjin, in first place. The city vertical assessment since the "Twelfth Five-Year Plan" period used Wuhan, in first place, and the city vertical assessment since the "Eleventh Five-Year Plan" period used Hefei, in first place. However, in the city sub-report, the vertical assessment of the 2 years since the "Twelfth Five-Year" plan had a dynamic curve that was too short, and a poor mapping effect, so it was omitted, with special explanation added.
2. Municipalities are both major cities and provinces, but the base data from these two aspects have different sources and ranges. Data for cultural consumption and educational consumption were not distinguished, resulting in the widening of the urban-rural gap in provinces, especially the "Roles of Radiation and Spurring On" detected in major cities (for details see the B2 technical report regarding the special consideration in the evaluation of major cities). Therefore, the results of the two status evaluations are not the same; evaluating major cities by

Table 4.10 2013 forecast of cultural/educational consumption for major cities and 2014 estimates of growth trends

	2013 status forecast		2014 growth trend estimates					
			Forecast for national urban areas and major cities		Urban-rural gap in provinces or major cities and regional discrepancies in major cities			
Regions	Vertical assessment, 2012 base value = 100	Regional horizontal assessment; zero-difference Ideal value = 100	Total cultural/educational consumption	Per capita cultural/educational consumption (yuan)	Urban per capita cultural/educational consumption (yuan)	Rural per capita cultural/educational consumption (yuan)	Urban-rural ratio (rural = 1)	Regional discrepancy (no discrepancy = 1)
National cities	**98.14**	**78.54**	**18,208.73**	**2,425.35**	**2,473.50**	**514.97**	**4.8032**	**1.3217**
Harbin	98.46	88.61	113.89	2,214.69	1,431.91	636.43	2.2499	1.0869
Changchun	98.60	87.84	95.40	2,482.44	2,031.71	748.07	2.7159	1.0235
Shenyang	98.90	83.65	167.03	3,156.07	2,298.98	662.65	3.4694	1.3013
Dalian	98.18	78.56	86.88	2,786.33	2,298.98	662.65	3.4694	1.1488
Beijing	98.71	84.80	599.96	4,807.95	4,408.24	1,331.64	3.3104	1.9824
Tianjin	98.13	73.25	226.84	2,716.72	2,686.00	932.70	2.8798	1.1201
Shijiazhuang	97.71	65.51	42.54	1,645.32	1,380.46	424.14	3.2548	1.3216
Jinan	99.02	74.00	101.48	2,893.76	1,905.84	580.09	3.2855	1.1931
Qingdao	95.47	66.97	63.51	2,238.07	1,905.84	580.09	3.2855	1.0772
Nanjing	99.97	94.44	312.53	5,457.60	3,967.66	1,516.00	2.6172	2.2502
Shanghai	98.02	82.13	662.14	4,809.95	4,480.16	1,040.43	4.3061	1.9832
Hangzhou	96.73	69.74	136.82	3,010.36	3,650.22	1,067.97	3.4179	1.2412
Ningbo	98.28	77.01	88.55	3,844.40	3,650.22	1,067.97	3.4179	1.5851
Fuzhou	100.16	79.98	63.02	3,187.28	2,605.70	646.51	4.0304	1.3142
Xiamen	96.75	65.00	51.64	2,559.66	2,605.70	646.51	4.0304	1.0554
Guangzhou	99.71	108.82	511.12	7,306.71	3,587.21	498.62	7.1943	3.0126
Shenzhen	97.02	64.75	90.55	2,782.69	3,587.21	498.62	7.1943	1.1473

Haikou	95.57	59.35	25.55	1,501.37	1,565.63	270.39	5.7903	1.3810
Taiyuan	96.01	75.02	59.47	1,995.74	1,809.02	618.76	2.9236	1.1771
Zhengzhou	97.22	64.12	128.75	1,729.74	1,900.84	402.76	4.7195	1.2868
Hefei	103.37	92.24	100.62	4,098.90	2,414.37	454.07	5.3172	1.6900
Wuhan	97.71	77.60	125.89	3,008.88	1,951.89	438.42	4.4521	1.2406
Nanchang	98.32	73.51	46.36	2,109.25	1,842.32	380.05	4.8476	1.1303
Changsha	96.62	74.92	84.70	2,748.32	1,997.14	441.36	4.5250	1.1332
Hohhot	98.61	77.13	44.94	3,513.24	2,487.95	586.59	4.2414	1.4485
Xi'an	97.77	92.48	197.79	3,367.18	2,594.69	517.23	5.0165	1.3883
Yinchuan	98.89	83.14	26.85	2,510.14	1,802.54	437.12	4.1237	1.0350
Lanzhou	95.96	68.87	31.81	1,483.75	1,613.49	375.35	4.2986	1.3882
Xining	95.23	52.44	10.64	916.05	1,252.72	350.19	3.5773	1.6223
Urumqi	97.53	66.60	40.71	1,488.55	1,453.22	304.31	4.7755	1.3863
Chongqing	95.50	73.74	394.98	1,874.13	1,632.59	460.83	3.5427	1.2273
Chengdu	97.83	77.36	154.85	2,684.86	1,853.15	371.56	4.9875	1.1070
Guiyang	97.45	79.60	51.65	2,221.88	1,679.46	260.69	6.4424	1.0839
Nanning	97.74	87.90	79.68	2,514.35	1,927.74	287.40	6.7074	1.0367
Kunming	101.31	81.83	84.92	2,942.08	1,636.83	341.81	4.7887	1.2131
Lhasa	97.45	43.49	1.85	790.00	576.12	50.76	11.3487	1.6743

Note: The national urban areas and each city was calculated according to annual growth averages in related areas from 2005 to 2012 (because data was missing for Lhasa, it was calculated according to annual average growth from 2008 to 2012). The urban-rural gap in the province where each major city is located is also based on average annual growth data from 2005 to 2012. The total estimates do no cover population growth

municipalities is more stringent than evaluation them by province or region. In other words, this is the reason why using municipalities as the status of major cities is not as ideal as using provinces/regions.

Chapter 5
Provincial and Municipal Reports

5.1 Jiangsu: Maintaining First Place in the 2012 Urban and Rural Horizontal Assessment

This report fully shows the growth trends in Jiangsu Province between the years 2000 and 2012 for all related aspects, and fully analyzes and tests Jiangsu's urban and rural cultural consumption demand situation.

5.1.1 Jiangsu's Growth in Urban and Rural Cultural Consumption Demand

5.1.1.1 Change in Cultural Consumption Total Share Values

For changing trends in urban and rural cultural consumption total growth and shares in Jiangsu Province since the year 2000, see Fig. 5.1.

From 2000 to 2012, total cultural consumption in urban and rural Jiangsu grew from 20.236 billion yuan to 132.284 billion yuan, a growth of 112.048 billion yuan, a 12-year total growth of 553.71 %, an average annual growth of 16.94 %, and ranking first among 31 provinces in degree of growth. During the "Tenth Five-Year Plan" period, the average annual growth was 15.34 %; during the "Eleventh Five-Year Plan" period, the average annual growth was 16.35 %; during the first 2 years of the "Twelfth Five-Year Plan" period, the average annual growth rate was 22.56 %. The average annual growth rate during the first 2 years of the "Twelfth Five-Year Plan" period was higher than that during the "Eleventh Five-Year Plan" period by 6.21 percentage points, and higher than that during the "Tenth Five-Year Plan" period by 7.22 percentage points. The highest total growth occurred in 2005,

Y. Wang et al., *Annual Evaluation Report of China's Cultural Consumption Demand*, Research Series on the Chinese Dream and China's Development Path,
DOI 10.1007/978-981-10-0730-9_5

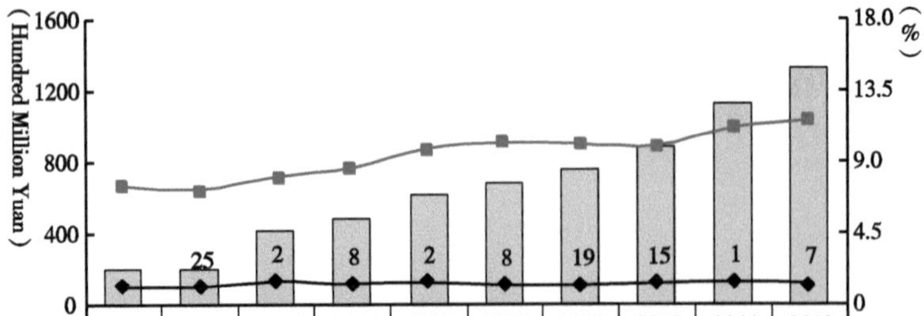

	2000	2001	2005	2006	2007	2008	2009	2010	2011	2012
Total Cultural Consumption	202.36	202.35	413.05	485.99	619.20	683.70	759.49	880.72	1125.92	1322.84
Total Annual Growth Index	100.00	100.00	132.26	117.66	127.41	110.42	111.09	115.96	127.84	117.49
Share of National Total	7.4828	7.2929	8.0570	8.6339	9.8556	10.2094	10.0977	10.0329	11.1189	11.5978

Fig. 5.1 Changing trends in urban and rural cultural consumption total growth and shares in Jiangsu province. *LHS cylindrical*: total urban and rural cultural consumption (hundreds of million yuan); *LHS curve*: annual growth coefficient (previous year = 100, lower than 100 becomes negative growth), marks the provincial/regional rank of annual growth, excluding the year 2000 starting point; *RHS curve*: share of the country's urban and rural areas (%)

with a growth rate of 32.36 %; the lowest total growth occurred during 2001, with a negative growth of 0.0049 %.

Over the same period, the national urban and rural total cultural consumption average annual growth rate was 12.74 %, significantly lower than that of Jiangsu, by 4.20 percentage points. Jiangsu's urban and rural cultural consumption total grew from 7.48 to 11.60 % of the national share, a growth degree of 54.99 %, ranking first place among 31 provinces in terms of growth degree and increase in share.

In the first 2 years of the "Twelfth Five-Year Plan" period, the national urban and rural cultural consumption total average annual growth rate was 13.99 %, and Jiangsu's urban and rural cultural consumption total average annual growth rate was 22.56 %, significantly higher than the national rate by 8.57 percentage points and an increase of 15.60 % in proportion of the national share in comparison to 2010. At the same time, Jiangsu's total growth was higher than its own average annual growth in the "Tenth Five-Year Plan" period by 7.22 percentage points, and was also higher than its own "Eleventh Five-Year Plan" period growth by 6.21 percentage points, and ranked 7th place among 31 provinces/regions in growth degree and in change in proportion of national share.

5.1.1.2 Per Capita Absolute Value Growth in Cultural Consumption

For Jiangsu's urban and rural per capita cultural consumption growth and change in growth degree trends since the year 2000, see Fig. 5.2.

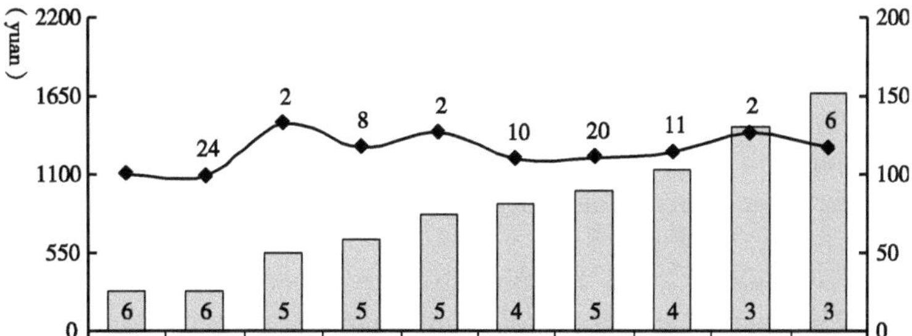

	2000	2001	2005	2006	2007	2008	2009	2010	2011	2012
Per Capita Cultural Consumption	278.35	275.65	554.12	646.91	816.08	893.60	986.22	1129.54	1428.10	1672.49
Annual Growth Coefficient	100.00	99.03	131.65	116.75	126.15	109.50	110.37	114.53	126.43	117.11

Fig. 5.2 Jiangsu's urban and rural Per capita cultural consumption growth and change in growth degree. *LHS cylindrical*: urban-rural per capita cultural consumption (yuan); *RHS curve*: annual growth data (previous year = 100, lower than 100 represents negative growth); annual growth for provinces are ranked, excluding the starting year 2000

From 2000 to 2012, Jiangsu's urban and rural per capita cultural consumption grew from 278.35 to 1,672.49 yuan, a growth of 1,394.14 yuan, a total growth of 500.86 %, an average annual growth of 16.12 %, and a degree of growth in first place among 31 provinces. During the "Tenth Five-Year Plan" period, the per capita total growth rate was 99.07 %, with an average annual growth of 14.76 %; during the "Eleventh Five-Year Plan" period, the per capita growth rate was 103.84 %, an average annual growth of 15.31 %. During the "Eleventh Five-Year Plan" period, the average annual growth rate was higher than that during the "Tenth Five-Year Plan" by 0.55 percentage points. The highest per capita growth rate took place during 2005, when there was a growth rate of 31.65 %; the lowest per capita growth rate took place during 2001, when there was a negative growth rate of 0.97 %.

Over the same period, the national urban and rural per capita cultural consumption average annual rate was 12.11 %, significantly lower than that of Jiangsu. Jiangsu's urban and rural per capita cultural consumption grew from being 19.96 % of the national urban and rural per capita value to 198.06 % of it (see Table 6 of this paper for comparison), and its rank among 31 provinces/regions in terms of per capita absolute value went from 6th place to 3rd place.

In the first 2 years of the "Twelfth Five-Year Plan" period, the national urban and rural per capita cultural consumption average annual growth rate was 13.44 %. Jiangsu's growth rate was 21.68 %, significantly higher than the national rate, and also higher than its own average annual growth rate during the "Tenth Five-Year Plan" period, as well as being higher than its own average annual growth rate during the "Eleventh Five-Year Plan" period, and the growth degree ranks in 6th place among 31 provinces and regions.

5.1.2 *Related Background Situation of Jiangsu's Urban and Rural Cultural Consumption*

For trends in relationships in Jiangsu province between per capita GDP and urban and rural per capita income (separating for non-cultural and cultural consumption) and savings, see Fig. 5.3.

From 2000 to 2012, Jiangsu's average annual growth in per capita GDP was 15.79 %; average annual growth in urban and rural per capita income was 13.81 %, lower than the GDP growth by 1.98 percentage points; average annual growth in total per capita consumption was 12.89 %, significantly lower than the per capita GDP growth by 2.90 percentage points, and slightly lower than growth in income by 0.92 percentage points; average annual growth in per capita savings was 15.92 %, slightly higher than GDP growth by 0.13 percentage points, significantly higher than income growth by 2.11 percentage points, and significantly higher than total consumption growth by 3.03 percentage points; average growth of per capita cultural consumption was 16.12 %, slightly higher than GDP growth by 0.33 percentage points, significantly higher than income growth by 2.31 percentage points, significantly higher than total consumption growth by 3.23 percentage points, and slightly higher than savings growth by 0.20 percentage points.

In the first 2 years of the "Twelfth Five-Year Plan" period, Jiangsu's average annual growth in per capita GDP was 13.73 %, average annual growth in urban and rural per capita income was 16.95 %, average annual per capita total consumption was 17.82 %, average annual growth in per capita savings was 15.34 %, and average annual growth in per capita cultural consumption was 21.68 %. The degree of

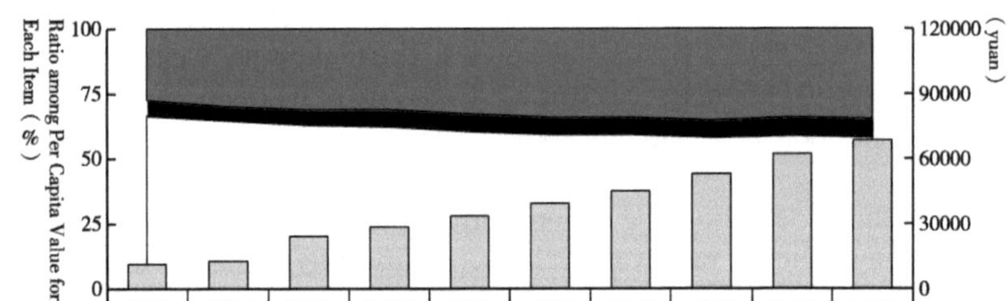

	2000	2001	2005	2006	2007	2008	2009	2010	2011	2012
(1) Per Capita Savings	1346.43	1593.09	2687.85	3094.78	3818.01	4540.50	5056.49	5958.79	6780.53	7927.22
(2) Cultural Consumption	278.35	275.65	554.12	646.91	816.08	893.60	986.22	1129.54	1428.10	1672.49
(3) Non-Cultural Consumption	3267.44	3436.17	5501.92	6290.20	7085.76	8008.98	8856.54	9811.67	11829.28	13515.15
(4) Per Capita GDP	11765.00	12882.00	24560.00	28814.00	33928.00	39622.00	44744.00	52840.00	62290.00	68347.00

Fig. 5.3 Relationship trends between per capita GDP, per capita income, consumption, and savings in Jiangsu Province. *LHS area*: urban and rural per capita savings, cultural consumption, and non-cultural consumption (yuan are converted to %), (1) + (2) + (3) = income, (2) + (3) = total consumption, (1) + (2) = non-cultural consumption surplus. Over the years the values of each indicator exhibited a direct proportion; *RHS cylinder*: per capita GDP (yuan)

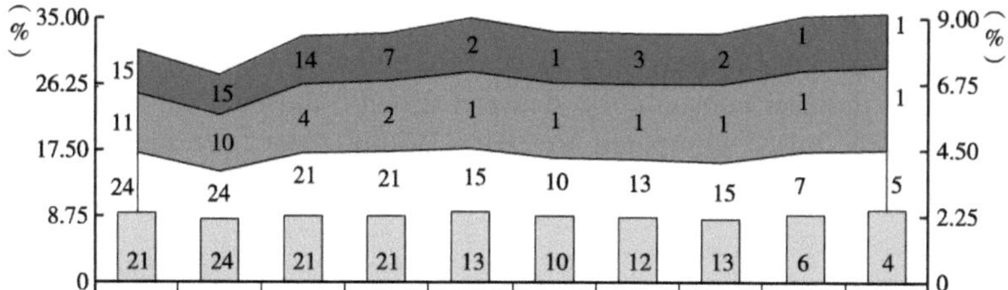

	2000	2001	2005	2006	2007	2008	2009	2010	2011	2012
Proportion of Income	5.6897	5.1962	6.3372	6.4485	6.9633	6.6473	6.6193	6.6837	7.1270	7.2356
Proportion of Total Consumption Ratio	7.8502	7.4263	9.1499	9.3254	10.3277	10.0376	10.0198	10.3237	10.7721	11.0122
Ratio to Non-Surplus	17.1316	14.7507	17.0920	17.2892	17.6104	16.4443	16.3209	15.9352	17.3976	17.4223
Ratio to GDP	2.3659	2.1398	2.2562	2.2451	2.4053	2.2553	2.2041	2.1377	2.2927	2.4471

Fig. 5.4 Changing trends in Jiangsu's urban and rural cultural consumption proportions. *LHS area*: urban and rural per capita cultural consumption as proportion of income, total consumption, and surplus non-cultural consumption (referred to in the graph as "non-surplus") ratio. The annual rise of each indicators proportion is superimposed. *RHS cylinder*: ratio of urban and rural per capita cultural consumption and GDP (%). Sorted by annual ratios for each indicator and by province/region

average annual growth in cultural consumption was higher than degree of GDP growth by 7.95 percentage points, higher than degree of income growth by 4.73 percentage points, higher than degree of growth in total consumption by 3.86 percentage points, and higher than degree of growth in savings by 6.34 percentage points. The ratio relationship between cultural consumption and various aspects shows an overall trend of increase.

All of this was shown in the analysis and calculation of related ratios of Jiangsu Province's urban and rural per capita cultural consumption. For changing trends in Jiangsu's urban and rural cultural consumption proportions since the year 2000, see Fig. 5.4.

5.1.2.1 Ratio of Per Capita Cultural Consumption to Per Capita GDP

From 2000 to 2012, the proportion of Jiangsu's urban and rural per capita cultural consumption in per capita GDP increased from 2.37 % to 2.45 %, and increased from 20th to 4th place in a ranking of 31 provinces and regions. Looking at the years listed in Table 4, this indicator ratio increased in the years 2005, 2007, and from 2011 to 2012, and decreased in the other years. Jiangsu's urban and rural ratio of this indicator increased to 3.43 %, and its degree of change was ranked 2nd place out of 31 provinces and regions.

Looking at each time period, Jiangsu's ratio for this indicator during the "Tenth Five-Year Plan" period decreased by 0.11 percentage points; during the "Eleventh Five-Year Plan" period it decreased by 0.12 percentage points. During the first

2 years of the "Twelfth Five-Year Plan" period, Jiangsu's urban and rural ratio for this indicator increased by 0.31 percentage points, a 14.47 % increase, and coordination of cultural consumption demand growth and economic development was significantly raised compared to 2010. Within these, the highest value was in 2002 at 2.48 %, and the lowest value was in 2004 at 2.08 %.

5.1.2.2 Proportion of Per Capita Income Comprised of Per Capita Cultural Consumption

From 2000 to 2012, Jiangsu's proportion of per capita income made up of per capita cultural consumption in urban and rural areas increased from 5.69 % to 7.24 %, increasing in rank from 15th place to 1st place among 31 provinces. Looking at the listed years in Chart 4, this indicator ratio increased in 2005–1007 and 2010–2012, and decreased during the other years. Jiangsu's urban and rural proportion for this indicator is 27.17 %, and the degree of change ranked 1st place out of 31 provinces and regions.

Looking at different time periods, Jiangsu's indicator for this ratio in urban and rural areas during the "Tenth Five-Year Period" increased by 0.65 percentage points; during the "Eleventh Five-Year Plan" it increased by 0.35 percentage points. During the first 2 years of the "Twelfth Five-Year Plan" period, Jiangsu's ratio for this indicator in urban and rural areas increased by 0.55 percentage points, with a degree of increase of 8.26 %, and the coordination of cultural consumption demand growth with income growth was significantly higher than that in 2010. The highest value was in 2012 at 7.24 %, and the lowest was in 2001 at 5.20 %.

5.1.2.3 Proportion of Total Per Capita Consumption Made Up by Per Capita Cultural Consumption

From 2000 to 2012, Jiangsu's proportion of per capita total consumption comprised of per capita cultural consumption in urban and rural areas grew from 7.85 to 11.01 %, moving from 11th place to 1st place among 31 provinces and regions. In looking at the list of years in Table 4, this indicator value increased from 2005 to 2007 and from 2010 to 2012, while decreasing in the other years. Jiangsu's urban and rural proportion for this indicator was 40.28 %, ranking 1st place in degree of change among 31 provinces.

Looking at each time period, during the "Tenth Five-Year Plan" Jiangsu's proportion for this indicator in urban and rural areas increased by 1.30 percentage points; during the "Eleventh Five-Year Period" it increased 1.17 percentage points. During the first 2 years of the "Twelfth Five-Year Plan" period, Jiangsu's proportion for this indicator in urban and rural areas increased by 0.69 percentage points, with a degree of increase of 6.67 %; the coordination of cultural consumption demand and total consumption growth was significantly higher than that in 2010. The highest value was in 2012 at 11.01 %, and the lowest was in 2001 at 7.43 %.

5.1.2.4 Ratio of Per Capita Cultural Consumption and Non-cultural Consumption Surplus

From 2000 to 2012, Jiangsu's proportion of per capita cultural consumption and per capita non-cultural consumption surplus in urban and rural areas increased from 17.13 to 17.42 %, moving from 24th place to 5 place among 31 provinces and regions. Looking at the years listed in Chart 4, the ratio for this indicator increased during 2005–2007 and 2011–2012, and decreased during the other years. The ratio for this indicator increased by 1.70 % in Jiangsu's urban and rural areas, and the degree of change ranked 1st place among 31 provinces and regions.

Looking at each time period, this indicator ratio in Jiangsu's urban and rural areas during the "Tenth Five-Year Plan" period decreased by 0.04 percentage points; during the "Eleventh Five-Year Plan" it decreased by 1.16 percentage points. During the first 2 years of the "Twelfth Five-Year Plan" period, this indicator ratio in Jiangsu's urban and rural areas increased by 1.49 percentage points, with a degree of increase of 9.33 %, and the coordination of cultural consumption demand growth and growth of "surplus funds" other than "essential consumption" was significantly higher than that in 2010. The highest value was in 2007 at 17.61 %, and the lowest was in 2001 at 14.75 %.

5.1.3 Urban/Rural and Regional Cultural Consumption Coordination in Jiangsu Province

5.1.3.1 Urban-Rural Ratio of Per Capita Cultural Consumption

For changing trends in Jiangsu's urban-to-rural ratio of per capita cultural consumption since the year 2000, see Fig. 5.5.

From 2000 to 2012, Jiangsu's urban-to-rural ratio of per capita cultural consumption expanded from 1.0860 to 1.6603, and because the urban-to-rural ratio of cultural consumption of other provinces or regions experienced more extreme expansions, Jiangsu's urban-to-rural ratio went up from 9th place to 4th place among 31 provinces and regions. The lowest urban-to-rural ratio was in 2001 at 0.9764, and the highest urban rural ratio was in 2012 at 1.6603. In looking at the list of years in Fig. 5.4, the urban-to-rural ratios in 2001 and 2008–2009 were reduced, while they were expanded in all other years. Since the "Tenth Five-Year Plan" period, Jiangsu's urban-to-rural ratio in cultural consumption expanded by 52.88 %, ranked 15th place out of 31 provinces and regions in urban-to-rural ratio change. This means that Jiangsu is one of the provinces or regions with the largest degree of urban-to-rural ratio changes.

While Jiangsu's urban-to-rural ratio in cultural consumption experienced changes, it also felt the dynamic effects of its own urban and rural areas. Over the same period, Jiangsu's urban and rural per capita cultural consumption grew from 292.12 to 1,966.12 yuan, a 573.05 % growth within the 12 years, and an average

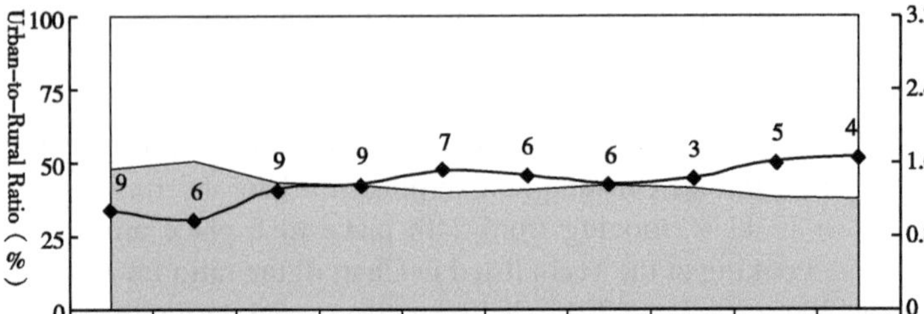

	2000	2001	2005	2006	2007	2008	2009	2010	2011	2012
Urban Per Capita	292.12	271.87	631.62	745.63	972.80	1048.78	1123.75	1301.54	1689.87	1966.12
Rural Per Capita	268.99	278.43	478.94	544.14	642.52	713.23	818.45	908.10	1044.64	1184.18
Jiangsu's Urban and Rural Per Capita	1.0860	0.9764	1.3188	1.3703	1.5140	1.4705	1.3730	1.4333	1.6177	1.6603

Fig. 5.5 Changing trends in Jiangsu's urban-to-rural ratio of per capita cultural consumption. *LHS area*: urban and rural per capita cultural consumption (yuan are converted to %), the Ratio to direct annual increase between urban and rural areas; *RHS curve*: urban-to-rural ratio of per capita cultural consumption (rural = 1, a number lower than 1 signifies an "urban-rural reversal", that is, the urban per capita is lower than that of the rural areas), and provinces and regions are ranked by annual urban-to-rural ratio

annual growth rate of 17.22 %. Urban per capita values had the highest growth in 2002, with a growth rate of 45.48 %; the lowest growth was in 2001, with a negative growth rate of 6.93 %. Rural per capita cultural consumption grew from 268.99 to 1,184.18 yuan, a growth of 915.19 yuan, a total 12-year growth of 340.23 %, and an average annual growth rate of 13.15 %. Rural per capita values had the highest growth in 2005, with a growth rate of 28.27 %; the lowest growth was in 2005, with a negative growth of 1.52 %. Jiangsu's average annual growth in its urban per capita cultural consumption demand was significantly higher than growth in rural areas, by 4.07 percentage points, resulting in a significant expansion in Jiangsu's urban-to-rural ratio of cultural consumption demand.

In the first 2 years of the "Twelfth Five-Year Plan" period, Jiangsu's average annual growth rate of urban per capita cultural consumption was 22.91 %, higher than that during the "Tenth Five-Year Plan" period by 6.23 percentage points, and also higher than that during the "Eleventh Five-Year Plan" period by 7.35 percentage points; the average annual growth rate of rural per capita cultural consumption was 14.19 %, higher than that during the "Tenth Five-Year Plan" period by 1.96 percentage points, and also higher than that during the "Eleventh Five-Year Plan" period by 0.54 percentage points. During this time, Jiangsu's urban per capita values were higher than rural ones, and the urban annual degree of growth was significantly higher than the rural growth degree, by 8.72 percentage points, signifying the expansion of the urban-rural gap. Jiangsu's urban-to-rural ratio in cultural consumption was significantly expanded compared to 2010, by 15.84 %, and Jiangsu was ranked 4th out of 31 provinces and regions in terms of urban-to-rural ratio.

5.1.3.2 Regional Discrepancies in Urban and Rural Per Capita Cultural Consumption

For changing trends in Jiangsu's urban and rural per capita cultural consumption and national regional discrepancies since the year 2000, see Fig. 5.6.

From 2000 to 2012, Jiangsu's urban and rural per capita cultural consumption and national urban and rural regional discrepancies expanded from 1.2996 to 1.9806, decreasing in rank from 21st to 29th place among 31 provinces and regions. The lowest regional discrepancy took place in 2004 at 1.2354, and the highest regional discrepancy was in 2012 at 1.9806. The list of years in Fig. 5.6 shows that the regional discrepancies in 2001 and from 2009 to 2010 were reduced, while they were expanded for all other years. Since the "Tenth Five-Year Plan" period, Jiangsu's urban and rural cultural consumption regional discrepancy expanded by 52.40 %, ranking in 31st place among 31 provinces and regions in terms of degree of change in regional discrepancies. This means that Jiangsu was one of the provinces with the largest degrees of change in regional discrepancies in urban and rural cultural consumption.

Jiangsu's urban and rural cultural consumption discrepancies changes, are dynamic in terms the province as well as the nation. For a comparison of detailed calculations of urban and rural per capita cultural consumption annual growth of Jiangsu Province as well as the nation, see Chapter One on Per Capita Absolute Values in this paper, which places an emphasis on examining the growth in discrepancies. From 2000 to 2012, Jiangsu's urban and rural per capita average annual growth in cultural consumption was significantly higher than the national growth, by 4.01 percentage points. The regional discrepancy of Jiangsu's urban and

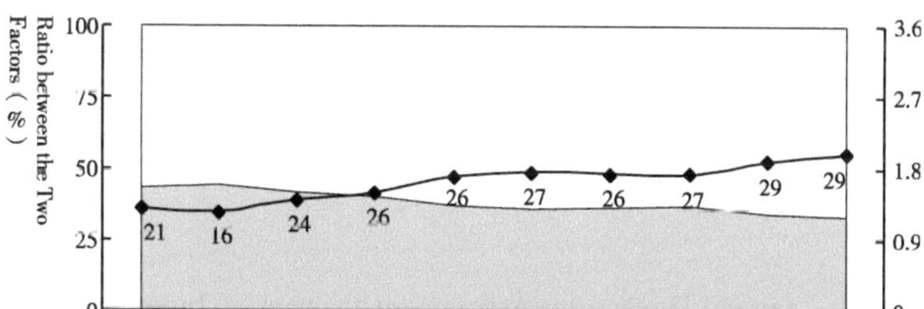

	2000	2001	2005	2006	2007	2008	2009	2010	2011	2012
Jiangsu's Urban and Rural Per Capita	278.35	275.65	554.12	646.91	816.08	893.60	986.22	1129.54	1428.10	1672.49
National Urban and Rural Per Capita	214.18	218.16	393.23	429.35	476.73	505.55	564.94	656.16	753.36	844.45
Urban–Rural Gap	1.2996	1.2636	1.4092	1.5067	1.7118	1.7676	1.7457	1.7214	1.8956	1.9806

Fig. 5.6 Jiangsu's urban and rural per capita cultural consumption and changing trends in national regional discrepancies. *LHS area*: urban and rural per capita cultural consumption (yuan are converted to %), direct ratio to local and national annual data; *RHS curve*: regional discrepancies in urban and rural per capita cultural consumption (no discrepancy = 1), annual regional discrepancies ranked by province and region

rural cultural consumption demand and that of the nation was expanded significantly.

In the first 2 years of the “Twelfth Five-Year Plan” period, Jiangsu’s urban and rural per capita cultural consumption annual growth was higher than its average annual growth during the “Tenth Five-Year Plan” by 6.92 percentage points, and also higher than its average annual growth during the “Eleventh Five-Year Plan” period by 6.37 percentage points; it was also significantly higher than national growth, by 8.24 percentage points. During this period, Jiangsu’s urban and rural per capita value was higher than the national urban and rural average value; its growth being higher than the national growth means that the regional discrepancy had expanded, and the national urban and rural regional discrepancy compared to that in 2012 was expanded significantly, by 15.06 %, with a ranking in regional discrepancy of 29th place out of 31 provinces and regions.

5.1.4 Assessment of Prosperity in Jiangsu’s Urban and Rural Cultural Consumption Demand

In the above overall analysis: Jiangsu’s overall urban and rural cultural consumption average annual growth since the “Tenth Five-Year Plan” period was significantly higher than the national growth, and per capita average annual growth was significantly higher than national average annual growth; the relative proportions show a slight rising trend, with each indicator proportion’s change during the “Eleventh Five-Year Plan Period” not being as great as those during the “Tenth Five-Year Plan” period; the urban-to-rural ratio was expanded significantly, and was very much expanded compared to the national urban and rural regional discrepancies. All of these findings were realized in the assessment and calculation of Jiangsu’s urban and rural cultural consumption demand prosperity index. For changing trends in Jiangsu’s urban and rural cultural consumption demand prosperity index since the year 2000, see Fig. 5.7.

5.1.4.1 Annual Horizontal Assessment Prosperity Index

With the national urban and rural cultural consumption overall share value, per capita absolute value, and proportion of each index as a base, and balanced by the “ideal value” of 100 of no discrepancy between urban/rural areas and regions, Jiangsu’s urban and rural prosperity index for 2012 was 102.73, higher than the ideal value by 2.73, and also higher than the previous year by 1.15. In a ranking of all 31 provinces and regions, Jiangsu’s urban and rural prosperity index for this indicator was ranked 14th place in the year 2000, 12th place in 2005, 2nd place in 2010, and the year 2012 was the same as the previous year, both 1st place.

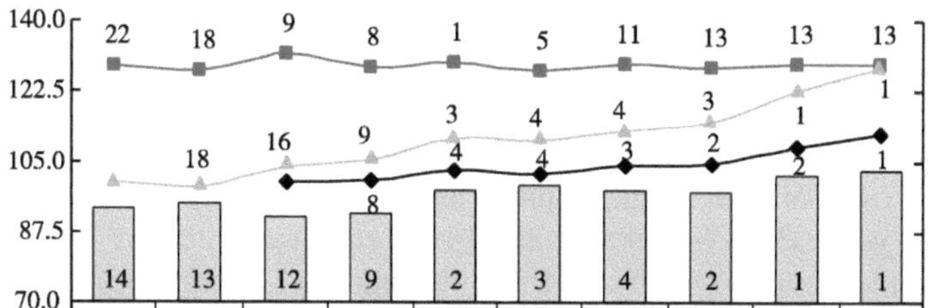

	2000	2001	2005	2006	2007	2008	2009	2010	2011	2012
Horizontal Assessment	93.06	94.33	91.10	91.83	97.54	98.96	97.93	97.15	101.58	102.73
Vertical Assessment (1)	100.00	98.46	103.70	105.27	110.45	110.11	112.71	114.90	122.57	128.58
Vertical Assessment (2)	0.00	0.00	100.00	100.29	102.89	101.90	103.85	104.39	108.34	111.71
Vertical Assessment (3)	100.59	98.46	105.53	100.29	102.00	98.81	101.84	99.88	101.65	101.32

Fig. 5.7 Changing trends in Jiangsu's urban and rural cultural consumption demand prosperity index. *LHS cylindrical*: horizontal assessment (ideal value for no discrepancy between urban/rural areas, regions = 100); *LHS curve*: vertical assessment (starting year base value =100), (*1*) starting year is 2000 (*2*) starting year is 2005; *RHS curve*: vertical assessment (*3*) starting from previous year. Assessed indexes for marked years are ranked in terms of provinces and regions

5.1.4.2 Vertical Assessment Prosperity Index Since the "Tenth Five-Year Plan" Period

With the year 2000, the last year of the "Ninth Five-Year Plan" period, having a starting base value of 100, Jiangsu's urban and rural prosperity index for this indicator for 2012 was 128.58, higher than the year 2000 starting base value by 28.58, and also higher than the previous year by 6.01. In a ranking of 31 provinces and regions, Jiangsu's urban and rural prosperity index was ranked 18th place in 2001, 16th place in 2005, 3rd place in 2010, and the year 2012 was the same as the previous year, both 1st place.

5.1.4.3 Vertical Assessment Prosperity Index Since the "Eleventh Five-Year Plan" Period

Setting the starting base value of 2005, the last year of the "Tenth Five-Year Plan" period, as 100, Jiangsu's urban and rural prosperity index for this indicator in 2012 was 111.71, higher than the starting base value for 2005 by 11.71, and also higher than the previous year by 3.37. Among 31 provinces and regions, Jiangsu's urban and rural prosperity index for this indicator was ranked 8th place in 2006, 2nd place in 2010, and in 2012 moved to first place from second place the year before.

5.1.4.4 Vertical Assessment of Prosperity Index Since the "Eleventh Five-Year Plan" Period

Setting 2010, the last year of the "Eleventh Five-Year Plan" period, with a starting base value of 100, Jiangsu's urban and rural prosperity index for this indicator in 2012 was 103.49, higher than the 2010 starting base value by 3.49, and also higher than the previous year by 1.84. In a ranking of 31 provinces and regions, Jiangsu's urban and rural prosperity index for this indicator ranked 13th in 2011, and fell to 14th place in 2012. This evaluation index is better explained by text than in a table; see Report B3 on the provincial and regional urban and rural ranking.

5.1.4.5 Annual Vertical Assessment of Prosperity Index

Setting the previous year, 2011, with a starting base value of 100, Jiangsu's urban and rural prosperity index for this indicator for 2012 was 101.32, higher than the 2011 starting base value by 1.32. In a ranking of 31 provinces and regions, Jiangsu's urban and rural prosperity index was ranked 22nd in the year 2000, 9th in 2005, 13th in 2010, and in 2012, 13th place (the same as the year before).

Jiangsu: Remaining in the First in the 2012 Horizontal Urban and Rural Status Assessment

5.2 Tianjin: Rising to the Top of the 2012 Urban and Rural Vertical Assessment of Prosperity Index

This paper fully shows growth trends across all related aspects in Tianjin from 2000 to 2012, and fully analyzes and assesses Tianjin's urban and rural cultural consumption demand situation.

5.2.1 Tianjin's Urban and Rural Cultural Consumption Demand Growth

5.2.1.1 Changes in Cultural Consumption Total Share Value

For changing trends in Total growth in cultural consumption and shares in Tianjin's urban and rural areas since 2000, see Fig. 5.8.

From 2000 to 2012, Tianjin's urban and rural total cultural consumption grew from 3.417 billion yuan to 16.917 billion yuan, an increase of 13.5 billion, a total growth of 395.08 % over 12 years, an average annual growth rate of 14.26 %, and rank of 6th place out of 31 provinces and regions in terms of growth degree. The

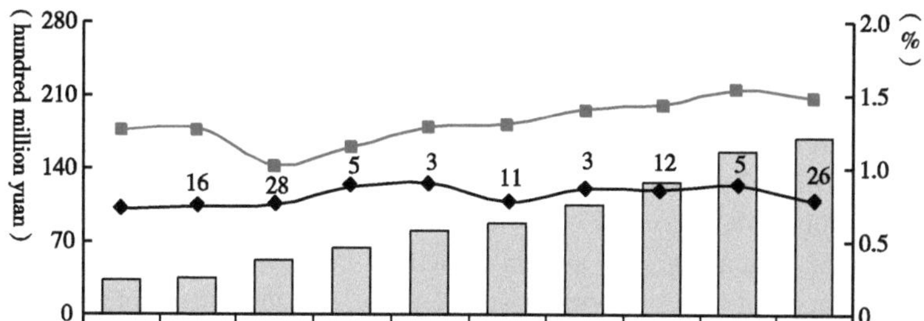

	2000	2001	2005	2006	2007	2008	2009	2010	2011	2012
Total Cultural Consumption	34.17	35.38	52.42	64.33	80.30	87.23	105.51	126.22	155.74	169.17
Total Annual Growth Coefficient	100.00	103.54	104.57	122.72	124.83	108.63	120.96	119.63	123.39	108.62
Share of National Total	1.2635	1.2751	1.0225	1.1429	1.2781	1.3026	1.4028	1.4379	1.5380	1.4832

Fig. 5.8 Changing trends in total growth in Tianjin's urban and rural cultural consumption and shares. *LHS cylindrical*: total amount in urban and rural cultural consumption (hundred million yuan); *LHS curve*: annual growth coefficient (previous year = 100), annual growth is ranked by province or region, not counting the starting year of 2000; *RHS curve*: portion of national urban and rural share (%)

average annual growth during the "Tenth Five-Year Plan" period was 8.94 %; during the "Eleventh Five-Year Plan" period it was 19.21 %; and during the first 2 years of the "Twelfth Five-Year Plan" period it was 15.77 %. Average annual growth during the first 2 years of the "Twelfth Five-Year Plan" period was 3.44 percentage points lower than that during the "Eleventh Five-Year Plan" period and higher than the "Tenth Five-Year Plan" period by 6.83 percentage points. The highest total growth occurred in 2007, with a growth rate of 24.83 %; the lowest growth rate occurred in 2003, with a negative growth of 0.16 %.

Over the same period, the total average annual growth rate of national urban and rural cultural consumption was 12.74 %, significantly lower than Tianjin's, by 1.52 percentage points. Tianjin's urban and rural cultural consumption as proportion of the entire nation's share increased from 1.26 % to 1.48 %, an increase of 17.38 %, a growth degree and proportion increase that was in 6th place among 31 provinces and regions.

During the first 2 years of the "Twelfth Five-Year Plan" period, national urban and rural total cultural consumption had an average annual growth of 13.99 %, and Tianjin's urban and rural total cultural consumption had an average annual growth of 15.77 %, significantly higher than the national growth by 1.78 percentage points, and growing to 3.15 % of the total country share. At the same time, Tianjin's total growth was higher than its growth during the "Tenth Five-Year Plan" period average annual growth by 6.83 percentage points, but lower than its own growth during the "Eleventh Five-Year Plan" period average annual growth by 3.44 percentage points. Tianjin's degree of growth and the proportion of total country share came in 26th place among a ranking of 31 provinces and regions.

5.2.1.2 Growth in Per Capita Absolute Values in Cultural Consumption

For Tianjin's urban and rural per capita cultural consumption growth and changing trends in growth degree, see Fig. 5.9.

From 2000 to 2012, Tianjin's urban and rural per capita cultural consumption grew from 348.67 to 1,222.22 yuan, an increase of 873.55 yuan, a total growth of 250.54 %, and an average annual growth of 11.02 %; the growth degree was ranked 18th place out of 31 provinces and regions. Among these, total per capita growth during the "Tenth Five-Year Plan" period increased by 45.48 %, with an average annual growth rate of 7.79 %; total per capita growth during the "Eleventh Five-Year Plan" period was 96.91 %, with an average annual growth rate of 14.51 %. The average annual growth rate during the "Eleventh Five-Year Plan" was higher than that during the "Tenth Five-Year Plan" by 6.72 percentage points. Growth in per capita values were highest during the year 2002, with a growth rate of 21.90 %; the year of the least growth was 2003, with a negative growth of 0.53 %.

Over the same period, the average annual national urban and rural per capita cultural consumption growth was 12.11 %, relatively higher than that in Tianjin. Tianjin's urban and rural per capita cultural consumption decreased from a national urban and rural per capita value of 162.79 % to 144.74 % (see Fig. 5.13 in this paper for a comparison); its rank among 31 provinces and regions in per capita absolute value went down to 6th place from 5th place.

During the first 2 years of the "Twelfth Five-Year Plan" period, the average annual growth rate in national urban and rural per capita cultural consumption was 13.44 %, and Tianjin's average annual growth rate was 10.62 %, significantly lower than the national rate yet higher than its own average annual growth rate during the "Tenth Five-Year Plan" period, lower than its own average annual growth rate

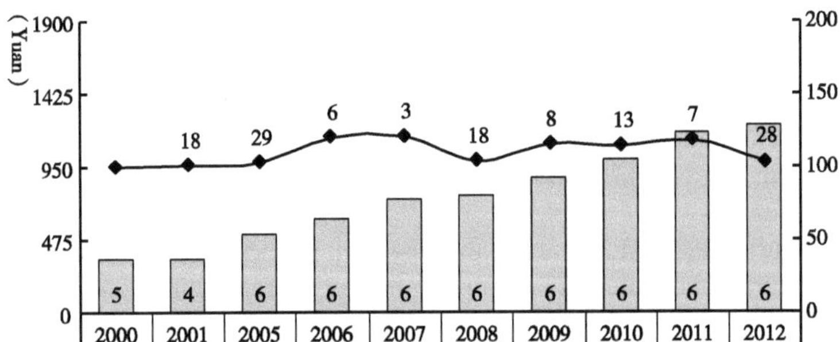

	2000	2001	2005	2006	2007	2008	2009	2010	2011	2012
Per Capita Cultural Consumption	348.67	353.00	507.25	607.49	733.38	761.54	877.77	998.83	1173.53	1222.22
Annual Growth Coefficient	100.00	101.24	102.96	119.76	120.72	103.84	115.26	113.79	117.49	104.15

Fig. 5.9 Changing trends in Tianjin's urban and rural per capita cultural consumption growth and growth degree. *LHS cylindrical*: urban per capita cultural consumption (yuan); *RHS curve*: annual growth value (previous year = 100), marks ranking of annual growth of provinces and regions, not counting the 2000 starting year

during the "Eleventh Five-Year Plan" period, with a growth rate ranking 28th out of 31 provinces and regions.

5.2.2 *Related Background Situation of Tianjin's Urban and Rural Cultural Consumption*

For trends in the relationships between Tianjin's per capita GDP and urban and rural per capita income, consumption (separated into non-cultural and cultural consumption), and savings, see Fig. 5.10.

From 2000 to 2012, the average annual growth in Tianjin's per capita GDP was 15.03 %; average annual growth in urban and rural per capita income was 11.99 %, significantly lower than GDP growth, by 3.04 percentage points; average annual growth in per capita total consumption grew 13.65 %, fairly significantly lower than GDP growth by 1.38 percentage points, fairly significantly higher than income growth, by 1.66 percentage points, and significantly higher than total consumption growth, by 2.38 percentage points; the average annual growth in per capita cultural consumption was 11.02 %, notably lower than GDP growth, by 4.01 percentage points, slightly lower than income growth by 0.97 percentage points, slightly lower than total consumption growth by 0.25 percentage points, significantly lower than savings growth by 2.63 percentage points.

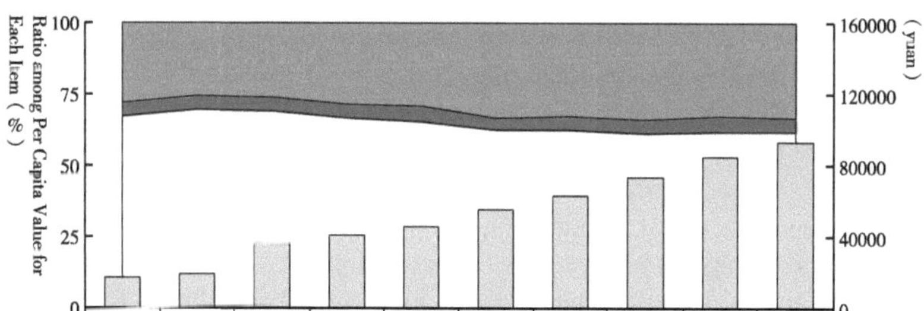

	2000	2001	2005	2006	2007	2008	2009	2010	2011	2012
(1) Per Capita Savings	1907.66	1950.81	2874.11	3526.58	4123.09	5555.44	6111.39	7169.92	7905.51	8860.07
(2) Cultural Consumption	348.67	353.00	507.25	607.49	733.38	761.54	877.77	998.83	1173.53	1222.22
(3) Non-Cultural Consumption	4597.83	5267.45	7479.22	8169.14	9260.09	10432.37	11567.43	13047.96	14866.19	16585.54
(4) Per Capita GDP	17353.00	19141.00	35783.00	41163.00	46122.00	55473.00	62574.00	72994.00	85213.00	93173.00

Fig. 5.10 Relationships between Tianjin's per capita GDP and urban and rural per capita income, consumption, and savings. *LHS area*: urban and rural per capita savings, cultural consumption, non-cultural consumption (yuan are converted to %). (1) + (2) + (3) = income, (2) + (3) = total consumption, (1) + (2) = non-cultural consumption surplus. There was a direct increase in ratio throughout the years; *RHS cylinder*: per capita GDP (yuan)

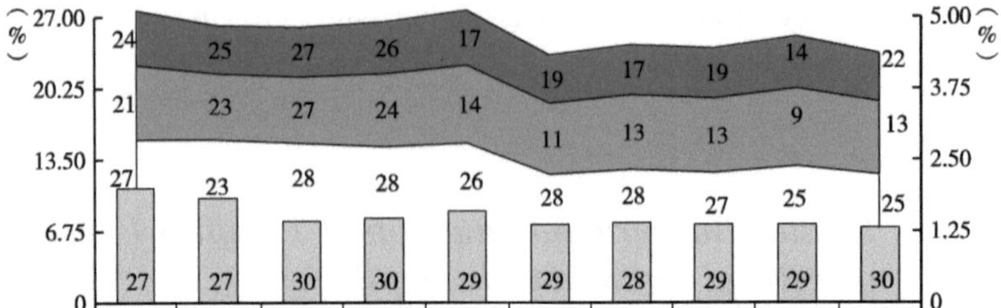

	2000	2001	2005	2006	2007	2008	2009	2010	2011	2012
Proportion of Income	5.0870	4.6624	4.6705	4.9377	5.1951	4.5467	4.7303	4.7077	4.9009	4.5831
Proportion of Total Consumption	7.0489	6.2807	6.3513	6.9217	7.3386	6.8032	7.0531	7.1107	7.3164	6.8634
Ratio to Non-Surplus	15.4531	15.3225	15.0013	14.6948	15.1010	12.0555	12.5591	12.2274	12.9257	12.1225
Ratio to GDP	2.0093	1.8442	1.4176	1.4758	1.5901	1.3728	1.4028	1.3684	1.3772	1.3118

Fig. 5.11 Changing trends in Tianjin's urban and rural cultural consumption proportions. *LHS area*: urban and rural per capita cultural consumption as proportion of income, proportion of total consumption, and non-cultural consumption surplus (called "non-surplus" in the figure) proportion (%). Each annual proportion's rise or fall is superimposed. *RHS cylinder*: ratio of urban and rural per capita cultural consumption and GDP(%). Each proportion of the indicated years is ranked by province or region

During the first 2 years of the "Twelfth Five-Year Plan" period, Tianjin's average annual growth in per capita GDP was 12.98 %, its average annual growth in urban and rural per capita income was 12.11 %, its average annual growth in per capita total consumption was 12.59 %, its average annual growth in per capita savings was 11.16 %, and its average annual growth in per capita cultural consumption was 10.62 %. The average annual degree of growth in cultural consumption was lower than the degree of growth of GDP by 2.36 percentage points, lower than the degree of growth in income by 1.49 percentage points, lower than the degree of growth in total consumption by 1.97 percentage points, and lower than the degree of growth in savings by 0.54 percentage points. The proportional relationship between cultural consumption and various factors completely showed a declining trend.

All of this was realized when doing analysis and calculation for Tianjin's urban and rural cultural consumption's related proportions. For the changing situation of proportions of Tianjin's urban and rural cultural consumption see Fig. 5.11.

5.2.2.1 Ratio of Per Capita Cultural Consumption to Per Capita GDP

From 2000 to 2012, the proportion of Tianjin's urban and rural per capita cultural consumption as part of per capita GDP decreased from 2.01 % to 1.31 %.

Looking at this across time periods, Tianjin's urban and rural ratios in this indicator decreased by 0.59 percentage points during the "Tenth Five-Year Plan" period; during the "Eleventh Five-Year Plan" period they decreased by 0.05 percentage points. During the first 2 years of the "Twelfth Five-Year Plan" period, these indicator ratios for Tianjin's urban and rural areas decreased by 0.06 percentage points, with a degree of decrease of 4.14 %; the coordination of cultural consumption demand growth and economic development was slightly decreased from that in 2010. The highest value was in 2002 at 2.01 %, and the lowest was in 2012 at 1.31 %.

5.2.2.2 Per Capita Cultural Consumption as Proportion of Per Capita Income

From 2000 to 2012, the proportion of per capita income made up of per capita cultural consumption in urban and rural areas in Tianjin decreased from 5.09 % to 4.58 %. Because the decrease in proportion of other provinces and regions was more obvious, Tianjin's ranking fell from 24th place to 22nd place. When looking at the years listed in Fig. 5.11, this indicator proportion showed increases from 2005 to 2007, in 2009, and in 2011, while all other years showed decreases. Since the "Tenth Five-Year Plan" period, Tianjin's urban and rural proportion for this indicator decreased by 9.91 %, and its degree of change was ranked 10th place among 31 provinces and regions.

Looking at it across time periods, this indicator proportion for Tianjin's urban and rural areas decreased by 0.42 percentage points during the "Tenth Five-Year Plan" period; during the "Eleventh Five-Year Plan" period it increased 0.04 percentage points. During the first 2 years of the "Twelfth Five-Year Plan" period, Tianjin's urban and rural areas' proportion for this indicator decreased by 0.12 percentage points, a degree of increase of 2.65 %. The coordination of cultural consumption demand growth and income growth was slightly decreased from 2010. The highest value was in 2002 at 5.40 %, and the lowest was in 2008 at 4.55 %.

5.2.2.3 Per Capita Cultural Consumption as Proportion of Per Capita Total Consumption

From 2000 to 2012, Tianjin's urban and rural per capita cultural consumption as proportion of per capita total consumption fell from 7.05 % to 6.86 %; because the proportion decrease of other provinces or regions was more obvious, Tianjin went up from 21st place to 13th place. Looking at the years listed in Fig. 5.11, we see that from 2005 to 2007 and from 2009 to 2011 this proportion indicator showed an increased, and during the other years in decreased. Since the "Tenth Five-Year Plan" period, Tianjin's proportion indicator in its urban and rural areas decreased by 2.63 %, with a degree of change that placed 14th place among 31 provinces and regions.

Looking across time periods, during the "Tenth Five-Year Plan" period, Tianjin's proportion for this indicator decreased by 0.70 percentage points; during the "Eleventh Five-Year Plan" period, it increased by 0.76 percentage points. During the first 2 years of the "Twelfth Five-Year Plan" period, Tianjin's urban and rural proportion for this indicator decreased by 0.25 percentage points, a degree of decrease of 3.48 %. Coordination of cultural consumption growth and total consumption growth decreased significantly in 2010. During this period, the highest value was seen in 2002 at 7.38 %, and the lowest in 2001 at 6.28 %.

5.2.2.4 Ratio of Per Capita Cultural Consumption to Per Capita Non-cultural Consumption Surplus

From 2000 to 2012, the ratio of Tianjin's urban and rural per capita cultural consumption to per capita non-cultural consumption surplus decreased from 15.45 % to 12.12 %, and because the decreases of other provinces and areas was more obvious, Tianjin went from 27th place to 25th place. When looking at the years listed in Fig. 5.11, this indicator proportion was shown to have increased in 2007, 2009, and 2011, while decreasing during the other years. Since the "Tenth Five-Year Plan" period, Tianjin's proportion of this indicator has decreased by 21.55 %, with a degree of change ranking 10th place among 31 provinces and regions.

Looking across time periods, during the "Tenth Five-Year Plan" period, Tianjin's urban and rural proportion for this indicator decreased by 0.45 percentage points; during the "Eleventh Five-Year Plan" period, it decreased by 2.77 percentage points. During the first 2 years of the "Twelfth Five-Year Plan" period, Tianjin's urban and rural proportion for this indicator fell 0.10 percentage points, a degree of decrease of 0.86 %, with the coordination of cultural consumption growth and growth of "surplus money" outside of "essential consumption" having slightly decreased from 2010. The highest value was seen in 2002 at 16.76 %, and the lowest in 2008 at 12.06 %.

5.2.3 Coordination Situation of Tianjin's Urban and Rural and Regional Cultural Consumption

5.2.3.1 Urban-to-Rural Ratio of Per Capita Cultural Consumption

For changes in Tianjin's urban-to-rural ratio of per capita cultural consumption in the year 2000 see Fig. 5.12.

From 2000 to 2012, Tianjin's urban-to-rural ratio of per capita cultural consumption expanded from 1.6743 to 1.7348, and due to the urban-to-rural ratio of cultural consumption of other provinces or regions experiencing a more serious expansion, Tianjin's urban-to-rural ratio increased from 23rd to 6th place among 31 provinces and regions. The smallest urban-to-rural ratio took place in 2003 at 1.1741, and the largest took place in 2007 at 2.7757. Looking at the years listed in Fig. 5.12, in 2005 and from 2008 to 2012, the urban-to-rural ratio was reduced, and in all other years it expanded. Since the "Tenth Five-Year Plan" period, Tianjin's

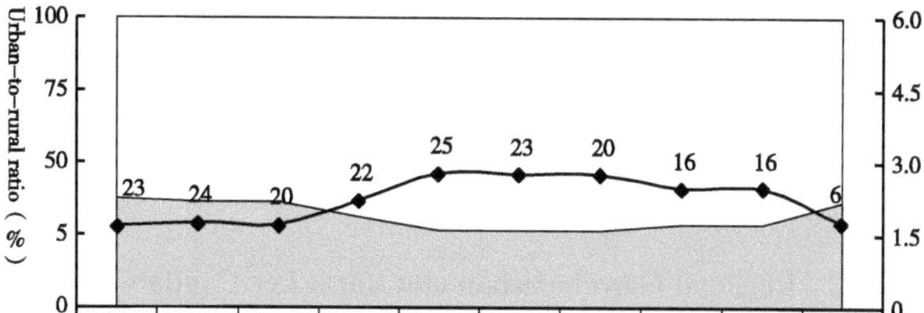

	2000	2001	2005	2006	2007	2008	2009	2010	2011	2012
Urban Per Capita	393.83	399.95	567.31	702.62	866.22	893.73	1023.64	1146.96	1335.16	1328.97
Rural Per Capita	235.22	230.39	328.86	315.59	312.07	324.47	371.85	462.25	542.12	766.08
Tianjin's Urban–to–Rural Ratio	1.6743	1.7360	1.7251	2.2264	2.7757	2.7544	2.7528	2.4813	2.4628	1.7348

Fig. 5.12 Changes in Tianjin's urban-to-rural ratio of per capita cultural consumption. *LHS area*: urban, rural per capita cultural consumption (yuan converted to %), direct proportional relationship between annual urban and rural values; *RHS curve*: urban-to-rural ratio of per capita cultural consumption (rural = 1); years are ranked according to urban-to-rural ratio of provinces or regions

urban-to-rural ratio of cultural consumption has expanded by 3.61 %, and its degree of change in the urban-to-rural ratio was 3rd place among 31 provinces and regions. This signifies that in terms of changes in urban-to-rural ratio of cultural consumption, Tianjin's status is one of the provinces with a relatively good status.

Tianjin's changes in urban-to-rural ratio of cultural consumption were influenced by its own changes both in urban and rural areas. Over this period, Tianjin's urban and rural per capita cultural consumption increased from 292.83 to 1,328.97 yuan, an increase of 935.14 yuan, a 12-year total growth of 237.45 %, and an average annual increase of 10.67 %. The largest urban per capita growth occurred in 2006, with a growth rate of 23.85 %; the lowest growth occurred in 2003, with a negative growth of 9.09 %. Rural per capita cultural consumption grew from 235.22 to 766.08 yuan, an increase of 530.86 yuan, a total 12-year growth of 225.69 %, and an average annual growth of 10.34 %. The largest rural per capita growth occurred in 2012, with a growth rate of 41.31 %; the smallest growth occurred in 2005, with a negative growth of 12.74 %. The average annual growth of Tianjin's urban per capita cultural consumption demand was slightly higher than the rural average annual growth, by 0.33 percentage points, resulting in a slight expansion of Tianjin's urban-to-rural ratio of cultural consumption demand.

During the first 2 years of the "Twelfth Five-Year Plan" period, the average annual growth of Tianjin's urban per capita cultural consumption was 7.64 %, higher than that during the "Tenth Five-Year Plan" period by 0.07 percentage points, but lower than that during the "Eleventh Five-Year Plan" period by 7.48 percentage points; average annual growth in rural per capita cultural consumption was 28.74 %, higher than that during the "Tenth Five-Year Plan" period by 21.81 percentage points, and also higher than that during the "Eleventh Five-Year Plan" period by 21.69 percentage points. Over this time, Tianjin's urban per capita values were higher than the rural ones, and the urban annual growth was noticeably lower than rural growth, by 21.20 percentage points, signifying a reduction of the urban-rural gap. Tianjin's urban-to-rural ratio of cultural consumption was significantly reduced, by 30.09 %, from 2010, and its urban-to-rural ratio was ranked 6th place out of 31 provinces and regions.

5.2.3.2 Regional Gaps in Urban and Rural Per Capita Cultural Consumption

For urban and rural per capita cultural consumption in Tianjin and changing statuses in national regional discrepancies, see Fig. 5.13.

From 2000 to 2012, Tianjin's urban and rural per capita cultural consumption and the national urban and rural regional discrepancy was reduced from 1.6279 to 1.4474, rising from 26th place to 23rd place among 31 provinces and regions. During this time, the smallest regional discrepancy was seen in 2005 at 1.2900, and the largest was seen in 2000 at 1.6279. Looking at the years listed in Table 6, in 2001, 2008, 2010, and 2012, the regional discrepancy was reduced, while in the rest of the years in expanded. Since the "Tenth Five-Year Plan" period, Tianjin's urban and rural cultural consumption regional discrepancy was reduced by 11.09 %, and its degree of change in regional discrepancy was ranked 3rd place out of 31 provinces and regions. This signifies that in terms of changes in regional discrepancy in urban and rural cultural consumption, Tianjin's status is relatively good compared to other provinces and regions.

Tianjin's changes in regional discrepancies in urban and rural cultural consumption are impacted both by its own as well as the national status. For calculations of

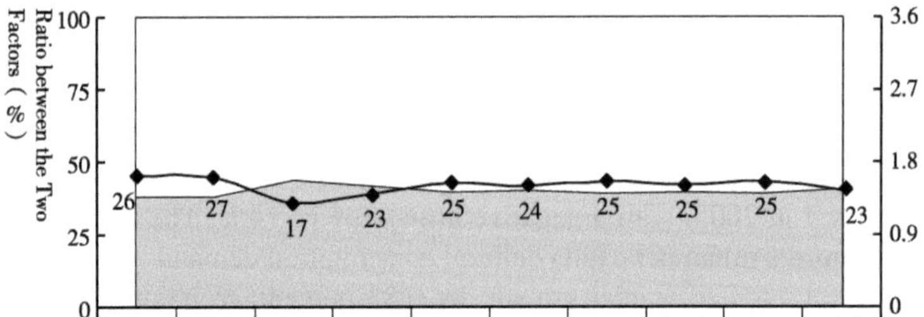

	2000	2001	2005	2006	2007	2008	2009	2010	2011	2012
Tianjin's Urban and Rural Per Capita	348.67	353.00	507.25	607.49	733.38	761.54	877.77	998.83	1173.53	1222.22
National Urban and Rural Per Capita	214.18	218.16	393.23	429.35	476.73	505.55	564.94	656.16	753.36	844.45
Urban–Rural Gap	1.6279	1.6181	1.2900	1.4149	1.5384	1.5064	1.5538	1.5222	1.5577	1.4474

Fig. 5.13 Tianjin's urban and rural per capita cultural consumption and changing status in national regional discrepancies. *LHS area*: urban and rural per capita cultural consumption (yuan are converted to %), annual proportional relationship between regional and national values; *RHS curve*: regional discrepancies in urban and rural per capita cultural consumption (no discrepancy = 1), annual regional discrepancies are ranked by province or region

Tianjin's, as well as the national, annual growth in urban and rural per capita cultural consumption see the first article on per capita absolute values in this paper for a focused inspection of the specific situation of growth discrepancies. From 2000 to 2012, Tianjin's average annual growth degree in urban and rural per capita cultural consumption was obviously lower than the national degree of growth, by 1.09 percentage points, and the regional discrepancies between Tianjin's urban and rural cultural consumption demand and the national cultural consumption demand was significantly reduced.

During the first 2 years of the "Twelfth Five-Year Plan" period, the average annual growth of Tianjin's urban and rural per capita cultural consumption was higher than its average annual growth during the "Tenth Five-Year Plan" period by 2.83 percentage points, but lower than the average annual growth during the "Eleventh Five-Year Plan" period by 3.89 percentage points, and significantly lower than the national growth degree, by 2.82 percentage points. Over this time, Tianjin's urban and rural per capita values were higher than the national urban and rural average values; growth lower than the national growth signifies that the regional discrepancies were reduced, and in comparing the national urban and rural regional discrepancies, there was a significant reduction in 2010 of 4.91 %, with a regional discrepancy rank of 23 out of 31 provinces and regions.

5.2.4 Prosperity Evaluation of Tianjin's Urban and Rural Cultural Consumption

To sum up the above analysis: The average annual growth in Tianjin's urban and rural cultural consumption since the "Tenth Five-Year Plan" period was fairly significantly higher than national growth, and average annual growth in per capita values was significantly lower than the national average annual growth; a broad overview of related proportions reveals a slight downward trend, and when comparing the "Eleventh Five-Year Plan" period with GDP, income ratio, total consumption ratio, the situation of increase and decrease was improved over the "Tenth Five-Year Plan" period, with the changing status of the proportion of surplus not as good as the "Tenth Five-Year Plan" period; the urban-to-rural ratio was expanded slightly, and the national urban-rural regional discrepancy was significantly reduced. All of this is expressed in the evaluation and calculation of Tianjin's urban and rural cultural consumption demand prosperity index. Changes in Tianjin's urban and rural cultural consumption prosperity index since 2000 are shown in Fig. 5.14.

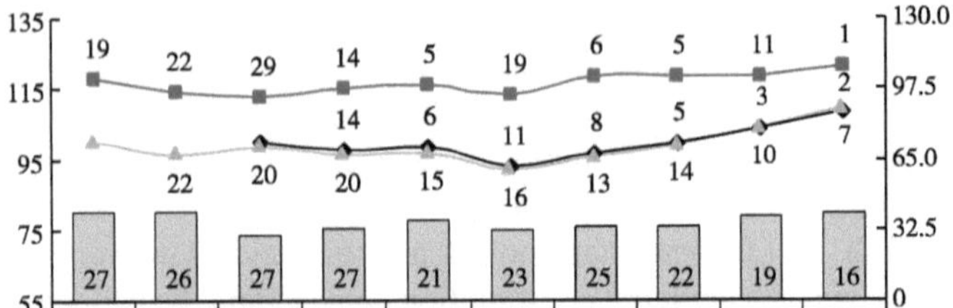

	2000	2001	2005	2006	2007	2008	2009	2010	2011	2012
Horizontal Assessment	80.23	80.00	73.64	75.42	77.54	74.72	75.78	75.70	78.45	79.50
Vertical Assessment (1)	100.00	96.34	98.51	96.04	96.53	92.02	95.54	99.23	103.90	109.51
Vertical Assessment (2)	—	—	100.00	97.79	98.55	93.09	96.51	99.56	103.76	108.62
Vertical Assessment (3)	102.31	96.34	93.49	97.79	99.15	95.00	102.77	103.29	103.02	107.81

Fig. 5.14 Changing status of Tianjin's urban and rural cultural consumption demand. *LHS cylindrical*: horizontal assessment (urban/rural, regional zero-difference ideal value = 100); *LHS curve*: vertical assessment (starting base value = 100), (*1*) starting value for the year 2000, (*2*) starting value for the year 2005; *RHS curve*: vertical assessment (*3*) starting from previous year. Assessed indexes for marked years are ranked in terms of provinces and regions

5.2.4.1 Annual Horizontal Assessment of Prosperity Index

According to the national urban and rural cultural consumption total share value, per capita absolute value, each index proportion base value, and according to the actual discrepancy between urban and rural areas and regions "ideal value" being 100 for balance, in 2012 Tianjin's urban and rural prosperity index value was 79.50, lower than the ideal value by 20.50, but higher than the previous year by 1.05. Tianjin's urban and rural prosperity index, among 31 provinces and regions, was ranked 27th in the year 2000, the same in the year 2005, 22nd in 2010, and in 2012 the rank went up to 16th place from 19th place the previous year.

5.2.4.2 Vertical Prosperity Index Assessment of Since the "Tenth Five-Year Plan" Period

According to a base value of 100 during the year 2000, the last year of the "Ninth Five-Year Plan" period, in the year 2012 Tianjin's urban and rural prosperity index value was 109.51, higher than the year 2000 starting value by 9.51, and also higher than the previous year by 5.61. Among 31 provinces and regions, Tianjin's urban and rural prosperity index value was ranked 22nd in 2001, 20th in 2005, 14th in 2010, and in 2012 went up to 7th place from the previous year ranking of 10th place.

5.2.4.3 Vertical Prosperity Index Assessment Since the "Eleventh Five-Year Plan" Period

When setting the last year of the "Tenth Five-Year Plan" period, 2005, with a starting value of 100, Tianjin's 2012 urban and rural prosperity index was 108.62, higher than that in 2005s starting base value by 8.62, and also higher than the previous year by 4.86. In a ranking of 31 provinces and regions, Tianjin's urban and rural prosperity index was ranked 14th in 2006, 5th in 2010, and in 2012 it went up to 2nd place from 3rd place the previous year.

5.2.4.4 Vertical Prosperity Index Assessment Since the "Twelfth Five-Year Plan"

With the last year of the "Eleventh Five-Year Plan" period, 2010, set with a base value of 100, Tianjin's urban and rural prosperity index was 110.78, higher than 2010s base value by 10.78, and also higher than the previous year by 7.76. In a ranking of 31 provinces and regions, Tianjin's urban and rural prosperity index was ranked 11th in 2011, and increased to 1st place in 2010. This evaluation index is better explained by text as opposed to in a table; see Report B3 on the provincial and regional urban and rural ranking with the previous year, 2011, having a starting base value of 100, Tianjin's urban and rural prosperity index was 107.81 in 2010, higher than the 2011 starting base value by 7.81. In a ranking of 31 provinces and regions, Tianjin's urban and rural prosperity index was ranked 19th in the year 2000, 29th in 2005, 5th in 2010, and went up from 11th place the previous year to 1st place in 2012.

5.3 Xinjiang: Rising to Second Place in the Urban and Rural Evaluation of Prosperity After the "Twelfth Five-Year Plan" Period

5.3.1 Growth in Xinjiang's Urban and Rural Cultural Consumption

5.3.1.1 Changes in Total Share Values of Cultural Consumption

See Fig. 5.15 for Xinjiang's urban and rural total cultural consumption growth and changes in shares since the year 2000.

From 2000 to 2012, Xinjiang's total urban and rural cultural consumption rose from 2.904 billion yuan to 9.885 billion yuan, an increase of 6.981 billion yuan, a total 12-year growth of 240.39 %, an average annual growth rate of 10.75 %, and a growth degree ranking 24th place out of 31 provinces and regions. Average annual

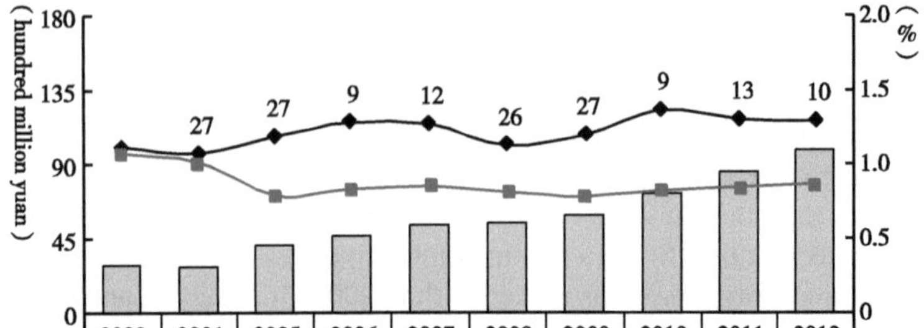

	2000	2001	2005	2006	2007	2008	2009	2010	2011	2012
Total Cultural Consumption	29.04	28.15	40.85	47.17	53.75	54.55	58.94	72.64	85.36	98.85
Total Annual Coefficient	100.00	96.94	106.69	115.47	113.95	101.49	108.05	123.24	117.51	115.80
Share of National Total	1.0738	1.0146	0.7968	0.8380	0.8555	0.8146	0.7836	0.8275	0.8430	0.8667

Fig. 5.15 Xinjiang's urban and rural total cultural consumption growth and changes in shares. *LHS cylindrical*: urban and rural total cultural consumption (hundreds of million yuan); *LHS curve*: annual growth coefficient (previous year = 100, less than 100 is negative growth), of the marked years' provincial and regional ranking in growth, the year 2000 starting point does not count; *RHS curve*: proportion share of national urban and rural areas (%)

growth during the "Tenth Five-Year Plan" period was 7.06 %; average annual growth during the "Eleventh Five-Year Plan" period was 7.06 %; average annual growth during the "Eleventh Five-Year Plan" period was 12.20 %; average annual growth during the first 2 years of the "Twelfth Five-Year Plan" period was 16.65 %. During the first 2 years of the "Twelfth Five-Year Plan" period, average annual growth degree was higher than that during the "Eleventh Five-Year Plan" period by 4.45 percentage points, and higher than that during the "Tenth Five-Year Plan" period by 9.59 percentage points. The highest total growth took place in 2002, with a growth rate of 40.32 %; the lowest annual growth was in 2003, with a negative growth of 12.58 %.

Over the same period, the average annual growth rate for national urban and rural total cultural consumption was 12.74 %, relatively significantly higher than that of Xinjiang by 1.99 percentage points. Xinjiang's total urban and rural cultural consumption feel from 1.07 % of the national share to 0.87 %, a degree of decrease of 19.29 %, and a growth degree and change in share that was ranked 24th place out of 31 provinces and regions.

In the first 2 years of the "Twelfth Five-Year Plan" period, the average annual growth for the national urban and rural cultural consumption total was 13.99 %, and Xinjiang's urban and rural cultural consumption total average annual growth rate was 16.65 %, significantly higher than the national rate by 2.66 percentage points, and an increase of 4.74 % from 2010 in terms of national share. At the same time, Xinjiang's overall growth was higher than its own average annual growth during the "Tenth Five-Year Plan" period by 9.59 percentage points, and also higher than its average annual growth during the "Eleventh Five-Year Plan" period by 4.45

percentage points, and the rank of change in growth degree and proportion of national share was 10th place out of 31 provinces and regions.

5.3.1.2 Growth in Per Capita Absolute Values of Cultural Consumption

See Fig. 5.16 for Xinjiang's urban and rural per capita cultural consumption growth and degree of changes in status since the year 2000.

From 2000 to 2012, Xinjiang's urban and rural per capita cultural consumption grew from 160.28 to 445.12 yuan, an increase of 284.84 yuan, a total growth of 177.71 %, an average annual growth of 8.88 %, and a growth degree ranked 29th place out of 31 provinces and regions. During the "Tenth Five-Year Plan" period, per capita total growth was 28.29 %, and average annual growth was 5.11 %; during the "Eleventh Five-Year Plan" period, per capita values had an overall growth of 62.63 %, and the average annual growth rate was 10.22 %. During the "Eleventh Five-Year Plan" period, average annual growth rate was higher than that during the "Tenth Five-Year Plan" period by 5.11 percentage points. The highest annual growth of per capita values took place in 2002, with a annual growth rate of 38.28 %; and the lowest annual growth was in 2003, with a negative growth of 13.91 %.

Over the same period, the annual average growth in national urban and rural per capita cultural consumption was 12.11 %, significantly higher than that of Xinjiang. Xinjiang's urban and rural per capita cultural consumption decreased from being 74.84 % of the national urban and rural per capita value to 52.71 % of it (see Fig. 5.20 in this paper for a comparison), and its per capita absolute value decreased from 22nd place to 30th place among 31 provinces and regions.

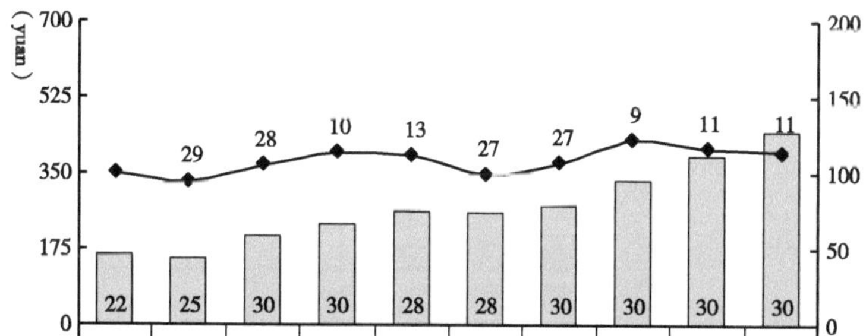

	2000	2001	2005	2006	2007	2008	2009	2010	2011	2012
Per Capita Cultural Consumption	160.28	151.10	205.63	232.39	259.38	258.15	274.76	334.42	388.53	445.12
Annual Growth Coefficient	100.00	94.27	104.64	113.01	111.61	99.53	106.43	121.71	116.18	114.57

Fig. 5.16 Xinjiang's urban and rural per capita cultural consumption growth and degree of status change. *LHS cylindrical*: urban and rural per capita cultural consumption (yuan); *RHS curve*: annual growth coefficient (previous year = 100, less than 100 is negative growth); of annual growth of provinces and regions ranked, the starting year of 2000 is not counted

In the first 2 years of the "Twelfth Five-Year Plan" period, the average annual growth rate of the national urban and rural per capita cultural consumption was 13.44 %, and Xinjiang's growth rate was 15.37 %, relatively significantly higher than the national rate, and also higher than its own "Tenth Five-Year Plan" and "Eleventh Five-Year Plan" period average annual growths, with a growth rate ranked 11th out of 31 provinces and regions.

5.3.2 *Related Background Situation of Xinjiang's Urban and Rural Cultural Consumption*

The relationship between Xinjiang's per capita GDP and urban and rural per capita income, consumption (separated into non-cultural and cultural consumption), and savings is shown in Fig. 5.17.

From 2000 to 2012, Xinjiang's average annual growth in per capita GDP was 13.54 %; the average annual growth in urban and rural per capita income was 11.90 %, relatively significantly lower than the GDP growth, by 1.63 percentage points; the average annual growth in per capita total consumption was 12.09 %, relatively significantly lower than the GDP growth by 1.44 percentage points, and slightly higher than income growth by 0.19 percentage points; the average annual growth in per capita savings was 11.23 %, significantly lower than GDP growth by 2.30 percentage points, slightly lower than income growth by 0.67 percentage points, and slightly lower than total consumption growth by 0.86 percentage points; the average annual growth in per capita cultural consumption was 8.88 %, significantly lower than GDP growth by 4.65 percentage points, significantly lower than income growth by 3.02 percentage points, significantly lower than total

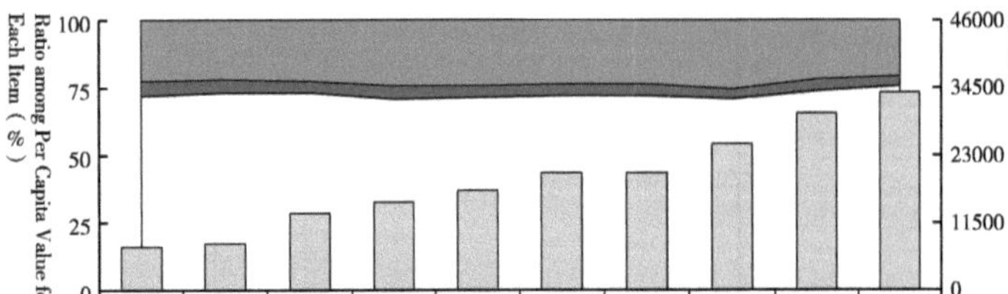

	2000	2001	2005	2006	2007	2008	2009	2010	2011	2012
(1) Per Capita Savings	663.07	737.03	1008.69	1244.33	1451.84	1580.03	1726.35	2093.52	2149.81	2377.49
(2) Cultural Consumption	160.28	151.10	205.63	232.39	259.38	258.15	274.76	334.42	388.53	445.12
(3) Non-Cultural Consumption	2143.40	2422.09	3295.64	3564.16	4220.72	4788.74	5210.29	5831.00	7137.38	8615.42
(4) Per Capita GDP	7372.00	7945.00	13108.00	15000.00	16999.00	19893.00	19942.00	25034.00	30087.00	33796.00

Fig. 5.17 The relationship between Xinjiang's per capita GDP and urban and rural per capita income, consumption, and savings. *LHS area*: urban and rural per capita savings, cultural consumption, non-cultural consumption (yuan are converted to %), (1) + (2) + (3) = income, (2) + (3) = total consumption, (1) + (2) = non-cultural consumption surplus, and the direct ratio between each value throughout the years

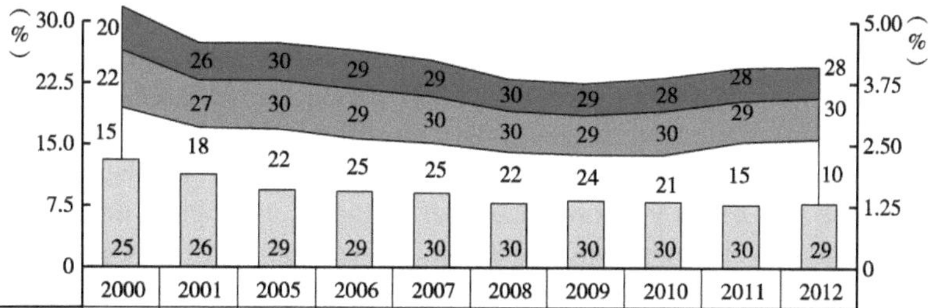

	2000	2001	2005	2006	2007	2008	2009	2010	2011	2012
Proportion of Income	5.4027	4.5646	4.5594	4.6101	4.3726	3.8955	3.8101	4.0492	4.0155	3.8916
Proportion of Total Consumption	6.9578	5.8720	5.8729	6.1210	5.7896	5.1151	5.0093	5.4241	5.1625	4.9127
Ratio to Non–Surplus	19.4673	17.0132	16.9335	15.7367	15.1575	14.0439	13.7305	13.7738	15.3064	15.7698
Ratio to GDP	2.1742	1.9018	1.5687	1.5492	1.5258	1.2977	1.3778	1.3359	1.2913	1.3171

Fig. 5.18 Changes in Xinjiang's urban and rural cultural consumption ratio. *LHS area*: urban and rural per capita cultural consumption as proportion of income, overall consumption, and ratio to non-cultural consumption surplus (called "Non Surplus" on the chart) (%). Each annual proportion's rise or fall is superimposed; *RHS cylinder*: ratio of urban and rural per capita cultural consumption and GDP (%). Years are ranked according to urban-to-rural ratio of provinces or regions years are ranked according to urban-to-rural ratio of provinces or regions

consumption growth by 3.21 percentage points, and significantly lower than savings growth by 2.35 percentage points.

During the first 2 years of the "Twelfth Five-Year Plan" period, Xinjiang's average annual growth in per capita GDP was 16.19 %, its average annual growth in urban and rural per capita income was 17.68 %, its average annual growth in per capita total consumption was 21.23 %, its average annual growth in per capita savings was 6.57 %, and its average annual growth in per capita cultural consumption was 15.37 %.

In the analysis and calculation of related ratios of Xinjiang's urban and rural per capita cultural consumption, these figures were arrived at. For a look at the changing proportions of Xinjiang's urban and rural cultural consumption since the year 2000, see Fig. 5.18.

5.3.2.1 Ratio of Per Capita Cultural Consumption to Per Capita GDP

From 2000 to 2012, the ratio of Xinjiang's urban and rural per capita cultural consumption and per capita GDP decreased from 2.17 % to 1.32 %, its rank falling from 25th to 29th place out of 31 provinces and regions. Looking at the years listed in Table 4, in 2009 and 2012, this index ratio saw an increase, while in other years it decreased. Since the "Tenth Five-Year Plan" period, Xinjiang's urban and rural ratio for this index decreased 39.42 %, with a degree of change ranking 18th among 31 provinces and regions.

Looking at this across time periods, during the "Tenth Five-Year Plan" period, Xinjiang's urban and rural proportion for this index decreased by 0.61 percentage points; in the "Eleventh Five-Year Plan" period, it decreased by 0.23 percentage points. During the first 2 years of the "Twelfth Five-Year Plan" period, Xinjiang's proportion for this index decreased by 0.02 percentage points, with a degree of decrease of 1.41 %; the coordination of cultural consumption demand growth and economic development was slightly decreased from 2010. During this period, the highest value was in 2002 at 2.47 %, and the lowest was in 2011 at 1.29 %.

5.3.2.2 Per Capita Cultural Consumption as Proportion of Per Capita Income

From 2000 to 2012, Xinjiang's per capita urban and rural cultural consumption as proportion of per capita income fell from 5.40 % to 3.89 %, and from 20th place to 28th place among 31 provinces and regions. From the years listed in Fig. 5.18 we can see that this index proportion showed increases in 2006 and 2010, with decreases during the other years. Since the "Tenth Five-Year Plan" period, Xinjiang's urban and rural proportion for this index decreased by 27.97 %, with a degree of change ranked 27th out of 31 provinces and regions.

Looking at this across time periods, during the "Tenth Five-Year Plan" period, Xinjiang's urban and rural proportion for this index decreased by 0.84 percentage points; during the "Eleventh Five-Year Plan" period, it decreased by 0.51 percentage points. During the first 2 years of the "Twelfth Five-Year Plan" period, Xinjiang's urban and rural proportion for this index decreased by 0.16 percentage points, with a degree of decrease of 3.89 %. The coordination of cultural consumption growth and income growth was slightly lower than that in 2010. During this period, the highest value took place in 2002 at 5.78 %, and the lowest was in 2009 at 3.81 %.

5.3.2.3 Per Capita Cultural Consumption as Proportion of Total Per Capita Consumption

From 2000 to 2012, Xinjiang's per capita cultural consumption as proportion of total per capita consumption decreased from 6.96 % to 4.91 %, and its rank among 31 provinces and regions went down from 22nd to 30th place. From looking at the years listed in Fig. 5.18, this proportion saw an increase from 2005 to 2006 and in 2010, while decreasing the rest of the years. Since the "Tenth Five-Year Plan" period, Xinjiang's urban and rural proportion for this index decreased by 29.39 %, and the degree of change ranked 31st place out of 31 provinces and regions.

Looking at this across time periods, Xinjiang's proportion for this index during the "Tenth Five-Year Plan" period decreased by 1.08 percentage points; during the "Eleventh Five-Year Plan" period it decreased by 0.45 percentage points. During the first 2 years of the "Twelfth Five-Year Plan" period, the urban and rural index for Xinjiang decreased by 0.51 percentage points, a degree of decrease of 9.45 %, with its coordination of cultural consumption growth and overall consumption growth significantly decreased from that of 2010. During this period, the highest value was in 2002 at 7.25 %, and the lowest was in 2012 at 4.91 %.

5.3.2.4 Ratio of Per Capita Cultural Consumption to Per Capita Non-cultural Surplus

From 2000 to 2012, the ratio of Xinjiang's urban and rural per capita cultural consumption and per capita non-cultural consumption surplus fell from 19.47 % to 15.77 %, and because the decreases in values of other provinces or regions were more significant, Xinjiang went up from 15th to 10th place. In looking at the years listed in Table 4, we see that this ratio increased from the year 2010–2012, while decreasing in other years. Since the "Tenth Five-Year Plan" period, Xinjiang's urban and rural proportion decreased by 18.99 %, with a degree of change ranked 7th among 31 provinces and regions.

Looking at this across time periods, during the "Tenth Five-Year Plan" period, Xinjiang's urban and rural index proportion fell by 2.53 percentage points; during the "Eleventh Five-Year Plan" period, it fell by 3.16 percentage points. During the first 2 years of the "Twelfth Five-Year Plan" period, Xinjiang's urban and rural index proportion increased by 2.00 percentage points, a degree of increase of 14.49 %, with a coordination of cultural consumption growth and growth in "surplus money" from "necessary consumption" being significantly enhanced. During this period, the highest value was in 2002 at 22.16 %, and the lowest was in 2009 at 13.73 %.

5.3.3 Xinjiang's Coordination of Urban/Rural and Regional Cultural Consumption

5.3.3.1 Urban/Rural Ratio of Per Capita Cultural Consumption

See Fig. 5.19 for Changes in Xinjiang's Urban-to-rural Ratio of Per Capita Cultural Consumption since 2000.

From 2000 to 2012, Xinjiang's urban-to-rural ratio of per capita cultural consumption expanded from 2.5299 to 2.6010, and because the urban-to-rural ratio of cultural consumption in other provinces and regions expanded more greatly, Xinjiang's urban-to-rural ratio rose from 29th to 20th place in a ranking of 31 provinces and regions. During this time, the lowest urban-to-rural ratio occurred in 2005 at 1.7895, and the highest was in 2002 at 3.7978. From looking at the years listed in Table 5, we see that in 2001, 2005, 2008, and from 2011 to 2012, the urban-to-rural ratio was reduced, and in all other years it was expanded. Since the "Tenth Five-Year Plan" period, Xinjiang's urban-to-rural ratio of cultural consumption expanded by 2.81 %, its urban-to-rural ratio change being ranked 2nd place out of

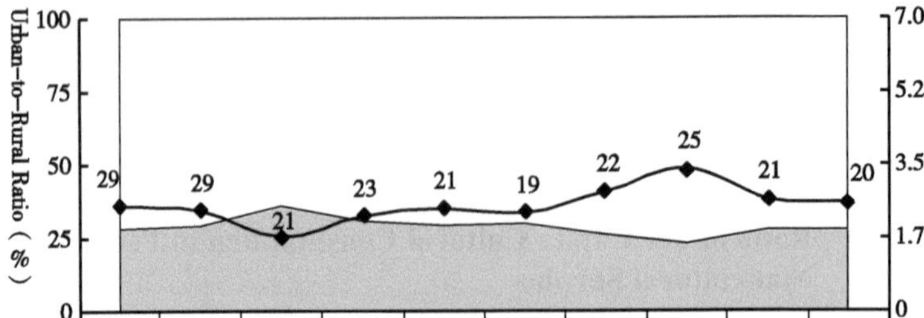

	2000	2001	2005	2006	2007	2008	2009	2010	2011	2012
Urban Per Capita	268.12	245.37	285.10	357.74	407.78	395.30	451.59	579.03	607.60	680.79
Rural Per Capita	105.98	102.21	159.32	157.00	166.27	168.99	158.13	170.15	229.66	261.74
Xinjiang's Urban–to–Rural Ratio	2.5299	2.4006	1.7895	2.2786	2.4525	2.3392	2.8558	3.4031	2.6457	2.6010

Fig. 5.19 Changing status of the urban-to-rural ratio of Xinjiang's per capita cultural consumption. *LHS area*: urban, rural per capita cultural consumption (yuan converted to %), direct proportional relationship between annual urban and rural values; *RHS curve*: urban-to-rural ratio of per capita cultural consumption (rural = 1), years ranked according to urban-to-rural ratio of provinces or regions

31 provinces and regions. This signifies that Xinjiang's status as a province is among the best in terms of changes in urban-to-rural ratio of cultural consumption.

As Xinjiang experienced changes in urban-to-rural ratio of cultural consumption, it also felt the influence of change in both urban and rural areas. Over this period, Xinjiang's urban per capita cultural consumption rose from 268.12 to 680.79 yuan, an increase of 412.67 yuan, a 12-year overall increase of 153.91 %, and an average annual growth rate of 8.07 %. The highest urban per capita values occurred in 2002, with a growth rate of 63.83 %; the lowest growth occurred in 2003, with a negative growth of 24.96 %. Rural per capita cultural consumption grew from 105.98 to 261.74 yuan, a growth of 155.76 yuan, an 12-year overall increase of 146.97 %, and an average annual growth rate of 7.83 %. The highest rural per capita values occurred in 2011, with a growth rate of 34.98 %; the lowest occurred in 2009, with a negative growth rate of 6.43 %. In this period, Xinjiang's average annual growth in urban per capita cultural consumption demand was slightly higher than that of rural growth, by 0.24 percentage points, resulting in a slight expansion in Xinjiang's urban-to-rural ratio of cultural consumption demand.

During the first 2 years of the "Twelfth Five-Year Plan" period, the average annual growth rate of Xinjiang's urban per capita cultural consumption was 8.43 %, higher than that of the "Tenth Five-Year Plan" period by 7.19 %, but lower than that of the "Eleventh Five-Year Plan" period by 6.79 percentage points; average annual growth rate in rural per capita cultural consumption was 24.03 %, higher than that of the "Tenth Five-Year Plan" period by 15.54 percentage points, and also higher than that of the "Eleventh Five-Year Plan" period by 22.71 percentage points. At this time, Xinjiang's urban per capita values were higher than those of rural areas, but annual growth in urban areas was much lower than that of rural areas, by 15.60 percentage points, signifying that the urban-rural gap was lessoning. Xinjiang's urban-to-rural ratio of cultural consumption was significantly reduced when compared with that of 2010, with an urban-to-rural ratio rank of 20th out of 31 provinces and regions.

5.3.3.2 Regional Discrepancies in Urban and Rural Per Capita Cultural Consumption

See Fig. 5.20 for the Changing Status of Xinjiang's Urban and Rural Per Capita Cultural Consumption and National Regional Discrepancy.

From 2000 to 2012, the regional discrepancy between Xinjiang's urban and rural per capita cultural consumption and national urban and rural areas expanded from 1.2516 to 1.4729, falling from 16th place among 31 provinces and regions to 25th place. During this period, the smallest regional discrepancy was in the year 2000 at 1.2516, and the largest was in 2009 at 1.5136. Looking at the years listed in Table 6, from 2006 to 2007 and 2010–2012, the regional discrepancy saw a reduction, while during the rest of the years it expanded. Since the "Tenth Five-Year Plan" period, Xinjiang's regional discrepancy in urban and rural cultural consumption expanded by 17.68 %, and its degree of changes in regional discrepancy was ranked 28th among 31 provinces and regions. This signifies that Xinjiang's degree of change in regional discrepancy in urban and rural cultural consumption is one of the most serious out of the provinces.

While Xinjiang's regional discrepancies in urban and rural cultural consumption experience changes, the province is both influenced by its own status as well as that of the nation. For a comparison and detailed calculation of both Xinjiang's and the

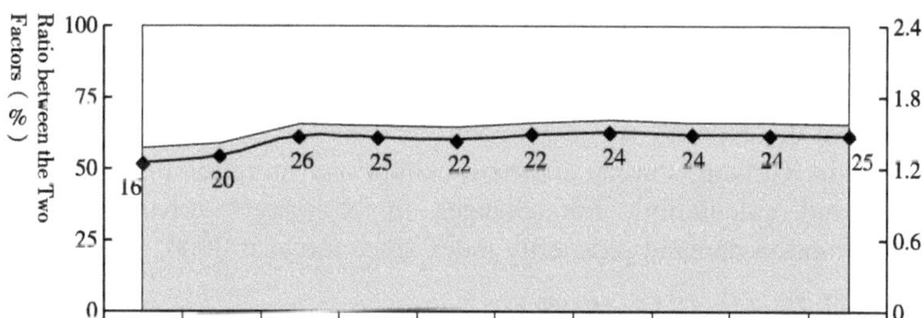

	2000	2001	2005	2006	2007	2008	2009	2010	2011	2012
Xinjiang's Urban–Rural Per Capita	160.28	151.10	205.63	232.39	259.38	258.15	274.76	334.42	388.53	445.12
National Urban–Rural Per Capita	214.18	218.16	393.23	429.35	476.73	505.55	564.94	656.16	753.36	844.45
Urban–Rural Gap	1.2516	1.3074	1.4771	1.4587	1.4559	1.4894	1.5136	1.4903	1.4843	1.4729

Fig. 5.20 The changing status of Xinjiang's urban and rural per capita cultural consumption and national regional discrepancy. LHS area: urban and rural per capita cultural consumption (yuan converted to %), rising ratio to local and national annual values; RHS curve: regional discrepancies in urban and rural per capita cultural consumption (no discrepancy = 1), marked years are ranked by regional discrepancies

nation's annual growth in urban and rural per capita cultural consumption, see the chapter on per capita absolute values in this paper for a focused investigation of the specific situation of growth discrepancies. From 2000 to 2012, Xinjiang's average annual growth in urban and rural per capita cultural consumption was significantly lower than that of the nation, by 3.23 percentage points, and the regional discrepancy between Xinjiang's urban and rural cultural consumption demand and that of the nation was broadened considerably.

In the first 2 years of the "Twelfth Five-Year Plan" period, the average annual growth of Xinjiang's urban and rural per capita cultural consumption grew by 5.15 percentage points, fairly higher than the national growth, by 1.93 percentage points. At this time, Xinjiang's urban and rural per capita values being lower than the national urban and rural average values, and its growth higher than that of the nation, indicates that the regional discrepancy was lessoning, and the national urban and rural regional discrepancy was significantly lessoned from that of 2010, by 1.17 %, with a regional discrepancy ranking of 25th out of 31 provinces and regions.

5.3.4 Xinjiang's Urban and Rural Cultural Consumption Prosperity Evaluation

To sum up the above: since the "Tenth Five-Year Plan" period, the average annual growth of Xinjiang's total urban and rural cultural consumption was significantly lower than national growth, with changes in average annual growth in per capita values, proportion of income, and proportion of overall consumption being better than those during the "Tenth Five-Year Plan" period, with all other proportion changes being not as favorable as those during the "Tenth Five-Year Plan" period; the urban-to-rural ratio was slightly expanded, and the national urban and rural regional discrepancy was significantly expanded. All of these results are concentrated in Xinjiang's urban and rural cultural consumption prosperity index evaluation and calculation. For changes in Xinjiang's urban and rural cultural consumption demand prosperity index since the year 2000, see Fig. 5.21.

5.3.4.1 Annual Horizontal Prosperity Assessment

With the national urban and rural cultural consumption overall share value, per capita absolute value, and proportion of each index as a base, and balanced by the "ideal value" of 100 of no discrepancy between urban/rural areas and regions, in 2012 Xinjiang's urban and rural index was 69.04, lower than the ideal value by 30.96, but higher than the previous year by 0.89. Among 31 provinces and regions, Xinjiang's urban and rural index was ranked 28th in 2000, 30th in 2005, and in 2010 and the previous years, as well as in 2012, in 29th place.

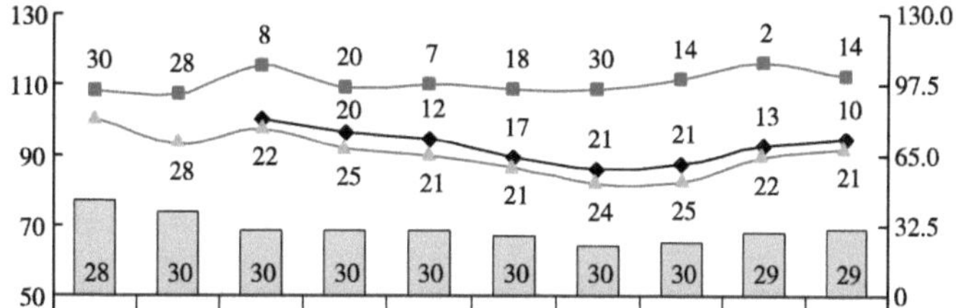

	2000	2001	2005	2006	2007	2008	2009	2010	2011	2012
Horizontal Assessment	77.12	73.48	68.26	68.44	68.47	66.96	64.16	65.28	68.15	69.04
Vertical Assessment (1)	100.00	93.30	97.35	91.86	89.78	86.25	81.81	82.35	89.33	91.75
Vertical Assessment (2)	—	—	100.00	96.41	94.43	89.44	86.07	87.41	92.61	94.57
Vertical Assessment (3)	94.41	93.30	105.86	96.41	97.58	95.16	95.61	99.83	107.77	101.31

Fig. 5.21 Changes in Xinjiang's urban and rural cultural consumption demand prosperity index. *LHS cylindrical*: horizontal assessment (urban/rural, regional zero-difference ideal value = 100); *LHS curve*: vertical assessment (starting base value = 100), (*1*) starting value for the year 2000, (*2*) starting value for the year 2005; *RHS curve*: vertical assessment (*3*) starting from previous year. Assessed indexes for marked years are ranked in terms of provinces and regions

5.3.4.2 Vertical Prosperity Index Assessment Since the "Tenth Five-Year Plan" Period

Based on a starting base value of 100 in the year 2000, the last year of the "Ninth Five-Year Plan" period, Xinjiang's urban and rural prosperity index in 2012 was 91.75, lower than the starting base value of the year 2000 by 8.25, but higher than the previous year by 2.42. Xinjiang's urban and rural prosperity index, out of 31 provinces and regions, was ranked 28th in 2001, 22nd in 2005, 25th in 2010, and in 2012 went up to 21st place from 22nd place in the previous year.

5.3.4.3 Vertical Prosperity Index Assessment Since the "Eleventh Five-Year Plan" Period

Setting the year 2005, the last year of the "Tenth Five-Year Plan" period, with a base value of 100, Xinjiang's urban and rural index in 2012 was 94.57, lower than that of the 2005 base value by 5.43, but higher than that of the previous year by 1.96. In a ranking of 31 provinces and regions, Xinjiang's urban and rural index was in 20th place in 2006, 21st place in 2010, and in 2012 went up to 10th place from 13th place the previous year.

5.3.4.4 Vertical Prosperity Index Assessment Since the "Twelfth Five-Year Plan" Period

Setting the year 2010, the last year of the "Eleventh Five-Year Plan" period, with a starting base value of 100, Xinjiang's urban and rural index for 2012 was 109.39, higher than the base value of 2010 by 9.39, and also higher than that of the previous year by 1.62. In a ranking of 31 provinces and regions, Xinjiang's urban and rural index was 2nd place in 2011 as well as 2012. This evaluation index is better explained by text than in a table; see Report B3 on the provincial and regional urban and rural ranking.

5.3.4.5 Annual Vertical Assessment of Prosperity Index

Setting the previous year, 2011, with a base value of 100, Xinjiang's urban and rural prosperity index in 2012 was 101.31, higher than the 2011 starting base value by 1.31. In a ranking of 31 provinces and regions, Xinjiang's prosperity index was 30th in 2000, 8th in 2005, 14th in 2010, and in 2010 fell from 2nd place the previous year to 14th place.

5.4 Qinghai: Rising to Third Place in the Urban and Rural Prosperity After the "Eleventh Five-Year Plan"

5.4.1 Qinghai's Urban and Rural Cultural Consumption Demand Growth

5.4.1.1 Changes in Overall Cultural Consumption Share

See Fig. 5.22 for Qinghai's urban and rural total cultural consumption growth and changes in shares since the year 2000.

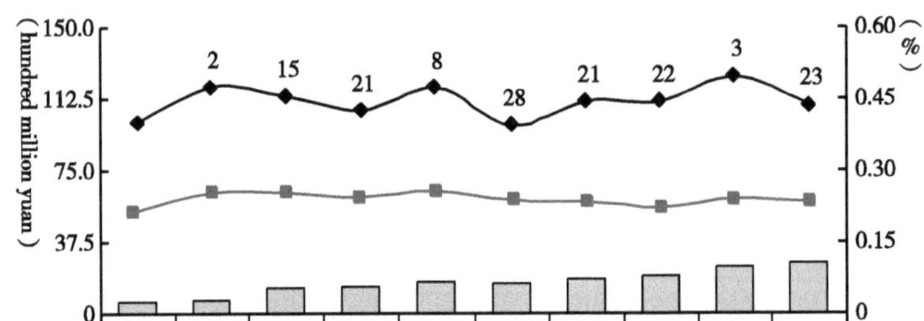

	2000	2001	2005	2006	2007	2008	2009	2010	2011	2012
Total Cultural Consumption	5.87	6.99	12.92	13.71	16.15	15.92	17.67	19.61	24.41	26.64
Share of Total Annual Growth	100.00	119.08	114.13	106.11	117.80	98.58	110.99	110.98	124.48	109.14
Share of National Total	0.2171	0.2519	0.2520	0.2436	0.2571	0.2377	0.2349	0.2234	0.2411	0.2336

Fig. 5.22 Qinghai's urban and rural total cultural consumption growth and changes in share. *LHS cylindrical*: overall urban and rural cultural consumption (in hundred million yuan); *LHS curve*: annual growth coefficient (previous year = 100, lower than 100 represents negative growth), of the marked years' provincial and regional ranking in growth, the year 2000 starting point does not count; *RHS curve*: proportion of national urban and rural share (%)

From 2000 to 2012, Qinghai's overall urban and rural cultural consumption grew from 587 million yuan to 2.664 billion yuan, an increase of 2.077 billion yuan, a 12-year total growth of 353.83 %, and average annual growth of 13.43 %, and a growth degree ranked 8th out of 31 provinces and regions. Average annual growth during the "Tenth Five-Year Plan" period was 17.09 %, during the "Eleventh Five-Year Plan" period it was 8.70 %; during the first 2 years of the "Twelfth Five-Year Plan" period it was 16.55 %. Average annual growth of the first 2 years of the "Twelfth Five-Year Plan" period was higher than that of the "Eleventh Five-Year Plan" period by 7.85 percentage points, and lower than that during the "Tenth Five-Year Plan" period by 0.54 percentage points. The highest annual growth rate took place during 2002, at a growth rate of 46.07 %; the lowest annual growth rate took place during 2008, with a negative rate of growth of 1.42 %.

Over the same period, average annual growth of national urban and rural overall cultural consumption was 12.74 %, slightly lower than Qinghai's growth by 0.69 percentage points. Qinghai's overall urban and rural cultural consumption as proportion of the national share increased from 0.22 % to 0.23 %, a growth rate of 7.60 %, with its degree of growth and change in share ranked 8th place out of 31 provinces and regions.

During the first 2 years of the "Twelfth Five-Year Plan" period, the average annual growth rate of national urban and rural overall cultural consumption was 13.99 %, and Qinghai's average annual growth in urban and rural overall cultural consumption was 16.55 %, significantly higher than the national value, by 2.56 percentage points, and in 2010 increasing 4.57 % in proportion of national share. At the same time, Qinghai's overall growth was lower than that of its "Tenth Five-Year Plan" period average annual growth by 0.54 percentage points, but higher than its "Eleventh Five-Year Plan" period average annual growth by 7.85 percentage points, with a growth degree ranked 23rd out of 31 provinces and regions in terms of changes in proportion of national share.

5.4.1.2 Growth in Cultural Consumption Per Capita Absolute Values

See Fig. 5.23 for Qinghai's urban and rural per capita cultural consumption growth and degree of changes in status since the year 2000.

From 2000 to 2012, Qinghai's urban and rural per capita cultural consumption grew from 114.34 to 466.91 yuan, a growth of 352.57 yuan, a total growth of 308.35 %, an average annual growth of 12.44 %, with a degree of growth ranked 8th among 31 provinces and regions. During the "Tenth Five-Year Plan" period, total per capita values grew 108.77 %, with an average annual growth rate of 15.86 %; during the "Eleventh Five-Year Plan" period, total per capita values grew 46.72 %, with an average annual growth rate of 7.97 %. Average annual growth during the "Eleventh Five-Year Plan" was lower than that during the "Tenth Five-Year Plan" by 7.89 percentage points. The highest per capita value growth occurred in 2002, with a growth rate of 44.27 %; the lowest per capita value occurred in 2008, with a negative growth of 1.94 %.

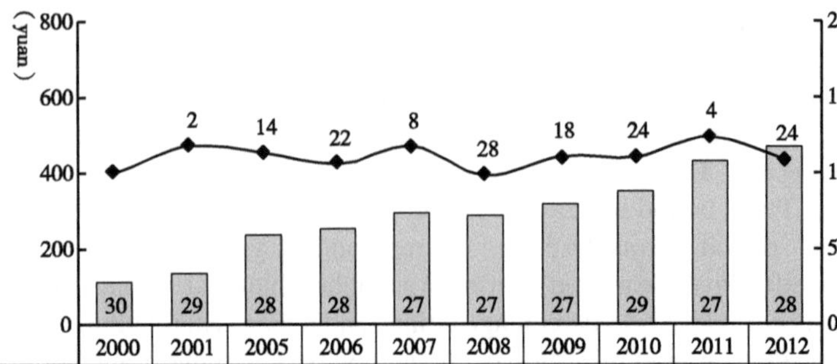

	2000	2001	2005	2006	2007	2008	2009	2010	2011	2012
Per Capita Cultural Consumption	114.34	134.45	238.71	251.44	293.50	287.81	317.97	350.23	431.53	466.91
Annual Growth Coefficient	100.00	117.58	113.09	105.34	116.72	98.06	110.48	110.14	123.21	108.20

Fig. 5.23 Qinghai's urban and rural per capita cultural consumption growth and degree of changes in status. *LHS cylindrical*: urban and rural per capita cultural consumption (yuan); *RHS curve*: annual growth coefficient (previous year = 100, less than 100 is negative growth); of annual growth of provinces and regions ranked, the starting year of 2000 is not counted

Over the same period, the average annual growth rate of national urban and rural cultural consumption was 12.11 %, slightly lower than that of Qinghai. Qinghai's urban and rural per capita cultural consumption went from being 53.39 % of the national urban and rural per capita value to 55.29 % of that value (for the comparison see Fig. 5.27 in this paper). Qinghai's per capita absolute value increased from a rank of 30th out of 31 provinces and regions, to 28th.

During the first 2 years of the "Twelfth Five-Year Plan" period, average annual growth for national urban and rural per capita cultural consumption was 13.44 %, and Qinghai's average annual growth rate was 15.46 %, significantly higher than that of the nation, also lower than its own "Tenth Five-Year Plan" period average annual growth, but higher than its own "Eleventh Five Year Plan" period average annual growth, with a growth rate ranking 24th out of 31 provinces and regions.

5.4.2 Related Background Situation of Qinghai's Urban and Rural Cultural Consumption

For the relationship between Qinghai's per capita GDP and urban and rural per capita income consumption since the year 2000, (separated into non-cultural and cultural consumption), and savings is shown in Fig. 5.24.

From 2000 to 2012, Qinghai's average annual growth in per capita GDP was 16.82 %; its average annual growth in urban and rural per capita income was 12.32 %, significantly lower than GDP growth, by 4.50 percentage points; average annual growth in per capita savings was 13.90 %, significantly lower than GDP growth, by 2.92 percentage points, and significantly higher than income growth, by

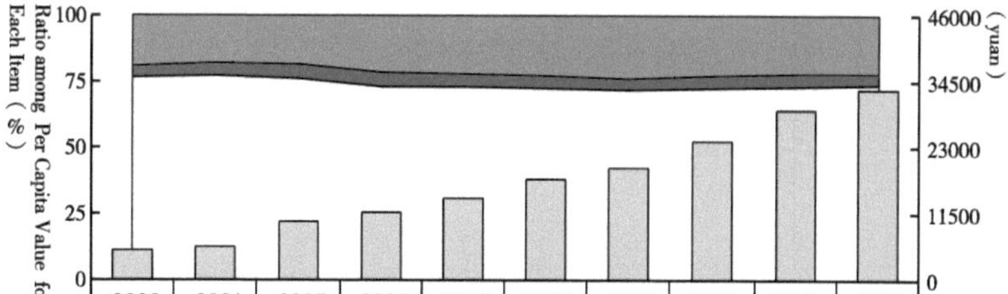

	2000	2001	2005	2006	2007	2008	2009	2010	2011	2012
(1) Per Capita Savings	515.74	553.63	810.46	1078.31	1238.65	1494.54	1697.09	1839.10	2102.77	2459.38
(2) Cultural Consumption	114.34	134.45	238.71	251.44	293.50	287.81	317.97	350.23	431.53	466.91
(3) Non-Cultural Consumption	2118.72	2381.64	3393.30	3634.85	4160.94	4754.00	5200.60	5886.13	6954.17	8155.33
(4) Per Capita GDP	5138.00	5774.00	10045.00	11762.00	14257.00	17389.00	19454.00	24115.00	29522.00	33181.00

Fig. 5.24 The relationship between Qinghai's per capita GDP and urban and rural per capita income, consumption, and savings. *LHS area*: urban and rural per capita savings, cultural consumption, non-cultural consumption (yuan are converted to %), (1) + (2) + (3) = income, (2) + (3) = total consumption, (1) + (2) = non-cultural consumption surplus, and the direct ratio between each value throughout the years

1.58 percentage points, also relatively significantly higher than overall consumption growth, by 1.98 percentage points; the average annual growth in per capita cultural consumption was 12.44 %, significantly lower than GDP growth, by 4.38 percentage points, slightly higher than income growth, by 0.12 percentage points, slightly higher than overall consumption growth, by 0.52 percentage points, and relatively significantly lower than savings growth, by 1.46 percentage points.

During the first 2 years of the "Twelfth Five-Year Plan" period, Qinghai's average annual growth in per capita GDP was 17.30 %, its average annual growth in urban and rural per capita income was 17.14 %, its average annual growth per capita overall consumption was 17.58 %, its average annual growth in per capita savings was 15.64 %, and its average annual growth in per capita cultural consumption was 15.46 %. The average annual growth in cultural consumption was lower than GDP growth by 1.84 percentage points, lower than income growth by 1.68 percentage points, lower than overall consumption growth by 2.12 percentage points, and lower than savings by 0.18 percentage points. The proportional relationship between cultural consumption and various factors completely showed a declining trend.

In the analysis and calculation of related ratios of Qinghai's urban and rural per capita cultural consumption, these figures were arrived at. For a look at the changing proportions of Qinghai's urban and rural cultural consumption since the year 2000, see Fig. 5.25.

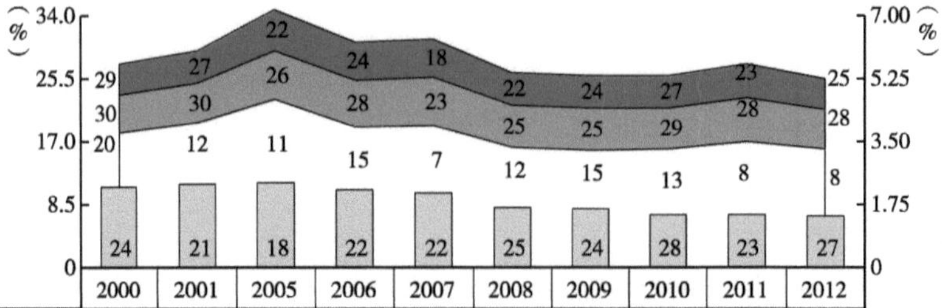

	2000	2001	2005	2006	2007	2008	2009	2010	2011	2012
Proportion of Income	4.1598	4.3798	5.3733	5.0647	5.1553	4.4033	4.4067	4.3369	4.5479	4.2134
Proportion of Total Consumption	5.1205	5.3436	6.5723	6.4700	6.5889	5.7085	5.7618	5.6159	5.8427	5.4152
Ratio to Non-Surplus	18.1474	19.5397	22.7520	18.9091	19.1559	16.1479	15.7796	15.9970	17.0274	15.9557
Ratio to GDP	2.2255	2.3285	2.3764	2.1378	2.0586	1.6551	1.6345	1.4523	1.4617	1.4072

Fig. 5.25 Changes in Qinghai's urban and rural cultural consumption ratio. *LHS area*: urban and rural per capita cultural consumption as proportion of income, overall consumption, and ratio to non-cultural consumption surplus (called "Non Surplus" on the chart) (%). Each annual proportion's rise or fall is superimposed; *RHS cylinder*: ratio of urban and rural per capita cultural consumption and GDP (%). Years are ranked according to urban-to-rural ratio of provinces or regions years are ranked according to urban-to-rural ratio of provinces or regions

5.4.2.1 Ratio of Per Capita Cultural Consumption and Per Capita GDP

From 2000 to 2012, the ratio of Qinghai's urban and rural cultural consumption and per capita GDP decreased from 2.23 % to 1.41 %, and decreased in ranking from 24th to 27th place in a ranking of 31 provinces and regions. Looking at the years listed in Fig. 5.25, we seen that in 2001, 2005, and 2011, this ratio increased, while in the other years it decreased. Since the "Tenth Five-Year Plan" period, this ratio in Qinghai's urban and rural areas decreased by 36.77 %, with a degree of change ranked 17th out of 31 provinces and regions.

Looking at it across time periods, during the "Tenth Five-Year Plan" period, this ratio in Qinghai's urban and rural areas increased by 0.15 percentage points; over the "Eleventh Five-Year Plan" period, it decreased by 0.92 percentage points. During the first 2 years of the "Twelfth Five-Year Plan" period, Qinghai's urban and rural ratio decreased by 0.05 percentage points, with a degree of decrease of 3.11 %, and a coordination of cultural consumption demand growth and economic growth that was slightly lower than that in 2010. During this period, the highest value occurred in 2002 at 2.99&, and the lowest value occurred in 2012 at 1.41 %.

5.4.2.2 Per Capita Cultural Consumption as Proportion of Per Capita Income

From 2000 to 2012, Qinghai's urban and rural per capita cultural consumption as proportion of per capita income increased from 4.16 % to 4.21 %, and increased in rank from 29th to 25th place out of 31 provinces and regions. By looking at the years listed in Table 4, we see that in 2001, 2005, 2007, 2009, and 2011, this proportion increased, while during the other years it decreased. Since the "Tenth Five-Year Plan" period, Qinghai's urban and rural ratio for this indicator increased 1.29 %, with a degree of change ranked 5th place out of 31 provinces and regions.

Looking at it across time periods, during the "Tenth Five-Year Plan" period, Qinghai's urban and rural ratio for this indicator increased by 1.21 percentage points; during the "Eleventh Five-Year Plan" period it decreased 1.04 percentage points. During the first 2 years of the "Eleventh Five-Year Plan" period, Qinghai's ratio for this indicator decreased by 0.12 percentage points, a degree of decrease of 2.85 %, and the coordination of cultural consumption demand growth and income growth was slightly decreased from that of 2010. During this period, the highest value occurred in 2002 at 5.89 %, and the lowest value occurred in 2000 at 4.16 %.

5.4.2.3 Per Capita Cultural Consumption as Proportion of Total Per Capita Consumption

From 2000 to 2012, Qinghai's urban and rural per capita cultural consumption as proportion of per capita total consumption increased from 5.12 to 5.42 %, and increased in rank from 28th place to 30th place among 31 provinces and regions. Looking at the years listed in Table 4, in 2001, 2005, 2007, 2009, and 2011, there was an increase, while all other years showed a decrease. Since the "Tenth Five-Year Plan" period, Qinghai's urban and rural proportion for this indicator increased by 5.76 %, with a degree of change ranking 9th out of 31 provinces and regions.

Looking at this across time periods, during the "Tenth Five-Year Plan" period, Qinghai's urban and rural ratio for this indicator increased by 1.45 percentage points; during the "Eleventh Five-Year Plan" period, it decreased by 0.96 percentage points. During the first 2 years of the "Twelfth Five-Year Plan" period, Qinghai's proportion for this indicator decreased by 0.20 percentage points, a degree of decrease of 3.57 %, and the coordination of cultural consumption demand growth and overall consumption growth was significantly decreased from that of 2010. During this period, the highest value occurred in 2002 at 7.17 %, and the lowest value occurred during 2000 at 5.12 %.

5.4.2.4 The Ratio of Per Capita Cultural Consumption to Per Capita Non-cultural Surplus

From 2000 to 2012, Qinghai's ratio of urban and rural per capita cultural consumption to per capita non-cultural consumption decreased from 18.15 % to 15.96 %, and because other provinces and regions had ratios for this indicator that decreased more significantly, Qinghai's went from 20th place to 8th place. Looking at the years listed in Fig. 5.25, we see that this ratio indicator was increased in 2001, 2005, 2007, and 2010–2011, while in all other years it decreased. Since the "Tenth Five-Year

Plan" period, Qinghai's urban and rural ratio for this indicator was 12.08 %, and its degree of change was ranked 4th place out of 31 provinces and regions.

5.4.3 *Xinjiang's Coordination of Urban/Rural and Regional Cultural Consumption*

5.4.3.1 Urban/Rural Ratio of Per Capita Cultural Consumption

See Fig. 5.26 for Changes in Qinghai's Urban-to-rural ratio of Per Capita Cultural Consumption since 2000.

From 2000 to 2012, Qinghai's urban-to-rural ratio of per capita cultural consumption expanded from 2.2880 to 2.3835, and because other provinces and regions had an urban-to-rural ratio of cultural consumption that expanded more seriously, Qinghai's urban-to-rural ratio rank moved up to 14th place from 28th out of 31 provinces and regions. During this time, the smallest urban-to-rural ratio occurred in 2000, at 2.2880, and the largest occurred in 2005 at 4.0405. Looking at the years listed in Fig. 5.26, we see that the urban-to-rural ratios in 2006 and 2008–2012 were slightly reduced, while they expanded during the rest of the years. Since the "Tenth Five-Year Plan" period, Qinghai's urban-to-rural ratio of cultural consumption expanded 4.17 %, and its changing status in urban-to-rural ratio ranked 4th place out of 31 provinces and regions. This signifies that Qinghai's status as a province is among the best in terms of changes in urban-to-rural ratio of cultural consumption.

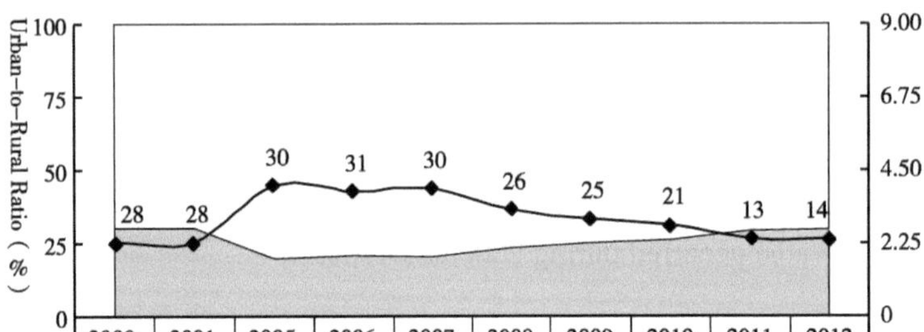

	2000	2001	2005	2006	2007	2008	2009	2010	2011	2012
Urban–Rural Per Capita	181.62	212.92	442.56	457.06	534.68	491.90	522.07	558.34	639.65	675.19
Rural Per Capita	79.38	91.82	109.53	118.66	135.13	148.86	173.75	198.53	265.43	283.28
Qinghai's Urban-to-Rural Ratio	2.2880	2.3189	4.0405	3.8518	3.9568	3.3044	3.0047	2.8124	2.4099	2.3835

Fig. 5.26 Changes in Qinghai's urban-to-rural ratio of per capita cultural consumption. *LHS area*: urban, rural per capita cultural consumption (yuan converted to %), direct proportional relationship between annual urban and rural values; *RHS curve*: urban-to-rural ratio of per capita cultural consumption (rural = 1), years ranked according to urban-to-rural ratio of provinces or regions

Qinghai's changes in urban-to-rural ratio of cultural consumption were influenced by its own changes both in urban and rural areas. Over the same period, Qinghai's urban per capita cultural consumption grew from 181.62 to 675.19 yuan, a growth of 493.57 yuan, a 12-year overall growth of 271.76 %, and an average annual growth rate of 11.56 %. The largest growth in urban per capita values took place in 2002, with a growth rate of 62.71 %; the lowest growth rate took place in 2008, with a negative growth of 8.00 %. Rural per capita cultural consumption increased from 79.38 to 283.28 yuan, a growth of 203.90 yuan, a 12-year overall growth of 256.87 %, and an average annual growth rate of 11.18 %. Average annual rural per capita growth was highest in 2000, with a growth rate of 58.22; it was lowest in 2004, with a negative growth of 17.90 %. During this time, Qinghai's average annual growth in urban per capita cultural consumption demand was slightly higher than average annual growth in rural areas, by 0.38 percentage points, resulting in a slight expansion of Qinghai's urban-to-rural ratio of cultural consumption demand.

During the first 2 years of the "Twelfth Five-Year Plan" period, Qinghai's average annual growth in urban per capita cultural consumption was 9.97 %, lower than that during the "Tenth Five-Year Plan period by 9.53 percentage points, but higher that that during the "Eleventh Five-Year Plan" period by 5.21 percentage points; average annual growth in rural per capita cultural consumption was 19.45 %, higher than that during the "Tenth Five-Year Plan" period by 12.80 percentage points, and also higher than that during the "Eleventh Five-Year Plan" period, by 6.82 percentage points. At the same time, Qinghai's urban per capita values were higher than those in rural areas, but the annual urban growth degree was very significantly lower than the rural growth rate, by 9.48 percentage points, signifying that the urban-rural gap is shrinking. Qinghai's urban-to-rural ratio in cultural consumption shrunk significantly compared to that in 2010, by 15.25 %, with an urban-to-rural ratio rank of 14th out of 31 provinces and regions.

5.4.3.2 Regional Gaps in Urban and Rural Per Capita Cultural Consumption

See Fig. 5.27 for the Changing Status of Qinghai's Urban and Rural Per Capita Cultural Consumption and the National Regional Discrepancy since the year 2000.

From 2000 to 2012, Qinghai's urban and rural per capita cultural consumption and the national urban and rural regional discrepancy was reduced from 1.4661 to 1.4471, its ranking moving up from 25th to 22nd place among 31 provinces and regions. During this time, the smallest regional discrepancy was in 2003 at 1.3171, and the largest was in 2010 at 1.4662. By looking at the years listed in Fig. 5.27, we see that in 2001, 2007, and 2011 the regional discrepancy was reduced, while in all other years it expanded. Since the "Tenth Five-Year Plan" period, Qinghai's regional discrepancy in urban and rural cultural consumption was reduced by 1.30 %, and its situation of change in regional discrepancy was ranked 11th out of 31 provinces and regions. This signifies that in terms of changes in regional

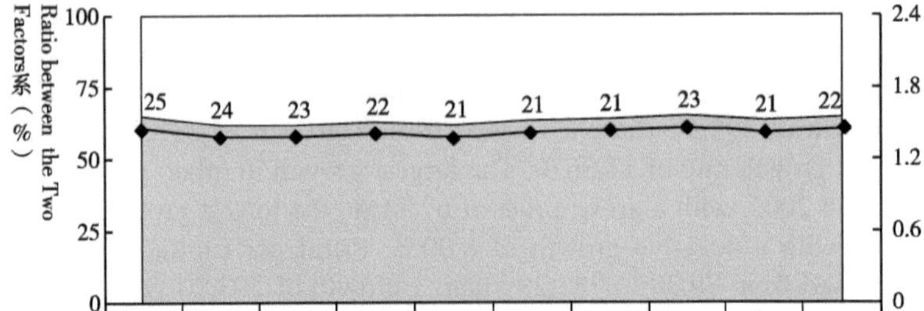

	2000	2001	2005	2006	2007	2008	2009	2010	2011	2012
Qinghai's Urban–Rural Per Capita	114.34	134.45	238.71	251.44	293.50	287.81	317.97	350.23	431.53	466.91
National Urban–Rural Per Capita	214.18	218.16	393.23	429.35	476.73	505.55	564.94	656.16	753.36	844.45
Urban–Rural Gap	1.4661	1.3837	1.3929	1.4144	1.3844	1.4307	1.4372	1.4662	1.4272	1.4471

Fig. 5.27 The changing status of Qinghai's urban and rural per capita cultural consumption and the national regional discrepancy. *LHS area*: urban and rural per capita cultural consumption (yuan converted to %), directly increasing ratio to local and national annual values; *RHS curve*: regional discrepancies in urban and rural per capita cultural consumption (no discrepancy = 1), marked years are ranked by regional discrepancies

discrepancy in urban and rural cultural consumption, Qinghai's status is relatively good compared to other provinces and regions.

While Qinghai's regional discrepancies in urban and rural cultural consumption experience changes, the province is influenced by its own status as well as that of the nation. For a comparison and detailed calculation of both Qinghai's and the nation's annual growth in urban and rural per capita cultural consumption, see the chapter on per capita absolute values in this paper for a focused investigation of the specific situation of growth discrepancies. From 2000 to 2012, Qinghai's average annual growth degree in urban and rural per capita cultural consumption was slightly higher than the national growth degree, by 0.33 percentage points, and the regional discrepancy between Qinghai's urban and rural cultural consumption demand and that of the nation was reduced relatively significantly.

During the first 2 years of the "Twelfth Five-Year Plan" period, Qinghai's average annual growth in urban and rural per capita cultural consumption was lower than its own average annual growth during the "Tenth Five-Year Plan" period, by 0.40 percentage points, but higher than its average annual growth during the "Eleventh Five-Year Plan" period, by 7.49 percentage points, and significantly higher than the national growth degree over the same period, by 2.02 percentage points. During this time, Qinghai's urban and rural per capita values were lower than the national urban and rural average values, and that its growth was higher than the national growth signifies that the regional gap was reduced, and the national urban and rural regional discrepancy was significantly reduced from that of 2010, by 1.30 %, with a ranking of the regional discrepancy of 22nd out of 31 provinces and regions.

5.4.4 *Prosperity Evaluation of Qinghai's Urban and Rural Cultural Consumption*

To sum up the above: Since the "Tenth Five-Year Plan" period, the average annual growth of Qinghai's total urban and rural cultural consumption was slightly higher than average national growth; proportion of income, proportion of consumption both increased, while GDP ratio and non-cultural consumption surplus had a downward trend. During the "Eleventh Five-Year Plan" period, each indicator proportion change was not as much as those during the "Tenth Five-Year Plan" period; the urban-to-rural ratio was slightly expanded, and the regional discrepancy with national urban and rural regions was relatively significantly reduced. All of these results are concentrated in Qinghais's urban and rural cultural consumption prosperity index evaluation and calculation. For changes in Qinghais's urban and rural cultural consumption demand prosperity index since the year 2000, see Fig. 5.28.

5.4.4.1 Annual Horizontal Assessment of Prosperity Index

With the national urban and rural cultural consumption overall share value, per capita absolute value, and proportion of each index as a base, and balanced by the "ideal value" of 100 of no discrepancy between urban/rural areas and regions, in 2012 Qinghai's urban and rural prosperity index was 71.57, lower than the ideal value by 28.43, and lower than the previous year by 3.16. Qinghai's urban and rural prosperity index, in a ranking of 31 provinces and regions, was ranked 20th in the year 2000, 28th in 2005, 29th in 2010, and in 2012, it went down to 27th from 24th the previous year.

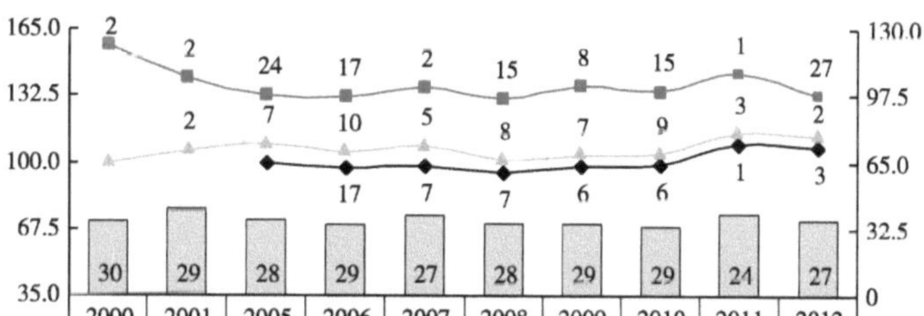

	2000	2001	2005	2006	2007	2008	2009	2010	2011	2012
Horizontal Assessment	71.20	77.28	71.93	69.75	74.08	70.01	70.18	68.85	74.73	71.57
Vertical Assessment (1)	100.00	105.90	109.02	104.98	107.98	100.91	103.49	104.01	114.07	112.66
Vertical Assessment (2)	—	—	100.00	96.97	98.41	94.96	98.00	98.83	108.63	107.12
Vertical Assessment (3)	122.08	105.90	98.04	96.97	101.44	95.88	102.31	99.67	108.11	97.39

Fig. 5.28 Changes in Qinghai's urban and rural cultural consumption demand prosperity index. *LHS cylindrical*: horizontal assessment (urban/rural, regional zero-difference ideal value = 100); *LHS curve*: vertical assessment (starting base value = 100), (*1*) starting value for the year 2000, (*2*) starting value for the year 2005; *RHS curve*: vertical assessment (*3*) starting from previous year. Assessed indexes for marked years are ranked in terms of provinces and regions

5.4.4.2 Vertical Assessment of Prosperity Since the "Tenth Five-Year Plan" Period

Based on a starting base value of 100 in the year 2000, the last year of the "Ninth Five-Year Plan" period, Qinghai's urban and rural prosperity index in 2012 was 112.66, higher than that of the starting base value of the year 2000 by 12.66, but lower than that the previous year by 1.41. In a ranking of 31 provinces and regions, Qinghai's urban and rural prosperity index was ranked 2nd in 2001, 7th in 2005, 9th in 2010, and in 2012 increased from 3rd place the previous year to 2nd place.

5.4.4.3 Vertical Assessment of Prosperity Index Since the "Eleventh Five-Year Plan" Period

Based on a starting base value of 100 in 2005, the last year of the "Tenth Five-Year Plan" period, in 2012 Qinghai's urban and rural prosperity index for this indicator was 107.12, higher than the 2005 starting base value by 7.12, but lower than the previous year by 1.51. In a ranking of 31 provinces and regions, Qinghai's urban and rural prosperity index for this indicator was ranked 17th in 2006, 6th in 2010, and in 2012 went down from 1st place the previous year to 3rd place.

5.4.4.4 Vertical Assessment of Prosperity Index Since the "Twelfth Five-Year Plan" Period

Setting 2010, the last year of the "Eleventh Five-Year Plan" period, with a starting base value of 100, in 2012 Qinghai's urban and rural prosperity index for this indicator was 105.49, higher than the 2010 starting base value by 5.49, but lower than the previous year by 2.62. In a ranking of 31 provinces and regions, Qinghai's urban and rural prosperity index for this indicator was ranked 1st place in 2011, and in 2012 went down to 10th place. This evaluation index is better explained by text than in a table; see Report B3 on the provincial and regional urban and rural ranking.

5.4.4.5 Annual Vertical Assessment of Prosperity Index

With the previous year, 2011, having a starting base value of 100, in 2012 Qinghai's urban and rural prosperity index for this indicator was 97.39, lower than the 2011 starting base value by 2.61. Qinghai's urban and rural prosperity index or this indicator, in a ranking of 31 provinces and regions, was ranked 2nd in 2000, 24th in 2005, 15th in 2010, and in 2012 decreased from 1st place the previous year to 27th place.

5.5 Liaoning: Rising to Third Place in Urban and Rural Prosperity Index After the "Tenth Five-Year Plan"

This paper presents related growth trends across all aspects in Liaoning from 2000 to 2012, fully analyzing and assessing Liaoning's urban and rural cultural consumption status.

5.5.1 Liaoning's Urban and Rural Cultural Consumption Growth

5.5.1.1 Changes in Overall Cultural Consumption Share Values

See Fig. 5.29 for Liaoning's urban and rural total cultural consumption growth and changes in shares since the year 2000.

From 2000 to 2012, Liaoning's total urban and rural cultural consumption grew from 7.582 billion yuan to 37.8 billion yuan, an increase of 30.218 billion yuan, a 12-year overall growth of 398.55 %, an average annual growth rate of 14.33 %, with a growth degree ranked 5th place out of 31 provinces and regions. During the "Tenth Five-Year Plan" period, average annual growth was 13.87 %; during the "Eleventh Five-Year Plan" period, average annual growth was 14.59 %; during the first 2 years of the "Twelfth Five-Year Plan" period, average annual growth was 14.81 %. The average annual growth degree during the first 2 years of the "Twelfth Five-Year Plan" period was higher than that during the "Eleventh Five-Year Plan"

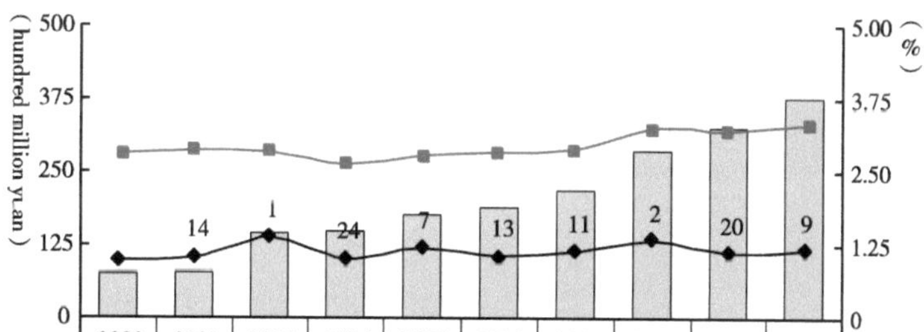

	2000	2001	2005	2006	2007	2008	2009	2010	2011	2012
Cultural Consumption Total	75.82	79.34	145.13	147.58	175.85	189.51	218.05	286.78	324.62	378.00
Total Annual Growth Coefficient	100.00	104.64	137.96	101.69	119.16	107.77	115.06	131.52	113.19	116.44
Share of National Total	2.8036	2.8595	2.8309	2.6219	2.7989	2.8299	2.8990	3.2669	3.2057	3.3141

Fig. 5.29 Liaoning's urban and rural total cultural consumption growth and changes in shares. *LHS cylindrical*: total amount in urban and rural cultural consumption (hundred million yuan); *LHS curve*: annual growth coefficient (previous year = 100), marked annual growth ranked by province or region, not counting the starting year of 2000; *RHS curve*: portion of national urban and rural share (%)

period by 0.22 percentage points; higher than that during the "Tenth Five-Year Plan" period by 0.94 percentage points.

Over the same period, the average annual growth rate in national overall urban and rural cultural consumption was 12.74 %, relatively significantly lower than that of Liaoning, by 1.59 percentage points. Liaoning's overall urban and rural cultural consumption as proportion of the national share increased from 2.80 to 3.31 %, a degree of increase of 18.19 %, a growth degree and share increase change ranked 5th place out of 31 provinces and regions.

During the first 2 years of the "Twelfth Five-Year Plan" period, the average annual growth in overall national urban and rural cultural consumption was 13.99 %, and the average annual growth Liaoning's overall urban and rural cultural consumption was 14.81 %, slightly higher than the national growth, by 0.82 percentage points, making up a proportion of 1.44 % of the national share in 2010. Over the same time, Liaoning's total growth was higher than its own average annual growth during the "Tenth Five-Year Plan" period, by 0.94 percentage points, and also higher than its own average annual growth during the "Eleventh Five-Year Plan" period, by 0.22 percentage points, with a growth degree and degree of change in the national share ranked 9th out of 31 provinces and regions.

5.5.1.2 Growth in Cultural Consumption Per Capita Absolute Values

See Fig. 5.30 for Liaoning's urban and rural per capita cultural consumption growth and degree of changes in status since the year 2000.

From 2000 to 2012, Liaoning's urban and rural per capita cultural consumption grew from 181.51 to 861.84 yuan, an increase of 680.33 yuan, a total growth of 374.82 %, an average annual growth of 13.86 %, and a growth degree ranked 2nd

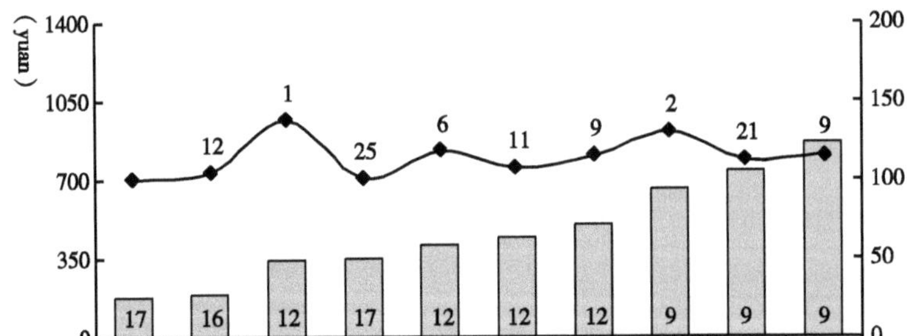

	2000	2001	2005	2006	2007	2008	2009	2010	2011	2012
Per Capita Cultural Consumption	181.51	189.41	344.00	347.58	410.43	440.05	505.10	659.74	741.33	861.84
Annual Growth Coefficient	100.00	104.35	137.79	101.04	118.08	107.22	114.78	130.62	112.37	116.26

Fig. 5.30 Liaoning's urban and rural per capita cultural consumption growth and degree of change in status. *LHS cylindrical*: urban per capita cultural consumption (yuan); *RHS curve*: annual growth value (previous year = 100), showing ranking of annual growth of provinces and regions, not counting the 2000 starting year

place out of 31 provinces and regions. During the "Tenth Five-Year Plan" period, total growth in per capita values was 89.52 %, an average annual growth of 13.64 %; during the "Eleventh Five-Year Plan" period, total growth in per capita values was 91.78 %, with an average annual growth of 13.91 %. During the "Eleventh Five-Year Plan" period the average annual growth rate was higher than that during the "Tenth Five-Year Plan" period, by 0.27 percentage points. The highest growth in per capita values occurred in 2005, with a growth rate of 37.79 %; the lowest growth occurred in 2004 with a growth rate of 0.46 %.

Over the same period, the average annual growth rate in national urban and rural cultural consumption was 12.11 %, relatively significantly lower than that of Liaoning. Liaoning's urban and rural per capita cultural consumption went from being 84.75 % of the national urban and rural per capita value to 103.06 % of it (See Fig. 5.34 for a comparison). The per capita absolute value rank went up from 17th to 9th place among 31 provinces and regions.

In the first 2 years of the "Twelfth Five-Year Plan" period, the average annual growth rate in national urban and rural per capita cultural consumption was 13.44 %, and Liaoning's growth rate was 14.29 %, slightly higher than that of the nation, and also higher than its own average annual growth during the "Tenth Five-Year Plan" period, as well as being higher than its own growth during the "Eleventh Five-Year Plan" period, with a growth rate ranked 9th place out of 31 provinces and regions.

5.5.2 Related Background Situation of Liaoning's Urban and Rural Cultural Consumption

The relationship between Liaoning's per capita GDP and urban and rural per capita income, consumption (separated into non-cultural and cultural consumption), and savings is shown in Fig. 5.31.

From 2000 to 2012, Liaoning's average annual growth in per capita GDP was 14.48 %; the average annual growth in urban and rural per capita income was 13.62 %, slightly lower than GDP growth, by 0.86 percentage points; the average annual growth in per capita overall consumption was 12.44 %, significantly lower than GDP growth by 2.04 percentage points, relatively significantly lower than income growth, by 1.18 percentage points; average annual growth in per capita savings was 17.21 %, significantly higher than GDP growth by 2.73 percentage points, and significantly higher than income growth, by 3.59 percentage points, and very significantly higher than total consumption growth, by 4.77 percentage points; the average annual growth in per capita cultural consumption was 13.86 %, slightly lower than GDP growth, by 0.62 percentage points, slightly higher than income growth, by 0.24 percentage points, relatively significantly higher than overall consumption growth, by 1.42 percentage points, and significantly lower than savings growth, by 3.35 percentage points.

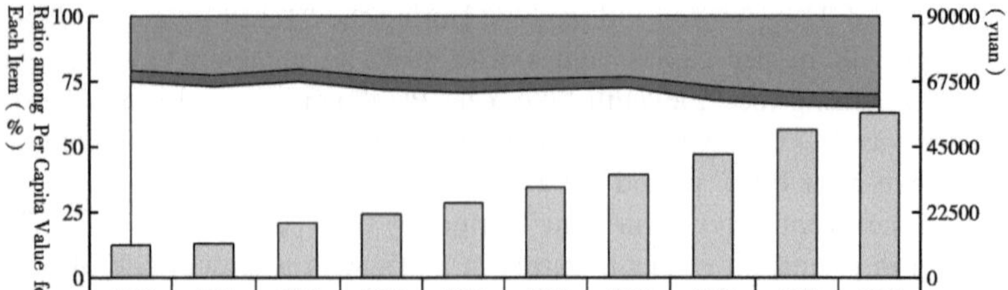

	2000	2001	2005	2006	2007	2008	2009	2010	2011	2012
(1) Per Capita Savings	816.61	974.53	1381.78	1822.90	2271.10	2596.38	2747.20	3638.35	4629.65	5488.91
(2) Cultural Consumption	181.51	189.41	344.00	347.58	410.43	440.05	505.10	659.74	741.33	861.84
(3) Non–Cultural Consumption	2969.16	3165.52	5120.35	5614.52	6539.21	7796.20	8607.71	9154.09	10521.46	12007.60
(4) Non–Cultural Consumption	11177.00	12015.00	18632.00	21788.00	25729.00	31259.00	35239.00	42355.00	50760.00	56649.00

Fig. 5.31 The relationship between Liaoning's per capita GDP and urban and rural per capita income, consumption, and savings. *LHS area*: urban and rural per capita savings, cultural consumption, non-cultural consumption (yuan are converted to %), (1) + (2) + (3) = income, (2) + (3) = total consumption, (1) + (2) = non-cultural consumption surplus, and the direct proportion between each value throughout the years

In the first 2 years of the "Twelfth Five-Year Plan" period, Liaoning's average annual growth in per capita GDP was 15.65 %, its average annual growth in urban and rural per capita income was 16.82 %, its average annual growth in per capita overall consumption was 14.51 %, its average annual growth in per capita savings was 22.83 %, and its average annual growth in per capita cultural consumption was 14.29 %.

In the analysis and calculation of related ratios of Liaoning's urban and rural per capita cultural consumption, these figures came about. For a look at the changing proportions of Liaoning's urban and rural cultural consumption since the year 2000, see Fig. 5.32.

5.5.2.1 Ratio of Per Capita Cultural Consumption and Per Capita GDP

From 2000 to 2012, the ratio of Liaoning's urban and rural per capita cultural consumption to per capita GDP decreased from 1.62 % to 1.52 %, and because the proportion for this indicator for other provinces and regions was lowered more significantly, Liaoning's ranking went up from 30th place to 24th place.

Looking at this across time periods, during the "Tenth Five-Year Plan" period, Lioaning's urban and rural ratio for this indicator increased by 0.22 percentage points; during the "Eleventh Five-Year Plan" period, it decreased by 0.29 percentage points. During the first 2 years of the "Twelfth Five-Year Plan" period, Liaoning's urban and rural ratio for this indicator decreased by 0.04 percentage points, a degree of decrease of 2.32 %, with a coordination of cultural consumption

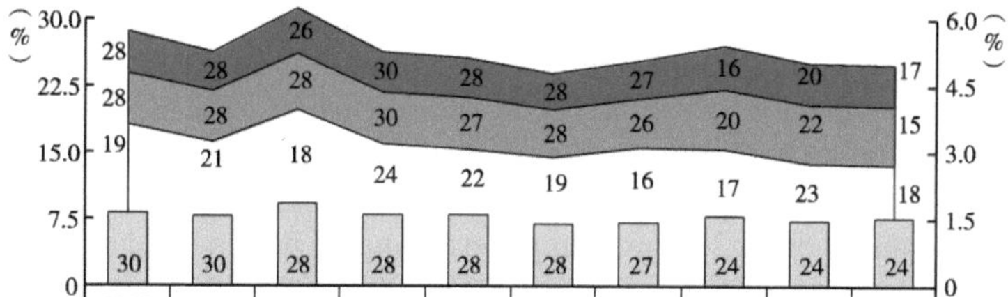

	2000	2001	2005	2006	2007	2008	2009	2010	2011	2012
Proportion of Income	4.5753	4.3750	5.0247	4.4648	4.4512	4.0623	4.2588	4.9043	4.6646	4.6946
Total Consumption Ratio	5.7611	5.6458	6.2953	5.8299	5.9058	5.3429	5.5427	6.7226	6.5821	6.6968
Ratio to Surplus	18.1855	16.2735	19.9329	16.0140	15.3059	14.4924	15.5305	15.3496	13.8024	13.5707
Ratio to GDP	1.6240	1.5765	1.8463	1.5953	1.5952	1.4078	1.4333	1.5576	1.4605	1.5214

Fig. 5.32 Changes in Liaoning's urban and rural cultural consumption ratio. *LHS area*: urban and rural per capita cultural consumption as proportion of income, overall consumption, and ratio to non-cultural consumption surplus (called "Non Surplus" on the chart) (%). Each annual proportion's rise or fall is superimposed; *RHS cylinder*: ratio of urban and rural per capita cultural consumption and GDP (%). Years are ranked according to urban-to-rural ratio of provinces or regions

demand growth and economic development slightly decreased from that of 2010. During this period, the highest value occurred in 2005 at 1.85 %, while the lowest value occurred in 2008 at 1.41 %.

5.5.2.2 Per Capita Cultural Consumption as Proportion of Per Capita Income

From 2000 to 2012, Liaoning's urban and rural per capita cultural consumption as proportion of per capita income increased from 4.58 to 4.69 %, and experienced an increase in rank from 28th to 17th place in a ranking of 31 provinces and regions. By looking at the years listed in Fig. 5.32, in 2005, 2009–2010, and 2012, the ratio for this indicator increased, and during all other years the annual average decreased. Since the "Tenth Five-Year Plan" period, Liaoning's urban and rural indicator for this ratio increased by 2.61 %, with a degree of change tanked 4th place out of 31 provinces and regions.

Looking at it across time periods, Liaoning's urban and rural ratio for this indicator, during the "Tenth Five-Year Plan" period, increased by 0.45 percentage points; in the "Eleventh Five-Year Plan" period, it decreased by 0.12 percentage points. In the first 2 years of the "Twelfth Five-Year Plan" period, Liaoning's urban and rural ratio for its indicator decreased by 0.21 percentage points, with a degree of decrease of 4.28 %, and a coordination of cultural consumption demand and income growth that was relatively significantly decreased from that of 2010. During this period, the highest value occurred in 2005 at 5.02 %, and the lowest was in 2008 at 4.06 %.

5.5.2.3 Per Capita Cultural Consumption as Proportion of Total Per Capita Consumption

From 2000 to 2012, Liaoning's urban and rural per capita cultural consumption as proportion of total per capita consumption increased from 5.76 to 6.70 %, moving up in ranking from 28th to 15th place among 31 provinces and regions. By looking at the years listed in Fig. 5.32, in 2005, 2007, 2009–2010, and 2012, this indicator ratio increased, while in all other years in decreased. Since the "Tenth Five-Year Plan" period, Liaoning's urban and rural indicator for this ratio increased by 16.24 %, with a degree of change ranked 5th among 31 provinces and regions.

Looking at this across time periods, Liaoning's urban and rural ratio for this indicator increased 0.53 percentage points in the "Tenth Five-Year Plan" period; in the "Eleventh Five-Year Plan" period, it increased by 0.43 percentage points. During the first 2 years of the "Twlefth Five-Year Plan" period, Liaoning's urban and rural ratio for this indicator decreased by 0.03 percentage points, a degree of decrease of 0.38 %, and a coordination of cultural consumption growth and overall consumption growth that is slightly lower than that in 2010. During this period, the highest value occurred in 2010 at 6.72 %, and the lowest value in 2008 at 5.34 %.

5.5.2.4 The Ratio of Per Capita Cultural Consumption to Per Capita Non-cultural Surplus

From 2000 to 2012, the ratio of Liaoning's urban and rural per capita cultural consumption and non-cultural consumption surplus fell from 18.19 % to 13.57 %, and because the ratio decrease of other provinces and regions was more significant, Liaoning's rank went up from 19th to 18th place. Looking at the years listed in Fig. 5.32, this ratio indicator, in 2005 and 2009 saw an increase, while in all other years it decreased. Since the "Tenth Five-Year Plan" period, Liaoning's urban and rural ratio for this indicator decreased by 25.38 %, with a degree of changed ranked 14th out of 31 provinces and regions.

Looking at this across time periods, during the "Tenth Five-Year Plan" period, Liaoning's ratio for this indicator increased by 1.75 percentage points; during the "Eleventh Five-Year Plan" period, it decreased by 4.58 percentage points. During the first 2 years of the "Twelfth Five-Year Plan" period, Liaoning's urban and rural ratio for this indicator decreased by 1.78 percentage points, a degree of decrease of 11.59 %, and the coordination of cultural consumption demand growth and "money left over" after "essential consumption" was very significantly decreased compared to 2010. During this period, the highest value occurred in 2005 at 19.93 %, and the lowest value occurred in 2012 at 13.57 %.

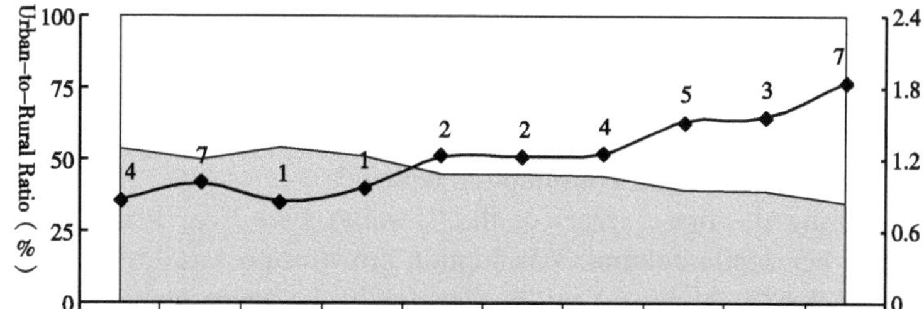

	2000	2001	2005	2006	2007	2008	2009	2010	2011	2012
Urban per capita	169.55	189.54	320.40	342.68	443.43	475.33	549.59	763.55	856.57	1027.31
Rural per capita	195.38	189.26	376.93	354.59	362.78	387.97	437.79	500.28	549.96	556.56
Liaoning's Urban-to-Rural Ratio	0.8678	1.0015	0.8500	0.9664	1.2223	1.2252	1.2554	1.5262	1.5575	1.8458

Fig. 5.33 Changes in Liaoning's urban-to-rural ratio of per capita cultural consumption. *LHS area*: urban and rural per capita cultural consumption (yuan are converted to %), the ratio annual between direct annual increase in urban and rural areas; *RHS curve*: urban-to-rural ratio of per capita cultural consumption (rural = 1, a number lower than 1 signifies an "urban-rural reversal", that is, the urban per capita is lower than that of the rural areas), and provinces and regions are ranked by annual urban-to-rural ratio

5.5.3 Liaoning's Coordination of Urban/Rural and Regional Cultural Consumption

5.5.3.1 Urban/Rural Ratio of Per Capita Cultural Consumption

See Fig. 5.33 for Changes in Liaoning's Urban-to-rural ratio of Per Capita Cultural Consumption since 2000.

From 2000 to 2012, Liaoning's urban-to-rural ratio of per capita cultural consumption expanded from 0.8678 to 1.8458, and its rank went down from 4th to 7th place among 31 provinces and regions. During this period, the smallest urban-to-rural ratio occurred in 2005, at 0.8500, and the largest occurred in 2012 at 1.8458. Looking at the years listed in Fig. 5.33, we see that in 2005 the urban-to-rural ratio was reduced, but during all other years it expanded. Since the "Tenth Five-Year Plan" period, Liaoning's urban-to-rural ratio of cultural consumption expanded 112.70 %, with a change in urban-to-rural ratio ranked 22nd out of 31 provinces and regions. This signifies that Liaoning is one of the provinces or regions with the largest serious degree of change in urban-to-rural ratio of cultural consumption.

Liaoning's changes in urban-to-rural ratio of cultural consumption were influenced by its own changes both in urban and rural areas. Over the same period, Liaoning's urban per capita cultural consumption grew from 169.55 yuan to 1.027.31 yuan, an increase of 857.76 yuan, a 12-year overall growth of 505.90 %, and an average annual growth rate of 16.20 %. The highest average annual growth in per capita urban values occurred in 2005, with a growth rate of 72.94 %. The lowest average annual growth occurred in 2006, with a negative growth of 5.93 %. During this period, Liaoning's average annual growth in urban and rural cultural consumption was very significantly higher average annual growth for rural areas, by 7.08 percentage points, resulting in significantly broadened urban-to-rural ratio of Liaoning's cultural consumption demand.

During the first 2 years of the "Twelfth Five-Year Plan" period, Liaoning's urban per capita cultural consumption growth rate was 15.99 %, higher than that during the "Tenth Five-Year Plan" period by 2.42 percentage points, but lower than that during the "Eleventh Five-Year Plan" period by 2.98 percentage points; the average annual growth in rural per capita cultural consumption was 5.47 %, lower than that during the "Tenth Five-Year Plan" period by 8.57 percentage points, and also lower than that during the "Eleventh Five-Year Plan" period by 0.36 percentage points. At this time, Liaoning's urban and rural per capita values were higher than those in rural areas, and the annual growth degree of urban areas was significantly higher than that of rural areas, by 10.52 percentage points, signifying that the urban-rural gap had widened. Compared to that in 2010, Liaoning's urban-to-rural ratio of cultural consumption was very significantly expanded, by 20.94 %; its urban-to-rural ratio was ranked 7th out of 31 provinces and regions.

5.5.3.2 Regional Gaps in Urban and Rural Per Capita Cultural Consumption

See Fig. 5.34 for the Changing Status of Liaoning's Urban and Rural Per Capita Cultural Consumption and the National Regional Discrepancy since the year 2000.

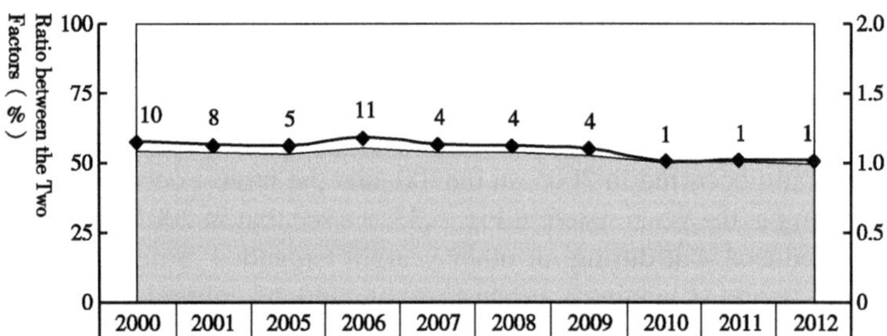

	2000	2001	2005	2006	2007	2008	2009	2010	2011	2012
Liaoning's Urban and Rural Per Capita	181.51	189.41	344.00	347.58	410.43	440.05	505.10	659.74	741.33	861.84
National Urban and Rural Per Capita	214.18	218.16	393.23	429.35	476.73	505.55	564.94	656.16	753.36	844.45
Urban–Rural Gap	1.1525	1.1318	1.1252	1.1904	1.1391	1.1296	1.1059	1.0055	1.0160	1.0206

Fig. 5.34 Changing status of Liaoning's urban and rural per capita cultural consumption and the national regional discrepancy. *LHS area*: urban and rural per capita cultural consumption (yuan converted to %), a direct rising proportional relationship between local and national annual values; *RHS curve*: regional discrepancies in urban and rural per capita cultural consumption (no discrepancy = 1), marked years are ranked by regional discrepancies

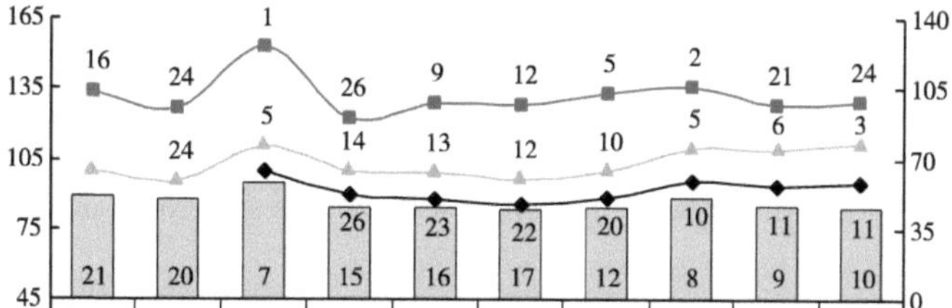

	2000	2001	2005	2006	2007	2008	2009	2010	2011	2012
Horizontal Assessment	89.22	87.59	94.57	84.03	83.80	83.42	84.37	88.19	84.69	84.13
Vertical Assessment (1)	100.00	95.60	110.66	99.90	98.76	96.08	100.01	109.79	109.13	111.80
Vertical Assessment (1)	—	—	100.00	89.89	87.93	85.20	88.02	95.15	93.56	94.46
Vertical Assessment (1)	103.15	95.60	126.17	89.89	97.47	96.69	102.87	105.72	97.27	98.27

Fig. 5.35 Changes in Liaoning's urban and rural cultural consumption demand prosperity index. *LHS cylindrical*: horizontal assessment (urban/rural, regional zero-difference ideal value = 100); *LHS curve*: vertical assessment (starting base value = 100), (*1*) starting value for the year 2000, (*2*) starting value for the year 2005; *RHS curve*: vertical assessment (*3*) starting from previous year. Assessed indexes for marked years are ranked in terms of provinces and regions

From 2000 to 2012, the regional discrepancy between Liaoning's urban and rural per capita cultural consumption and the national urban and rural regions was reduced from 1.1525 to 1.0206, and its ranking among 31 provinces and regions rose from 10th place to 1st. During this period, the smallest regional discrepancy was in 2010 at 1.0055, and the largest was in 2004 at 1.2672. Just by looking at the years listed in Fig. 5.35, we see that in 2001, 2005, and 2007–2010, the regional discrepancy was reduced, and it all other years it expanded. Since the "Tenth Five-Year Plan" period, Liaoning's regional discrepancy in urban and rural cultural consumption was reduced by 11.44 %, and was ranked 2nd among 31 provinces and regions in terms of changes in regional discrepancy. This signifies that Liaoning is one of the provinces with a relatively good status in terms of changes in regional discrepancy of urban and rural cultural consumption.

While Liaoning's regional discrepancies in urban and rural cultural consumption experience changes, the province also is influenced by its own status as well as that of the nation. For a comparison and detailed calculation of both Liaoning's and the nation's annual growth in urban and rural per capita cultural consumption, see the chapter on per capita absolute values in this paper for a focused investigation of the specific situation of growth discrepancies. From 2000 to 2012, Liaoning's average annual growth in urban and rural per capita cultural consumption was significantly higher than the national growth, by 1.75 percentage points, and the regional discrepancy between Liaoning's urban and rural cultural consumption demand and that of the nation was significantly reduced.

During the first 2 years of the "Twelfth Five-Year Plan" period, the average annual growth in Liaoning's urban and rural cultural consumption was higher than that during "Tenth Five-Year Plan" period, by 0.65 percentage points, and also higher than that during the "Eleventh Five-Year Plan" period, by 0.38 percentage points, and also slightly higher than the national growth degree, by 0.85 percentage points. During this time, Liaoning's urban and rural per capita values were higher than the national urban and rural average values; the higher growth compared to the nation signifies that the regional discrepancy expanded, and the regional discrepancy with the nation was significantly expanded from that of 2010, by 1.50 %, with a regional discrepancy ranking 1st among 31 provinces and regions.

5.5.4 *Prosperity Status Evaluation of Liaoning's Urban and Rural Cultural Consumption*

To sum up the above: since the "Tenth Five-Year Plan" period, Liaoning's average annual growth in overall urban and rural cultural consumption was significantly higher than national growth, with average annual growth in per capita values being significantly higher than the national average annual growth; proportion of income, proportion of consumption both increased, while GDP ratio and non-cultural consumption surplus had a downward trend. During the "Eleventh Five-Year Plan" period, each indicator proportion change was not as much as those during the "Tenth Five-Year Plan" period; the urban-to-rural ratio was very significantly expanded, and the regional discrepancy with the national urban and rural areas was very significantly reduced. All of these results are concentrated in Liaoning's urban and rural cultural consumption prosperity index evaluation and calculation. For changes in Liaoing's urban and rural cultural consumption demand prosperity index since the year 2000, see Fig. 5.35.

5.5.4.1 Annual Horizontal Prosperity Assessment

With the national urban and rural cultural consumption overall share value, per capita absolute value, and proportion of each index as a base, and balanced by the "ideal value" of 100 of no discrepancy between urban/rural areas and regions, in 2012 Liaoning's urban and rural prosperity index was 84.13, lower than the ideal value by 15.87, and also lower than the previous year by 0.56. In a ranking of 31 provinces and regions, Liaoning's urban and rural index was ranked 21st in 2000, 7th in 2005, 8th in 2010, and in 2012 its ranking fell from 9th to 10th place.

5.5.4.2 Vertical Prosperity Assessment Since the "Tenth Five-Year Plan" Period

With the last year of the "Ninth Five-Year Plan" period, 2000, with a starting base value of 100, in 2012 Liaoning's urban and rural prosperity index was 111.80, higher than the starting base value in 2000 by 11.80, and higher than that of the previous year by 2.67. In a ranking of 31 provinces and regions, Liaoning's urban and rural prosperity index was ranked 24th in 2001, 5th in 2005, the same in 2010, and in 2012 it went down from 6th place the previous year to 3rd place.

5.5.4.3 Vertical Prosperity Assessment Since the "Eleventh Five-Year Plan" Period

With 2005, the last year of the "Tenth Five-Year Plan" period, having a starting base value of 100, in 2012 Liaoning's urban and rural prosperity index was 94.46, lower than the 2005 starting base value by 5.54, but higher than that of the previous year by 0.90. In a ranking of 31 provinces and regions, Liaoning's urban and rural prosperity index was ranked 26th in 2006, 10th in 2010, and in 2012 was the same as the previous year, 11th place.

5.5.4.4 Vertical Prosperity Assessment Since the "Twelfth Five-Year Plan" Period

With 2010, the last year of the Eleventh Five-Year Plan" period, with a starting base value of 100, in 2012 Liaoning's urban and rural prosperity index was 95.70, lower than the starting base value in 2010 by 4.30, and also lower than the previous year by 1.57. This evaluation index is better explained by text than in a table; see Report B3 on the provincial and regional urban and rural ranking.

5.5.4.5 Annual Vertical Assessment of Prosperity Index

Setting 2011 with a starting base value of 100, in 2012 Liaoning's urban and rural prosperity index was 98.27, lower than the 2011 starting base value by 1.73. In a ranking of 31 provinces and regions, Liaoning's urban and rural prosperity index was ranked 16th in 2000, 1st in 2005, 2nd in 2010, and in 2012 went down from the previous year from 21st place to 24th.

Chapter 6
Key City Reports

6.1 Guangzhou: Maintaining First Place in the 2012 Horizontal City Prosperity Evaluation

Guangzhou: Maintaining First Place in the 2012 Horizontal Urban and Rural Prosperity Evaluation

6.1.1 Guangzhou's Growth in Cultural and Educational Consumption Demand

6.1.1.1 Changing Shares of Overall Cultural and Educational Consumption

See Fig. 6.1 for Guangzhou's overall growth in cultural and educational consumption and changes in share since 2005.

From 2000 to 2012, Guangzhou's overall cultural and educational consumption increased from 14.174 to 38.436 billion yuan, an increase of 24.262 billion yuan, a total growth of 171.17 %, an average annual growth of 15.32 %, and a growth degree ranked 7th out of 36 major cities. The largest growth occurred in 2007, with a growth rate of 31.17 %, and the lowest growth occurred in 2008, with a growth rate of 9.46 %.

During this period, the average annual growth in national urban and rural overall cultural and educational consumption was 13.00 %; Guangzhou's average annual growth degree was significantly higher than that of the nation, by 2.32 percentage points. Guangzhou's overall cultural and educational consumption as proportion of the national urban share increased from 2.34 to 2.70 %, a degree of increase of

Y. Wang et al., *Annual Evaluation Report of China's Cultural Consumption Demand*,
Research Series on the Chinese Dream and China's Development Path,
DOI 10.1007/978-981-10-0730-9_6

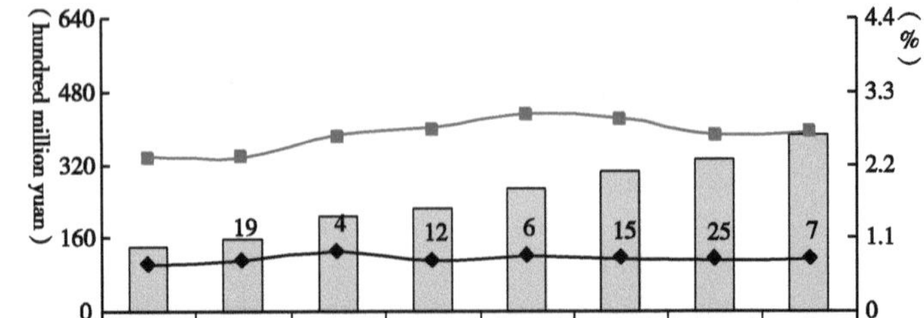

	2005	2006	2007	2008	2009	2010	2011	2012
Total Cultural and Educational Consumption	141.74	157.23	206.25	225.76	268.98	304.11	333.31	384.36
Annual Growth Coefficient	100.00	110.93	131.17	109.46	119.14	113.06	109.60	115.32
Proportion of National Urban–Rural Total	2.3377	2.2945	2.6506	2.7692	2.9733	2.8931	2.6459	2.6952

Fig. 6.1 Guangzhou's overall growth in cultural and educational consumption and changes in share. *LHS cylindrical*: total cultural and educational consumption (hundred million yuan); *LHS curve*: annual growth coefficient (previous year = 100), annual growth of cities is ranked, except for 2005; *RHS curve*: proportion of national urban share

15.29 %, and a growth degree and share increase that was ranked 7th out of 36 major cities.

In the first 2 years of the "Twelfth Five-Year Plan" period, the average annual growth in overall national urban cultural and educational consumption was 16.48 %, while Guangzhou's overall average annual growth was 12.42 %, very significantly lower than the national growth degree, by 4.06 percentage points, and also very significantly lower than its own average annual growth during the "Eleventh Five-Year Plan" period by 4.08 percentage points. Guangzhou's proportion of the national urban share decreased by 6.84 % from 2010, with a growth degree and proportion share changed ranked 7th out of 36 provinces and regions.

6.1.1.2 Growth in Per Capita Absolute Values of Cultural and Educational Consumption

See Fig. 6.2 for growth in per capita absolute values of cultural and educational consumption in Guangzhou since 2005.

From 2005 to 2012, Guangzhou's per capita value of cultural and educational consumption increased from 2,328.97 to 5,667.29 yuan, an increase of 3,338.32 yuan, a total growth of 143.34 %, and average annual growth rate of 13.55 %, and a growth degree ranked 4th place out of 36 major cities. The highest annual per capita growth growth occurred in 2007, with a growth rate of 29.15 %, and the lowest occurred in 2008, with a growth rate of 7.71 %.

Over the same period, the average annual growth in national urban per capita educational and cultural consumption was 9.21 %. Guangzhou's average annual growth was very significantly higher than the national urban average annual growth, with per capita value increasing from 212.21 % of the national urban per

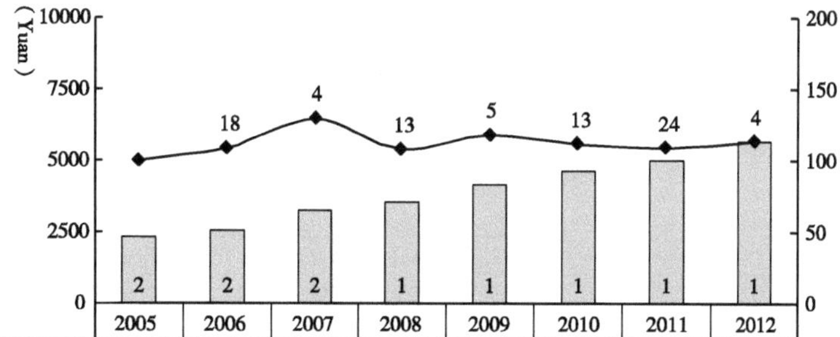

	2005	2006	2007	2008	2009	2010	2011	2012
Per Capita Cultural and Educational Consumption	2328.97	2530.69	3268.39	3520.45	4136.58	4611.35	4991.17	5667.29
Annual Growth Index	100.00	108.66	129.15	107.71	117.50	111.48	108.24	113.55

Fig. 6.2 Per capita cultural and educational consumption growth and changing growth trends in Guangzhou. *LHS cylindrical*: per capita cultural and educational consumption (yuan), ranking of annual per capita values of marked cities; RHS curve: annual growth coefficient (previous year = 100), ranking of annual growth of marked 36 cities, not counting the starting year of 2005

capita value to 278.70 % of it (for a comparison see Fig. 6.6 of this paper), and a per capita absolute value rank among 36 major cities increasing from 2nd place to 1st place.

During the first 2 years of "Twelfth Five-Year Plan" period, the average annual growth in national urban per capita cultural and educational consumption was 11.77 %, and Guangzhou's average annual growth in per capita value was 10.86 %, slightly lower than the national urban average annual growth. Guangzhou's annual growth in per capita values was also significantly lower than its own average annual growth during the "Eleventh Five-Year Plan" period, with a growth degree ranked 4th out of 36 major cities.

6.1.2 Related Background Situation of Guangzhou's Cultural and Educational Consumption

See Fig. 6.3 for the trends in relationships between Guangzhou's per capita GDP and urban per capita income, consumption (separated into non-cultural consumption and educational/cultural consumption) since 2005.

From 2005 to 2012, the average annual growth of Guangzhou's per capita GDP was 13.26; the average annual growth in urban per capita income was 11.13 %, significantly lower than GDP growth, by 2.13 percentage points; overall per capita consumption growth was 11.77 %, relatively significantly lower than GDP growth by 1.49 percentage points, and slightly higher than income growth, by 0.64 percentage points; the average annual growth in per capita savings was 8.45 %, very significantly lower than overall consumption growth, by 3.32 percentage points; average annual growth in per capita cultural and educational consumption was

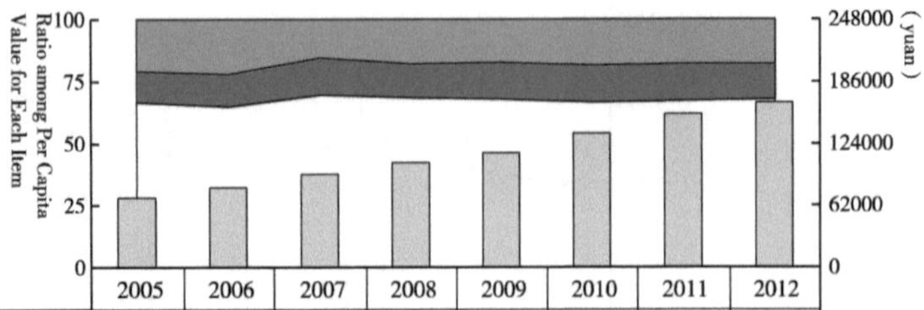

	2005	2006	2007	2008	2009	2010	2011	2012
(1) Urban Per Capita Savings	3819.00	4405.73	3517.90	4480.77	4788.71	5646.88	6228.34	6739.20
(2) Per Capita Cultural and Educational Consumption	2328.97	2530.69	3268.39	3520.45	4136.58	4611.35	4991.17	5667.29
(3) Per Capita Non-Cultural Consumption	12139.27	12914.24	15682.93	17315.50	18684.30	20400.26	23218.57	25863.12
(4) Urban Per Capita GDP	69268.00	80382.00	92676.00	105492.00	115734.00	134258.00	153308.00	165574.00

Fig. 6.3 Status of relationship of Guangzhou's per capita GDP to urban per capita income, consumption, and savings. *LHS area*: rural per capita savings, cultural consumption, non-cultural consumption (yuan converted to %), (1) + (2) + (3) = income, (2) + (3) = overall consumption, (1) + (2) = non-cultural consumption surplus; direct ratio in annual changes in index *RHS cylinder*: per capita GDP (yuan)

13.55 %, slightly higher than GDP growth, by 0.29 percentage points, and significantly higher than income growth, by 2.42 percentage points, relatively significantly higher than overall consumption growth, by 1.78 percentage points, notably higher than savings growth, by 5.10 percentage points.

During the "Eleventh Five-Year Plan" period, Guangzhou's average annual growth in per capita GDP was 14.15 %, average annual growth in urban per capita income was 10.89 %, average annual growth in per capita overall consumption was 11.57 %, average annual growth in per capita savings was 8.14 %, and average annual growth in per capita cultural and educational consumption was 14.64 %. Average annual growth in cultural and educational consumption was higher than GDP growth by 0.49 percentage points, higher than income growth by 3.75 percentage points, higher than overall consumption growth by 3.07 percentage points, and higher than savings growth by 6.50 percentage points.

During the first 2 years of the "Twelfth Five-Year Plan" period, Guangzhou's average annual growth in per capita GDP was 11.05 %, its average annual growth in urban per capita income was 11.73 %, average annual growth in per capita overall consumption was 12.28 %, average annual growth in per capita savings was 9.24 %, and average annual growth in per capita cultural and educational consumption was 10.86 %. Average annual growth in cultural and educational consumption was lower than GDP growth by 0.19 percentage points., lower than income growth by 0.87 percentage points, lower than overall consumption growth by 1.42 percentage points, and higher than savings growth by 1.62 percentage points. In 2012, the proportional relationship between Guangzhou's cultural and educational consumption and savings showed a rising trend.

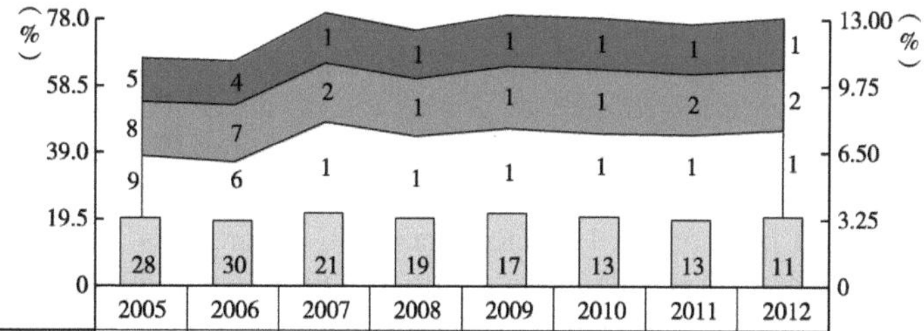

	2005	2006	2007	2008	2009	2010	2011	2012
Ratio of Cultural and Educational Consumption to Income	12.7355	12.7486	14.5461	13.9056	14.9824	15.0410	14.4932	14.8089
Cultural and Educational Consumption as Proportion of Consumption	16.0971	16.3852	17.2462	16.8960	18.1263	18.4368	17.6931	17.9740
Ratio of Non-Cultural Consumption to Surplus	37.8819	36.4841	48.1617	43.9989	46.3467	44.9527	44.4865	45.6800
Cultural and Educational Consumption and GDP	3.3623	3.1483	3.5267	3.3372	3.5742	3.4347	3.2557	3.4228

Fig. 6.4 Changing trends in Guangzhou's cultural and educational consumption ratio. *LHS area*: per capita cultural/educational as proportion of income, overall consumption, and non-cultural consumption surplus (%), the ratios of each indicator over the years are superimposed; *RHS cylinder*: per capita cultural/educational consumption and GDP (%). The ratio for each year is ranked within 36 major cities

These results were seen in the calculation and analysis of each indicator's proportion in Guangzhou's cultural and educational consumption. For the changing trends of proportions since 2005 in Guangzhou's cultural and educational consumption, see Fig. 6.4.

6.1.2.1 Ratio of Per Capita Cultural and Educational Consumption and Per Capita GDP

From 2005 to 2012, the ratio of Guangzhou's per capita cultural and educational consumption to per capita GDP increased from 3.36 to 3.46 %, its rank increasing from 28th place to 11th place out of 36 major cities. Since the "Eleventh Five-Year Plan" period, Guangzhou's ratio for this indicator increased by 0.06 percentage points, a degree of increase of 1.80 %, and a degree of change ranked 3rd place among 36 major cities.

During this period, in 2007, 2009, and 2012, Guangzhou's ratio for this indicator showed an increase, while in other years it decreased. The highest value occurred in 2009 at 3.57 %, and the lowest value in 2006 at 3.15 %. During the "Eleventh Five-Year Plan" period, it increased by 0.07 percentage points, with a degree of increase of 2.15 %; during the first 2 years of the "Twelfth Five-Year Plan" period, it decreased by 0.0119 percentage points, a degree of decrease of 0.35 %. In terms of the changes in the relationship of coordination between cultural and educational consumption demand growth and urban economic development, during the "Eleventh Five-Year Plan" period it was slightly increased, and during the first 2 years of the "Twelfth Five-Year Plan" period, it reverted to a slight decrease.

6.1.2.2 Per Capita Cultural and Educational Consumption as Proportion of Per Capita Income

From 2005 to 2012, Guangzhou's per capita cultural and educational consumption as proportion of per capita income increased from 12.74 to 14.81 %, and its ranking increased from 5th to 1st place among 36 major cities. Since the "Eleventh Five-Year Plan" period, Guanghou's ratio for this indicator increased by 2.07 percentage points, with a degree of increase of 16.28 %, and a degree of change ranked 2nd out of 36 major cities.

During this time, Guangzhou's ratio for this indicator showed increases from 2006–2007, 2009–2010, and in 2012, with a decrease in all other years. The highest value occurred in 2010 at 15.04 %, and the lowest value occurred in 2005 at 12.74 %. During the "Eleventh Five-Year Plan" period, it increased by 2.31 percentage points, a growth degree of 18.10 %; in the first 2 years of the "Twelfth Five-Year Plan" period, it decreased by 0.23 percentage points, with a degree of decrease of 1.54 %. In terms of the change in the relationship of coordination between cultural and educational consumption demand growth and growth in income of urban citizens, it was very significantly increased during the "Eleventh Five-Year Plan" period, and during the first 2 years of the "Twelfth Five-Year Plan" period it reverted to a relatively significant decrease.

6.1.2.3 Per Capita Cultural and Educational Consumption as Proportion of Per Capita Overall Consumption

From 2005 to 2012, Guangzhou's per capita cultural and educational consumption as proportion of overall consumption increased from 16.10 to 17.97 %, its rank increasing from 8th to 2nd place among 36 major cities. Since the "Eleventh Five-Year Plan" period, Guangzhou's ratio for this index increased by 1.88 percentage points, a degree of increase of 11.66 %, and a degree of change ranked 4th place out of 36 major cities.

During this period, Guangzhou's ratio for this indicator, from 2006–2007, 2009–2010, and 2012, showed an increase, while it decreased during all other years. The highest value occurred in 2010 at 18.44 %, and the lowest in 2005 at 16.10 %. During the "Eleventh Five-Year Plan" period, there was an increase of 2.34 percentage points, and a degree of increase of 14.53 %; during the first 2 years of the "Twelfth Five-Year Plan" period, there was a decrease of 0.46 percentage points, with a degree of decrease of 2.51 %. In terms of the changes in the coordination relationship between cultural and educational consumption demand growth and the growth in overall income of urban citizens, during the "Eleventh Five-Year Plan" period, it very significantly increased, while during the first 2 years of the "Twelfth Five-Year Plan" period it reverted to a significant decrease.

6.1.2.4 Ratio of Per Capita Cultural and Educational Consumption and Per Capita Non-cultural Consumption Surplus

From 2005 to 2012, Guangzhou's ratio of per capita cultural and educational consumption to per capita non-cultural consumption surplus increased from 37.88 to 45.68 %, and its ranked went up from 9th to 1st place out of 36 major cities. Since the "Eleventh Five-Year Plan" period, Guangzhou's ratio for this index went up 7.80 percentage points, a degree of increase of 20.59 %, and a degree of fluctuation ranked 3rd among 36 major cities.

Throughout this period, in 2007, 2009, and 2012 Guangzhou's ratio for this index increased, and in all other years it decreased. The highest value occurred in 2007 at 48.16 %, and the lowest in 2006 at 36.48 %. During the "Eleventh Five-Year Plan" period there was an increase of 7.07 percentage points, with a degree of increase of 18.67 %; during the first 2 years of the "Twelfth Five-Year Plan" period, there was an increase of 0.73 percentage points, with an increase degree of 1.62 %. As for the change in the coordination relationship of cultural and educational consumption growth and growth in "surplus money" left over from "essential consumption", there was a notable growth enhancement during the "Eleventh Five-Year Plan" period, and during the first 2 years of the "Twelfth Five-Year Plan" period, a significant enhancement trend continued.

6.1.3 Coordination Status of Urban/Rural and Regional Cultural and Educational Consumption

6.1.3.1 Urban-to-Rural Ratio of Per Capita Cultural and Educational Consumption Within the Provinces

For changing trends in urban-to-rural ratio of per capita cultural and educational consumption within the provinces since 2005, see Fig. 6.5.

From 2005 to 2012, Guangdong's urban-to-rural ratio of per capita cultural and educational consumption expanded from 4.6270 to 6.3308, with its ranking among 31 provinces and regions going down to 30th from 26th place. During this period, in 2008, and from 2010 to 2012, the urban-to-rural ratio was reduced, while in all other years it expanded. The smallest urban-to-rural ratio occurred in 2005 at 4.6270, and the largest occurred in 2007 at 7.8248. Since the "Eleventh Five-Year Plan" period, the urban-to-rural ratio of Guangdong Province's cultural and educational consumption expanded 36.82 %, with the degree of change in the urban-to-rural ratio ranked 26th out of 31 provinces and regions.

While the urban-to-rural ratio of Guangdong's cultural and educational consumption experiences changes, it is also under the influence of its own annual demand changes in both urban and rural aspects. In terms of the role they play within the provinces, major cities not only directly stimulate urban growth, but also drive rural growth.

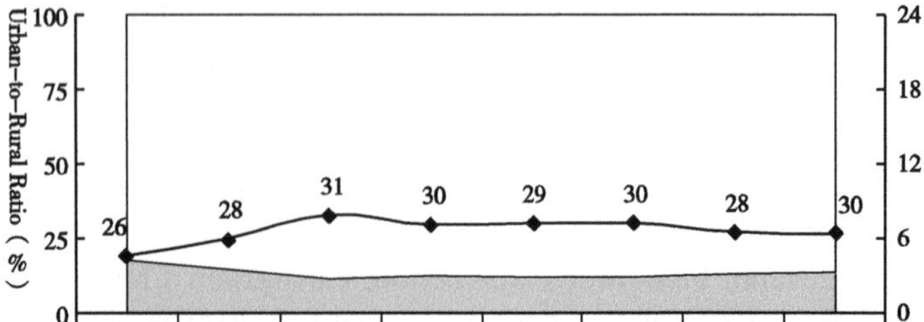

	2005	2006	2007	2008	2009	2010	2011	2012
Provincial/ Urban Per Capita	1669.09	1813.86	1994.86	1936.38	2168.88	2375.96	2647.94	2954.13
Provincial/Rural Per Capita	360.73	303.37	254.94	272.87	296.72	326.53	404.15	466.63
Provincial Urban–to–Rural Ratio	4.6270	5.9790	7.8248	7.0963	7.3095	7.2764	6.5519	6.3308

Fig. 6.5 Urban-to-rural ratio of per capita cultural and educational consumption within the provinces. *LHS area*: provincial and regional urban and rural per capita cultural and educational consumption (yuan converted to %), proportional relationship between urban and rural areas for each year superimposed; *RHS curve*: urban-to-rural ratio of per capita cultural and educational consumption; *RHS curve*: urban-to-rural ratio of per capita cultural and educational consumption (rural = 1). The urban-to-rural ratios of the marked years are ranked among 31 provinces and regions

From 2005 to 2012, Guangdong's urban per capita cultural and educational consumption grew from 1,669.09 to 2,954.13 yuan, a growth of 1,285.04 yuan, and an overall growth of 76.99 %, with an average annual growth of 8.50 %. The highest urban per capita growth occurred in 2009, with a growth rate of 12.01 %; the lowest growth occurred in 2008, with a negative growth of 2.93 %. Rural per capita cultural and educational consumption grew from 360.73 to 466.63, a growth of 105.90 yuan, a total growth of 29.36 %, and an average annual growth of 3.75 %. The highest rural per capita growth occurred in 2011, with a growth rate of 23.77 %; the lowest growth occurred in 2007 with a negative growth of 15.96 %. Within the 7 years, urban per capita cultural and educational consumption demand average annual growth was notably higher than rural average annual growth, by 4.75 percentage points, resulting in a significant expansion of the urban-to-rural ratio of cultural and educational consumption demand in Guangdong.

In the first 2 years of the "Twelfth Five-Year Plan" period, Guangdong's urban per capita average annual growth was 11.51 %, higher than its own average annual growth during the "Eleventh Five-Year Plan" period by 4.19 percentage points; rural per capita average annual growth was 19.54 %, higher than its own average annual growth during the "Eleventh Five-Year Plan" period by 21.51 percentage points. In 2012, urban per capita values were higher than rural ones, and the urban average annual growth degree was higher than rural growth by 8.03 percentage points, indicating that the gap was narrowing. Guangdong's urban-to-rural ratio in cultural and educational consumption demand was significantly reduced from that in 2010, by 13.00 %, and the urban-to-rural ratio was ranked 30th out of 31 provinces and regions.

6.1.3.2 Regional Discrepancies in Urban Per Capita Cultural and Educational Consumption

For Guangzhou's per capita cultural and educational consumption and the national urban regional discrepancy since 2005, see Fig. 6.6.

From 2005 to 2012, the regional discrepancy between Guangzhou's per capita cultural and educational consumption and that of the nation expanded from 2.1221 to 2.7870, and its ranked decreased from 35th to 36th place out of 36 major cities. During this period, Guangzhou's regional discrepancy was reduced in 2006 and 2011, while in all other years it expanded. The smallest regional discrepancy was in 2006 at 2.1036, and the largest regional discrepancy was in 2010 at 2.8332. Since the "Eleventh Five-Year Plan" period, the regional discrepancy between Guangzhou's cultural and educational consumption and that of the nation was expanded by 31.33 %, and Guangzhou's status of changes in regional discrepancy was ranked 36th out of 36 provinces and regions. This signifies that Guangzhou is considered one of the cities with the most serious degree of changes in cultural and educational consumption.

While regional discrepancy of Guangzhou's cultural and educational consumption experienced changes, it was also under the influence of its own as well as the national urban annual change in demand. See the chapter in this paper on per capita values for more detailed comparative calculations on national urban growth in per capita cultural and educational consumption, where a closer look is taken at growth discrepancies.

From 2005 to 2012, Guangzhou's average annual growth was notably higher than the national urban average growth, by 4.34 percentage points, and the regional

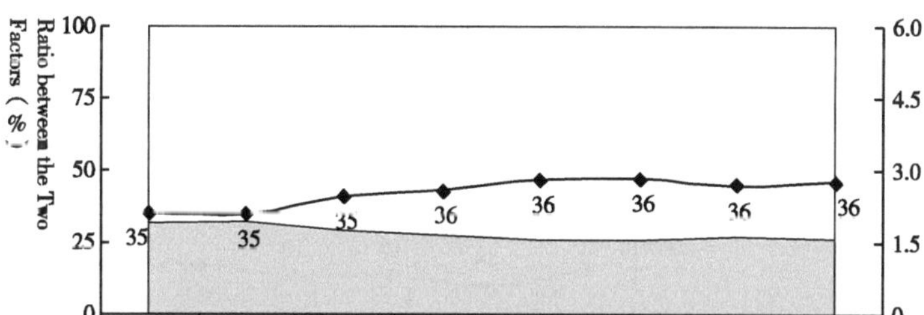

	2005	2006	2007	2008	2009	2010	2011	2012
Local Urban Per Capita	2328.97	2530.69	3268.39	3520.45	4136.58	4611.35	4991.17	5667.29
National Urban Per Capita	1097.46	1203.03	1329.16	1358.26	1472.76	1627.64	1851.74	2033.50
Local Regional Discrepancy	2.1221	2.1036	2.4590	2.5919	2.8087	2.8332	2.6954	2.7870

Fig. 6.6 Changing trends in regional discrepancies between Guangzhou's cultural and educational consumption and national urban values. *LHS area*: per capita cultural and educational consumption (yuan converted to %), direct proportional relationship between local and national annual values; *RHS curve*: regional discrepancy in per capita cultural and educational consumption (no discrepancy = 1). Regional discrepancies of the marked years are ranked among 36 major cities

discrepancy between Guangzhou's cultural and educational consumption demand and that of the nation's urban areas was expanded by an extreme amount.

In the first 2 years of the "Twlefth Five-Year Plan" period, Guangzhou's average annual growth was significantly lower than its own average annual growth during the "Eleventh Five-Year Plan" period, by 3.78 percentage points, and also slightly lower than the national urban average annual growth by 0.91 percentage points. In 2012, Guangzhou's per capita values were higher than national urban average values, the average annual growth was lower than the national urban average growth, signifying that the discrepancy was reduced. The regional discrepancy between Guangzhou's cultural and educational consumption and that of national urban areas was reduced significantly from that of 2010, by 1.63 %, with a regional discrepancy ranked 36th out of 36 major cities.

6.1.4 Prosperity Assessment of Guangzhou's Cultural and Educational Consumption Demand

To sum up the above: Since the "Eleventh Five-Year Plan" period, Guangzhou's average annual growth in cultural and educational consumption was significantly higher than the national urban average annual growth, and average annual growth in per capita values was notably higher than average annual growth in national urban areas; the cultural and educational ratio for this indicator has experienced a significant upward trend; the urban-to-rural ratio in provinces and regions significantly expanded, and the discrepancy with the national urban regions was notably expanded. All of this is shown in the assessment and calculation of that prosperity index of Guangzhou's cultural and educational consumption demand (Fig. 6.7).

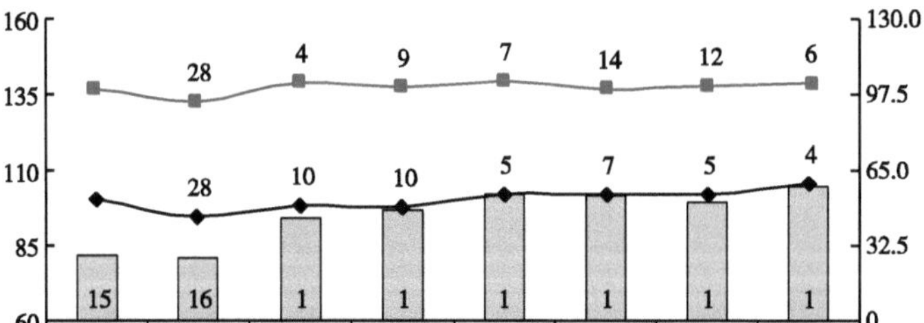

	2005	2006	2007	2008	2009	2010	2011	2012
Horizontal Assessment	81.48	80.41	93.84	96.75	101.92	101.40	99.34	104.50
Vertical Assessment (1)	100.00	94.49	98.29	97.42	101.65	101.75	101.96	105.30
Vertical Assessment (2)	100.00	94.49	102.73	100.08	102.91	99.76	101.27	102.48

Fig. 6.7 Changing trends in the prosperity index of Guangzhou's cultural and educational consumption. *LHS cylindrical*: horizontal assessment (urban-rural and zero-difference ideal value = 100); *LHS curve*: vertical assessment (starting base value = 100), (1) 2005 starting point; RHS curve: (2) Starting from previous year; shows assessed 36 cities in a ranking

6.1.4.1 Annual Horizontal Assessment of Prosperity Index

With the national urban cultural and educational consumption overall share value, per capita absolute value, and proportion of each index as a base, and balanced by the "ideal value" of 100 of no discrepancy between urban/rural areas and regions, in 2012 Guangzhou's prosperity index for this indicator was 104.50, higher than the ideal value by 4.50, and also higher than the previous year by 5.16. In an annual comparison, Guangzhou's prosperity index for this indicator, out of 36 major cities, ranked 15th in 2005, 1st in 2010, and in 2012 maintained the same place as the previous year, 1st.

6.1.4.2 Vertical Assessment of Prosperity Index Since the "Eleventh Five-Year Plan" Period

With the last year of the "Tenth Five-Year Plan" period, 2005, having a starting base value of 100, in 2012 Guangzhou's prosperity index for this indicator was 105.30, higher than the 2005 starting base value by 5.30, and also higher than the previous year by 3.34. In a comparison since the "Eleventh Five-Year Plan" period, in a ranking of 36 major cities, Guangzhou's prosperity index for this indicator was ranked 28th in 2006, 7th in 2010, and in 2012 went up to 4th place from 5th place the previous year.

6.1.4.3 Vertical Assessment of Prosperity Index Since the "Twelfth Five-Year Plan" Period

With the last year of the "Eleventh Five-Year Plan" period, 2010, with a starting base value of 100, in 2012 Guangzhou's prosperity index for this indicator was 103.80, higher than the starting base value of 2010 by 3.80, and also higher than the previous year by 2.53. In a comparison since the "Twelfth Five-Year Plan" period, in a ranking of 36 major cities, Guangzhou's prosperity index for this indicator was ranked 12th in 2011 and 9th in 2012. This evaluation index is better explained by text than in a table; see Report B3 on the ranking of major cities.

6.1.4.4 Annual Vertical Assessment of Prosperity Index

With the previous year, 2011, with a starting base value of 100, in 2012 Guangzhou's prosperity index for this indicator was 102.48, higher than the starting base value of 2011 by 2.48. In a annual comparison, in a ranking of 36 major cities, Guangzhou's prosperity index of this indicator was 28th in 2006, 14th in 2010, and in 2012 went up to 6th place from 12th place the previous year.

6.2 Tianjin: Rising to the Top in the 2012 Vertical Assessment of City Prosperity Indexes

Tianjin: Rises to First Place in the 2012 Vertical Assessment of Prosperity in Major Cities

6.2.1 Tianjin's Growth in Cultural and Educational Consumption Demand

6.2.1.1 Changing Shares of Overall Cultural and Educational Consumption

See Fig. 6.8 for Tianjin's overall growth in cultural and educational consumption and changes in share since 2005.

From 2005 to 2012, Tianjin's cultural and educational totals grew from 9.846 to 18.844 billion yuan, an increase of 8.998 billion yuan, a total growth of 91.39 %, and average annual growth rate of 9.72 %, and a growth degree ranked 21st among 36 major cities. The highest annual growth was in 2007, at a growth rate of 14.14 %; the lowest annual growth was in 2008, at a negative growth rate of 0.88 %.

Over the same period, the total average annual growth in national urban cultural and educational consumption was 13.00 %, and Tianjin's average annual growth degree was significantly lower than the national growth degree by 3.28 percentage points. Tianjin's total cultural and educational consumption as proportion of the national urban share decreased from 1.62 % to 1.32 %, a degree of decrease of 18.63 %, and a growth degree and change in share ranked 21st among 36 major cities.

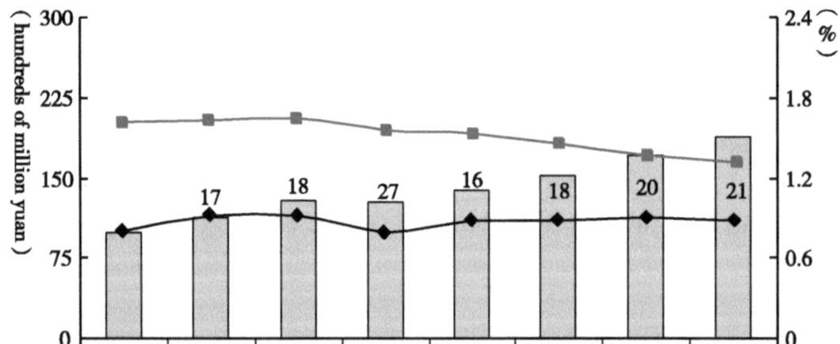

	2005	2006	2007	2008	2009	2010	2011	2012
Total Cultural and Educational Consumption	98.46	112.36	128.26	127.12	138.99	152.90	171.75	188.44
Annual Growth Coefficient	100.00	114.12	114.14	99.12	109.33	110.01	112.33	109.72
Share of National Total	1.6239	1.6397	1.6483	1.5592	1.5364	1.4546	1.3634	1.3214

Fig. 6.8 Tianjin's overall growth in cultural and educational consumption and changes in share. *LHS cylindrical*: cultural and educational total (hundreds of million yuan); *LHS curve*: annual growth coefficient (previous year = 100, lower than 100 is negative growth), marked annual growth is ranked by city, not counting the starting year of 1005; *RHS curve*: proportion of national urban share

During the first 2 years of the "Twelfth Five-Year Plan" period, the average annual growth in total national urban cultural and educational consumption was 16.48 %, and Tianjin's total average annual growth was 11.02 %, notably lower than the national growth degree by 5.46 percentage points, and also significantly higher than its own average annual growth during the "Eleventh Five-Year Plan" by 1.82 percentage points. Tianjin's proportion of the national urban share decreased by 9.16 % from 2010, and its growth degree and change in share was ranked 21st out of 36 major cities.

6.2.1.2 Growth in Per Capita Absolute Values of Cultural and Educational Consumption

See Fig. 6.9 for changing growth trends in Tianjin's per capita cultural and educational consumption growth since 2005.

From 2005 to 2012, Tianjin's per capita value in cultural and educational consumption increased from 1,283.70 to 2,299.83 yuan, an increase of 1,016.12 yuan, a total growth of 79.16 %, an average annual growth rate of 8.69 %, and a growth degree ranked 18th among 36 major cities. The highest per capita value occurred in 2006, with a growth rate of 13.12 %, and the lowest value occurred in 2008, with a negative growth of 1.88 %.

Over the same period, the average annual growth in national urban per capita cultural and educational consumption was 9.21 %. Tianjin's average annual growth degree was slightly lower than the national urban average growth, and the per capita values went down from being 116.97 % of the national urban per capita value, to 113.10 % (for a comparison, see Fig. 6.13). The per capita absolute value went down from 14th place to 18th place among 36 major cities.

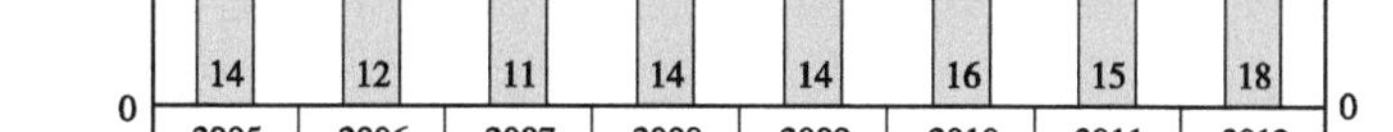

	2005	2006	2007	2008	2009	2010	2011	2012
Per Capita Cultural Consumption	1283.70	1452.17	1639.83	1608.97	1740.85	1899.50	2116.01	2299.82
Annual Growth Coefficient	100.00	113.12	112.92	98.12	108.20	109.11	111.40	108.69

Fig. 6.9 Per capita cultural and educational consumption growth and changing growth trends in Tianjin. *LHS cylindrical*: per capita cultural and educational consumption (yuan), per capita values of marked years are ranked among 36 cities; *RHS curve*: annual growth coefficient (previous year = 100, lower than 100 is negative growth), ranking of annual growth of marked 36 cities, not counting the starting year of 2005

During the first 2 years of the "Twelfth Five-Year Plan" period, the average annual growth in national urban per capita cultural and educational consumption was 11.77 %, and Tianjin's average annual growth in per capita values was 10.03 %, relatively significantly lower than the national urban average growth. Tianjin's average annual growth in per capita values was also relatively significantly higher than its own average annual growth during the "Eleventh Five-Year Plan" period, with a growth degree ranked 18th out of 36 major cities.

6.2.2 *Related Background Situation of Tianjin's Cultural and Educational Consumption*

See Fig. 6.10 for the trends in relationships between Tianjin's per capita GDP and urban per capita income, consumption (separated into non-cultural consumption and educational/cultural consumption) since 2005.

From 2005 to 2012, Tianjin's average annual growth in per capita GDP was 18.50 %; average annual growth in urban per capita income was 13.43 %, notably lower than GDP growth, by 5.07 percentage points; average annual growth in per capita overall consumption was 11.37 %, very significantly lower than GDP growth, by 7.13 percentage points, and significantly lower than income growth, by 2.06 percentage points; average annual growth in per capita savings was 18.88 %, slightly higher than GDP growth, by 0.38 percentage points, notably higher than income growth, by 5.45 percentage points, and very significantly higher than overall consumption growth, by 7.51 percentage points; average annual growth in per capita cultural and educational consumption was 8.69 %, very significantly lower than GDP growth, by 9.81 percentage points, very significantly lower than income growth, by 4.74 percentage points, significantly lower than

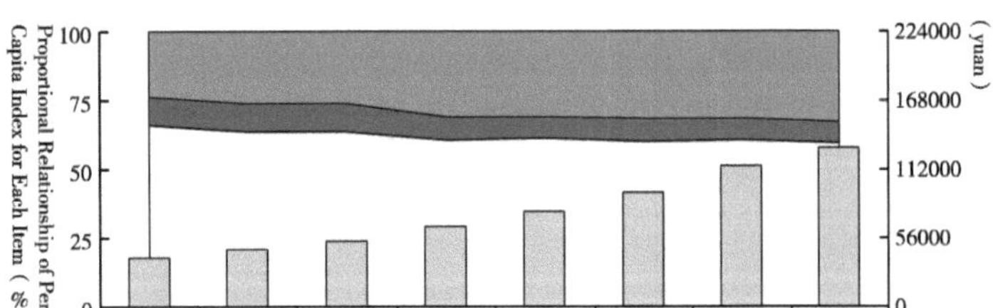

	2005	2006	2007	2008	2009	2010	2011	2012
(1) Urban Per Capita Savings	2985.29	3735.04	4328.47	6000.06	6600.66	7730.83	8496.77	10016.90
(2) Per Capita Cultural and Educational Consumption	1283.70	1452.17	1639.83	1608.97	1740.85	1899.50	2116.01	2299.82
(3) Per Capita Non-Cultural Consumption	8369.56	9095.88	10389.05	11813.50	13060.50	14662.27	16308.08	18219.90
(4) Urban Per Capita GDP	39507.00	46173.00	52939.00	65918.00	77193.00	93895.00	114141.00	129610.00

Fig. 6.10 Relationship of Tianjin's per capita GDP to urban per capita income, consumption, and savings. *LHS area*: rural per capita savings, cultural consumption, non-cultural consumption (yuan converted to %), (1) + (2) + (3) = income, (2) + (3) = overall consumption, (1) + (2) = non-cultural consumption surplus; direct ratio in annual changes in index. *RHS cylinder*: per capita GDP (yuan)

overall consumption, by 2.68 percentage points, and very significantly lower than savings growth, by 10.19 percentage points.

During the "Eleventh Five-Year Plan" period, Tianjin's average annual growth in per capita GDP was 18.90 %, average annual growth in urban per capita income was 13.96 %, average annual growth in per capita overall consumption was 11.40 %, average annual growth in per capita savings was 20.96 %, and average annual growth in per capita cultural and educational consumption was 8.15 %. The average annual growth in cultural and educational consumption was lower than GDP growth by 10.75 percentage points, lower than income growth by 5.81 percentage points, lower than overall consumption growth by 3.25 percentage points, and lower than savings growth by 12.81 percentage points.

During the first 2 years of the "Twelfth Five-Year Plan" period, the average annual growth in Tianjin's per capita GDP was 17.49 %, average annual growth in urban per capita income was 12.12 %, average annual growth in per capita overall consumption was 11.31 %, average annual growth in per capita savings was 13.83 %, and average annual growth in per capita cultural and educational consumption was 10.03 %. Average annual growth in cultural and educational consumption was lower than GDP growth by 7.46 percentage points, lower than income growth by 2.09 percentage points, lower than overall consumption growth by 1.28 percentage points, and lower than savings growth by 3.80 percentage points. In 2012, the proportional relationship between Tianjin's educational and cultural consumption showed a downward trend.

All of the preceding was figured out in an analysis and calculation of various proportions for Tianjin's per capita cultural and educational consumption. See Fig. 6.11 for Tianjin's changes in cultural and educational consumption since 2005.

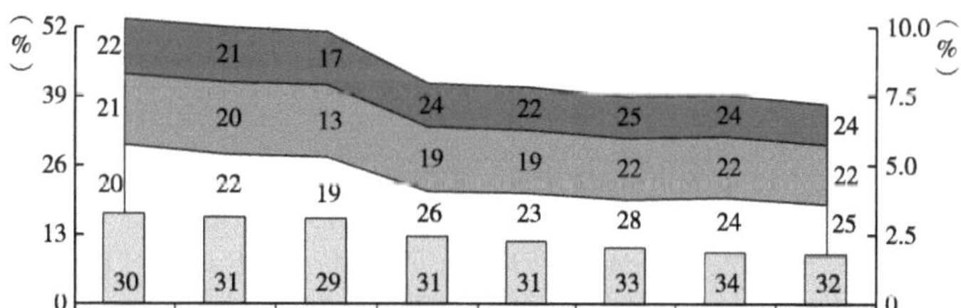

	2005	2006	2007	2008	2009	2010	2011	2012
Cultural and Educational Consumption as Proportion of Income	10.1570	10.1671	10.0250	8.2840	8.1340	7.8193	7.8601	7.5313
Cultural and Educational Consumption as Proportion of Consumption	13.2981	13.7672	13.6324	11.9871	11.7614	11.4692	11.4850	11.2078
Ratio of Non-Cultural Consumption to Surplus	30.0703	27.9952	27.4757	21.1455	20.8697	19.7241	19.9383	18.6723
Ratio of Cultural and Educational Consumption to GDP	3.2493	3.1451	3.0976	2.4409	2.2552	2.0230	1.8539	1.7744

Fig. 6.11 Changing trends in Tianjin's cultural and educational consumption ratio. *LHS area*: per capita cultural/educational as proportion of income, overall consumption, and non-cultural consumption surplus (%), the ratios of each indicator over the years are superimposed; *RHS cylinder*: per capita cultural/educational consumption and GDP (%). The ratio for each year is ranked within 36 major cities

6.2.2.1 Ratio of Per Capita Cultural and Educational Consumption and Per Capita GDP

From 2005 to 2012, the ratio of Tianjin's per capita cultural and educational consumption and per capita GDP decreased from 3.25 % to 1.77 %, and its ranking decreased from 30th to 32nd place in a ranking of 36 major cities. Since the "Eleventh Five-Year Plan" period, Tianjin's proportion for this indicator decreased by 1.47 percentage points, a degree of decrease o 45.39 %, and a degree of change ranked 28th place out of 36 major cities.

During this period, Tianjin's proportion for this indicator was reduced. The highest value occurred in 2005 at 3.25 %, and the lowest value in 2012 at 1.77 %. During the "Eleventh Five-Year Plan" period, there was a decrease of 1.23 percentage points, and a degree of decrease of 37.74 %; during the first 2 years of the "Twelfth Five-Year Plan" period, there was a decrease of 0.25 percentage points, and a degree of decrease of 12.29 %. In terms of the changes in the coordinated relationship between cultural and educational consumption demand growth and urban economic development, during the "Eleventh Five-Year Plan" it decreased significantly, and during the first 2 years of the "Twelfth Five-Year Plan" period, it maintained a significant decreasing trend.

6.2.2.2 Per Capita Cultural and Educational Consumption as Proportion of Per Capita Income

From 2005 to 2012, Tianjin's per capita cultural and educational consumption as proportion of per capita income decreased from 10.16 % to 7.53 %, and its rank fell from 22nd to 24th place among 36 major cities. Since the "Eleventh Five-Year Plan" period, Tianjin's proportion for this indicator decreased by 2.63 percentage points, a degree of decrease of 25.85 % and a rank in degree of change of 22nd out of 36 major cities.

During this period, Tianjin's proportion for this indicator increased in 2006 and 2011, and decreased during all other years. The highest value occurred in 2006 at 10.17 %, and the lowest in 2012 at 7.53 %. During the "Eleventh Five-Year Plan" period there was a decrease of 2.34 percentage points, with a degree of decrease of 23.02 %; during the first 2 years of the "Twelfth Five-Year" plan there was a decrease of 0.29 percentage points, with a degree of decrease of 3.68 % In terms of the changes in the coordinated relationship between cultural and educational consumption demand growth and the growth of income of urban citizens, during the "Eleventh Five-Year Plan" period it decreased notably, and during the first 2 years of the "Twelfth Five-Year Plan" period it maintained a decreasing trend.

6.2.2.3 Per Capita Cultural and Educational Consumption as Proportion of Per Capita Overall Consumption

From 2005 to 2012, Tianjin's per capita cultural and educational consumption as proportion of per capita overall consumption decreased from 13.30 % to 11.21 %, with a rank among 36 major cities that decreased from 21st place to 22nd place. Since the "Eleventh Five-Year Plan" period, Tianjin's ratio for this indicator decreased by 2.09 percentage points, a degree of decrease of 15.72 %, and a degree of change ranked 18th out of 36 major cities.

During this period, Tianjin's ratio for this indicator increased in 2006 and 2011, and decreased in all other years. The highest value occurred in 2006 at 13.77 %, and the lowest in 2012 at 11.21 %. During the "Eleventh Five-Year Plan" period, there was a decrease of 1.83 percentage points, a degree of decrease of 13.75 %; during the first 2 years of the "Twelfth Five-Year Plan" period. There was a decrease of 0.26 percentage points, a degree of decrease of 2.28 %. In terms of the changing relationship of coordination between cultural and educational consumption demand growth and the growth in income of urban citizens, during the "Eleventh Five-Year Plan" period there was a notable decrease, and during the first 2 years of the "Twelfth Five-Year Plan" period there was still a significant decrease.

6.2.2.4 Ratio of Per Capita Cultural and Educational Consumption and Per Capita Non-cultural Consumption Surplus

From 2005 to 2012, the ratio of Tianjin's per capita cultural and educational consumption and per capita non-cultural consumption surplus decreased from 30.07 % to 18.67 %, with a ranking among 36 major cities falling from 20th to 25th place. Since the "Eleventh Five-Year Plan" period, Tianjin's ratio for this indicator fell 11.40 percentage points, a degree of decrease of 37.90 %, a degree of change ranked 23rd out of 36 major cities.

During this period, Tianjin's ratio of this indicator showed an increase, and during all other years it decreased. The highest value occurred in 2005 at 30.07 %, and lowest occurred in 2012 at 18.67 %. During the "Eleventh Five-Year Plan" period there was a decrease of 10.35 percentage points, and a degree of decrease of 34.41 %; during the first 2 years of the "Twelfth Five-Year Plan" period there was a decrease of 1.05 percentage points, and a degree of decrease of 5.33 %. In terms of the changing growth relationship of coordinated growth between cultural and educational consumption demand growth and urban citizens' "surplus money" outside of "essential consumption", during the "Eleventh Five-Year Plan" period there was a significant decrease, and during the first 2 years of the "Twelfth Five-Year Plan" period, there was a still a trend of significant decrease.

6.2.3 *Coordination Status of Urban/Rural and Regional Cultural and Educational Consumption*

6.2.3.1 Urban-to-Rural Ratio of Overall Per Capita Cultural and Educational Consumption

For Tianjin's urban-to-rural ratio of overall per capita cultural and educational consumption since 2005, see Fig. 6.12.

From 2005 to 2012, Tianjin's urban-to-rural ratio of overall per capita cultural and educational consumption was reduced from 3.9035 to 2.9425, its ranking increasing from 20th to 4th place among 31 provinces and regions. During this time, the urban-to-rural ratio was reduced from 2008 to 2012, while it expanded during all other years. The smallest urban-to-rural ratio occurred in 2012, at 2.9425, and the largest urban-to-rural ratio occurred in 2007 at 5.2547. Since the "Eleventh Five-Year Plan" period, Tianjin's urban-to-rural ratio of overall cultural and educational consumption was reduced by 24.62 %, and the change in urban-to-rural ratio was ranked 4th place out of 31 provinces and regions. This signifies that Tianjin's change in urban-to-rural ratio of overall cultural and educational consumption signifies one of the most favorable statuses out of all provinces and regions.

Along with the changes in the urban-to-rural ratio of cultural and educational consumption, Tianjin was also affected by its own urban and rural annual demand. The central role of major cities is not only to stimulate urban growth, but also to drive rural growth.

From 2005 to 2012, Tianjin's overall urban per capita cultural and educational consumption grew from 1,283.70 to 2,254,22, a growth of 970.52 yuan, a total growth of 75.60 %, and an average annual growth of 8.38 %. Rural per capita cultural and

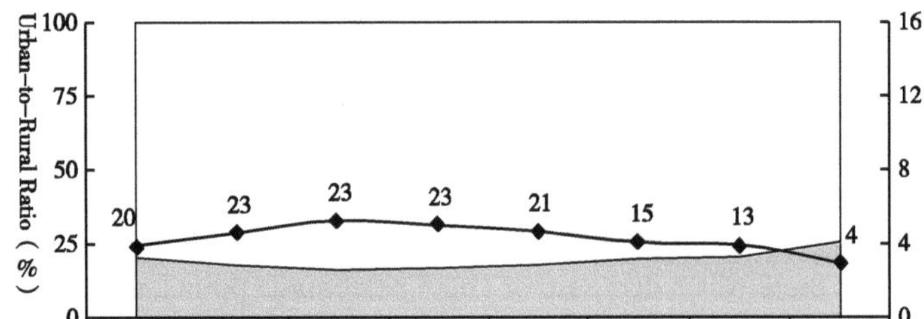

	2005	2006	2007	2008	2009	2010	2011	2012
National Urban Per Capita	1283.70	1452.17	1639.83	1608.97	1740.85	1899.50	2116.01	2254.22
National Rural Per Capita	328.86	315.59	312.07	324.47	371.85	462.25	542.12	766.08
National Urban-to-Rural Ratio	3.9035	4.6014	5.2547	4.9588	4.6816	4.1092	3.9032	2.9425

Fig. 6.12 Changing trends in the urban-to-rural ratio of overall per capita cultural and educational consumption. *LHS area*: overall urban/rural per capita cultural and educational consumption (yuan converted to %), proportional relationship between urban and rural areas for each year superimposed; *RHS curve*: urban-to-rural ratio of per capita cultural and educational consumption (rural = 1). The urban-to-rural ratios of the marked years are ranked among 31 provinces and regions

educational consumption grew from 328.86 to 766.08 yuan, a growth of 437.22 yuan, a total growth of 132.95 %, and an average annual growth of 12.84 %. The highest rural per capita value occurred in 2012, with a growth rate of 41.31 %; the lowest growth occurred in 2006, with a negative growth of 4.04 %. During the 7-year period, the average annual growth in urban per capita cultural and educational consumption demand was significantly lower than average annual rural growth, by 4.46 percentage points, resulting in a pretty significant reduction in Tianjin's urban-to-rural ratio of overall cultural and educational consumption demand.

During the first 2 years of the "Twelfth Five-Year Plan" period, the average annual growth of Tianjin's overall urban per capita value was 8.94 %, higher than its own average annual growth during the "Eleventh Five-Year Plan" period by 0.79 percentage points; average annual rural per capita growth was 28.74 %, higher than its own average annual growth during the "Eleventh Five-Year Plan" period by 21.69 percentage points. In 2012, urban per capita values were higher than rural values, and the urban per capita average annual growth degree was lower than the rural per capita growth degree, by 19.80 percentage points, signifying that the discrepancy was reduced. Tianjin's urban-to-rural ratio of cultural and educational consumption demand was very significantly reduced from that of 2010, by 28.39 %, and the urban-to-rural ratio was ranked 4th out of 31 provinces and regions.

6.2.3.2 Regional Discrepancies in Urban Per Capita Cultural and Educational Consumption

See Fig. 6.13 for changing trends in discrepancies between Tianjin's per capita cultural and educational consumption and national urban per capita amounts.

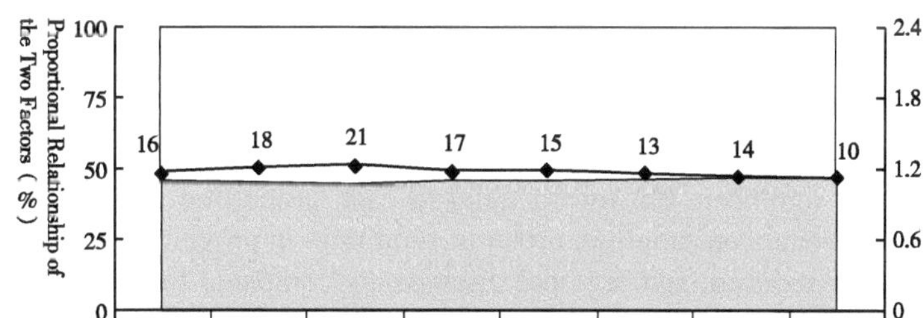

	2005	2006	2007	2008	2009	2010	2011	2012
Local Urban Per Capita	1283.70	1452.17	1639.83	1608.97	1740.85	1899.50	2116.01	2299.82
National Urban Per Capita	1097.46	1203.03	1329.16	1358.26	1472.76	1627.64	1851.74	2033.50
Local Regional Discrepancy	1.1697	1.2071	1.2337	1.1846	1.1820	1.1670	1.1427	1.1310

Fig. 6.13 Tianjin's regional discrepancies in urban per capita cultural and educational consumption and national urban consumption. *LHS area*: per capita cultural and educational consumption (yuan converted to %), direct proportional relationship between local and national annual values; *RHS curve*: regional discrepancy in per capita cultural and educational consumption (no discrepancy = 1). Regional discrepancies of the marked years are ranked among 36 major cities

From 2005 to 2012, the discrepancy between Tianjin's urban per capita cultural consumption and the national urban consumption was reduced from 1.1697 to 1.1310, its rank rising from 16th to 10th place. During this period, Tianjin's regional discrepancy showed a reduction from 2008 to 2012, while in all other years it expanded. The smallest regional discrepancy occurred in 2012 at 1.1310, and the largest occurred in 2007 at 1.2337. Since the "Eleventh Five-Year Plan" period, Tianjin's cultural and educational consumption and national urban consumption regional discrepancy was reduced by 3.31 %, and Tianjin's degree of change in regional discrepancy was ranked 15th out of 36 major cities. This signifies that Tianjin is among the cities in a better situation in terms of regional discrepancy in cultural and educational consumption.

While changes occurred in Tianjin's regional discrepancy in cultural and educational consumption, the influence of annual demand of Tianjin's and the national urban areas was also felt. See this paper's chapter on per capita values for detailed calculations of a comparison between per capita cultural and educational consumption growth in national urban areas and in Tianjin, which examines the specific discrepancies in growth.

From 2005 to 2012, Tianjin's average annual growth degree was slightly lower than the national urban average growth degree, by 0.52 percentage points, and the discrepancy between Tianjina's cultural and educational consumption demand and that of the national urban areas was significantly reduced.

During the first 2 years of "Twelfth Five-Year Plan" period,

6.2.4 *Prosperity Assessment of Tianjin's Cultural and Educational Consumption Demand*

To sum up the above: During the "Eleventh Five-Year Plan" period, Tianjin's average annual growth in total cultural and educational consumption was significantly lower than the national urban average growth, and average annual per capita value growth was also slightly lower than the national urban average growth; there was a significant downward trend in each proportion in relation to cultural and educational consumption; urban-to-rural ratio in provinces and regions was significantly reduced, and regional discrepancy compared to national urban areas was significantly reduced. These results are all collectively are seen in the assessment and calculation of Tianjin's cultural and educational consumption demand prosperity index. See Fig. 6.14 for changing trends in prosperity index of Tianjin's cultural and educational consumption.

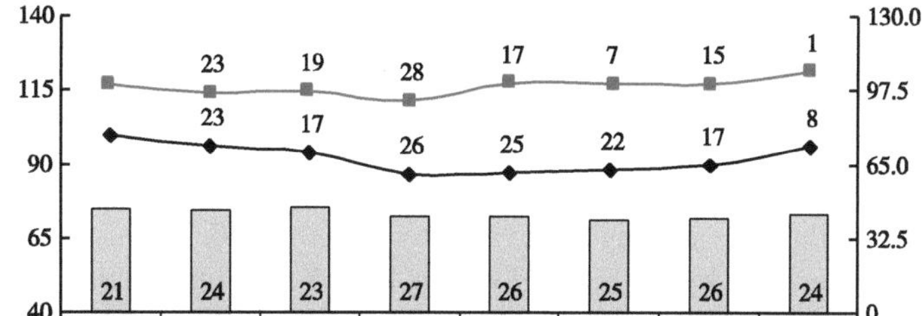

	2005	2006	2007	2008	2009	2010	2011	2012
Horizontal Assessment	74.74	74.49	75.68	72.30	72.19	71.37	71.86	73.51
Vertical Assessment (1)	100.00	96.23	93.79	86.82	87.22	88.33	89.67	96.28
Vertical Assessment (2)	100.00	96.23	97.01	93.13	100.24	100.76	100.73	105.65

Fig. 6.14 Changing trends in the prosperity index of Tianjin's cultural and educational consumption. *LHS cylindrical*: horizontal assessment (urban-rural and zero-difference ideal value = 100); *LHS curve*: vertical assessment (starting base value = 100), (1) 2005 starting point; *RHS curve*: (2) Starting from previous year; shows assessed 36 cities in a ranking

6.2.4.1 Annual Horizontal Assessment of Prosperity Index

With the national urban cultural and educational consumption overall share value, per capita absolute value, and proportion of each index as a base, and balanced by the "ideal value" of 100 of no discrepancy between urban/rural areas and regions, in 2012 Tianjin's prosperity index for this indicator was 73.51, lower than the ideal value by 26.49, but higher than the previous year by 1.65. In a annual comparison, Tianjin's prosperity index for this indicator, in a ranking of 36 major cities, was ranked 21st in 2005, 25th in 2010, and in 2012 went up to 24th place from 26th place the previous year.

6.2.4.2 Vertical Assessment Status Since the "Eleventh Five-Year Plan" Period

Setting the last year of the "Tenth Five-Year Plan" period, 2005, with a starting base value of 100, in 2012 Tianjin's prosperity index for this indicator was 96.28, lower than the 2005 starting base value by 3.72, but higher than the previous year by 6.61. In a comparison since the "Eleventh Five-Year Plan" period, Tianjin's prosperity index for this indicator, in a ranking of 36 major cities, was ranked 23rd in 2006, 22nd in 2010, and in 2012 its ranked went up to 8th place from 17th place the previous year.

6.2.4.3 Vertical Assessment Status Since the "Twelfth Five-Year Plan" Period

Giving the last year of the "Eleventh Five-Year Plan" period, 2010, a starting base value of 100, Tianjin's prosperity index for this indicator in 2012 was 106.88, higher than the starting base value by 6.88 in 2010, and also higher than that of the previous year by 6.15. In "Twelfth Five-Year Plan" period, Tianjin's prosperity index for this indicator, in a ranking of 36 major cities, was ranked 15th in 2011 and went up to 6th place in 2012. This evaluation index is better explained by text than in a table; see Report B3 on the ranking of major cities.

6.2.4.4 Annual Vertical Assessment of Prosperity Index

Setting a starting base value of 100 to the previous year, 2011, in 2012 Tianjin's prosperity index for this indicator was 105.65, higher than the 2011 starting base value by 5.65. In a annual comparison, Tianjin's prosperity index for this indicator, in a ranking of 36 major cities, was ranked 23rd in 2006, 7th in 2010, and in 2012 went up from 15th place the previous year to 1st place.

6.3 Wuhan: Rising to First Place in Evaluation of Cities After the "Twelfth Five-Year Plan"

This paper presents growth trends of Wuhan (and municipalities) in all areas from 2005 to 2012, and fully analyzes and assesses Wuhan's cultural and educational consumption demand situation.

6.3.1 Wuhan's Growth in Cultural and Educational Consumption Demand

6.3.1.1 Changing Shares of Overall Cultural and Educational Consumption

See Fig. 6.15 for Wuhan's overall growth in cultural and educational consumption and changes in share since 2005.

From 2005 to 2012, Wuhan's total cultural and educational consumption grew from 8.105 to 11.415 billion, a growth of 3.310 billion, a total growth of 40.84 %, an average annual growth rate of 5.01 %, and a growth degree ranked 34th out of 36 major cities. The largest annual growth occurred in 2011, with a growth rate of

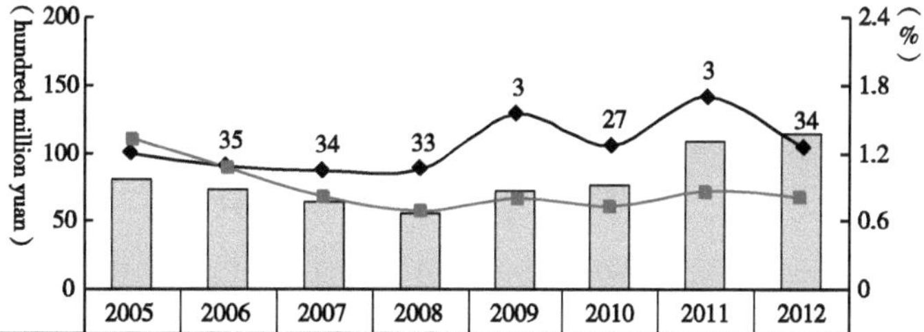

	2005	2006	2007	2008	2009	2010	2011	2012
Total Cultural and Educational Consumption	81.05	73.29	63.65	56.02	72.27	76.68	108.70	114.15
Annual Growth Coefficient	100.00	90.43	86.84	88.02	129.01	106.10	141.77	105.02
Share of National Total	1.3368	1.0696	0.8180	0.6871	0.7989	0.7295	0.8629	0.8004

Fig. 6.15 Tianjin's overall growth in cultural and educational consumption and changes in share. *LHS cylindrical*: cultural and educational total (hundreds of million yuan); *LHS curve*: annual growth coefficient (previous year = 100, lower than 100 is negative growth), annual growth of cities is ranked, not counting the starting year of 2005; *RHS curve*: proportion of national urban share

41.77; the smallest annual growth rate occurred in 2007, with a negative growth of 13.16 %.

During this period, the average annual growth of national urban total cultural and educational consumption was 13.00 %, and Wuhan's average annual growth was very significantly lower than that of the nation, by 7.99 percentage points. Wuhan's total cultural and educational consumption as proportion of the national urban share decreased from 1.34 % to 0.80 %, a degree of decrease of 40.13 %, and a change n growth degree and share that was ranked 34th out of 36 major cities.

During the first 2 years of the "Twelfth Five-Year Plan" period, the average annual growth in total national cultural and educational consumption was 16.48 %, Wuhan's total average annual growth was 22.01 %, significantly higher than the national growth degree, by 5.53 percentage points, and also significantly higher than its own average annual growth during the "Eleventh Five-Year Plan" period, by 23.11 percentage points. Wuhan's proportion of the national urban share increased 9.73 % in 2010, with a change in growth degree and share that was ranked 34th out of 36 major cities.

6.3.1.2 Growth in Per Capita Absolute Values of Cultural and Educational Consumption

See Fig. 6.16 for changing growth trends in Wuhan's per capita cultural and educational consumption growth since 2005.

From 2005 to 2012, Wuhan's per capita cultural and educational consumption grew from 1,021.21 to 2,366.57 yuan, an increase of 1,345.36 yuan, and a total growth of 131.74 %. The average annual growth rate was 12.76 %, and the growth degree was ranked 8th out of 36 major cities. The largest per capita annual growth

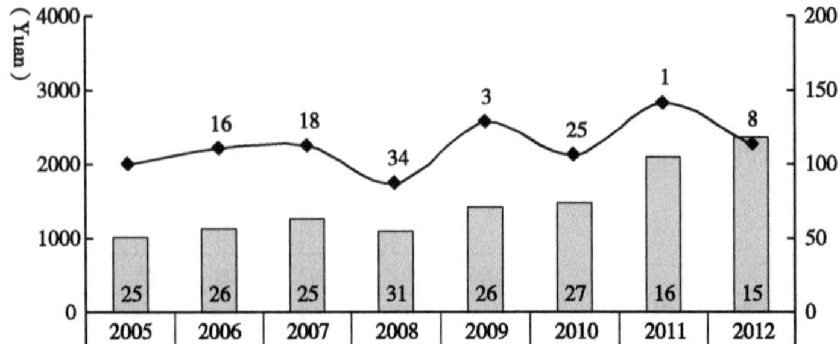

	2005	2006	2007	2008	2009	2010	2011	2012
Per Capita Cultural and Educational Consumption	1021.21	1125.33	1258.37	1095.43	1406.89	1480.81	2098.82	2366.57
Annual Growth Index	100.00	110.20	111.82	87.05	128.43	105.25	141.73	112.76

Fig. 6.16 Per capita cultural and educational consumption growth and changing growth trends in Wuhan. *LHS cylindrical*: per capita cultural and educational consumption (yuan), per capita values of marked years are ranked among 36 cities; *RHS curve*: annual growth coefficient (previous year = 100, lower than 100 is negative growth), ranking of annual growth of marked 36 cities, not counting the starting year of 2005

occurred in 2011, with a growth rate of 41.73 %; the lowest was in 2008, with a negative growth of 12.95 %.

During this period, the average annual growth in national urban per capita cultural and educational consumption was 9.21 %. Wuhan's average annual growth was significantly higher than the national urban average growth, increasing from 93.05 % of the national urban per capita value, to 116.38 % of it (see Fig. 6.21 in this article for a comparison). The per capita absolute value went from 25th place to 15th place out of 36 major cities.

During the first 2 years of the "Twelfth Five-Year Plan" period, the average annual growth in national urban per capita cultural and educational consumption was 11.77 %, and Wuhan's average annual growth in per capita values was 26.42 %, significantly higher than the national urban average annual growth.

6.3.2 *Related Background Situation of Wuhan's Cultural and Educational Consumption*

See Fig. 6.17 for the trends in relationships between Wuhan's per capita GDP and urban per capita income, consumption (separated into non-cultural consumption and educational/cultural consumption) since 2005.

From 2005 to 2012, Wuhan's average annual growth in per capita GDP was 19.32 %; average annual growth in urban per capita income was 13.94 %, significantly lower than GDP growth, by 5.38 percentage points; average annual growth in per capita total consumption was 13.00 %, significantly lower than GDP growth, by 6.32 percentage points, and slightly lower than income growth, by 0.94 percentage points; average annual growth in per capita savings was 16.63 %, significantly

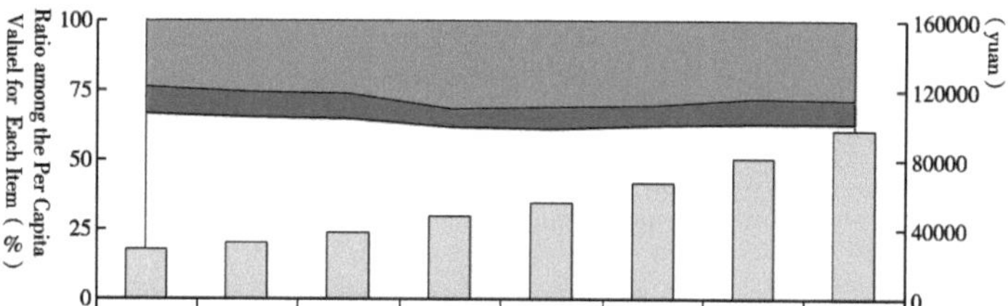

	2005	2006	2007	2008	2009	2010	2011	2012
(1) Urban Per Capita Savings	2615.35	3175.23	3757.64	5279.47	5678.84	6316.25	6597.13	7678.06
(2) Per Capita Cultural and Educational Consumption	1021.21	1125.33	1258.37	1095.43	1406.89	1480.81	2098.82	2366.57
(3) Per Capita Non-Cultural Consumption	7213.54	8055.15	9341.63	10337.54	11303.40	13009.26	15042.14	17002.08
(4) Urban Per Capita GDP	28200.00	31981.00	38152.00	47670.00	55367.00	66549.00	81278.00	97078.00

Fig. 6.17 Status of relationship of Wuhan's per capita GDP to urban per capita income, consumption, and savings. *LHS area*: per capita savings, cultural and educational consumption, non-cultural consumption (yuan converted to %), (1) + (2) + (3) = income, (2) + (3) = total consumption, (1) + (2) = non-cultural consumption surplus, direct ratio in annual changes in index. *RHS cylinder*: per capita GDP (yuan)

lower than GDP growth, by 2.69 percentage points, significantly higher than income growth, by 2.69 percentage points, and significantly higher than total consumption growth, by 3.63 percentage points; average annual growth in per capita cultural and educational consumption was 12.76 %, significantly lower than GDP growth, by 6.56 percentage points, significantly lower than income growth, by 1.18 percentage points, slightly lower than total consumption growth by 0.24 percentage points, and significantly lower than savings growth, by 3.87 percentage points.

During the "Eleventh Five-Year Plan" period, Wuhan's average annual growth in per capita GDP was 18.74 %, average annual growth in urban per capita income was 13.91 %, average annual growth in per capita total consumption was 11.97 %, average annual growth in per capita savings was 19.29 %, and average annual growth in per capita cultural and educational consumption was 7.72 %. The average annual growth in cultural and educational consumption was 11.02 percentage points lower than GDP growth. 6.19 percentage points lower than income growth, 4.25 percentage points lower than total consumption growth, and 11.57 percentage points lower than savings growth.

During the first 2 years of the "Twelfth Five-Year Plan" period, the average annual growth in Wuhan's per capita GDP was 20.78 %, average annual growth in urban per capita income was 14.01 %, average annual growth in per capita total consumption was 15.62 %, average annual growth in per capita savings was 10.25 %, and average annual growth in per capita cultural and educational consumption was 26.42 %. Average annual growth in cultural and educational consumption was 5.64 percentage points higher than GDP growth, 12.41 percentage points higher than income growth, 10.80 percentage points higher than total consumption growth, and 16.17 percentage points higher than savings growth. In

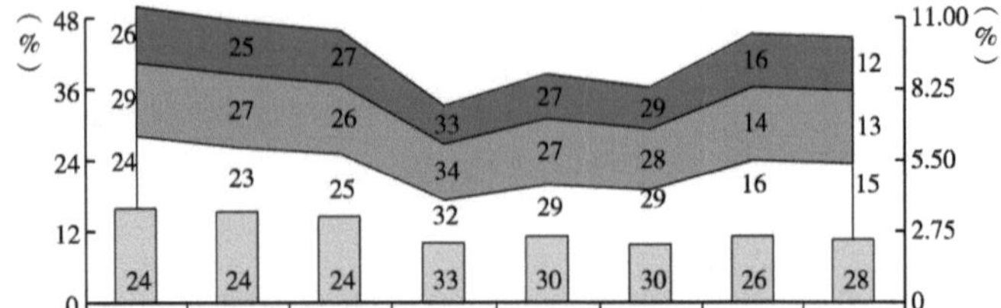

	2005	2006	2007	2008	2009	2010	2011	2012
Cultural and Educational Consumption as Proportion of Income	9.4120	9.1078	8.7645	6.5546	7.6507	7.1171	8.8416	8.7499
Cultural and Educational Consumption as Proportion of Consumption	12.4012	12.2579	11.8714	9.5813	11.0689	10.2195	12.2445	12.2185
Ratio of Non-Cultural Consumption to Surplus	28.0818	26.1671	25.0871	17.1835	19.8553	18.9919	24.1356	23.5605
Ratio of Cultural and Educational Consumption and GDP	3.6214	3.5188	3.2983	2.2979	2.5410	2.2251	2.5823	2.4378

Fig. 6.18 Changing trends in Wuhan's cultural and educational consumption ratio. *LHS area*: per capita cultural/educational as proportion of income, overall consumption, and non-cultural consumption surplus (%), the ratios of each indicator over the years are superimposed; *RHS cylinder*: per capita cultural/educational consumption and GDP (%). The ratio for each year is ranked within 36 major cities

2012, the proportional relationship among Wuhan's cultural and educational consumption and various factors saw a complete increasing trend.

All of this was realized in an analysis and calculation of various proportions for Wuhan's per capita cultural and educational consumption. See Fig. 6.18 for Wuhan's changes in cultural and educational consumption since 2005.

6.3.2.1 Ratio of Per Capita Cultural and Educational Consumption and Per Capita GDP

From 2005 to 2012, the proportion of Wuhan's per capita cultural and educational consumption within per capita GDP decreased from 3.62 % to 2.44 %, and its ranking decreased from 24th to 28th place out of 36 major cities. Since the "Eleventh Five-Year Plan" period, Wuhan's ratio for this index decreased by 1.18 percentage points, a degree of decrease of 32.68 %, and a degree of change ranked 15th out of 36 major cities.

During this period, Wuhan's indicator for this ratio increased in 2009 and 2011, while decreasing during all other years. The highest value occurred in 2005, at 3.62 %, and the lowest in 2010, at 2.23 %. During the "Eleventh Five-Year Plan" period there was a decrease of 1.40 percentage points, a decrease of 38.56 %; during the first 2 years of the "Twelfth Five-Year Plan" period, there was an increase of 0.21 percentage points, a degree of increase of 9.56 %. In terms of the changes in the coordinated relationship between cultural and educational consumption demand growth and urban economic development, during the "Eleventh Five-Year Plan" there was a significant decrease, and during the first 2 years of the "Twelfth-Year Plan" period, there was a reversal to a significant increase.

6.3.2.2 Per Capita Cultural and Educational Consumption as Proportion of Per Capita Income

From 2005 to 2012, Wuhan's per capita cultural and educational consumption as proportion of per capita income decreased from 9.41 % to 8.75 %, and because other cities had decreases in proportion that were more significant, Wuhan's rank went up from 26th place to 12th place. Since the "Eleventh Five-Year Plan" period, Wuhan's proportion for this indicator decreased by 0.66 percentage points, a degree of decrease of 7.03 %, and a degree of change in growth ranked 7th out of 36 major cities.

During this period, Wuhan's ratio for this indicator increased in 2009 and 2011, and decreased during all others years. The highest value occurred in 2005 at 9.41 %, and the lowest in 2008 at 6.55 %. During the "Eleventh Five-Year Plan" period, there was a decrease of 2.29 percentage points, a degree of decrease of 24.38 %; during the first 2 years of the "Twelfth Five-Year Plan" period, there was an increase of 1.63 percentage points, a degree of increase of 22.94 %. In terms of the coordinated relationship between cultural and educational consumption demand growth and the growth of income of urban citizens, during the "Eleventh Five-Year Plan" period there was a significant decrease, and during the first 2 years of the "Twelfth Five-Year Plan" period there was again a significant increase.

6.3.2.3 Per Capita Cultural and Educational Consumption as Proportion of Per Capita Overall Consumption

From 2005 to 2012, Wuhan's per capita cultural and educational consumption as proportion of per capita overall consumption decreased from 12.40 % to 12.22 %, and because the ratio for this indicator for other cities was more significant, Wuhan's rank went up from 29th place to 13th place. Since the "Eleventh Five-Year Plan" period, Wuhan's proportion for this indicator decreased 0.18 percentage points, a degree of decrease of 1.47 %, and a degree of change ranked 6th out of 36 major cities.

During this period, Wuhan's proportion for this indicator increased in 2009 and 2011, and decreased in all other years. The highest value occurred in 2005, at 12.40 %, and the lowest in 2008 at 9.58 %. During the "Eleventh Five-Year Plan" period, there was a decrease of 2.18 percentage points, and a degree of decrease of 17.59; during the first 2 years of the "Twelfth Five-Year Plan" period, there was an increase of 2.00 percentage points, a degree of increase of 19.56 %. In terms of the coordinated relationship between cultural and educational consumption demand growth and growth in overall consumption of urban citizens, during the "Eleventh Five-Year Plan" there was a significant decrease, and during the first 2 years of the "Twelfth Five-Year Plan" period there was a again a significant increase.

6.3.2.4 Ratio of Per Capita Cultural and Educational Consumption and Per Capita Non-cultural Consumption Surplus

From 2005 to 2012, Wuhan's ratio of per capita cultural and educational consumption and per capita non-cultural consumption surplus decreased from 28.09 % to 23.56 %, and because other cities had a ratio for this indicator that decreased significantly, Wuhan increased to 15th place from 24th place. Since the "Eleventh Five-Year Plan" period, Wuhan's ratio for this indicator decreased by 4.52 percentage points, a degree of decrease of 16.10 %, and a degree of change ranked 8th out of 36 major cities.

During this period, Wuhan's ratio increased in 2009 and 2011, and decreased during all other years. The highest value occurred in 2005 at 28.08 %, and the lowest in 2008 at 17.18 %. During the "Eleventh Five-Year Plan" period, there was a decrease of 9.09 percentage points, a decrease degree of 32.37 %; during the first 2 years of the "Twelfth Five-Year Plan" period, there was an increase of 4.57 percentage points, a degree of increase of 24.06 %. In terms of the changing growth relationship of coordinated growth between cultural and educational consumption demand growth and urban citizens' "surplus money" outside of "essential consumption", during the "Eleventh Five-Year Plan" period, there was a significant decrease, and during the first 2 years of the "Twelfth Five-Year Plan" period, there was again a significant increase.

6.3.3 Coordination Status of Urban/Rural and Regional Cultural and Educational Consumption

6.3.3.1 Urban-to-Rural Ratio of Per Capita Cultural and Educational Consumption Within the Provinces

For changing trends in urban-to-rural ratio of per capita cultural and educational consumption within the Hubei Province since 2005, see Fig. 6.19.

From 2005 to 2012, Hubei's urban-to-rural ratio of per capita cultural and educational consumption expanded from 3.3280 to 4.1860, and its rank fell from 14th to 17th place among 31 provinces and regions. During this period, in 2008 and 2011–2012, the urban-to-rural ratio was reduced, while in all other years it expanded. The smallest urban rural ratio occurred in 2005 at 3.3280, and the largest in 2010 at 4.3841. Since the "Eleventh Five-Year Plan" period, the urban-to-rural ratio of Hubei Province's cultural and educational consumption expanded 25.78 %, and its change in urban-to-rural ratio was ranked 22nd out of 31 provinces and regions. This signifies that that Hubei Province is considered to have a relatively serious status of changing urban-to-rural ratios in terms of cultural and educational consumption.

While the urban-to-rural ratio of Hubei's cultural and educational consumption experiences changes, it is also under the influence of its own annual demand

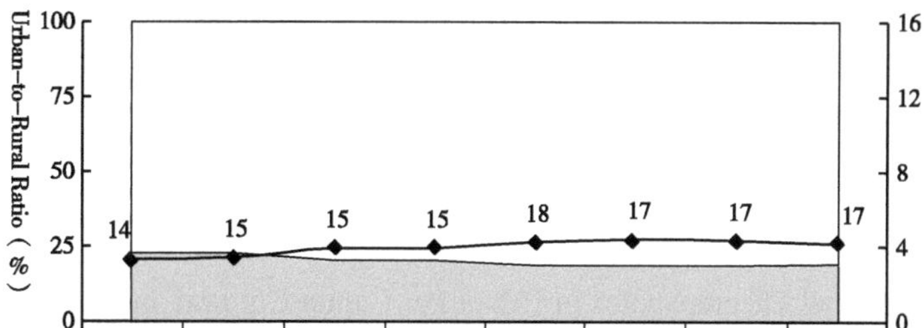

	2005	2006	2007	2008	2009	2010	2011	2012
Provincial and Regional Urban Per Capita	904.76	997.74	1120.29	1037.24	1208.46	1263.16	1489.67	1651.92
Provincial and Regional Rural Per Capita	271.86	292.34	284.13	267.13	281.68	288.12	341.87	394.63
Provincial/Regional Urban–to–Rural Ratio	3.3280	3.4129	3.9429	3.8829	4.2902	4.3841	4.3574	4.1860

Fig. 6.19 Changing trends in the urban-to-rural ratio of per capita cultural and educational consumption in Hubei Province. *LHS area*: provincial and regional urban and rural per capita cultural and educational consumption (yuan converted to %), proportional relationship between urban and rural areas for each year superimposed; *RHS curve*: urban-to-rural; ratio of per capita cultural and educational consumption; *RHS curve*: urban-to-rural ratio of per capita cultural and educational consumption (rural = 1). The urban-to-rural ratios of the marked years are ranked among 31 provinces and regions

changes in both urban and rural aspects. In terms of the role they play within the provinces, major cities not only directly stimulate urban growth, but also drive rural growth.

From 2005 to 2012, Hubei's urban per capita cultural and educational consumption grew from 904.76 to 1,651.92 yuan, an increase of 747.16 yuan, a total growth of 82.58 %, and an average annual growth of 8.98 %. The highest urban per capita growth occurred in 2011, with a growth of 17.93 %; the lowest growth occurred in 2008, with a negative growth of 7.41 %. Rural per capita cultural and educational consumption grew from 271.86 to 394.63 yuan, an increase of 122.77 yuan, a total growth of 45.16 %, and an average annual growth of 5.47 %. The highest rural per capita growth occurred in 2011, with a growth rate of 18.66 %; the lowest growth occurred in 2008, with a negative growth of 5.98 %. During the 7 years, average annual growth degree in urban per capita cultural and educational consumption demand was significantly higher than rural growth, by 3.51 percentage points, resulting in a significant expansion in Hubei's urban-to-rural ratio of cultural and educational consumption demand.

During the first 2 years of the "Twelfth Five-Year Plan" period, Hubei's average annual growth in urban per capita values was 14.36 %, 7.46 percentage points higher than its own average annual growth during the "Eleventh Five-Year Plan" period; the average annual growth in rural per capita values was 17.03 %, 15.86 percentage points higher than its own average annual growth during the "Eleventh Five-Year Plan" period. In 2012, urban per capita values were higher than rural ones, yet the urban average annual growth degree 2.67 percentage points lower than the rural one, signifying that the regional discrepancy was reduced. Compared to that of 2010, Hubei's urban-to-rural ratio in cultural and educational consumption demand was reduced by 4.52 %, and its urban-to-rural ratio was ranked 17th out of 31 provinces and regions.

Regional Discrepancies in Urban Per Capita Cultural and Educational Consumption

See Fig. 6.20 for changing trends in discrepancies between Wuhan's per capita cultural and educational consumption and national urban per capita amounts.

From 2005 to 2012, Wuhan's regional discrepancy between per capita cultural and educational consumption and national urban consumption expanded from 1.0695 to 1.1638, with its rank decreasing from 15th to 6th place among 36 major cities. During this period, Wuhan's regional discrepancy was reduced from 2006 to 2007 and in 2009, while in all other years it expanded. The smallest regional discrepancy occurred in 2009 at 1.0447, and the largest occurred in 2008 at 1.1935. Since the "Eleventh Five-Year Plan" period, the regional discrepancy between Wuhan's cultural and educational consumption and national urban consumption expanded 8.82 %, and Wuhan's degree of change in regional discrepancy was ranked 24th out of 36 major cities. This signifies that Wuhan's changing trends in regional discrepancy of cultural and educational consumption is considered to be among the most serious of the cities.

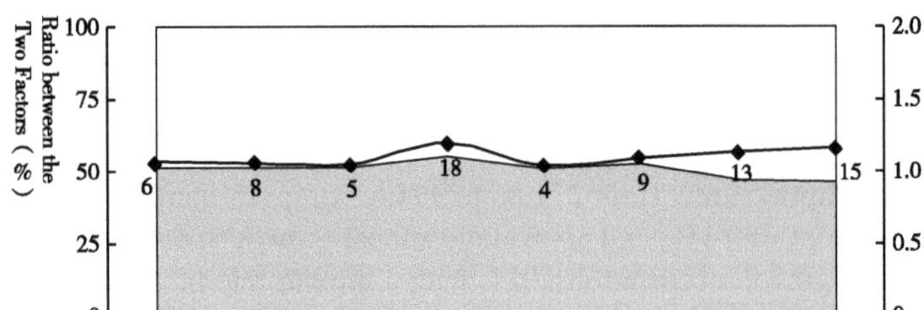

	2005	2006	2007	2008	2009	2010	2011	2012
Local Urban Per Capita	1021.21	1125.33	1258.37	1095.43	1406.89	1480.81	2098.82	2366.57
National Urban Per Capita	1097.46	1203.03	1329.16	1358.26	1472.76	1627.64	1851.74	2033.50
Local Regional Gap	1.0695	1.0646	1.0533	1.1935	1.0447	1.0902	1.1334	1.1638

Fig. 6.20 Wuhan's regional discrepancies in urban per capita cultural and educational consumption and national urban consumption. *LHS area*: per capita cultural and educational consumption (yuan converted to %), direct proportional relationship between local and national annual values; *RHS curve*: regional discrepancy in per capita cultural and educational consumption (no discrepancy = 1). Regional discrepancies of the marked years are ranked among 36 major cities

While changes occur in Wuhan's regional discrepancy in cultural and educational consumption, the influence of annual demand of Wuhan's and the nationwide urban areas is also felt. See this paper's chapter on per capita values for detailed calculations of a comparison between per capita cultural and educational consumption growth in national urban areas and in Wuhan, which examines the specific discrepancies in growth.

From 2005 to 2012, Wuhan's average annual growth degree was significantly higher than the national urban average growth degree, by 3.55 percentage points, and the regional discrepancy between Wuhan's cultural and educational consumption demand and national urban consumption was significantly expanded.

In the first 2 years of the "Twelfth Five-Year Plan", Wuhan's average annual growth degree was very significantly higher than the average annual growth degree during the "Eleventh Five-Year Plan", by 18.70 percentage points, and also very extremely significantly higher than the national urban average growth, by 14.65 percentage points. In 2012, Wuhan's per capita value was higher than the national urban average value, with an average annual growth higher than the national urban average growth, signifying that the regional discrepancy expanded. Compared to that in 2010, the regional discrepancy of Wuhan's cultural and educational consumption and national urban consumption significantly expanded, by 6.75 %, with a ranking of 15th out of 36 major cities in terms of regional discrepancy.

6.3.4 *Prosperity Assessment of Wuhan's Cultural and Educational Consumption Demand*

To sum up the above: since the "Eleventh Five-Year Plan" period, Wuhan's average annual growth in overall cultural and educational consumption was extremely significantly lower than the national urban average growth, and average annual growth in per capita values was significantly higher than the national urban average growth; the proportion of cultural and educational consumption to each indicator showed a significant decreasing trend, but during the first 2 years of the "Twelfth Five-Year Plan" period, it returned to an increase; the urban-to-rural ratio in the provinces was significantly expanded, and the regional discrepancy with national urban areas was significantly expanded. These results are all collectively seen in the assessment and calculation of Wuhan's cultural and educational consumption demand prosperity index. See Fig. 6.21 for changing trends in prosperity index of Wuhan's cultural and educational consumption since 2005.

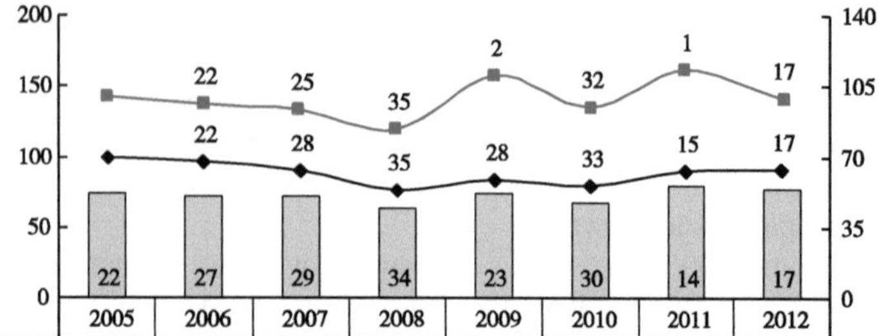

	2005	2006	2007	2008	2009	2010	2011	2012
Horizontal Assessment	74.50	71.66	71.53	63.52	73.98	68.22	79.72	77.17
Vertical Assessment	100.00	96.31	90.35	75.82	83.20	79.24	90.17	90.59
Vertical Assessment	100.00	96.31	93.31	84.07	110.14	94.66	113.54	99.35

Fig. 6.21 Changing trends in the prosperity Index of Wuhan's cultural and educational Consumption. *LHS cylindrical*: horizontal assessment (urban-rural and zero-difference ideal value = 100); *LHS curve*: vertical assessment (starting base value = 100), (1) 2005 starting point; *RHS curve*: (2) Starting from previous year; shows assessed 36 cities in a ranking

6.3.4.1 Annual Horizontal Assessment Prosperity Index

With the national urban cultural and educational consumption overall share value, per capita absolute value, and proportion of each index as a base, and balanced by the "ideal value" of 100 of no discrepancy between urban/rural areas and regions, in 2012 Wuhan's prosperity index for this indicator was 77.17, lower than the ideal value by 22.83, and also lower than the previous year by 2.55. In a annual comparison, Wuhan's prosperity index for this indicator, out of 36 major cities, was ranked 22nd in 2005, 30th in 2010, and in 2012 went down from 14th the previous year to 17th place.

6.3.4.2 Vertical Assessment of Prosperity Since the "Eleventh Five-Year Plan" Period

Setting the last year of the "Tenth Five-Year Plan" period, 2005, with a starting base value of 100, in 2012 Wuhan's prosperity index for this indicator was 90.59, lower than the 2005 starting base value by 9.41, and higher than the previous year by 0.42. Compared with the period since "Eleventh Five-Year Plan" period, Wuhan's prosperity index for this indicator, out of 36 major cities, was ranked 22nd in 2006, 33rd in 2010, and in 2012 went down from 15th place the previous year to 17th place.

6.3.4.3 Vertical Assessment of Prosperity Since the "Twelfth Five-Year Plan" Period

Setting the last year of the "Eleventh Five-Year Plan" period, 2010, with a starting base value of 100, in 2012 Wuhan's prosperity index for this indicator was 112.86, higher than the 2010 starting base value by 12.86, but lower than that of the previous year by 0.68. In the "Twelfth Five-Year Plan" period, Wuhan's prosperity index for this indicator was ranked 1st in 2011, and in 2012 maintained the same ranking. This evaluation index is better explained by text than in a table; see Report B3 on the ranking of major cities.

6.3.4.4 Annual Vertical Assessment of Prosperity Index

Setting the previous year, 2011, with a starting base value of 100, in 2012 Wuhan's prosperity index for this indicator was 99.35, lower than the 2011 starting base value by 0.65. In a annual comparison, in a ranking of this prosperity index among 36 major cities, Wuhan was ranked 22nd in 2006, 32nd in 2010, and in 2012 went down from 1st place the previous year to 17th place.

6.4 Hefei: Rising to Third Place in Status of Cities After the "Eleventh Five-Year Plan"

Hefei: Ranked the First in Prosperity Evaluation of Major Cities Since the "Eleventh Five-Year Plan"

This paper fully presents Hefei's (and its municipalities) growth trends in all areas from 2005 to 2012, and fully analyzes and assesses Hefei's cultural and educational consumption demand situation.

6.4.1 Hefei's Growth in Cultural and Educational Consumption Demand

6.4.1.1 Changing Shares of Overall Cultural and Educational Consumption

See Fig. 6.22 for Hefei's overall growth in cultural and educational consumption and changes in share since 2005.

From 2005 to 2012, Hefei's overall cultural and educational consumption grew from 965 million yuan to 5.976 billion yuan, a total growth of 519.27 %, an average annual growth rate of 29.76 %, and a growth degree ranked 1st among 36 major

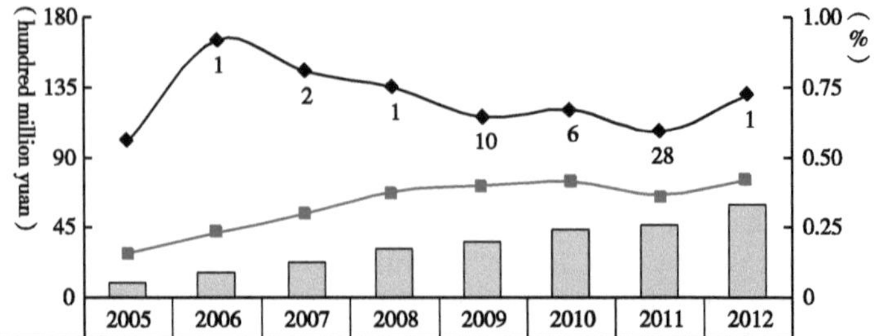

	2005	2006	2007	2008	2009	2010	2011	2012
Total Cultural and Educational Consumption	9.65	15.90	23.03	30.93	35.87	43.34	46.05	59.76
Annual Growth Index	100.00	164.88	144.81	134.32	115.97	120.81	106.26	129.76
Share National Total	0.1592	0.2320	0.2960	0.3794	0.3965	0.4123	0.3656	0.4190

Fig. 6.22 Hefei's overall growth in cultural and educational consumption and changes in share. *LHS cylindrical*: total cultural and educational consumption (hundred million yuan); *LHS curve*: annual growth coefficient (previous year = 100), annual growth of cities is ranked, except for 2005; *RHS curve*: proportion of national urban share

cities. The highest annual growth occurred in 2006, with a growth rate of 64.88 %; the lowest annual growth occurred in 2011, with a growth rate of 6.26 %.

During this period, the overall national urban cultural and educational average annual growth was 13.00 %, and Hefei's average annual growth was very significantly higher than the national growth degree, by 16.76 percentage points. Hefei's total cultural and educational consumption as proportion of the national urban share increased from 0.16 % to 0.42 %, a degree of increase of 163.19 %, a growth degree and degree of change in share ranked first out of 36 major cities.

During the first 2 years of the "Twelfth Five-Year Plan" period, the average annual growth in overall national urban educational and cultural consumption was 16.48 %, and Hefei's overall average annual growth was 17.43 %, slightly higher than the national growth degree by 0.95 percentage points, and also very significantly lower than its own average annual growth during the "Eleventh Five-Year Plan" period, by 17.61 percentage points. Hefei's proportion of the national urban share was 1.63 % higher than that of 2010, and the growth degree and share change was ranked 1st out of 36 major cities.

6.4.1.2 Growth in Per Capita Absolute Values of Cultural and Educational Consumption

See Fig. 6.23 for changing growth trends in Hefei's per capita cultural and educational consumption growth since 2005.

From 2005 to 2012, Hefei's per capita values of cultural and educational consumption grew from 569.32 to 2,643.34 yuan, a growth of 2,074 yuan, a total growth of 364.30 %, an average annual growth rate of 24.53 %, and a growth degree

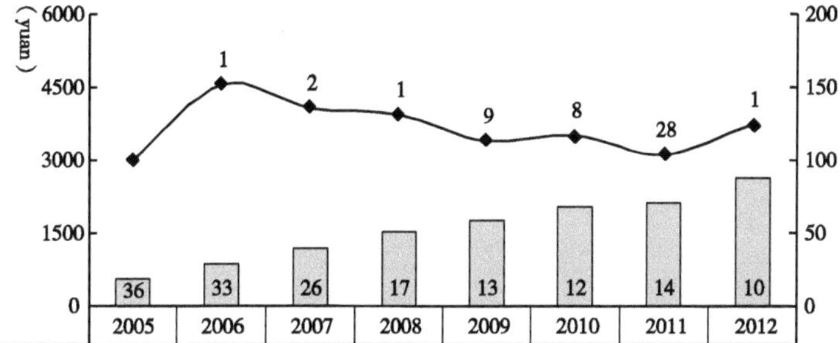

	2005	2006	2007	2008	2009	2010	2011	2012
Per Capita Cultural and Educational Consumption	569.32	863.21	1176.30	1539.40	1741.16	2043.47	2122.74	2643.34
Annual Growth Coefficient	100.00	151.62	136.27	130.87	113.11	117.36	103.88	124.53

Fig. 6.23 Per capita cultural and educational consumption growth and changing growth trends in Hefei. *LHS cylindrical*: per capita cultural and educational consumption (yuan), ranking of annual per capita values of marked cities; *RHS curve*: annual growth coefficient (previous year = 100), ranking of annual growth of marked 36 cities, not counting the starting year of 2005

ranked 1st place out of 36 major cities. The highest growth in per capita values occurred in 2006, with a growth rate of 51.62 %; the lowest growth occurred in 2011, with a growth rate of 3.88 %.

During this period, the average annual growth in national urban per capita cultural and educational consumption was 9.21 %, and Hefei's average annual growth degree was significantly higher than the national urban average growth. Hefei's per capita values increased from 51.88 % of the national urban per capita value to 129.99 % of it (see Fig. 6.27 for a comparison). In a ranking of 36 major cities, the per capita absolute value's rank increased from 36th place to 10th place.

During the first 2 years of the "Twelfth Five-Year Plan" period, the average annual growth in national urban per capita cultural and educational consumption increased 11.77 %, and Hefei's average annual growth in per capita values increased 13.73 %, relatively significantly higher than the national urban average growth. Hefei's average annual growth in per capita values were significantly lower than its own average annual growth during the "Eleventh Five-Year Plan" period, with a growth degree ranked 1st place out of 36 major cities.

6.4.2 *Related Background Situation of Hefei's Cultural and Educational Consumption*

See Fig. 6.24 for the trends in relationships between Hefei's per capita GDP and urban per capita income, consumption (separated into non-cultural consumption and educational/cultural consumption) since 2005.

From 2005 to 2012, Hefei's average annual growth in per capita GDP was 17.55 %; average annual growth in urban per capita income was 15.05 %,

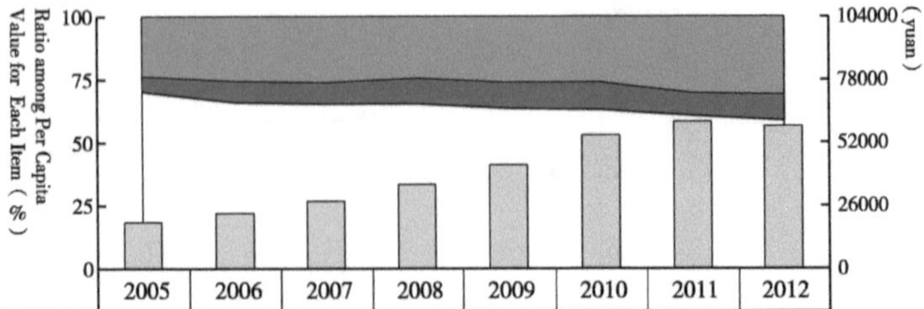

	2005	2006	2007	2008	2009	2010	2011	2012
(1) Urban Per Capita Savings	2285.93	2847.94	3490.05	3838.63	4463.65	5038.71	6761.82	8045.31
(2) Per Capita Cultural and Educational Consumption	569.32	863.21	1176.30	1539.40	1741.16	2043.47	2122.74	2643.34
(3) Per Capita Non-Cultural Consumption	6828.42	7302.25	8760.12	10212.56	10953.66	11968.32	13574.35	15150.61
(4) Urban Per Capita GDP	18960.00	23203.00	28134.00	34482.00	42998.00	54802.00	60556.00	58790.00

Fig. 6.24 Status of relationship of Hefei's per capita GDP to urban per capita income, consumption, and savings. *LHS area*: per capita savings, cultural and educational consumption, non-cultural consumption (yuan converted to %), (1) + (2) + (3) = income, (2) + (3) = total consumption, (1) + (2) = non-cultural consumption surplus, direct ratio in annual changes in index. *RHS cylinder*: per capita GDP (yuan)

significantly lower than the GDP growth, by 2.50 percentage points; average annual growth in overall per capita consumption was 13.36 %, significantly lower than GDP growth, by 4.19 percentage points, relatively significantly lower than income growth, by 1.69 percentage points; average annual growth in per capita savings was 19.69 %, significantly higher than GDP growth, by 2.14 percentage points, significantly higher than income growth, by 4.64 percentage points, and very significantly higher than overall consumption growth, by 6.33 percentage points; average annual growth in per capita cultural and educational consumption was 24.53 %, significantly higher than GDP growth, by 6.98 percentage points, significantly higher than the average annual growth in per capita income, by 9.48 percentage points, and very significantly higher than average annual growth in overall consumption, by 11.17 percentage points, very significantly higher than savings growth, by 4.84 percentage points.

During the "Eleventh Five-Year Plan" period, Hefei's average annual growth in per capita GDP was 23.65 %, average annual growth in urban per capita income was 14.49 %, average annual growth in overall per capita consumption was 13.63 %, average annual growth in per capita savings was 17.13 %, and average annual growth in per capita cultural and educational consumption was 29.12 %. The average annual growth degree of cultural and educational consumption was 5.47 percentage points higher GDP growth degree, 14.63 percentage points higher than income growth degree, 15.49 percentage points higher than overall consumption growth degree, and 11.99 percentage points higher than savings growth degree.

During the first 2 years of the "Twelfth Five-Year Plan" period, Hefei's average annual growth in per capita GDP was 3.57 %, average annual growth in urban per

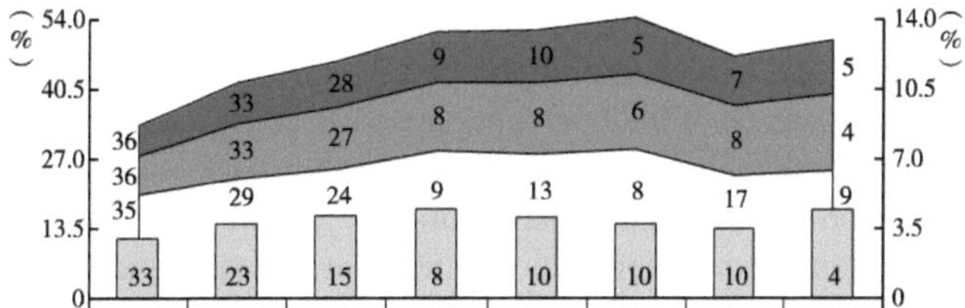

	2005	2006	2007	2008	2009	2010	2011	2012
Cultural and Educational Consumption as Proportion of Income	5.8792	7.8378	8.7611	9.8739	10.1475	10.7266	9.4517	10.2299
Cultural and Educational Consumption as Proportion of Consumption	7.6959	10.5715	11.8383	13.0991	13.7155	14.5839	13.5231	14.8553
Ratio of Cultural Consumption to Surplus	19.9394	23.2599	25.2081	28.6239	28.0615	28.8537	23.8925	24.7304
Ratio of Cultural and Educational Consumption to GDP	3.0027	3.7203	4.1811	4.4644	4.0494	3.7288	3.5054	4.4962

Fig. 6.25 Changing trends in Hefei's cultural and educational consumption ratio. *LHS area*: per capita cultural/educational as proportion of income, overall consumption, and non-cultural consumption surplus (%), the ratios of each indicator over the years are superimposed; *RHS cylinder*: per capita cultural/educational consumption and GDP (%). The ratio for each year is ranked within 36 major cities

capita income was 16.46 %, average annual growth in per capita overall consumption was 12.69 %, average annual growth in per capita savings was 26.36 %, and average annual growth in per capita cultural and educational consumption was 13.73 %. The average annual growth in cultural and educational consumption was higher than GDP growth by 10.16 percentage points, lower than income growth by 2.73 percentage points, higher than overall consumption by 1.04 percentage points, and lower than savings growth by 12.63 percentage points. In 2012, the relationship between Hefei's cultural and educational consumption and GDP and overall consumption showed a direct trend of increase.

All of this was realized in an analysis and calculation of various proportions for Hefei's per capita cultural and educational consumption. See Fig. 6.25 for Hefei's changes in cultural and educational consumption since 2005.

6.4.2.1 Ratio of Per Capita Cultural and Educational Consumption and Per Capita GDP

From 2005 to 2012, Hefei's ratio of per capita cultural and educational consumption and per capita GDP grew from 3.00 to 4.50 %, and its rank went up from 33rd to 4th out of 36 major cities. Since the "Eleventh Five-Year Plan" period, Hefei's indicator for this ratio increased by 1.49 percentage points, a degree of increase of 49.74 %, and a degree of change ranked first place out of 36 major cities.

During this period, Hefei's ratio, from 2006 to 2008, and in 2012, experienced increases, while from 2009 to 2011 experienced decreases. The highest value occurred in 2012 at 4.50 %, and the lowest in 2005 at 3.00 %. During the "Eleventh

Five-Year Plan" period, there was an increase of 0.73 percentage points, a degree of increase of 24.18 %; during the first 2 years of the "Twelfth Five-Year Plan", there was an increase of 0.77 percentage points, a degree of increase of 20.58 %. In terms of the changes in coordinated relationship between cultural and educational consumption growth and urban economic development, during the "Eleventh Five-Year Plan" period there was a significant increase, and during the first 2 years of the "Twelfth Five-Year Plan" period a significant trend of increase was maintained.

6.4.2.2 Per Capita Cultural and Educational Consumption as Proportion of Per Capita Income

From 2005 to 20012, Hefei's per capita cultural and educational consumption as proportion of per capita income grew from 5.88 to 10.23 %, and its rank increased from 36th to 5th place among 36 major cities. Since the "Eleventh Five-Year Plan" period, Hefei's indicator for this ratio increased by 4.35 percentage points, a degree of increase of 74.00 %, and a degree of change ranked 1st among 36 major cities.

During this period, Hefei's ratio, from 2006 to 2010 and in 2010, experienced increases, while in 2011 it experienced a decrease. The highest value occurred in 2010 at 10.73 %, and the lowest value in 2005 at 5.88 %. During the "Eleventh Five-Year Plan" period, there was an increase of 4.85 percentage points, a degree of increase of 82.45 %; during the first 2 years of the "Twelfth Five-Year Plan" period, there was a decrease of 0.50 percentage points, a decrease degree of 4.63 %. In terms of the change in coordinated relationship between cultural and educational consumption growth and the growth in income of urban citizens, during the "Eleventh Five-Year Plan" period, there was a very significant increase, and during the first 2 years of the "Twelfth Five-Year Plan" period there was again a significant decrease.

6.4.2.3 Per Capita Cultural and Educational Consumption as Proportion of Per Capita Overall Consumption

From 2005 to 2012, Hefei's per capita cultural and educational consumption as proportion of per capita overall consumption grew from 7.70 to 14.86 %, and its rank went up from 36th place to 4th place among 36 major cities. Since the "Eleventh Five-Year Plan" period, Hefei's ratio for this indicator went up by 7.16 percentage points, an increase degree of 93.03 %, and a degree of change ranked first out of 36 provinces and regions.

During this period, Hefei's ratio experienced increases from 2006 to 2010 and in 2012, while in 2011 it decreased. The highest value occurred in 2012, at 14.86 %, and the lowest in 2005 at 7.70 %. During the "Eleventh Five-Year Plan" period, there was an increase of 6.89 percentage points, and a degree of increase of 89.50 %; during the first 2 years of the "Twelfth Five-Year Plan" period, there was an increase of 0.27 percentage points, and a degree of increase of 1.86 %. In terms of the coordinated relationship between cultural and educational consumption demand growth and total consumption of urban citizens, during the "Eleventh Five-Year Plan" period there was a very significant increase, and during the first 2 years of the "Twelfth Five-Year Plan" period, a significant increase was maintained.

6.4.2.4 Ratio of Per Capita Cultural and Educational Consumption and Per Capita Non-cultural Consumption Surplus

From 2005 to 2012, Hefei's ratio of per capita cultural and educational consumption and per capita non-cultural consumption increased from 19.94 to 24.73 %, moving up from 35th to 9th place among 26 major cities. Since the "Eleventh Five-Year Plan" period, Hefei's ratio for this indicator increased by 4.79 percentage points, a degree of increase of 24.03 %, and a degree of increase ranked first out of 35 major cities.

During this period, Hefei's ratio increased from 2006 to 2008, in 2010, and in 2012, while in 2009 and 2011 it decreased. The highest value occurred in 2010 at 28.85 %, and the lowest in 2005 at 19.94 %. During the "Eleventh Five-Year Plan" period there was an increase of 8.91 percentage points, and a degree of growth of 44.71 %; during the first 2 years of the "Twelfth Five-Year Plan" period, there was a decrease of 4.12 percentage points, a degree of decrease of 14.29 %. In terms of the changes in the coordinated relationship of cultural and educational consumption demand and the growth of "surplus money" outside of the "essential consumption" of urban citizens, during the "Eleventh Five-Year Plan" period there was a significant increase, though during the first 2 years of the "Twelfth Five-Year Plan" period there was a reversion to a significant decrease.

6.4.3 Coordination Status of Urban/Rural and Regional Cultural and Educational Consumption

6.4.3.1 Urban-to-Rural Ratio of Per Capita Cultural and Educational Consumption Within the Provinces

For changing trends in urban-to-rural ratio of per capita cultural and educational consumption within the provinces since 2005, see Fig. 6.26.

From 2005 to 2012, Anhui's urban-to-rural ratio of per capita cultural and educational consumption expanded from 2.5951 to 5.0081, its rank falling from 4th to 26th out of 31 provinces and regions. During this period, the urban-to-rural ratio was reduced from 2008 to 2009, while in all other years it expanded. The smallest urban-to-rural ratio occurred in 2005, at 2.5951, while the largest occurred in 2012 at 5.0081. Since the "Eleventh Five-Year Plan" period, Anhui's urban-to-rural ratio in cultural and educational consumption expanded by 92.98 %, with a

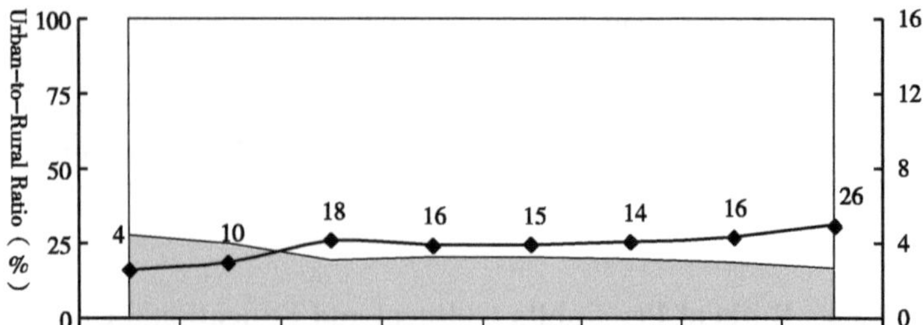

	2005	2006	2007	2008	2009	2010	2011	2012
Provincial/Regional Urban Per Capita	666.42	869.23	1169.99	1160.14	1225.36	1479.75	1631.28	1932.74
Provincial/Regional Rural Per Capita	256.80	290.74	283.17	294.84	312.05	363.92	376.18	385.92
Provincial/Regional Urban–Rural Ratio	2.5951	2.9897	4.1318	3.9348	3.9268	4.0661	4.3364	5.0081

Fig. 6.26 Urban-to-rural ratio of per capita cultural and educational consumption within the provinces. *LHS area*: provincial and regional urban and rural per capita cultural and educational consumption (yuan converted to %), proportional relationship between urban and rural areas for each year superimposed; *RHS curve*: urban-to-rural; ratio of per capita cultural and educational consumption; *RHS curve*: urban-to-rural ratio of per capita cultural and educational consumption (rural = 1). The urban-to-rural ratios of the marked years are ranked among 31 provinces and regions

rank of 31 out of 31 provinces and regions in terms of change in urban-to-rural ratio. This signifies that Anhui's situation is among the most serious of the provinces and regions in terms of change in reductions and expansions in urban-to-rural ratio.

While the urban-to-rural ratio of Anhui's cultural and educational consumption experienced changes, it was also under the influence of its own annual demand changes in both urban and rural aspects. In terms of the role they play within the provinces, major cities not only directly stimulate urban growth, but also drive rural growth.

From 2005 to 2012, Anhui's urban per capita cultural and educational consumption increased from 666.42 to 1,932.74 yuan, an increase of 1,266.32 yuan, a total increase of 190.02 %, and an average annual growth of 16.43 %. The highest urban per capita growth occurred in 2007, with a growth rate of 34.60 %; the lowest growth occurred in 2008, with a negative growth of 0.84 %. Rural per capita cultural and educational consumption grew from 256.80 to 385.92 yuan, a growth of 129.12 yuan, a total growth of 50.28 %, and an average annual growth of 5.99 %. The highest rural per capita growth occurred in 2010, with a growth rate of 16.62 %; the lowest growth occurred in 2007, with a negative growth of 2.60 %. Within the 7 years, urban per capita cultural and educational consumption demand average annual growth was significantly higher than rural average annual growth by 10.44 percentage points, signifying that the urban-to-rural ratio of Anhui's cultural and educational consumption demand was expanded significantly.

During the first 2 years of the "Twelfth Five-Year Plan" period, Anhui's average annual growth in urban per capita values was 14.29 %, lower than its own average annual growth during the "Eleventh Five-Year Plan" period by 3.01 percentage points; average annual growth of rural per capita values was 2.98 %, lower than its own average annual growth during the "Eleventh Five-Year Plan" period by 4.24 percentage points. In 2012, urban per capita values were higher than those in rural areas, with average urban annual growth being higher than rural growth by 11.31 percentage points, signifying that the gap was widening. The urban-to-rural ratio in Anhui's cultural and educational consumption demand has widened seriously, by 23.17 %, compared to that in 2010, and the urban-to-rural ratio ranked 26th among 31 provinces and regions.

6.4.3.2 Regional Discrepancies in Urban Per Capita Cultural and Educational Consumption

See Fig. 6.27 for changing trends in discrepancies between Hefei's per capita cultural and educational consumption and national urban per capita amounts.

From 2005 to 2012, the regional discrepancy between Hefei's per capita cultural and educational consumption was reduced from1.4812 to 1.2999, and its tanking went up from 28th to 22nd place among 36 major cities. During this period, Hefei's regional discrepancy was reduced from 2006 to 2007 and in 2011, while in all other years it expanded. The lowest regional discrepancy occurred in 2007 at 1.1150, and the largest in 2005 at 1.4812. Since the "Eleventh Five-Year Plan" period, the discrepancy between Hefei's cultural and educational consumption and the national urban value was reduced by 12.24 %, and Hefei's degree of change in regional discrepancies was ranked 8th out of 26 major cities. This signifies that Hefei is a

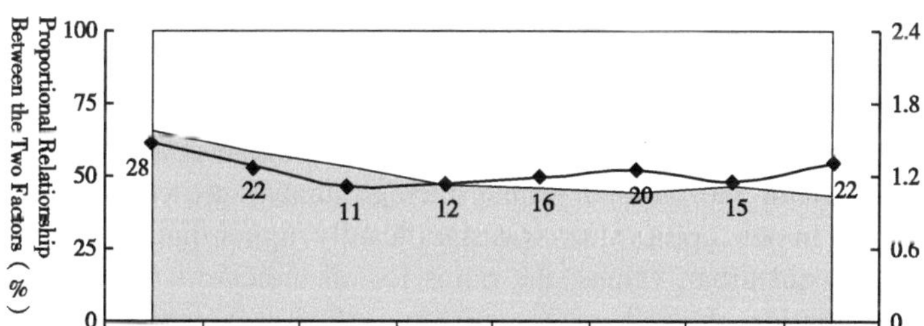

	2005	2006	2007	2008	2009	2010	2011	2012
Local Urban Per Capita	569.32	863.21	1176.30	1539.40	1741.16	2043.47	2122.74	2643.34
National Urban Per Capita	1097.46	1203.03	1329.16	1358.26	1472.76	1627.64	1851.74	2033.50
Local Regional Gap	1.4812	1.2825	1.1150	1.1334	1.1822	1.2555	1.1463	1.2999

Fig. 6.27 Hefei's regional discrepancies in urban per capita cultural and educational consumption and national urban consumption. *LHS area*: per capita cultural and educational consumption (yuan converted to %), direct proportional relationship between local and national annual values; *RHS curve*: regional discrepancy in per capita cultural and educational consumption (no discrepancy = 1). Regional discrepancies of the marked years are ranked among 36 major cities

city with one of the more favorable statuses in terms of regional discrepancy changes in cultural and educational consumption.

While changes occurred in Hefei's regional discrepancy in cultural and educational consumption, the influence of annual demand of Hefei's and of the national urban areas is also felt. See this paper's chapter on per capita values for detailed calculations of a comparison between per capita cultural and educational consumption growth in national urban areas and in Hefei, which examines the specific discrepancies in growth.

From 2005 to 2012, Hefei average annual growth was significantly higher than the national urban average annual growth, by 15.32 percentage points, and the discrepancy between Hefei's cultural and educational consumption demand and the national urban demand was reduced.

During the first 2 years of the "Twelfth Five-Year Plan" period, Hefei's average annual growth degree was significantly lower than its own average annual growth during the "Eleventh Five-Year Plan" period, by 15.39 percentage points, and also was higher than national urban average annual growth, by 1.96 percentage points. In 2012, Hefei's per capita value was higher than the national urban average value, its average annual growth was higher than the national urban average annual growth, signifying than the gap had expanded. The discrepancy between Hefei's cultural and educational consumption and the national urban cultural and educational consumption was widened significantly, by 3.54 %, in comparison with 2010, and the discrepancy ranked 22nd out of 36 major cities.

6.4.4 Prosperity Assessment of Hefei's Cultural and Educational Consumption Demand

To sum up the above: since the "Eleventh Five-Year Plan" period, Hefei's overall average annual growth in cultural and educational consumption was significantly higher than the national urban average annual growth, and its average annual growth in per capita values was significantly higher than the average annual growth of national urban values; the ratios for all indicators in cultural and educational consumption showed an overall trend of improvement; the urban-to-rural ratio within the province was significantly expanded, yet the discrepancy between the national urban values was significantly reduced. These results are all collectively seen in the assessment and calculation of Hefei's cultural and educational consumption demand prosperity index. See Fig. 6.28 for changing trends in prosperity index of Hefei's cultural and educational consumption since 2005.

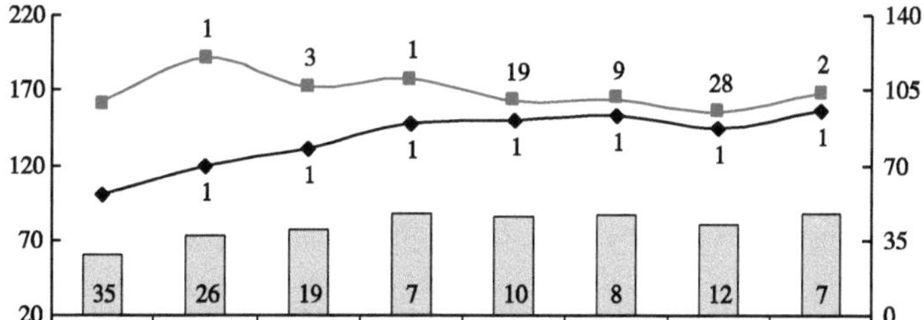

	2005	2006	2007	2008	2009	2010	2011	2012
Horizontal Assessment	60.14	72.46	77.24	88.15	85.11	86.62	80.15	87.33
Vertical Assessment (1)	100.00	119.98	131.42	148.00	149.86	153.79	144.75	156.77
Vertical Assessment (2)	100.00	119.98	106.38	110.54	100.17	100.44	94.45	103.58

Fig. 6.28 Changing trends in the prosperity index of Hefei's cultural and educational. *LHS cylindrical*: horizontal assessment (urban-rural and zero-difference ideal value = 100); *LHS curve*: vertical assessment (starting base value = 100), (*1*) 2005 starting point; *RHS curve*: (2) Starting from previous year; shows assessed 36 cities in a ranking

6.4.4.1 Annual Horizontal Assessment Prosperity Index

With the national urban cultural and educational consumption overall share value, per capita absolute value, and proportion of each index as a base, and balanced by the "ideal value" of 100 of no discrepancy between urban/rural areas and regions, in 2012 Hefei's prosperity index for this indicator was 87.33, lower than the ideal value by 12.67, but higher than the previous year by 7.18. In a annual comparison, Hefei's prosperity index, in a ranking of 36 major cities, was ranked 35th in 2005, 8th in 2010, and in 2012 had gone up from 12th place the previous year to 7th place.

6.4.4.2 Vertical Assessment of Prosperity Since the "Eleventh Five-Year Plan" Period

Setting the last year of the "Tenth Five-Year Plan" period, 2005, with a starting base value of 100, in 2012 Hefei's prosperity index for this indicator was 156.77, higher than the starting base value of 2005 by 56.77, and also 12.02 higher than the previous year. Since the "Eleventh Five-Year Plan" period, Hefei's status indicator for this index in a ranking of 36 major cities, was ranked first place in 2006, the same in 2010, and in 2012 was the same as the previous year, still first place.

6.4.4.3 Vertical Assessment of Prosperity Since the "Twelfth Five-Year Plan" Period

Setting the last year of the "Eleventh Five-Year Plan" period, 2010, with a starting base value of 100, in 2012 Hefei's prosperity index was 97.45, lower than the 2010 starting base value by 2.55, but higher than the previous year by 3.00. Compared with the period since the "Twelfth Five-Year Plan" period, Hefei's prosperity index for this indicator, in a ranking of 36 major cities, was ranked 28th in 2011, and in 2012 went up to 20th place. This evaluation index is better explained by text than in a table; see Report B3 on the ranking of major cities.

6.4.4.4 Annual Vertical Assessment of Prosperity Index

Setting the previous year, 2011, with a starting base value of 100, in 2012 Hefei's prosperity index for this indicator was 103.8, 3.58 higher than the 2011 starting base value. In a annual comparison, Hefei's prosperity index for this indicator, in a ranking of 36 major cities, was ranked first in 2006, 9th in 2010, and in 2012 went up to 2nd place from 28th place the previous year.

MIX
Papier aus verantwortungsvollen Quellen
Paper from responsible sources
FSC® C105338

FSC
www.fsc.org

If you have any concerns about our products,
you can contact us on
ProductSafety@springernature.com

In case Publisher is established outside the EU,
the EU authorized representative is:
Springer Nature Customer Service Center GmbH
Europaplatz 3, 69115 Heidelberg, Germany

Printed by Libri Plureos GmbH
in Hamburg, Germany